# THE ANCHOR ANTHOLOGY OF SEVENTEENTH-CENTURY VERSE

## Volume 2

*The Anchor Seventeenth-Century Series presents the major —and significant minor—texts in English of the seventeenth century in authoritative and inexpensive editions. Prepared especially for Anchor Books by a distinguished group of American and Canadian scholars, these newly edited texts meet the highest standards of scholarship and readability. Each volume incorporates the latest textual and critical discoveries, and the series as a whole is designed to provide a reliable access to the literature of the seventeenth century.*

Professor RICHARD S. SYLVESTER received his B.A. degree from St. Louis University, his B.A. and M.S. degrees from Oxford University, where he was a Rhodes scholar, and his Ph.D. degree from Yale. He has been a Professor of English at Yale since 1966. He is the Co-Editor of *Archives,* and Executive Editor of the Yale Edition of the Complete Works of St. Thomas More. His publications include *George Cavendish's "Life and Death of Cardinal Wolsey," Two Early Tudor Lives, Thomas More's "History of King Richard III,"* and an edition of Richard Pace's *The Benefit of a Liberal Education,* as well as numerous articles and reviews.

AD ÆTHERA VIRTUS
EX HIS
ORI-
DOCUIT
OVID'S
METAMORPHOSIS
Englished,
Mythologiz'd,
And
Represented
in figures
by
G. S.
MDCXXXII.
Francisco Clein Inv: Salamon Savery sculp:
formantur et
Amore
Sapientia
AFFIGIT HVMO DIVINÆ PARTICVLAM AVRÆ.
VNTVR
CVNCTA

# The Anchor Anthology of Seventeenth-Century Verse

## VOLUME 2

EDITED WITH AN
INTRODUCTION AND NOTES BY
RICHARD S. SYLVESTER

ANCHOR BOOKS
Doubleday & Company, Inc., Garden City, New York
1969

*The Anchor Seventeenth-Century Series*
*is published by Doubleday Anchor Books*
*under the General Editorship of*
*Professor* J. MAX PATRICK
*New York University*

*This edition has been especially prepared for*
*Anchor Books and has never appeared in book form.*

*Library of Congress Catalog Card Number 68–29286*

*Printed in the United States of America*
*First Edition*

FOR PATRICE

OBIIT

*June 20, 1964*

Farewell, thou child of my right hand, and Joy

# CONTENTS

# LIST OF ILLUSTRATIONS

Title Pages

# INTRODUCTION

When Michael Drayton, in 1627, sat down to write his verse-epistle to his "Most Dearely-loved Friend Henery Reynolds," he could look back, with considerable pride, on a fifty-year period of immense poetic achievement in English literature. Drayton himself had played a sturdy, if somewhat less than major, part in that achievement, but his reminiscent poem modestly declines to mention his own works and concentrates instead on praising "grave morrall Spencer" and "noble Sidney," Shakespeare and Marlowe and Jonson, together with lesser figures like Warner, Chapman, and Daniel. As the leisurely couplets of his epistle extend their survey to the contemporary scene, Drayton's nostalgia becomes somewhat petulant. The poetry of the 1620s was evidently not greatly to his taste; he can praise "modern" writers like Sandys, Alexander, Drummond and William Browne, but he senses that they are not the poets of the moment. Good professional that he is, Drayton pleads for those

> Whose workes oft printed, set on every post,
> To publique censure subject have bin most;

and he resents the "rich composures" of poets who are "incloistered" in private chambers and whose works circulate only in manuscript. "Let such Peeces," he wryly says, "bee spoke of by those that shall come after me, I passe [i.e. care] not for them."

Drayton was in many ways a better prophet than he knew. The future did indeed take care of those "private" poets from whom he so carefully disassociated himself. The poems of John Donne, which had circulated in manuscript for years, were published in 1633, two years after Donne's, and Drayton's, death. The "school" of metaphysical poetry, of which Donne was the major representative, was to flourish in the next decades as, one by one, the works of his successors began to appear in print. Most of these publications were posthumous: George Herbert's *The Temple* in 1633, Carew's *Poems* in 1640, Henry King's in 1657, Lord Herbert of Cherbury's in 1665 and, in the case of Aurelian Townshend, no edition at all save for the appearance of a few poems in anthologies of verse. Twentieth-century scholarship and criticism have done much to reaffirm the value of this body of poetry and, today, "the Metaphysical Poets" do not want for defenders, much less for readers. The more strictly religious poets of the Donne tradition—Herbert and Vaughan, Crashaw and Traherne—are generously represented in Volume 1 of the present collection; our concern in this volume is with the secular metaphysicals and with the social poets whom the century produced.

To distinguish among the various poetic traditions of the early seventeenth century invariably involves the critic—and the anthologist—in a number of compromises. Literary historians conveniently categorize the non-dramatic verse of the period by assigning individual poems or poets to one of three schools, that of Donne, that of Jonson, or that of Spenser. These broad groupings have their value; but, inevitably, they fail to do justice to the way in which any given poet, a Carew, for example, can draw his inspiration, his technique, and his mode from Donne, from Jonson, or from the Petrarchans, blending various features of many schools and thus making his own contribution to the rich complexity of the poetic scene. In selecting poems from the twenty authors presented here, we have tried, wherever possible, to suggest the broad range which their work comprehends. Secular metaphysical poetry, as embodied in the verse of Herbert of Cherbury, Henry King, John Cleveland, and Abraham Cowley, bulks large in this collection, but it yields space, on the whole to Jonson and his many followers. Poets writing, directly or indirectly, under Spenser's influence are less fully represented. We have included Habington, whose *Castara* looks back to Sidney's *Astrophil and Stella,* but have omitted poets like Giles and Phineas Fletcher, William Browne of Tavistock, and William Basse. Cavalier poetry, the songs of Carew, Lovelace, Suckling and Stanley, is well illustrated here; but we have not attempted to indicate the development of political and satiric verse, through Marvell, Butler, and Dryden, as the century progressed.

## INTRODUCTION

If any single theme can be said to dominate in this selection, its general nature is suggested at the outset by Drayton, whose importance in the development of the pentameter couplet has often been noted.[1] Despite his nostalgia for Elizabethan times, nowhere better manifested than in his last pastoral, *The Muses Elizium*, Drayton had already, in his *Heroicall Epistles* of the 1590s, employed the closed couplet to good effect. Behind his use of the form lay scattered experiments like Nicholas Grimald's in Tottel's *Songs and Sonnets* (1557) and Marlowe's translation of Ovid's *Amores;* but the future, for both Ovid and for the couplet, was immense. In the hands of Jonson ("To Penshurst," "To the Memory of . . . William Shakespeare,") and his successors, the pentameter couplet became the accepted vehicle for epigram, elegy and verse-epistle, and for other types of serious verse. The tetrameter couplet, often viewed as the hallmark of the Tribe of Ben, was generally reserved for lighter subjects; but it too flourished and, on occasion (King's "The Exequy," Crashaw's "A Hymn to St. Teresa," Marvell's "To his Coy Mistress"), was adapted to a great variety of subject matters. By the time of Dryden, the couplet, particularly the closed pentameter couplet, had become the dominant verse form. Perhaps the crowning moment in its triumph came with *Religio Laici* (1682), the last selection in this volume. Dryden transforms a whole tradition of personal, religious meditation[2] in verse by presenting his views in the form of a public debate, and he masterfully adapts the balanced metrics of his couplets to the shifting positions demanded by the rhetorical structure of his poem.

The distance travelled by the couplet in the course of the seventeenth century can be measured by comparing Dryden's use of the form in *Religio Laici* with Donne's employment of it in "Satyre III," an almost ferociously tender poem, also in couplets, which tersely covers the same subject—the nature of the true church—that Dryden deals with. Donne's pentameters are ruggedly irregular; one line runs on to another with an almost feverish energy that is accen-

[1] See particularly Ruth C. Wallerstein, "The Development of the Rhetoric and Metre of the Heroic Couplet," *Publications of the Modern Language Association*, L (1935), 166–209.

[2] For the meditative tradition, see Martz's Introduction to Volume 1 of this collection.

tuated by the urgent imperatives which the speaker, in his quest for truth, forces upon himself: "Know thy foes," "Seeke true religion," "aske thy father which is shee,"

> Yet strive so, that before age, deaths twilight,
> Thy Soule rest, for none can worke in that night.
> To will, implyes delay, therefore now doe:
> Hard deeds, the bodies paines; hard knowledge too
> The mindes indeavours reach, and mysteries
> Are like the Sunne, dazling, yet plaine to all eyes.

Dryden's balanced calmness, on the other hand, manifests itself in the even pace of his end-stopped couplets:

> And, after hearing what our Church can say,
> If still our Reason runs another way,
> That private Reason 'tis more Just to curb,
> Than by Disputes the publick Peace disturb.
> For points obscure are of small use to learn:
> But *Common quiet* is *Mankind's* concern.

In a sense, Ben Jonson's stricture on Donne's metrics ("that Done for not keeping of accent deserved hanging")[3] forecasts the way in which the couplet was to develop in the coming century. When Pope, discussing metrics in the *Essay on Criticism* (1711), praises "The easy vigour of a line, / Where Denham's strength, and Waller's sweetness join," he calls attention to that smoothing out of irregularities in accent and in syntax which both Waller and Denham had done much to effect. For Dryden and the eighteenth century, the sweetness and harmony of the new couplet were epitomized in Denham's famous lines on the Thames from *Cooper's Hill:*

> O could I flow like thee, and make thy stream
> My great example, as it is my theme!
> Though deep, yet clear, though gentle, yet not dull,
> Strong without rage, without ore-flowing full.

Samuel Johnson's comment on these two couplets succinctly indi-

[3] Ben Jonson, *The Works,* eds. C. H. Herford, Percy and Evelyn Simpson, I, 133.

cates the grounds upon which the Augustans based their admiration: "But so much meaning is comprised in so few words; the particulars of resemblance are so perspicaciously collected, and every mode of excellence separated from its adjacent fault by so nice a line of limitation; the different parts of the sentence are so accurately adjusted; and the flow of the last couplet is so smooth and sweet; that the passage, however celebrated, has not been praised above its merit."[4]

While Denham's lines did indeed provide both an example and a theme for the great age of the couplet,[5] the history of the form before *Cooper's Hill* shows how poets were feeling their way towards the kind of qualified balance which his couplets reflect. Here is Drayton, first of all, struggling along in the hexameters of *Polyolbion* (1622):

Give me those Lines (whose touch the skilfull eare to please)
That gliding flow in state, like swelling *Euphrates*,
In which things naturall be, and not in falsely wrong:
The Sounds are fine and smooth, the Sense is full and strong,
Not bumbasted with words, vaine ticklish eares to feed;
But such as may content the perfect man to read.[6]

About ten years later, Thomas Randolph, that comically effusive son of Ben, picks up the pattern in pentameters:

I meane the stile, being pure and strong and round,
Not long but Pythy: being short breath'd, but sound.
Such as the grave, acute, wise Seneca sings,
That best of Tutors to the worst of kings.

[4] *The Lives of the Poets* (Life of Denham).

[5] Among the many imitations, Pope's parody in *The Dunciad* (III, 169–72) is perhaps the best known:

Flow, Welsted, flow! like thine inspirer, beer,
Tho' stale, not ripe, tho' thin, yet never clear;
So sweetly mawkish, and so smoothly dull;
Heady, not strong; o'erflowing, tho' not full.

[6] *The Works of Michael Drayton*, ed. J. W. Hebel, Kathleen Tillotson, and B. H. Newdigate, IV, 422. I owe this reference to Mrs. Susan B. Holohan of Yale University.

> Not long and empty; lofty but not proud;
> Subtle but sweet, high but without a cloud.[7]

And, finally, William Cartwright, in his tribute to Ben Jonson (1638):

> But *thou* still put'st true passions on; dost *write*
> With the same courage that try'd Captaines fight;
> Giv'st the right blush and colour unto things;
> *Low* without *creeping, high* without losse of *wings;*
> *Smooth,* yet not *weake,* and by a thorough-care,
> *Bigge* without *swelling,* without *painting faire.*[8]

No account of the rise of the couplet can be complete without a careful consideration of the part played by George Sandys—for Dryden, "the best versifier of the former age"[9]—the golden translator of Ovid already praised by Drayton in the *Epistle to Reynolds.* Sandys' *Metamorphoses* had first appeared in 1626, but in 1632 he reissued the volume, adding a wealth of engravings and appending an extensive commentary to each book. In his couplets Sandys employed the "metaphrastic" method, endeavoring to stick as closely as possible to his original, and rendering word for word, line for line. If he never quite achieves the magnificent verbal eloquence of Ovid himself, he does capture much of the rhetorical pitch and pull of the Latin lines by using those devices of parallelism, balance, and antithesis which Dryden and Pope were so strongly to favor. Moreover, Sandys tends to make one pentameter couplet the equivalent of two Latin hexameters, thus compressing his original to an intense degree. Elisions and syntactical ellipses are frequent in his

[7] "To Mr. Feltham on his booke of Resolves," lines 89–94, in *The Poems and Amyntas of Thomas Randolph,* ed. J. J. Parry, p. 126. Randolph's poem was first published in 1638, three years after his death, but it was written some years earlier.

[8] From *Jonsonus Virbius,* 1638. Reprinted in Cartwright's *Poems* (1651), four years before Denham's lines first appeared in the 1655 edition of *Cooper's Hill.*

[9] Dryden makes this remark in the "Preface to the Fables" (1700). See *The Essays of John Dryden,* ed. W. P. Ker, II, 247. Sandys' *A Paraphrase upon the Divine Poems* (1638) was prefaced by eulogies from Henry King, Sidney Godolphin, Carew, Dudley Digges, Lord Falkland, and Waller. King's and Carew's poems are included in the present volume.

verse. Although his couplets are generally end-stopped, when he does allow run-on lines he usually achieves the same effect as that attained in closed couplets by introducing a heavy medial caesura. Where Ovid's Latin, for all its artifice, flows smoothly, Sandys' English line is segmented, with its rhetorical weight equalized through the deliberate balancing of phrase against phrase, half-line against half-line. In his passages of sustained dialogue, as in Philomela's speech to Tereus (VI, 576–95), Sandys' characters sound as if they were the heroes or heroines in one of Dryden's heroic plays.[10] Less magniloquent, but perhaps more indicative of Sandys' normal pace, are witty couplets like the following, from the story of Salmacis and Hermaphroditus in Book IV:

> So they, by such a strict embracement glew'd,
> Are now but one, with double forme indew'd.
> No longer he a Boy, nor she a maid;
> But neither, and yet either, might be said.

In addition to its importance in the development of the couplet, Sandys' *Metamorphoses* also reflects other important features of the "new poetry," tending towards neo-classical norms. His volume is a vast storehouse, a kind of final *summa,* of classical mythology. In his marginalia and commentaries, he summarized the wealth of Ovidian lore that had descended to the Renaissance through the Middle Ages, in the *Ovid Moralisé* and in a host of allegorizations. Sandys offers literal and historical interpretations of the fables, and he often analyzes them in their "natural" or "physical" senses, finding scientific "facts" beneath the fiction of the verse.[11] He is not very much interested in the theological aspects of the tales, but he does dredge up every possible moral lesson that he can extract from them. Thus, in Book VI, Arachne and Niobe stand out as types illustrating the dangers of self-sufficiency and self-reliance. Again and again, one feels, perhaps with Ovid as well as with Sandys, that

[10] It may be recalled that Dryden, in the *Preface to Annus Mirabilis* (1667), spoke of Ovid as expressing "the proper wit of Dialogue or Discourse, and, consequently, of the Drama."

[11] Here Sandys emerges as an early follower of Bacon, who had interpreted thirty-one myths along these lines in his *De Sapientia Veterum* of 1609.

man's chief concern should be his life on this earth. The gods are capriciously dangerous and man, like Milton's unfallen Adam, should be "lowlie wise," contented not to dream of other worlds.

Classical ideas like these, and the classical myths in which they are enshrined, are omnipresent in the verse of many of the poets presented here. Waller, seeking to describe the way in which nature itself is "civilized" by the presence of his mistress, recalls how

> *Amphion* so made stones and timber leap
> Into fair Figures from a confus'd heap:
> And in the symmetry of her parts is found
> A power, like that of harmony in sound.
>
> ("At Penshurst." [Had Sacharissa livd] lines 17–20)[12]

So, too, Lovelace forsakes his Aesopian grasshopper's "Peirch of Grasse" for the Horatian self-contentment of a life that, "asking nothing, nothing need[s]," and Herrick transforms "the dull and drooping west" of Devonshire into the golden gardens of the Hesperides. For poets writing in the traditions of Jonson and Spenser, the classics are constantly available. Their allusions to ancient myths or authors can be merely ornamental, but they often function as structural devices which help to generalize the poet's view in time and to harmonize his verse with the best of what "has oft been thought, but ne'er so well expressed." The massive example of Milton, who sums up so many different poetic traditions of the century, stands as a monumental reminder of the powerful resources that classical literature could offer to the poet who knew how to use them.

Yet the classical way had not been the way of the great metaphysical poets and it is not, in the main, the method of their lesser successors in this volume. Donne, though he tried classical forms (epigram, elegy, satire, and verse-epistle) constantly displaces the classical center with his own forceful techniques. Allusions to the classics in his verse, while certainly not rare, are seldom central to his concerns. Carew, in his "Elegie upon the death of . . . Donne,"

[12] See also Cowley's "Ode. Of Wit," lines 29–32, for another instance of Amphion as the civilizing power of poetry.

found this fact an occasion for praise and went on to prophesy that poets would now

> repeale the goodly exil'd traine
> Of gods and goddesses, which in thy just raigne
> Were banish'd nobler Poems.

The gods and goddesses, never completely exiled, did indeed come back, and Carew's own great elegy, which speaks of Donne's "Promethean breath" and likens his fire to that of the poet-priest Apollo, illustrates, as do many of Carew's other poems, the role that they would play in the verse of the new society.

With the huge interest in Donne and the metaphysical poets which has arisen in the last sixty years, we may perhaps have tended to underestimate the greatness of Ben Jonson's achievement as a poet. If the selections offered in this volume insist on his all-important role in the development of seventeenth-century verse, that emphasis should not be construed as a devaluation of Donne and his successors. A well-rounded view of the literary scene about 1630 would probably discern not a violent conflict between metaphysical and Jonsonian poetry, but rather a sort of lovers' quarrel between them. Lest we exaggerate the differences between the two schools, it is well to recall that one of Donne's elegies ("To make the Doubt cleare that no Woman's true") was printed in Jonson's *Under-wood* and that several of Jonson's elegies, including "'Tis true, I'm broke!" in this collection, have often been attributed to Donne.[13] Contemporaries referred to both Jonson and Donne as "strong-lined" poets, though the term was usually applied to metaphysical writers during the period.[14] Moreover, the two poets seem to have been relatively good friends. Donne addressed one poem to Jonson, a Latin epigram on *Volpone,* in which he praised Jonson for renovating the classics instead of merely imitating them. Jonson's

[13] The Donne elegy, usually referred to as "The Expostulation," is placed among doubtful poems by Helen Gardner (*The Elegies and the Songs and Sonnets of John Donne*); but it does appear in the first edition of Donne's verse, and it is included in the Donnean canon by John Shawcross and printed as No. 22 in his edition of *The Complete Poetry of John Donne.*

[14] See George Williamson, "Strong Lines," in *Seventeenth Century Contexts* (London, Faber, 1960).

admiration for Donne, on the other hand, is, characteristically, more direct and open. He recognized Donne's superb originality as a poet "Whose every worke . . . Came forth example, and remaines so, yet," even if his own poetry was to possess other virtues.

The truth of the matter is, as Jonson saw so well, that Donne was, in the last analysis, inimitable.[15] His greatest successors learned much from him, to be sure, but each blended his legacy with other traditions or adjusted it to suit the demands of his own talents. The minor metaphysicals, most of them well represented here, also depart from Donne in many ways, even when they are deliberately trying to echo one of his conceits or to catch the directly conversational flavor of his diction. As a group, they share Donne's privateness, his tendency to concentrate everything in his own consciousness and to pull all the world into the orbit of his verse. Donne's own tense energy may be beyond them, but they imitate his manner by mingling colloquial and arcane idioms, evolving highly individual and often unique verse forms, and justifying, at their best, their frequent outlandishness in terms of an overriding personal tone, a dramatically modulated speaker's voice to which language had, perforce, to submit.

Poetry like this, if we may extend C. S. Lewis' fine phrase, is an essentially "centripetal" poetry.[16] Its characteristic verse form is the variously developed and often highly complex stanza in which line lengths and rhyme schemes weave together to form idiosyncratic patterns. Poems written in the closed pentameter couplet tend to create an entirely different effect, for, in the world of the couplet, the reader usually knows where he stands from the beginning. The lines are the same length, the rhymes come at regular intervals. The poet need not write impersonally, though he often does, but the "set" qualities of his metrics normally work to regulate expectation and to generalize meaning. With the typical metaphysical stanza, however, one discovers the poet's pattern only as the form

[15] This point is also made, over and over again, by the poets whose elegies on Donne appeared in the early editions of his verse. See the poems by King, Herbert, Carew, and Corbett in this volume.

[16] Lewis applies this term only to Donne (*English Literature in the Sixteenth Century Excluding Drama*, Oxford University Press, 1954, p. 549).

itself develops through twelve or perhaps fourteen lines; there is no *donnée,* and nothing is "given" rhythmically until the poet himself has established it.

Of the poets presented in this volume, those who write primarily in the Donne tradition manifest their individuality in a variety of ways. Herbert of Cherbury, George Herbert's brother, is perhaps the most strictly "metaphysical" of them all. Important in the history of philosophy for his prose treatises, Herbert is often abstractedly concerned with problems of unity and multiplicity in his verse. His love poems plead, as in "The Thought," that they are "of more then vulgar kind"; he likes a "black beauty," opaquely mysterious, yet open to his dark speculations. His precision as a "Philosopher of Knowledge" can waste itself on a riddle in "A Vision," but it can also serve to delineate, as in his finest poem, "An Ode upon a Question moved,"[17] a subtle, "becalmed" kind of passion, aloof, but delicately articulated:

> So when from hence we shall be gone,
> And be no more, nor you, nor I,
> As one anothers mystery,
> Each shall be both, yet both but one.

Henry King, Donne's close friend and executor, is at his best in his many elegies, most of them written in freely moving and versatile couplets. King is a great poet of separation and parting; he writes of love affairs at the moment when they dissolve ("The Surrender," "The Retreat," "The Legacy") with a tough poise, and he shares something of Donne's fascination with the macabre horrors of the grave:

> With this cast ragge of my mortalitie
> Let all my faults and errours buried be.
> And as my sear-cloth rots, so may kind fate
> Those worst acts of my live incinerate.
> He shall in story fill a glorious room
> Whose ashes and whose sins sleep in one Tomb.
>
> ("The Legacy," lines 19–24)

[17] This poem can be profitably compared with its model, Donne's "dialogue of one," *The Extasie.*

The deaths of his friends seem inevitably to have moved King to verse, never more impressively than in the anguished, yet ultimately confident, tetrameters of "The Exequy." In this poem, with an intimate, and almost casual tone, King laments the death of his young wife, Anne, transforming his sad task into the triumphant expression of a love which conquers space and time:

So close the ground, and 'bout her shade
Black curtains draw, my *Bride* is laid.

But heark! My pulse like a soft Drum
Beats my approch, tells *Thee* I come;
And slow howere my marches be,
I shall at last sit down by *Thee*.

(lines 79–80, 111–14)

Two lesser poets, Sir Henry Wotton and Aurelian Townshend, who produced only a small body of verse, are often classed among the followers of Donne. Each has his great moment, Wotton in "On his Mistris, the Queen of Bohemia," and Townshend in "A Dialogue Betwixt Time and A Pilgrime," but neither poet achieved anything like the contemporary fame visited upon John Cleveland, the most flamboyantly conceited of Donne's successors. At one level, Cleveland's immense popularity during the middle years of the century can be attributed to his ardent pursuit of sensationally witty imagery. His former Cambridge pupils, who collected the 1677 edition of his verse, used Cleveland's own language in their preface to indicate the nature of his appeal:

> Some of these grand Sophys will not allow him the reputation of a wit at all: yet how many such authors must be creamed and spirited to make up his Fuscara? And how many of their slight productions may be gigged out of one of his pregnant words? There perhaps you may find some leaf-gold, here massy wedges; there some scattered rays, here a galaxy; there some loose fancy frisking in the air, here Wit's Zodiac.

Cleveland's effervescently recondite metaphors must have delighted the academic circles in which he moved, and it is hard to believe that he himself failed to sense the comic effect that such imagery can often have:

> If my Affection thou wouldst win,
> First cast thy Hieroglyphick Skin.
> My Modern lips know not, alack,
> The old religion of thy *Smack.*
> I count that Primitive Embrace,
> As out of Fashion, as thy Face;
> And yet so long 'tis since thy fall,
> Thy Fornication's Classical.
>
> ("A Young Man to an Old Woman Courting Him," lines 19–26)

To take Cleveland seriously, one must see him as a satirist, preparing the way, with his humorous incongruities, for Samuel Butler and the glories of *Hudibras.* Dryden put the situation very neatly when he remarked, in the *Essay on Dramatic Poesy,* that Donne "gives us deep thoughts in common language, though rough cadence," while Cleveland "gives us common thoughts in abstruse words."

If Cleveland led metaphysical poetry into the coteries of academic wit, then it was Abraham Cowley's unhappy task to attempt to naturalize its salient features in public-minded verse. Cowley was very much a modern spirit; like Dryden an early member of the Royal Society, he preferred men and manners to the giants and witches of older "Heroick poesie." The ode "To the Royal Society" sets forth his ideals most completely, but in his earlier work the reader often feels that Cowley, as he himself says in "The Request," is merely making "a *Mistress* of [his] own *Desire,*" rather than opening up new areas of personal, or social, experience. Theme and style clash constantly in his verse and the conflict sorely tries him:

> *Truth* gives a *dull propriety* to my stile,
> And all the *Metaphors* does spoil.
>
> ("The Dissembler," lines 17–18)

As the contrary example of Carew had shown earlier, Donne's poised cerebration could be combined with the lyric neatness of Jonsonian song; but it proved impossible to employ metaphysical techniques in the kind of serious, social performances to which Cowley addressed himself. Carew knew better, seldom failing to disinguish his private "Lyrique feet" from the public paces that did not arouse his interest:

I that ne're more of private sorrow knew
Then from my Pen some froward Mistresse drew,
And for the publike woe, had my dull sense
So sear'd with ever adverse influence,
As the invaders sword might have, unfelt,
Pierc'd my dead bosome, yet began to melt:

("Obsequies to the Lady Anne Hay," lines 7–12)

Or, as he more gently puts it in "To my Friend G. N. from Wrest,"

Thus I enjoy my selfe, and taste the fruit
Of this blest Peace, whilst toyl'd in the pursuit
Of Bucks, and Stags, th'embleme of warre, you strive
To keepe the memory of our Armes alive.

(lines 107–10)

Carew's gracefulness in both his songs and in poems like "From Wrest" and "To Saxham," takes us back to Jonson and to the kind of poem which his successors characteristically produced. In the lyric, Jonson stood for a formal, yet lively, elegance that, as he put it in "Still to be neat, still to be drest," was always endeavoring to make "simplicitie a grace." His songs, most of them based on classical models, speak to a public audience and were usually written for stage performance. Carefully controlled and superbly finished, they rarely attempt to analyze private and personal experience. Unlike Donne, Jonson is not a great love poet, but he is a great poet of friendship and of civilized society. Where Donne constantly strives to preserve the absolute monarchy of his own wit, Jonson characteristically adjusts his verse to the tempo of the world around him. Even when his subject is intensely personal, as in "On My First Sonne," Jonson struggles to disengage himself from his own grief; his greatest love, the child he has lost, becomes "his best piece of poetrie," and the discipline of his art transforms his private sorrow into an experience common to all men.

Thus the basic movement in most of Jonson's verse is towards, and not away from, society. In poem after poem, he builds a place for himself in a cultivated circle, where, as in "To Penshurst," a charitable openness keeps civilization in tune with itself. Jonson did not achieve such a perspective without an immense effort, as can be seen in "An Execration upon Vulcan," where, after starting with the idea that his works, of all poets', are least deserving of destruction by fire, he gradually comes to see that his lot is no different from that of other men. Vulcan has many ways of "massacring Mankind," but men are united in their opposition to his ravages. So, too, in the great Cary-Morison ode, Jonson moves outward from his fantastic opening conceit of the child who, at Saguntum, returned to the womb rather than face the horrors of the war into which he was born. The child "sums a circle" which the poem will expand and develop until its circumference can include the perfect life of the early-dead Morison:

> All Offices were done
> By him, so ample, full, and round,
> In weight, in measure, number, sound,
> As though his age imperfect might appeare,
> His life was of Humanitie the Spheare.

Here, as so often in Jonson, the ideal person and the ideal society are balanced and neatly structured, reflecting the form of the work of art in which he commemorates them.

Socially oriented poetry like Jonson's could be imitated successfully, as it was by the "Sons of Ben." Milton, in whose work so many poetic traditions of the Renaissance converge, was not attracted by the metaphysical mode, but he did pay his tribute to Jonson in *L'Allegro*, *Il Penseroso*, and particularly in *Comus*. Two of Jonson's masques, *Pleasure Reconciled To Vertue* (one of the sources for *Comus*) and *Pans Anniversarie*, are included in this volume. They show Jonson at his best as a public poet, celebrating through his art, "the rites of true society."

With Robert Herrick, perhaps Jonson's most thoroughgoing disciple, these social rites take on a new form. Herrick treasures the country customs and the local myths of the Devonshire to which he was "exiled," but he has no sympathy for the "warty incivility" of his parishioners. Their vulgarity threatens the imaginative harmony of his vision, and he neutralizes it by pinpointing them in the (often bawdy) epigrams which he scatters throughout the *Hes-*

*perides*. Where Jonson had placed his own epigrams (*the* classical form) at the head of his poems in the 1616 *Works*, Herrick interweaves the gross with the delicate, complicating the fabric of his volume and diversifying its texture. A poem like "The Hock-cart" combines both strands, glorifying the rustics and their farm implements as symbols of the natural process, but never forgetting the harsh toil that makes the harvest possible:

> And, you must know, your Lords word's true,
> Feed him ye must, whose food fils you.
> And that this pleasure is like raine,
> Not sent ye for to drowne your paine,
> But for to make it spring againe.
>
> (lines 51–55)

Perhaps Herrick's greatest theme is the "Times trans-shifting" which he mentions in "The Argument of his Book." In poem after poem he blends together pagan rites and Christian customs, never more artfully than in "Corinna's going a Maying." His lyrics are deceptively neat and simple as they sing of his airy mistresses or trace the way in which lilies first became white. Almost always a classical or Jonsonian model lies behind these poems, but Herrick is seldom content merely to imitate his sources. His classicism is enriched by his love for native myth at the same time that his sophistication prevents his affectionate intimacy from descending to sentimentality.

The *Hesperides* may well have seemed old-fashioned to many a reader when it was published in 1648. Herrick's world blossoms with a kind of Elizabethan charm; he values folk superstitions, magic, fairies and witches precisely for their imaginative beauty, and it was this beauty which, as Richard Corbett was to lament in "The Faeryes Farewell," was now departing from the English poetical scene. The kind of myth-making which Waller and Denham would concern themselves with was more "rational," more directly concerned with public life and the social spirit of town and court. Waller's "On St. James's Park" does not deal with the countryside, but with a London landscape that the king himself has regulated and controlled. The diversions which it offers to the court become transformed, as the poem proceeds, into the political acts of government:

Here *Charles* contrives the ordering of his States,
Here he resolves his neighb'ring Princes fates:
What Nation shall have Peace, where War be made,
Determin'd is in this oraculous shade.

Here, as in Denham's "Cooper's Hill," the prospect is wider, more impersonal and more patently optimistic, than it had ever been in the poetry of the earlier century. The new verse of the Augustans would continue Jonson's effort to express individuality in terms of a social, civilized context.

R. S. SYLVESTER

*Yale University*
*August 25, 1968*

# NOTE

In accordance with the principles adopted in the Anchor Seventeenth-Century Series, the texts presented here are given in the original spelling and punctuation. Long "ſ" has been rendered as "s" and u and v, i and j have been normalized to conform with modern usage. A few obvious printers' errors in spelling and punctuation have been silently corrected, but substantive emendations of the early editions are made only on rare occasions. In such cases the original reading is recorded in a note. The edition employed for each poet is indicated in the Commentary section which follows the texts.

# ACKNOWLEDGMENTS

I am deeply indebted to Professor Louis L. Martz of Yale University, who first suggested to me the compilation of this anthology and who has given me, generously and freely, the benefit of his time and advice as my work proceeded. Professor J. Max Patrick of New York University and Mr. Eugene Eoyang and Miss Susan Burchardt of Doubleday & Company staunchly encouraged my effort in its early stages. Miss Susanna Lesan has been an omnipresent editor as the volume has moved through the press. I am grateful to Mrs. Barbara Stern and to Mrs. Mary Ludlam for their skill in preparing accurate typescripts. The illustrations have been supplied from copies in the Beinecke Rare Book and Manuscript Library of Yale University, where the staff, here as on many other occasions, has been handsomely co-operative.

# MICHAEL DRAYTON
## 1563–1631

# To My Most Dearely-loved Friend Henery Reynolds Esquire, of Poets and Poesie

MY DEARELY loved friend how oft have we,
In winter evenings (meaning to be free,)
To some well chosen place us'd to retire;
And there with moderate meate, and wine, and fire,
Have past the howres contentedly with chat,
Now talk'd of this, and then discours'd of that,
Spoke our owne verses 'twixt our selves, if not
Other mens lines, which we by chance had got,
Or some Stage pieces famous long before,
Of which your happy memory had store;
And I remember you much pleased were,
Of those who lived long agoe to heare,
As well as of those, of these latter times,
Who have inricht our language with their rimes,
And in succession, how still up they grew,
Which is the subject, that I now pursue;
For from my cradle (you must know that) I,
Was still inclin'd to noble Poesie,
And when that once *Pueriles* I had read,
And newly had my *Cato* construed,
In my small selfe I greatly marveil'd then,
Amongst all other, what strange kinde of men

TO MY MOST DEARELY-LOVED FRIEND: Henry Reynolds, a poet and critic, was Drayton's close friend. He translated Tasso's *Aminta* and published an essay on poetry. Drayton's poem first appeared in 1627.

8 *got:* memorized.

18 *still:* always.

19 *Pueriles: Sententiae Pueriles,* a schoolboy Latin textbook compiled by Leonard Culman.

20 *Cato:* The *Disticha de Moribus* of Dionysius Cato was a standard text in Elizabethan schools.

These Poets were; And pleased with the name,
To my milde Tutor merrily I came,
(For I was then a proper goodly page,
Much like a Pigmy, scarse ten yeares of age)
Clasping my slender armes about his thigh.
O my deare master! cannot you (quoth I)
Make me a Poet, doe it; if you can,
And you shall see, Ile quickly be a man,
Who me thus answered smiling, boy quoth he,
If you'le not play the wag, but I may see
You ply your learning, I will shortly read
Some Poets to you; *Phoebus* be my speed,
Too't hard went I, when shortly he began,
And first read to me honest *Mantuan*,
Then *Virgils Eglogues*, being entred thus,
Me thought I straight had mounted *Pegasus*,
And in his full Careere could make him stop,
And bound upon *Parnassus* by-clift top.
I scornd your ballet then though it were done
And had for Finis, *William Elderton*.
But soft, in sporting with this childish jest,
I from my subject have too long digrest,
Then to the matter that we tooke in hand,
*Jove* and *Apollo* for the *Muses* stand.
   That noble *Chaucer*, in those former times,
The first inrich'd our *English* with his rimes,
And was the first of ours, that ever brake,
Into the *Muses* treasure, and first spake
In weighty numbers, delving in the Mine
Of perfect knowledge, which he could refine,
And coyne for currant, and asmuch as then
The *English* language could expresse to men,

36 *Mantuan:* Baptista Spagnuoli Mantuanus (1448–1516), whose *Eclogues* were often used in schools.

40 *by-clift:* Mount Parnassus was often referred to as having two peaks.

42 *Elderton:* d. 1592?, writer of popular ballads in the 1570s and 1580s.

48 *The first:* i.e. was the first who.

He made it doe; and by his wondrous skill,
Gave us much light from his abundant quill.
And honest *Gower*, who in respect of him,
Had only sipt at *Aganippas* brimme,
And though in yeares this last was him before,
Yet fell he far short of the others store.
When after those, foure ages very neare,
They with the Muses which conversed, were
That Princely *Surrey*, early in the time
Of the Eight *Henry*, who was then the prime
Of *Englands* noble youth; with him there came
*Wyat;* with reverence whom we still doe name
Amongst our Poets, *Brian* had a share
With the two former, which accompted are
That times best makers, and the authors were
Of those small poems, which the title beare,
Of songs and sonnets, wherein oft they hit
On many dainty passages of wit.
*Gascoine* and *Churchyard* after them againe
In the beginning of *Eliza's* raine,
Accoumpted were great Meterers many a day,
But not inspired with brave fier, had they
Liv'd but a little longer, they had seene,
Their workes before them to have buried beene.
Grave morrall *Spencer* after these came on
Then who am I perswaded there was none
Since the blind *Bard* his *Iliads* up did make,
Fitter a taske like that to undertake,
To set downe boldly, bravely to invent,
In all high knowledge, surely excellent.

57 *Gower:* John Gower (1325?–1408), Chaucer's contemporary.
58 *Aganippas:* the sacred poetic fountain on Mount Helicon.
67 *Brian:* Sir Francis Bryan (d. 1550), a minor poet and the friend of Wyatt.
68 *accoumpted:* accounted.
71 *songs and sonnets:* the title of the famous miscellany published by Richard Tottel in 1557.
73 *Gascoine and Churchyard:* George Gascoigne (1525?–1577) and Thomas Churchyard (1520?–1604).

The noble *Sidney,* with this last arose,
That *Heroe* for numbers, and for Prose.
That throughly pac'd our language as to show,
The plenteous *English* hand in hand might goe
With *Greeke* and *Latine,* and did first reduce
Our tongue from *Lillies* writing then in use;
Talking of Stones, Stars, Plants, of fishes, Flyes,
Playing with words, and idle Similies,
As th'*English,* Apes and very Zanies be
Of every thing, that they doe heare and see,
So imitating his ridiculous tricks,
They spake and writ, all like meere lunatiques.
Then *Warner* though his lines were not so trim'd,
Nor yet his Poem so exactly lim'd
And neatly joynted, but the Criticke may
Easily reproove him, yet thus let me say;
For my old friend, some passages there be
In him, which I protest have taken me,
With almost wonder, so fine, cleere, and new
As yet they have bin equalled by few.
Neat *Marlow* bathed in the *Thespian* springs
Had in him those brave translunary things,
That the first Poets had, his raptures were,
All ayre, and fire, which made his verses cleere,
For that fine madnes still he did retaine,
Which rightly should possesse a Poets braine.
And surely *Nashe,* though he a Proser were
A branch of Lawrell yet deserves to beare,
Sharply *Satirick* was he, and that way
He went, since that his being, to this day

89 *reduce:* lead back.

90 *Lillies:* John Lyly (1554?–1606), author of *Euphues* (1579); the following lines describe the Euphuistic style which Sidney had attacked in his *Apology for Poetry*.

97 *Warner:* William Warner (1558?–1609). His major work was *Albion's England* (1586).

98 *lim'd:* limbed, articulated.

111 *Nashe:* Thomas Nashe (1567–1601), notorious for his satirical writings.

Few have attempted, and I surely thinke
Those words shall hardly be set downe with inke;
Shall scorch and blast, so as his could, where he,
Would inflict vengeance, and be it said of thee,
*Shakespeare* thou hadst as smooth a Comicke vaine,
Fitting the socke, and in thy naturall braine,
As strong conception, and as Cleere a rage,
As any one that trafiqu'd with the stage.
  Amongst these *Samuel Daniel,* whom if I
May spake of, but to sensure doe denie,
Onely have heard some wisemen him rehearse,
To be too much *Historian* in verse;
His rimes were smooth, his meeters well did close,
But yet his maner better fitted prose:
Next these, learn'd *Johnson,* in this List I bring,
Who had drunke deepe of the *Pierian* spring,
Whose knowledge did him worthily prefer,
And long was Lord here of the Theater,
Who in opinion made our learn'st to sticke,
Whether in Poems rightly dramatique,
Strong *Seneca* or *Plautus,* he or they,
Should beare the Buskin, or the Socke away.
Others againe here lived in my dayes,
That have of us deserved no lesse praise
For their translations, then the daintiest wit
That on *Parnassus* thinks, he highst doth sit,
And for a chaire may mongst the Muses call,
As the most curious maker of them all;
As reverent *Chapman,* who hath brought to us,
*Musaeus, Homer,* and *Hesiodus*

125 *rehearse:* describe.

126 *Historian:* Daniel (1562–1619) was best known for his *Civill Warres* (1609).

133 *learn'st to sticke:* i.e. Jonson set a difficult problem for our most learned critics.

143 *Chapman:* George Chapman (1559?–1634), also well known as a dramatist.

Out of the Greeke; and by his skill hath reard
Them to that height, and to our tongue endear'd,
That were those Poets at this day alive,
To see their bookes thus with us to survive,
They would think, having neglected them so long,
They had bin written in the *English* tongue.
  And *Silvester* who from the *French* more weake,
Made *Bartas* of his sixe dayes labour speake
In naturall *English*, who, had he there stayd,
He had done well, and never had bewraid,
His owne invention, to have bin so poore
Who still wrote lesse, in striving to write more.
  Then dainty *Sands* that hath to *English* done,
Smooth sliding *Ovid*, and hath made him run
With so much sweetnesse and unusuall grace,
As though the neatnesse of the *English* pace,
Should tell the Jetting *Lattine* that it came
But slowly after, as though stiffe and lame.
  So *Scotland* sent us hither, for our owne
That man, whose name I ever would have knowne,
To stand by mine, that most ingenious knight,
My *Alexander*, to whom in his right,
I want extreamely, yet in speaking thus
I doe but shew the love, that was twixt us,
And not his numbers which were brave and hie,
So like his mind, was his cleare Poesie,
And my deare *Drummond* to whom much I owe
For his much love, and proud I was to know,

151 *Silvester:* Joshua Sylvester (1563–1618), who translated the *Semaines* of Guillaume de Saluste, seigneur du Bartas (collected edition, 1606) as the *Divine Weeks.* His version became more popular in England than the original had been in France.

154 *bewraid:* betrayed.

157 *Sands:* Sandys' *Ovid* first appeared in 1626.

166 *Alexander:* Sir William Alexander of Menstry, Earl of Stirling (1567?–1640), tutor to Prince Henry, the son of James I. He published many volumes of verse.

171 *Drummond:* William Drummond of Hawthornden (1585–1649).

His poesie, for which two worthy men,
I *Menstry* still shall love, and *Hauthorne-den*,
Then the two *Beamounts* and my *Browne* arose,
My deare companions whom I freely chose
My bosome friends; and in their severall wayes,
Rightly borne Poets, and in these last dayes,
Men of much note, and no lesse nobler parts,
Such as have freely tould to me their hearts,
As I have mine to them; but if you shall
Say in your knowledge, that these be not all
Have writ in numbers, be inform'd that I
Only my selfe, to these few men doe tye,
Whose workes oft printed, set on every post,
To publique censure subject have bin most;
For such whose poems, be they nere so rare,
In private chambers, that incloistered are,
And by transcription daintyly must goe;
As though the world unworthy were to know,
Their rich composures, let those men that keepe
These wonderous reliques in their judgement deepe,
And cry them up so, let such Peeces bee
Spoke of by those that shall come after me,
I passe not for them: nor doe meane to run,
In quest of these, that them applause have wonne,
Upon our Stages in these latter dayes,
That are so many, let them have ther bayes
That doe deserve it; let those wits that haunt
Those publique circuits, let them freely chaunt

175 *Beamounts:* Francis Beaumont (1584–1616), the dramatist, and his brother, Sir John Beaumont (1583–1627), the poet.

175 *Browne:* William Browne of Tavistock (1591–1643?), author of *Britannia's Pastorals* (1613 and 1616).

185 *set . . . post:* Titlepages were tacked up on posts to advertize new books.

187 ff. *such:* probably alluding to Donne, whose poems were not published during his lifetime.

191 *composures:* compositions.

195 *passe:* care.

200 *circuits:* playhouses.

Their fine Composures, and their praise pursue,
And so my deare friend, for this time adue.

# The Epistle of Rosamond to King Henry the Second

## *The Argument*

HENRY *the Second keepeth* (*with much care*)
*Lord* CLIFFORDS *daughter,* ROSAMOND *the faire;*
*And whilst his Sonnes doe* Normandie *invade,*
*He forc'd to* France, *with wond'rous cost had made*
*A Labyrinth in* Woodstock, *where unseene*
*His Love might lodge safe, from his jealous Queene:*
*Yet when he stay'd beyond his time abroad,*
*Her pensive Brest, his Darling to unload,*
*In this Epistle doth her Griefe complaine;*
*And his Rescription tells her his againe.*

IF YET thine Eyes (Great HENRY) may endure
These tainted Lines, drawne with a Hand impure,
(Which faine would blush, but Feare keeps Blushes backe,
And therefore suted in despairing Blacke)
Let me for Loves sake their acceptance crave,
But that sweet Name (vile) I prophaned have;
Punish my Fault, or pittie mine estate,
Reade them for Love, if not for Love, for Hate.

THE EPISTLE OF ROSAMOND: The Epistle of Rosamond and Henry's reply first appeared in 1597 and went through ten editions before the final one of 1619. Henry II (1133–1189) had Rosamond Clifford (d. 1176) as his mistress in the 1170s. The rebellion of his son, Henry, who was supported by the queen (Eleanor of Aquitaine), occurred in 1173–74. By Drayton's day the story of "fair Rosamond" had already become legendary.

10 *rescription:* return letter.

If with my Shame thine Eyes thou faine would'st feede,
Here let them surfet, of my Shame to reade:
This scribbled Paper which I send to thee,
If noted rightly, doth resemble mee:
As this pure Ground, whereon these Letters stand,
So pure was I, ere stayned by thy Hand;
Ere I was blotted with this foule Offence,
So cleere and spotlesse was mine Innocence:
Now, like these Markes which taint this hatefull Scroule,
Such the blacke sinnes which spot my leprous Soule.
What, by this Conquest, canst thou hope to winne,
Where thy best Spoyle, is but the Act of Sinne?
Why on my Name this slander do'st thou bring,
To make my Fault renowned by a King?
'Fame never stoopes to things, but meane and poore,
'The more our Greatnesse, our Fault is the more;
'Lights on the Ground, themselves doe lessen farre,
'But in the Ayre, each small Sparke seemes a Starre.
Why, on my Woman-frayltie should'st thou lay
So strong a Plot, mine Honour to betray?
Or thy unlawfull Pleasure should'st thou buy,
Both with thine owne shame, and my Infamie?
'Twas not my Minde consented to this Ill,
Then had I beene transported by my Will;
For, what my Bodie was inforc'd to doe,
(Heaven knowes) my Soule yet ne'r consented to:
For, through mine Eyes had she her liking seene,
Such as my Love, such had my Lover beene.
'True Love is simple, like his Mother Truth,
'Kindly Affection, Youth to love with Youth;
'No greater corsive to our blooming Yeeres,
'Then the cold Badge of winter-blasted Hayres.
'Thy Kingly Power makes to withstand thy Foes,
'But cannot keepe backe Age, with Time it growes;
'Though Honour our ambitious Sex doth please,
'Yet in that Honour, Age a foule Disease:

39 *corsive:* corrosive.

'Nature hath her free Course in all, and then
'Age is alike, in Kings, and other Men.
Which all the World will to my shame impute,
That I, my selfe did basely prostitute;
And say, that Gold was Fuell to the Fire,
Gray Hayres in Youth not kindling greene Desire.
O no; that wicked Woman, wrought by thee,
My Tempter was to that forbidden Tree;
That subtill Serpent, that seducing Devill,
Which bad me taste the Fruit of good and Evill;
That CIRCE, by whose Magicke I was charm'd,
And to this monstrous shape am thus transform'd;
That vip'rous Hag, the Foe to her owne Kind,
That divellish Spirit, to damne the weaker Mind;
Our Fraylties Plague, our Sexes onely Curse,
Hells deep'st Damnation, the worst Evils worse.
    But HENRY, how canst thou affect me thus,
T' whom thy remembrance now is odious?
My haplesse Name, with HENRIES Name I found,
Cut in the Glasse with HENRIES Diamond;
That Glasse from thence faine would I take away,
But then I feare the Ayre would me betray;
Then doe I strive to wash it out with Teares,
But then the same more evident appeares.
Then doe I cover it with my guiltie Hand,
Which that Names witnesse doth against me stand;
Once did I sinne, which Memorie doth cherish,
Once I offended, but I ever perish.
'What Griefe can be, but Time doth make it lesse?
'But Infamie, Time never can suppresse.
Sometimes, to passe the tedious irkesome Houres,
I climbe the top of *Woodstocks* mounting Towres,
Where, in a Turret, secretly I lye,
To view from farre such as doe travell by;
Whither (me thinkes) all cast their Eyes at mee,
As through the Stones my Shame did make them see,

51 *Woman:* She remains unidentified.

And with such Hate the harmelesse Walls doe view,
As e'vn to Death their Eyes would me pursue.
The married Women curse my hatefull Life,
Wronging a faire Queene, and a vertuous Wife;
The Maidens wish, I buried quicke may die,
And from each place neere my abode, doe flie.
Well knew'st thou what a Monster I would be,
When thou didst build this Labyrinth for me,
Whose strange *Meanders* turning ev'ry way,
Be like the course wherein my Youth did stray;
Onely a Clue doth guide me out and in,
But yet still walke I circular in sinne.
  As in the Gallerie this other day,
I and my Woman past the time away,
'Mongst many Pictures, which were hanging by,
The silly Girle at length hapt to espie
Chaste LUCRECE Image, and desires to know,
What shee should be, her selfe that murd'red so?
Why Girle (quoth I) this is that Roman Dame;
Not able then to tell the rest for shame,
My Tongue doth mine owne Guiltinesse betray;
With that I sent the prattling Wench away,
Lest when my lisping guiltie Tongue should hault,
My Lookes might prove the Index to my Fault.
As that Life-bloud which from the Heart is sent,
In Beauties Field pitching his Crimson Tent,
In lovely Sanguine sutes the Lillie Cheeke,
Whilst it but for a resting Place doth seeke;
And changing oftentimes with sweet Delight,
Converts the White to Red, the Red to White;
The Blush with Palenesse for the place doth strive,
The Palenesse thence the Blush would gladly drive;

88 *Labyrinth:* apparently a house built within a garden maze. Early writers refer to its "Daedalian craftsmanship."
91 *Clue:* thread.
98 *What:* Who.
103 *hault:* stumble.

Thus in my Brest a thousand Thoughts I carrie,
Which in my Passion diversly doe varie.
When as the Sunne hales tow'rds the Westerne slade,
And the Trees shadowes hath much taller made,
Forth goe I to a little Current neere,
Which like a wanton Trayle creepes here and there,
Where, with mine Angle casting in my Bait,
The little Fishes (dreading the deceit)
With fearefull nibbling flye th'inticing Gin,
By Nature taught what danger lies therein.
Things Reasonlesse, thus warn'd by Nature be,
Yet I devour'd the Bait was layd for me:
Thinking thereon, and breaking into Grones,
The bubbling Spring, which trips upon the Stones,
Chides me away, lest sitting but too nie,
I should pollute that Native puritie.
*Rose of the World,* so doth import my Name,
*Shame of the World,* my Life hath made the same.
And to th' unchaste this Name shall given be,
Of ROSAMOND, deriv'd from Sinne and Me.
The CLIFFORDS take from me that Name of theirs,
Which hath beene famous for so many yeeres:
They blot my Birth with hateful Bastardie,
That I sprang not from their Nobilitie;
They my alliance utterly refuse,
Nor will a Strumpet shall their Name abuse.
Here, in the Garden, wrought by curious hands,
Naked DIANA in the Fountaine stands,
With all her Nymphes got round about to hide her,
As when ACTEON had by chance espy'd her:

115 *slade:* open space in the woods.
119 *Angle:* fishing pole.
121 *Gin:* trap, net.
129–30 *Rose . . . same:* Drayton's lines translate the punning Latin inscription said to have been placed on Rosamond's tomb when she was buried at Godstow Abbey: *Rosa mundi sed non rosa munda.*

This sacred Image I no sooner view'd,
But as that metamorphos'd Man, pursu'd
By his owne Hounds; so, by my Thoughts am I,
Which chase me still, which way soe'r I flye.
Touching the Grasse, the Honey-dropping Dew,
Which falls in Teares before my limber shoo,
Upon my Foot consumes in weeping still,
As it would say, Why went'st thou to this Ill?
Thus, to no Place in safetie can I goe,
But every thing doth give me cause of Woe.
  In that faire Casket, of such wond'rous Cost,
Thou sent'st the Night before mine Honour lost,
AMIMONE was wrought, a harmelesse Maid,
By NEPTUNE, that adult'rous God, betray'd;
She prostrate at his Feet, begging with Prayers,
Wringing her Hands, her Eyes swolne up with Teares:
This was not an intrapping Bait from thee,
But by thy Vertue gently warning mee,
And to declare for what intent it came,
Lest I therein should ever keepe my shame.
And in this Casket (ill I see it now)
That JOVES Love Iö, turn'd into a Cow;
Yet was she kept with ARGUS hundred Eyes:
So wakefull still be JUNO'S Jealousies:
By this I well might have fore-warned beene,
T' have cleer'd my selfe to thy suspecting Queene,
Who with more hundred Eyes attendeth mee,
Then had poor ARGUS single Eyes to see.
In this thou rightly imitatest JOVE,
Into a Beast thou hast transform'd thy Love;
Nay, worser farre (beyond their beastly kind)
A Monster both in Bodie and in Mind.
  The Waxen Taper which I burne by Night,
With the dull vap'rie dimnesse mockes my Sight,
As though the Dampe which hinders the cleere Flame,
Came from my Breath, in that Night of my Shame;
When as it look'd with a darke lowring Eye,
To see the losse of my Virginitie.

And if a Starre but by the Glasse appeare,
I straight intreat it, not to looke in here;
I am alreadie hatefull to the Light,
And will it too, betray me to the Night?
  Then sith my Shame so much belongs to thee,
Rid me of that, by onely murd'ring mee;
And let it justly to my charge be layd,
That I thy Person meant to have betray'd:
Thou shalt not need by circumstance t'accuse me,
If I denie it, let the Heavens refuse me.
My Life's a Blemish, which doth cloud thy Name,
Take it away, and cleare shall shine thy Fame:
Yeeld to my Sute, if ever Pittie mov'd thee,
In this shew Mercie, as I ever lov'd thee.

## *Henry to Rosamond*

WHEN first the Post arrived at my Tent,
And brought the Letters ROSAMOND had sent,
Thinke from his Lips but what deare Comfort came,
When in mine Eare he softly breath'd thy Name:
Straight I injoyn'd him, of thy Health to tell,
Longing to heare my ROSAMOND did well;
With new Enquiries then I cut him short,
When of the same he gladly would report,
That with the earnest Haste, my Tongue oft trips,
Catching the words halfe spoke, out of his Lips:
This told, yet more I urge him to reveale,
To lose no time, whilst I unrip'd the Seale.
The more I reade, still doe I erre the more,
As though mistaking somewhat said before:
Missing the Point, the doubtfull Sense is broken,
Speaking againe what I before had spoken.
  Still in a Swoond, my Heart revives and faints,
'Twixt Hopes, Despaires, 'twixt Smiles and deepe Complaints.

As these sad Accents sort in my Desires,
Smooth Calmes, rough Stormes, sharpe Frosts, and raging Fires,
Put on with Boldnesse, and put backe with Feares,
For oft thy Troubles doe extort my Teares.
O, how my Heart at that blacke Line did tremble!
That blotted Paper should Thy Selfe resemble;
O, were there Paper but neere halfe so white!
The Gods thereon their sacred Lawes would write
With Pens of Angels Wings; and for their Inke,
That Heavenly *Nectar*, their immortall Drinke.
  Majestike Courage strives to have supprest
This fearefull Passion, stir'd up in my Brest;
But still in vaine the same I goe about,
My Heart must breake within, or Woes breake out.
Am I at home pursu'd with private Hate,
And Warre comes raging to my Palace Gate?
Is meager Envie stabbing at my Throne,
Treason attending when I walke alone?
And am I branded with the Curse of Rome,
And stand condemned by a Councels Doome?
And by the pride of my rebellious Sonne,
Rich *Normandie* with Armies over-runne?
Fatall my Birth, unfortunate my Life,
Unkind my Children, most unkind my Wife.
Griefe, Cares, old Age, Suspition to torment me,
Nothing on Earth to quiet or content me;
So many Woes, so many Plagues to find,
Sicknesse of Bodie, discontent of Mind;
Hopes left, Helps reft, Life wrong'd, Joy interdicted,
Banish'd, distress'd, forsaken, and afflicted.
Of all Reliefe hath Fortune quite bereft me?
Onely my Love yet to my Comfort left me:
And is one Beautie thought so great a thing,
To mitigate the Sorrowes of a King?

37 *Curse of Rome:* Pope Alexander III excommunicated Henry for his part in the death of Thomas à Becket.

53 *Bar'd:* Barred; *prove:* experience.

Bar'd of that Choice the Vulgar often prove;
Have we, then they, lesse priviledge in Love?
Is it a King the wofull Widdow heares?
Is it a King dryes up the Orphans Teares?
Is it a King regards the Clyents crie?
Gives Life to him, by Law condemn'd to die?
Is it his Care the Common-wealth that keepes,
As doth the Nurse her Babie, whilst it sleepes?
And that poore King of all those Hopes prevented,
Unheard, unhelp'd, unpitti'd, unlamented?
  Yet let me be with Povertie opprest,
Of Earthly Blessings rob'd, and dis-possest,
Let me be scorn'd, rejected, and revil'd,
And from my Kingdome let me live exil'd,
Let the Worlds Curse upon me still remaine,
And let the last bring on the first againe;
All Miseries that wretched Man may wound,
Leave for my Comfort onely ROSAMOND.
For Thee, swift Time his speedie course doth stay,
At thy Command, the Destinies obay;
Pittie is dead, that comes not from thine Eyes,
And at thy Feet ev'n Mercie prostrate lyes.
  If I were feeble, rheumatike, or cold,
These were true signes that I were waxed old:
But I can march all day in massie Steele,
Nor yet my Armes unwieldy weight doe feele;
Nor wak'd by Night with Bruise or bloudie Wound,
The Tent my Bed, no Pillow but the Ground:
For very Age had I layne Bedred long,
One Smile of Thine, againe could make me Yong.
Were there in Art a Power but so divine,
As is in that sweet Angell-Tongue of Thine,
That great Enchantresse, which once tooke such paines,
To put young Bloud into old AESONS Veines,
And in Groves, Mountaines, and the Moorish Fen,
Sought out more Hearbes then had been knowne to Men,

85 *Enchantresse:* Medea.

And in the pow'rfull Potion that she makes,
Put Bloud of Men, of Birds, of Beasts, and Snakes;
Never had needed to have gone so farre,
To seeke the Soyles where all those Simples are;
One Accent from thy Lips the Bloud more warmes,
Then all her Philters, Exorcismes, and Charmes.
Thy Presence hath repaired in one day,
What many Yeeres with Sorrowes did decay,
And made fresh Beautie in her flower to spring,
Out of the wrinckles of Times ruining.
Ev'n as the hungry Winter-starved Earth,
When she by nature labours towards her Birth,
Still as the Day upon the darke World creepes,
One Blossome forth after another peepes,
Till the small Flower, whose Root (at last) unbound,
Gets from the frostie Prison of the Ground,
Spreading the Leaves unto the pow'rfull Noone,
Deck'd in fresh Colours, smiles upon the Sunne.
  Never unquiet Care lodg'd in that Brest,
Where but one Thought of ROSAMOND did rest;
Nor Thirst, nor Travaile, which on Warre attend,
Ere brought the long Day to desired end;
Nor yet did pale Feare, or leane Famine live,
Where hope of Thee did any Comfort give:
Ah, what Injustice then is this of Thee,
That thus the Guiltlesse do'st condemne for me?
When onely she (by meanes of my Offence)
Redeemes thy Purenesse, and thy Innocence,
When to our Wills perforce obey they must,
That's just in them, what ere in us unjust,
Of what we doe, not them account we make;
The Fault craves pardon for th'Offendors sake:
'And what to worke, a Princes Will may merit,
'Hath deep'st impression in the gentlest Spirit.
  If 't be my Name, that doth Thee so offend,
No more my selfe shall be mine owne Names Friend;

92 *Simples:* herbs.

If it be that, which Thou do'st onely hate,
That Name, in my Name, lastly hath his date;
Say 'tis accurst, and fatall, and disprayse it,
If written, blot it, if engraven, raze it;
Say, that of all Names 'tis a Name of Woe,
Once a Kings Name, but now it is not so:
And when all this is done, I know 'twill grieve thee;
And therefore (Sweet) why should I now beleeve thee?
  Nor shouldst thou thinke, those Eyes with Envie lowre,
Which passing by thee, gaze up to thy Towre;
But rather prayse thine owne, which be so cleere,
Which from the Turret like two Starres appeare:
Above, the Sunne doth shine, beneath, thine Eye,
Mocking the Heav'n, to make another Skye.
  The little Streame which by thy Tow'r doth glide,
Where oft thou spend'st the wearie Ev'ning Tide,
To view thee well, his Course would gladly stay,
As loth from thee to part so soone away,
And with Salutes thy selfe would gladly greet,
And offer up some small Drops at thy Feet;
But finding, that the envious Bankes restraine it,
T' excuse it selfe, doth in this sort complaine it,
And therefore this sad bubbling Murmure keepes,
And for thy want, within the Channell weepes.
And as thou do'st into the Water looke,
The Fish which see thy shaddow in the Brooke,
Forget to feede, and all amazed lye,
So daunted with the lustre of thine Eye.
  And that sweet Name, which thou so much do'st wrong,
In time shall be some famous Poets Song;
And with the very sweetnesse of that Name,
Lyons and Tygers Men shall learne to tame.
The carefull Mother, at her pensive Brest,
With ROSAMOND shall bring her Babe to Rest;
The little Birds (by Mens continuall sound)
Shall learne to speake, and prattle ROSAMOND:

126 *date:* end.

And when in Aprill they begin to sing,
With ROSAMOND shall welcome in the Spring;
And she in whom all Rarities are found,
Shall still be said to be a ROSAMOND.
The little Flowers dropping their honied Dew,
Which (as thou writ'st) doe weepe upon thy Shoo,
Not for thy Fault (sweet ROSAMOND) doe moane,
Onely lament, that thou so soone art gone;
For if thy Foot touch Hemlocke as it goes,
That Hemlock's made more sweeter than the Rose.
Of JOVE, or NEPTUNE, how they did betray,
Speake not; of Iö, or AMIMONE,
When she, for whom JOVE once became a Bull,
Compar'd with Thee, had beene a Tawnie Trull;
He a white Bull, and she a whiter Cow,
Yet he nor she neere halfe so white as Thou.
Long since (thou know'st) my Care provided for
To lodge thee safe from jealous ELLINOR;
The Labyrinths Conveyance guides thee so,
(Which onely VAUGHAN, thou, and I doe know)
If she doe guard thee with an hundred Eyes,
I have a hundred subtill MERCURIES,
To watch that ARGUS which my Love doth keepe,
Untill Eye, after Eye, fall all to sleepe.
And those Starres which looke in, but looke to see,
(Wond'ring) what Starre here on the Earth should be;
As oft the Moone, amidst the silent Night,
Hath come to joy us with her friendly Light,
And by the Curtaine help'd mine Eye to see
What envious Night and Darkenesse hid from me;
When I have wish'd, that she might ever stay,
And other Worlds might still enjoy the Day.
What should I say? Words, Teares, and Sighes be spent,
And want of Time doth further Helpe prevent:

180 *Vaughan:* a trusted servant of Henry, who had charge of the palace at Woodstock.

My Campe resounds with fearefull shockes of Warre,
Yet in my Brest more dang'rous Conflicts are;
Yet is my Signall to the Battels sound,
The blessed Name of beautious ROSAMOND.
Accursed be that Heart, that Tongue, that Breath,
Should thinke, should speake, or whisper of thy Death;
For in one Smile, or Lowre from thy sweet Eye,
Consists my Life, my Hope, my Victorie.
Sweet *Woodstock,* where my ROSAMOND doth rest,
Be blest in Her, in whom thy King is blest:
For though in *France* a while my Body bee,
My Heart remaines (deare Paradise) in thee.

# The Muses Elizium

## *The Description of Elizium*

A PARADICE on earth is found,
Though farre from vulgar sight,
Which with those pleasures doth abound
That it *Elizium* hight.

Where, in Delights that never fade,
The Muses lulled be,
And sit at pleasure in the shade
Of many a stately tree,

Which no rough Tempest makes to reele
Nor their straight bodies bowes,
Their lofty tops doe never feele
The weight of winters snowes;

THE MUSES ELIZIUM: The text given here is that of the first edition (1630). "The Description of Elizium" functions as a preface to the ten "Nimphalls" which follow it.

In Groves that evermore are greene,
No falling leafe is there,
But *Philomel* (of birds the Queene)
In Musicke spends the yeare.

The *Merle* upon her mertle Perch,
There to the *Mavis* sings,
Who from the top of some curld Berch
Those notes redoubled rings;

There Daysyes damaske every place
Nor once their beauties lose,
That when proud *Phoebus* hides his face
Themselves they scorne to close.

The Pansy and the Violet here,
As seeming to descend,
Both from one Root, a very payre,
For sweetnesse yet contend,

And pointing to a Pinke to tell
Which beares it, it is loath,
To judge it; but replyes, for smell
That it excels them both,

Wherewith displeasde they hang their heads
So angry soone they grow
And from their odoriferous beds
Their sweets at it they throw.

The winter here a Summer is,
No waste is made by time,
Nor doth the Autumne ever misse
The blossomes of the Prime.

40 *Prime:* spring.

The flower that July forth doth bring
In Aprill here is seene,
The Primrose that puts on the spring
In July decks each Greene.

The sweets for soveraignty contend
And so abundant be,
That to the very Earth they lend
And Barke of every Tree:

Rills rising out of every Banck,
In wilde Meanders strayne,
And playing many a wanton pranck
Upon the speckled plaine,

In Gambols and lascivious Gyres
Their time they still bestow
Nor to their Fountaines none retyres,
Nor of their course will goe

Those Brooks with Lillies bravely deckt,
So proud and wanton made,
That they their courses quite neglect:
And seeme as though they stayde,

Faire *Flora* in her state to viewe
Which through those Lillies looks,
Or as those Lillies leand to shew
Their beauties to the brooks.

That *Phoebus* in his lofty race,
Oft layes aside his beames
And comes to coole his glowing face
In these delicious streames;

53 *Gyres:* turnings.

Oft spreading Vines clime up the Cleeves,
Whose ripned clusters there,
Their liquid purple drop, which drives
A Vintage through the yeere.

Those Cleeves whose craggy sides are clad
With Trees of sundry sutes,
Which makes continuall summer glad,
Even bending with their fruits,

Some ripening, ready some to fall,
Some blossom'd, some to bloome,
Like gorgeous hangings on the wall
Of some rich princely Roome:

*Pomegranates, Lymons, Cytrons,* so
Their laded branches bow,
Their leaves in number that outgoe
Nor roomth will them alow.

There in perpetuall Summers shade,
*Apolloes* Prophets sit
Among the flowres that never fade,
But flowrish like their wit;

To whom the Nimphes upon their Lyres,
Tune many a curious lay,
And with their most melodious Quires
Make short the longest day.

The *thrice three virgins* heavenly Cleere,
Their trembling Timbrels sound,
Whilst the three comely *Graces* there
Dance many a dainty Round,

69 *Cleeves:* slopes.
93 *virgins:* the nine muses.

Decay nor Age there nothing knowes,
There is continuall Youth,
As Time on plant or creatures growes,
So still their strength renewth.

The Poets Paradice this is,
To which but few can come;
The Muses onely bower of blisse
Their deare *Elizium.*

Here happy soules, (their blessed bowers,
Free from the rude resort
Of beastly people) spend the houres,
In harmlesse mirth and sport,

Then on to the *Elizian* plaines
*Apollo* doth invite you
Where he provides with pastorall straines,
In *Nimphals* to delight you.

## *The Second Nimphall*

### Lalus, Cleon, and Lirope

*The Muse new courtship doth devise,*
*By Natures strange varieties,*
*Whose rarieties she here relates,*
*And gives you pastorall delicates.*

LALUS a Jolly youthfull Lad,
With *Cleon,* no lesse crown'd
With vertues; both their beings had
On the Elizian ground.
Both having parts so excellent,
That it a question was,
Which should be the most eminent,
Or did in ought surpasse.

This *Cleon* was a Mountaineer,
And of the wilder kinde,
And from his birth had many a yeere
Bin nurst up by a Hinde:
And as the sequell well did show,
It very well might be;
For never Hart, nor Hare, nor Roe,
Were halfe so swift as he.
But *Lalus* in the Vale was bred,
Amongst the Sheepe and Neate,
And by those Nimphes there choicly fed,
With Hony, Milke, and Wheate;
Of Stature goodly, faire of speech,
And of behaviour mylde,
Like those there in the Valley rich,
That bred him of a chyld.
Of Falconry they had the skill,
Their Halkes to feed and flye,
No better Hunters ere clome Hill,
Nor hollowed to a Cry:
In Dingles deepe, and Mountains hore,
Oft with the bearded Speare
They cumbated the tusky Boare,
And slew the angry Beare.
In Musicke they were wondrous quaint,
Fine Aers they could devise;
They very curiously could Paint,
And neatly Poetize;
That wagers many time were laid
On Questions that arose,
Which song the witty *Lalus* made,
Which *Cleon* should compose.

LALUS, CLEON, AND LIROPE.
12 *Hinde:* peasant.
18 *Neate:* cattle.
27 *clome:* climbed.
28 *hollowed to a Cry:* hallooed to a pack of hounds.

The stately Steed they manag'd well,
Of Fence the art they knew,
For Dansing they did all excell
The Gerles that to them drew;
To throw the Sledge, to pitch the Barre,
To wrestle and to Run,
They all the Youth exceld so farre,
That still the Prize they wonne.
These sprightly Gallants lov'd a Lasse,
Cald *Lirope the bright*,
In the whole world there scarcely was
So delicate a Wight,
There was no Beauty so divine
That ever Nimph did grace,
But it beyond it selfe did shine
In her more hevenly face:
What forme she pleasd each thing would take
That ere she did behold,
Of Pebbles she could Diamonds make,
Grosse Iron turne to Gold:
Such power there with her presence came
Sterne Tempests she alayd,
The cruell Tigar she could tame,
She raging Torrents staid,
She chid, she cherisht, she gave life,
Againe she made to dye,
She raised a warre, apeasd a strife,
With turning of her eye.
Some said a God she did beget,
But much deceiv'd were they,
Her Father was a *Rivelet*,
Her Mother was a *Fay*.
Her Lineaments so fine that were,
She from the Fayrie tooke,
Her Beauties and Complection cleere,
By nature from the Brooke.

52 *wight:* creature.

These Ryvalls wayting for the houre
(The weather calme and faire)
When as she us'd to leave her Bower
To take the pleasant ayre,
Acosting her; their complement
To her their Goddesse done;
By gifts they tempt her to consent,
When *Lalus* thus begun.

*Lalus.* Sweet *Lirope* I have a Lambe
Newly wayned from the Damme,
Of the right kinde, it is notted,
Naturally with purple spotted,
Into laughter it will put you,
To see how prettily 'twill But you;
When on sporting it is set,
It will beate you a Corvet,
And at every nimble bound
Turne it selfe above the ground;
When tis hungry it will bleate,
From your hand to have its meate,
And when it hath fully fed,
It will fetch Jumpes above your head,
As innocently to expresse
Its silly sheepish thankfullnesse,
When you bid it, it will play,
Be it either night or day,
This *Lirope* I have for thee,
So thou alone wilt live with me.

*Cleon.* From him O turne thine eare away,
And heare me my lov'd *Lirope*,
I have a Kid as white as milke,
His skin as soft as *Naples* silke,

86 *wayned:* weaned.
87 *notted:* without horns.
92 *Corvet:* a leaping or frisking motion.

His hornes in length are wondrous even,
And curiously by nature writhen;
It is of th'Arcadian kinde,
Ther's not the like twixt either *Inde;*
If you walke, 'twill walke you by,
If you sit downe, it downe will lye,
It with gesture will you wooe,
And counterfeit those things you doe;
Ore each Hillock it will vault,
And nimbly doe the Summer-sault,
Upon the hinder Legs 'twill goe,
And follow you a furlong so,
And if by chance a Tune you roate,
'Twill foote it finely to your note,
Seeke the world and you may misse
To finde out such a thing as this;
This my love I have for thee
So thou'lt leave him and goe with me.

*Lirope.* Beleeve me Youths your gifts are rare,
And you offer wondrous faire;
*Lalus* for Lambe, *Cleon* for Kyd,
'Tis hard to judge which most doth bid,
And have you two such things in store,
And I n'er knew of them before?
Well yet I dare a Wager lay
That *Brag* my litle Dog shall play,
As dainty tricks when I shall bid,
As *Lalus* Lambe, or *Cleons* Kid.
But t'may fall out that I may need them
Till when yee may doe well to feed them;
Your Goate and Mutton pretty be
But Youths these are noe bayts for me,
Alasse good men, in vaine ye wooe,
'Tis not your Lambe nor Kid will doe.

121 *roate:* repeat.

*Lalus.* I have two Sparrowes white as Snow,
Whose pretty eyes like sparkes doe show;
In her Bosome *Venus* hatcht them
Where her little *Cupid* watcht them,
Till they too fledge their Nests forsooke
Themselves and to the Fields betooke,
Where by chance a Fowler caught them
Of whom I full dearely bought them;
They'll fetch you Conserve from the Hip,
And lay it softly on your Lip,
Through their nibling bills they'll Chirup
And fluttering feed you with the Sirup,
And if thence you put them by
They to your white necke will flye,
And if you expulse them there
They'll hang upon your braded Hayre;
You so long shall see them prattle
Till at length they'll fall to battle,
And when they have fought their fill,
You will smile to see them bill.
These Birds my *Lirope's* shall be
So thou'llt leave him and goe with me.

*Cleon.* His Sparrowes are not worth a rush
I'le finde as good in every bush,
Of Doves I have a dainty paire
Which when you please to take the Aier,
About your head shall gently hover
Your Cleere browe from the Sunne to cover,
And with their nimble wings shall fan you,
That neither Cold nor Heate shall tan you,
And like Umbrellas with their feathers
Sheeld you in all sorts of weathers:

147 *fledge:* with feathers on their wings.
151 *Hip:* red fruit of the smooth bramble.

They be most dainty Coloured things,
They have Damask backs and Chequerd wings,
Their neckes more Various Cullours showe
Then there be mixed in the Bowe;
*Venus* saw the lesser Dove
And therewith was farre in Love,
Offering for't her goulden Ball
For her Sonne to play withall;
These my *Liropes* shall be
So shee'll leave him and goe with me.

*Lirope.* Then for Sparrowes, and for Doves
I am fitted twixt my Loves,
But *Lalus,* I take noe delight
In Sparowes, for they'll scratch and bite
And though joynd, they are ever wooing
Alwayes billing if not doeing,
Twixt *Venus* breasts if they have lyen
I much feare they'll infect myne;
*Cleon* your Doves are very dainty,
Tame Pidgeons else you knowe are plenty,
These may winne some of your Marrowes
I am not caught with Doves, nor Sparrowes,
I thanke ye kindly for your Coste,
Yet your labour is but loste.

*Lalus.* With full-leav'd Lillies I will stick
Thy braded hayre all o'r so thick,
That from it a Light shall throw
Like the Sunnes upon the Snow.
Thy Mantle shall be Violet Leaves,
With the fin'st the Silkeworme weaves
As finly Woven; whose rich smell
The Ayre about thee so shall swell
That it shall have no power to moove.
A Ruffe of Pinkes thy Robe above

195 *Marrowes:* companions.

About thy necke so neatly set
That Art it cannot counterfet,
Which still shall looke so Fresh and new,
As if upon their Roots they grew:
And for thy head Ile have a Tyer
Of netting, made of Strawbery wyer,
And in each knot that doth compose
A Mesh, shall stick a halfe blowne Rose,
Red, damaske, white, in order set
About the sides, shall run a Fret
Of Primroses, the Tyer throughout
With Thrift and Daysyes frindgd about;
All this faire Nimph Ile doe for thee,
So thou'lt leave him and goe with me.

*Cleon.* These be but weeds and Trash he brings,
Ile give thee solid, costly things,
His will whither and be gone
Before thou well canst put them on;
With Currall I will have thee Crown'd,
Whose Branches intricatly wound
Shall girt thy Temples every way;
And on the top of every Spray
Shall stick a Pearle orient and great,
Which so the wandring Birds shall cheat,
That some shall stoope to looke for Cheries,
As other for tralucent Berries.
And wondring, caught e'r they be ware
In the curld Tramels of thy hayre:
And for thy necke a Christall Chaine
Whose lincks shapt like to drops of Raine,
Upon thy panting Breast depending,
Shall seeme as they were still descending,

219 *Tyer:* headdress.
220 *Thrift:* the sea pink or sea gillyflower.
227 *Currall:* coral.
234 *tralucent:* translucent.
239 *depending:* hanging down.

And as thy breath doth come and goe,
So seeming still to ebbe and flow:
With Amber Bracelets cut like Bees,
Whose strange transparancy who sees,
With Silke small as the Spiders Twist,
Doubled so oft about thy Wrist,
Would surely thinke alive they were,
From Lillies gathering hony there.
Thy Buskins Ivory, carv'd like Shels
Of Scallope, which as little Bels
Made hollow, with the Ayre shall Chime,
And to thy steps shall keepe the time:
Leave *Lalus, Lirope* for me
And these shall thy rich dowry be.

*Lirope. Lalus* for flowers *Cleon* for Jemmes,
For Garlands and for Diadems,
I shall be sped, why this is brave,
What Nimph can choicer Presents have,
With dressing, brading, frowncing, flowring,
All your Jewels on me powring,
In this bravery being drest,
To the ground I shall be prest,
That I doubt the Nimphes will feare me,
Nor will venture to come neare me;
Never Lady of the May,
To this houre was halfe so gay;
All in flowers, all so sweet,
From the Crowne, beneath the Feet,
Amber, Currall, Ivory, Pearle,
If this cannot winne a Gerle,
Thers nothing can, and this ye wooe me,
Give me your hands and trust ye to me,
(Yet to tell ye I am loth)
That I'le have neither of you both.

*Lalus.* When thou shalt please to stem the flood,
(As thou art of the watry brood)

I'le have twelve Swannes more white then snow,
Yokd for the purpose two and two,
To drawe thy Barge wrought of fine Reed
So well that it nought else shall need,
The Traces by which they shall hayle
Thy Barge; shall be the winding trayle
Of woodbynd; whose brave Tasseld Flowers
(The Sweetnesse of the Woodnimphs Bowres)
Shall be the Trappings to adorne,
The swannes, by which thy Barge is borne,
Of flowred Flags I'le rob the banke
Of water-Cans and King-cups ranck
To be the Covering of thy Boate,
And on the Streame as thou do'st Floate,
The *Naiades* that haunt the deepe,
Themselves about thy Barge shall keepe,
Recording most delightfull Layes,
By Sea Gods written in thy prayse,
And in what place thou hapst to land,
There the gentle Silvery sand,
Shall soften, curled with the Aier
As sensible of thy repayre:
This my deare love I'le doe for thee,
So Thou'lt leave him and goe with me:

*Cleon.* Tush Nimphe his Swannes will prove but Geese,
His Barge drinke water like a Fleece;
A Boat is base, I'le thee provide,
A Chariot, wherein *Jove* may ride;
In which when bravely thou art borne,
Thou shalt looke like the glory̆ous morne
Ushering the Sunne, and such a one
As to this day was never none,
Of the Rarest Indian Gummes,

281 *hayle:* pull along.
288 *water-Cans:* yellow water lilies; *King-cups:* buttercups.
302 *drinke:* soak up.

More pretious then your Balsamummes
Which I by Art have made so hard,
That they with Tooles may well be Carv'd
To make a Coach of: which shall be
Materyalls of this one for thee,
And of thy Chariot each small peece
Shall inlayd be with Amber Greece,
And guilded with the Yellow ore
Produc'd from *Tagus* wealthy shore;
In which along the pleasant Lawne,
With twelve white Stags thou shalt be drawne,
Whose brancht palmes of a stately height,
With severall nosegayes shall be dight;
And as thou ryd'st, thy Coach about,
For thy strong guard shall runne a Rout,
Of Estriges: whose Curled plumes
Sen'sd with thy Chariots rich perfumes,
The scent into the Aier shall throw;
Whose naked Thyes shall grace the show;
Whilst the Woodnimphs and those bred
Upon the mountayns, o'r thy head
Shall beare a Canopy of flowers,
Tinseld with drops of Aprill showers,
Which shall make more glorious showes
Then spangles, or your silver Oas;
This bright nimph I'le doe for thee
So thou'lt leave him and goe with me.

*Lirope*. Vie and revie, like Chapmen profer'd,
Would't be receaved what you have offer'd;
Ye greater honour cannot doe me,
If not building Altars to me:

316 *Amber Greece:* ambergris.
318 *Tagus:* Iberian river, famed for its golden gravel.
325 *Estriges:* ostriches.
326 *Sen'sd:* i.e. the perfumes act as incense.
334 *Oas:* small circular ornaments.
337 *Chapmen:* peddlers.

Both by Water and by Land,
Bardge and Chariot at command;
Swans upon the Streame to tawe me,
Stags upon the Land to draw me,
In all this Pompe should I be seene,
What a pore thing were a Queene:
All delights in such excesse,
As but yee, who can expresse:
Thus mounted should the Nimphes me see,
All the troope would follow me,
Thinking by this state that I
Would assume a Deitie.
There be some in love have bin,
And I may commit that sinne,
And if e'r I be in love,
With one of you I feare twill prove,
But with which I cannot tell,
So my gallant Youths farewell.

## *The Seventh Nimphall*

### FLORIMEL, LELIPA, NAIIS, CODRUS a FERIMAN

*The Nimphes, the Queene of love pursue,*
*Which oft doth hide her from their view:*
*But lastly from th' Elizian Nation,*
*She banisht is by Proclamation.*

*Florimel.* Deare *Lelipa*, where hast thou bin so long,
Was't not enough for thee to doe me wrong;
To rob me of thy selfe, but with more spight
To take my *Naiis* from me, my delight?
Yee lazie Girles, your heads where have ye layd,
Whil'st *Venus* here her anticke prankes hath playd?

343 *tawe:* pull.

*Lelipa.* Nay *Florimel,* we should of you enquire,
The onely Mayden, whom we all admire
For Beauty, Wit, and Chastity, that you
Amongst the rest of all our Virgin crue,
In quest of her, that you so slacke should be,
And leave the charge to *Naiis* and to me.

*Florimel.* Y'are much mistaken *Lelipa,* 'twas I,
Of all the Nimphes, that first did her descry,
At our great Hunting, when as in the Chase
Amongst the rest, me thought I saw one face
So exceeding faire, and curious, yet unknowne
That I that face not possibly could owne.
And in the course, so Goddesse like a gate,
Each step so full of majesty and state;
That with my selfe, I thus resolv'd that she
Lesse then a Goddesse (surely) could not be:
Thus as *Idalia,* stedfastly I ey'd,
A little Nimphe that kept close by her side
I noted, as unknowne as was the other,
Which *Cupid* was disguis'd so by his mother.
The little purblinde Rogue, if you had seene,
You would have thought he verily had beene
One of *Diana's* Votaries, so clad,
He every thing so like a Huntresse had:
And she had put false eyes into his head,
That very well he might us all have sped.
And still they kept together in the Reare,
But as the Boy should have shot at the Deare,
He shot amongst the Nimphes, which when I saw,
Closer up to them I began to draw;
And fell to hearken, when they naught suspecting,
Because I seem'd them utterly neglecting,
I heard her say, my little *Cupid* too't,
Now Boy or never, at the Bevie shoot.

FLORIMEL, LELIPA, NAIIS, CODRUS A FERIMAN.
23 *Idalia:* Venus.
32 *sped:* overcome.

Have at them *Venus,* quoth the Boy anon,
I'le pierce the proud'st, had she a heart of stone:
With that I cryde out, Treason, Treason, when
The Nimphes that were before, turning agen
To understand the meaning of this cry,
They out of sight were vanish't presently.
Thus but for me, the Mother and the Sonne,
Here in Elizium, had us all undone.

*Naiis.* Beleeve me gentle Maide, 'twas very well,
But now heare me my beauteous *Florimel.*
Great *Mars* his Lemman being cryde out here,
She to *Felicia* goes, still to be neare
Th' Elizian Nimphes, for at us in her ayme,
The fond *Felicians* are her common game.
I upon pleasure idly wandring thither,
Something worth laughter from those fooles to gather,
Found her, who thus had lately beene surpriz'd;
Fearing the like, had her faire selfe disguis'd
Like an old Witch, and gave out to have skill
In telling Fortunes either good or ill;
And that more neatly she with them might close,
She cut the Cornes, of dainty Ladies Toes:
She gave them Phisicke, either to coole or moove them,
And powders too to make their sweet Hearts love them.
And her sonne *Cupid,* as her Zany went,
Carrying her boxes, whom she often sent
To know of her faire Patients how they slept.
By which meanes she, and the blinde Archer crept
Into their favours, who would often Toy,
And tooke delight in sporting with the Boy;
Which many times amongst his waggish tricks,
These wanton Wenches in the bosome pricks;

51 *Lemman:* beloved; *cryde out:* discovered.
52 *Felicia:* Drayton's ironic name for the real world.
63 *Phisicke:* medicine.
65 *Zany:* attendant fool.

That they before which had some franticke fits,
Were by his Witchcraft quite out of their wits.
Watching this Wisard, my minde gave me still
She some Impostor was, and that this skill
Was counterfeit, and had some other end.
For which discovery, as I did attend,
Her wrinckled vizard being very thin,
My piercing eye perceiv'd her cleerer skin
Through the thicke Rivels perfectly to shine;
When I perceiv'd a beauty so divine,
As that so clouded, I began to pry
A little nearer, when I chanc't to spye
That pretty Mole upon her Cheeke, which when
I saw; survaying every part agen,
Upon her left hand, I perceiv'd the skarre
Which she received in the Trojan warre;
Which when I found, I could not chuse but smile,
She, who againe had noted me the while,
And by my carriage, found I had descry'd her,
Slipt out of sight, and presently doth hide her.

*Lelipa.* Nay then my dainty Girles, I make no doubt
But I my selfe as strangely found her out
As either of you both; in Field and Towne
When like a Pedlar she went up and downe:
For she had got a pretty handsome Packe,
Which she had fardled neatly at her backe:
And opening it, she had the perfect cry,
Come my faire Girles, let's see, what will you buy?
Here be fine night Maskes, plastred well within,
To supple wrinckles, and to smooth the skin:

79 *vizard:* mask.
81 *Rivels:* wrinkles.
88 *Trojan warre:* Venus, who favored the Trojans, had been wounded during the war.
98 *fardled:* carried as a bundle.

Heer's Christall, Corall, Bugle, Jet, in Beads,
Cornelian Bracelets, for my dainty Maids:
Then Periwigs and Searcloth-Gloves doth show,
To make their hands as white as Swan or Snow:
Then takes she forth a curious gilded boxe,
Which was not opened but by double locks;
Takes them aside, and doth a Paper spred,
In which was painting both for white and red:
And next a piece of Silke, wherein there lyes
For the decay'd, false Breasts, false Teeth, false Eyes:
And all the while shee's opening of her Packe,
*Cupid* with's wings bound close downe to his backe:
Playing the Tumbler on a Table gets,
And shewes the Ladies many pretty feats.
I seeing behinde him that he had such things,
For well I knew no boy but he had wings,
I view'd his Mothers beauty, which to me
Lesse then a Goddesse said, she could not be:
With that quoth I to her, this other day,
As you doe now, so one that came this way,
Shew'd me a neate piece, with the needle wrought,
How *Mars* and *Venus* were together caught
By polt-foot *Vulcan* in an Iron net;
It griev'd me after that I chanc't to let,
It to goe from me: whereat waxing red,
Into her Hamper she hung downe her head,
As she had stoup't some noveltie to seeke,
But 'twas indeed to hide her blushing Cheeke:
When she her Trinkets trusseth up anon,
E'r we were 'ware, and instantly was gone.

*Florimel.* But hearke you Nimphes, amongst our idle prate,
Tis current newes through the Elizian State,
That *Venus* and her Sonne were lately seene

103 *Bugle:* kind of glass bead, usually black.
105 *Searcloth-Gloves:* waterproof gloves made of cloth coated with wax.
110 *painting:* cosmetics.
125 *polt-foot:* with a crippled foot.

Here in *Elizium,* whence they oft have beene
Banisht by our edict, and yet still merry,
Were here in publique row'd o'r at the Ferry,
Where as 'tis said, the Ferryman and she
Had much discourse, she was so full of glee,
*Codrus* much wondring at the blind Boyes Bow.

*Naiis.* And what it was, that easly you may know,
*Codrus* himselfe comes rowing here at hand.

*Lelipa. Codrus* come hither, lett your Whirry stand,
I hope upon you, ye will take no state
Because two Gods have grac't your Boat of late;
Good Ferry-man I pray thee let us heare
What talke ye had, aboard thee whilst they were.

*Codrus.* Why thus faire Nimphes.
As I a Fare had lately past,
And thought that side to ply,
I heard one as it were in haste;
A Boate, a Boate, to cry,
Which as I was about to bring,
And came to view my Fraught,
Thought I, what more then heavenly thing,
Hath fortune hither brought.
She seeing mine eyes still on her were,
Soone, smilingly, quoth she;
Sirra, looke to your Roother there,
Why lookst thou thus at me?
And nimbly stept into my Boat,
With her a little Lad
Naked and blind, yet did I note,
That Bow and Shafts he had,

144 *Whirry:* little boat.
150 *past:* transported across.
155 *Fraught:* load.
160 *Roother:* rudder.

And two Wings to his Shoulders fixt,
Which stood like little Sayles,
With farre more various colours mixt,
Then be your Peacocks Tayles;
I seeing this little dapper Elfe,
Such Armes as these to beare,
Quoth I thus softly to my selfe,
What strange thing have we here,
I never saw the like thought I:
Tis more then strange to me,
To have a child have wings to fly,
And yet want eyes to see;
Sure this is some devised toy,
Or it transform'd hath bin,
For such a thing, halfe Bird, halfe Boy,
I thinke was never seene;
And in my Boat I turnd about,
And wistly viewd the Lad,
And cleerely saw his eyes were out,
Though Bow and Shafts he had.
As wistly she did me behold,
How likst thou him quoth she,
Why well, quoth I; and better should,
Had he but eyes to see.
How sayst thou honest friend, quoth she,
Wilt thou a Prentice take,
I thinke in time, though blind he be,
A Ferry-man hee'll make;
To guide my passage Boat quoth I,
His fine hands were not made,
He hath beene bred too wantonly
To undertake my trade;
Why helpe him to a Master then,
Quoth she, such Youths be scant,
It cannot be but there be men

186 *wistly:* intently.
194 *passage Boat:* passenger boat.

That such a Boy do want.
Quoth I, when you your best have done,
No better way you'll finde,
Then to a Harper binde your Sonne,
Since most of them are blind,
The lovely Mother and the Boy,
Laught heartily thereat,
As at some nimble jest or toy,
To heare my homely Chat.
Quoth I, I pray you let me know,
Came he thus first to light,
Or by some sicknesse, hurt, or blow,
Depryved of his sight;
Nay sure, quoth she, he thus was borne,
Tis strange borne blind, quoth I,
I feare you put this as a scorne
On my simplicity;
Quoth she, thus blind I did him beare,
Quoth I, if't be no lye,
Then he's the first blind man Ile sweare,
Ere practised Archery;
A man, quoth she, nay there you misse,
He's still a Boy as now,
Nor to be elder then he is,
The Gods will him alow;
To be no elder then he is,
Then sure he is some sprite
I straight replide, againe at this,
The Goddesse laught out right;
It is a mystery to me,
An Archer and yet blinde;
Quoth I againe, how can it be,
That he his marke should finde;
The Gods, quoth she, whose will it was
That he should want his sight,
That he in something should surpasse,
To recompence their spight,
Gave him this gift, though at his Game

He still shot in the darke,
That he should have so certaine ayme,
As not to misse his marke.
By this time we were come a shore,
When me my Fare she payd,
But not a word she uttered more,
Nor had I her bewrayd,
Of *Venus* nor of *Cupid* I
Before did never heare,
But that a Fisher comming by
Then, told me who they were.

*Florimel.* Well; against them then proceed
As before we have decreed,
That the Goddesse and her Child,
Be for ever hence exild,
Which *Lelipa* you shall proclaime
In our wise *Apollo's* name.

*Lelipa.* To all th' Elizian Nimphish Nation,
Thus we make our Proclamation,
Against *Venus* and her Sonne
For the mischeefe they have done,
After the next last of May,
The fixt and peremtory day,
If she or *Cupid* shall be found
Upon our Elizian ground,
Our Edict, meere Rogues shall make them,
And as such, who ere shall take them,
Them shall into prison put,
*Cupids* wings shall then be cut,
His Bow broken, and his Arrowes
Given to Boyes to shoot at Sparrowes,
And this Vagabund be sent,
Having had due punishment

245 *bewrayd:* revealed.
261 *peremtory:* decisive, final.

To mount *Cytheron,* which first fed him:
Where his wanton Mother bred him,
And there out of her protection
Dayly to receive correction;
Then her Pasport shall be made,
And to *Cyprus* Isle convayd,
And at *Paphos* in her Shryne,
Where she hath beene held divine,
For her offences found contrite,
There to live an Anchorite.

## *The Tenth Nimphall*

### NAIIS, CLAIA, CORBILUS, SATYRE

*A Satyre on* Elizium *lights,*
*Whose ugly shape the Nimphes affrights,*
*Yet when they heare his just complaint,*
*They make him an Elizian Saint.*

*Corbilus.* WHAT; breathles Nimphs? bright Virgins let me know
What suddaine cause constraines ye to this haste?
What have ye seene that should affright ye so?
What might it be from which ye flye so fast?
I see your faces full of pallid feare,
As though some perill followed on your flight;
Take breath a while, and quickly let me heare
Into what danger ye have lately light.

*Naiis.* Never were poore distressed Gerles so glad,
As when kinde, loved *Corbilus* we saw,
When our much haste us so much weakned had,
That scarcely we our wearied breathes could draw.
In this next Grove under an aged Tree,
So fell a monster lying there we found,

NAIIS, CLAIA, CORBILUS, SATYRE.
14 *fell:* ugly.

As till this day, our eyes did never see,
Nor ever came on the Elizian ground.
Halfe man, halfe Goat, he seem'd to us in show,
His upper parts our humane shape doth beare,
But he's a very perfect Goat below,
His crooked Cambrils arm'd with hoofe and hayre.

*Claia.* Through his leane Chops a chattering he doth make
Which stirres his staring beastly driveld Beard,
And his sharp hornes he seem'd at us to shake,
Canst thou then blame us though we were afeard.

*Corbilus.* Surely it seemes some Satyre this should be,
Come and goe back and guide me to the place,
Be not affraid, ye are safe enough with me,
Silly and harmelesse be their Silvan Race.

*Claia.* How *Corbilus;* a Satyre doe you say?
How should he over high *Parnassus* hit?
Since to these Fields ther's none can finde the way,
But onely those the Muses will permit.

*Corbilus.* Tis true; but oft, the sacred Sisters grace
The silly satyre, by whose plainesse, they
Are taught the worlds enormities to trace,
By beastly mens abhominable way;
Besyde he may be banisht his owne home
By this base time, or be so much distrest,
That he the craggy by-clift Hill hath clome
To finde out these more pleasant Fields of rest.

*Naiis.* Yonder he sits, and seemes himselfe to bow
At our approch, what doth our presence awe him?
Me thinks he seemes not halfe so ugly now,
As at the first, when I and *Claia* saw him.

20 *Cambrils:* hocks.
34 *silly:* simple.
39 *by-clift:* with two peaks (Parnassus).

*Corbilus.* Tis an old Satyre, Nimph, I now discerne,
Sadly he sits, as he were sick or lame,
His lookes would say, that we may easly learne
How, and from whence, he to Elizium came.
Satyre, these Fields, how cam'st thou first to finde?
What Fate first show'd thee this most happy shore?
When never any of thy Silvan kinde
Set foot on the Elizian earth before?

*Satyre.* O never aske, how I came to this place,
What cannot strong necessity finde out?
Rather bemoane my miserable case,
Constrain'd to wander the wide world about.
With wild *Silvanus* and his woody crue,
In Forrests I, at liberty and free,
Liv'd in such pleasure as the world ne'r knew,
Nor any rightly can conceive but we.
This jocond life we many a day enjoy'd,
Till this last age, those beastly men forth brought,
That all those great and goodly Woods destroy'd,
Whose growth their Grandsyres, with such sufferance sought,
That faire *Felicia* which was but of late,
Earth's Paradice, that never had her Peere,
Stands now in that most lamentable state,
That not a Silvan will inhabit there;
Where in the soft and most delicious shade,
In heat of Summer we were wont to play,
When the long day too short for us we made,
The slyding houres so slyly stole away;
By *Cynthia's* light, and on the pleasant Lawne,
The wanton Fayry we were wont to chase,
Which to the nimble cloven-footed Fawne,
Upon the plaine durst boldly bid the base.
The sportive Nimphes, with shouts and laughter shooke
The Hils and Valleyes in their wanton play,
Waking the Ecchoes, their last words that tooke,

76 *bid the base:* challenged in the game of prisoner's base.

Till at the last, they lowder were then they.
The lofty hie Wood, and the lower spring,
Sheltring the Deare, in many a suddaine shower;
Where Quires of Birds, oft wonted were to sing,
The flaming Furnace wholly doth devoure;
Once faire *Felicia,* but now quite defac'd,
Those Braveries gone wherein she did abound,
With dainty Groves, when she was highly grac'd
With goodly Oake, Ashe, Elme, and Beeches croun'd:
But that from heaven their judgement blinded is,
In humane Reason it could never be,
But that they might have cleerly seene by this,
Those plagues their next posterity shall see.
The little Infant on the mothers Lap
For want of fire shall be so sore distrest,
That whilst it drawes the lanke and empty Pap,
The tender lips shall freese unto the breast;
The quaking Cattle which their Warmstall want,
And with bleake winters Northerne winde opprest,
Their Browse and Stover waxing thin and scant,
The hungry Crowes shall with their Caryon feast.
Men wanting Timber wherewith they should build,
And not a Forrest in *Felicia* found,
Shall be enforc'd upon the open Field,
To dig them Caves for houses in the ground:
The Land thus rob'd, of all her rich Attyre,
Naked and bare her selfe to heaven doth show,
Begging from thence that *Jove* would dart his fire
Upon those wretches that disrob'd her so;
This beastly Brood by no meanes may abide
The name of their brave Ancestors to heare,
By whom their sordid slavery is descry'd,
So unlike them as though not theirs they were,
Nor yet they sense, nor understanding have,
Of those brave Muses that their Country song,

99 *Browse:* fodder; *Stover:* winter food.
114 *song:* sung.

But with false Lips ignobly doe deprave
The right and honour that to them belong;
This cruell kinde thus Viper-like devoure
That fruitfull soyle which them too fully fed;
The earth doth curse the Age, and every houre
Againe, that it these viprous monsters bred.
I seeing the plagues that shortly are to come
Upon this people cleerely them forsooke:
And thus am light into Elizium,
To whose straite search I wholly me betooke.

*Naiis.* Poor silly creature, come along with us,
Thou shalt be free of the Elizian fields:
Be not dismaid, nor inly grieved thus,
This place content in all abundance yeelds.
We to the cheerefull presence will thee bring,
Of *Joves* deare Daughters, where in shades they sit,
Where thou shalt heare those sacred Sisters sing,
Most heavenly Hymnes, the strength and life of wit.

*Claia.* Where to the Delphian God upon their Lyres
His Priests seeme ravisht in his height of praise:
Whilst he is crowning his harmonious Quiers,
With circling Garlands of immortall Bayes.

*Corbilus.* Here live in blisse, till thou shalt see those slaves,
Who thus set vertue and desert at nought:
Some sacrific'd upon their Grandsires graves,
And some like beasts in markets sold and bought.
Of fooles and madmen leave thou then the care,
That have no understanding of their state:
For whom high heaven doth so just plagues prepare,
That they to pitty shall convert thy hate.
And to Elizium be thou welcome then,
Untill those base Felicians thou shalt heare,
By that vile nation captived againe,
That many a glorious age their captives were.

# SIR HENRY WOTTON
1568–1639

## *A Hymn to my God in a night of my late Sicknesse*

*Oh thou great Power,* in whom I move,
For whom I *live,* to whom I *die,*
Behold me through thy beams of *love,*
Whilest on this *Couch* of tears I lye;
And Cleanse my sordid *soul* within,
By thy *Christs Bloud,* the *bath* of sin.

No hallowed oyls, no grains I need,
No rags of Saints, no purging fire,
One rosie drop from *Davids* Seed
Was worlds of seas, to quench thine Ire.
O pretious Ransome! which once paid,
That *Consummatum est* was said:

And said by *him,* that said no more,
But *seal'd* it with his sacred *breath.*
Thou then, that hast dispung'd my score,
And dying, wast the death of *death;*
Be to me now, on thee I call,
My Life, my Strength, my Joy, my All.

## A Poem *written by Sir* Henry Wotton, *in his youth*

O Faithless World, and thy more faithless Part,
a womans heart!
The true shop of variety, where sits
nothing but fits

A HYMN TO MY GOD.

12 *Consummatum est:* "It is consummated," Christ's dying words on the cross.

And feavers of desire, and pangs of love,
which toyes remove.
Why was she born to please, or I to trust
words writ in dust?
Suffering her Eys to govern my despair,
my pain for air;
And fruit of time rewarded with untruth,
the food of youth.
Untrue she was: yet, I beleev'd her eys
(instructed spies)
Till I was taught, that Love was but a scool
to breed a fool.
Or sought she more by triumphs of deniall,
to make a triall
How far her smiles commanded my weakness?
yeild and Confess:
Excuse no more thy folly; but for Cure,
blush and indure
As well thy shame, as passions that were vain:
and think, 'tis gain
To know, that Love lodg'd in a womans brest,
Is but a guest.

## *On his Mistris, the* Queen *of* Bohemia

You meaner *Beauties* of the *Night*,
That poorly satisfie our *Eies*
More by your *number*, then your *light*,
You *Common people* of the *Skies*;
What are you when the *Sun* shall rise?

ON HIS MISTRIS: The Queen of Bohemia was Elizabeth (1596–1662), daughter of James I. She married Frederick V, the Elector Palatine, in 1613. He became King of Bohemia for a brief period in 1619.

You Curious Chanters of the Wood,
That warble forth *Dame Natures* layes,
Thinking your Voyces understood
By your weake *accents;* whats your praise
When *Philomell* her voyce shal raise?

You *Violets,* that first apeare,
By your *pure purpel mantels* knowne,
Like the proud *Virgins* of the *yeare,*
As if the *Spring* were all your own;
What are you when the *Rose is* blowne?

So, when *my Mistris* shal be *seene*
In *form* and *Beauty* of her *mind,*
By *Vertue* first, then *Choyce* a *Queen,*
Tell me, if *she* were not design'd
Th'*Eclypse* and *Glory* of her kind.

## *Upon the sudden Restraint of the* Earle of Somerset, *then falling from favor*

Dazel'd thus, with height of place,
Whilst our hopes our wits beguile,
No man markes the narrow space
'Twixt a prison, and a smile.

Then, since fortunes favours fade,
You, that in her armes doe sleep,
Learne to swim, and not to wade;
For, the Hearts of Kings are deepe.

UPON THE SUDDEN RESTRAINT OF THE EARLE OF SOMERSET: Sir Robert Carr (d. 1645), who became Earl of Somerset on November 3, 1613, was accused of poisoning Sir Thomas Overbury in September 1615. His wife, the divorced Countess of Essex, pleaded guilty and received a pardon in 1616. Carr was tried and found guilty in the latter year and remained in prison until 1622.

But, if Greatness be so blind,
As to trust in towers of Aire,
Let it be with Goodness lin'd,
That at'least, the Fall be faire.

Then though darkened, you shall say,
When Friends faile, and Princes frowne,
*Vertue* is the roughest way,
But proves at night a *Bed* of *Downe.*

## *The Character of a Happy Life*

How *happy* is he born and taught,
That serveth not an others *will?*
Whose *Armour* is his *honest* thought:
And simple *Truth* his utmost Skill?

Whose *Passions* not his masters are,
Whose *soul* is still prepar'd for *Death;*
Untide unto the *world,* by care
Of *Publick fame,* or *private breath.*

Who *envies* none that *Chance* doth *raise,*
Nor *Vice* hath ever Understood;
How deepest wounds are given by *praise,*
Nor rules of State, but rules of *good.*

Who hath his *life* from rumors freed,
Whose *Conscience* is his strong retreat:
Whose *state* can neither *flatterers* feed,
Nor *ruine* make *oppressors great.*

THE CHARACTER OF A HAPPY LIFE.
7 *Untide:* not bound.

Who *God* doth late and early pray,
More of his *grace,* then *gifts* to lend:
And entertaines the harmless day
With a *Religious* Book, or Friend.

This man is freed from servile bands
Of hope to rise, or *feare* to fall:
*Lord* of himselfe, though not of *Lands,*
And having *nothing:* yet hath *all.*

## *On a* Banck *as I sate* a Fishing, *A Description of the* Spring

And now all *Nature* seem'd in *Love,*
The lusty *Sap* began to move;
New *Juice* did stirre th'embracing *Vines;*
And *Birds* had drawne their *Valentines:*
The *jealous Trout,* that low did lie,
Rose at a wel-dissembled *Flie:*
There stood my friend, with patient Skill
Attending of his trembling *quill.*
Already were the *Eaves* possest
With the swift *Pilgrims* daubed nest.
The *Groves* already did rejoyce
In *Philomels* triumphing *voyce.*
  The *showers* were short; the *weather* mild;
The *Morning* fresh; the *Evening* smil'd.
  *Jone* takes her neat-rub'd paile, and now
She trips to milk the Sand-red *Cow;*
Where, for some sturdy foot-ball *Swaine,*
*Jone* strokes a *sillibub,* or twaine.

ON A BANCK AS I SATE A FISHING.

10 *Pilgrims:* a bird who has just returned from the South.

18 *sillibub:* a drink made of fresh milk or cream, curdled with wine or cider, and often sweetened or flavored.

The *Fields* and *Gardens* were beset
With *Tulip, Crocus,* Violet.
And now, though late, the *Modest Rose*
Did more then halfe a blush disclose.
Thus all look't *gay,* all full of *Chear,*
To welcome the *New-liveri'd yeare.*

## *Tears at the Grave of Sr.* Albertus Morton (*who was buried at* Southampton) *wept by* Sir H. Wotton

*Silence* (in truth) would speak my Sorrow best,
For, deepest wounds can least their feelings tel:
Yet, let me borrow from mine own unrest,
But time to bid *Him,* whom I lov'd, Farwel.

O my unhappy Lines! you that before
Have serv'd my youth to vent some wanton Cries,
And now congeal'd with grief, can scarce implore
Strength to accent! Here my *Albertus* lies.

This is the Sable Stone, this is the Cave
And womb of Earth that doth his Corp's imbrace,
While others sing his praise, let me engrave
These bleeding Numbers, to adorn the Place.

Here will I paint the Characters of woe,
Here will I pay my Tribute to the Dead,
And here my faithfull Tears in showrs shal flow
To humanize the Flints whereon I tread.

TEARS AT THE GRAVE OF SR. ALBERTUS MORTON: Sir Albertus Morton (c. 1584–1625). He served with Wotton, his half-uncle, on many embassies.

Where though I mourn my matchlesse losse alone,
And none between my weaknesse judge and me,
Yet even these gentle walles allow my Mone,
Whose doleful Echoes to my Plaints agree.

But, is He gon? and live I Ryming here,
As if some Muse would listen to my Lay?
When all distun'd sit waiting for their Dear,
And bathe the Banks where he was wont to play?

Dwell thou in endlesse Light, discharged soul:
Freed now from Natures, & from Fortunes trust:
While on this fluent Globe, my Glasse shall role,
And run the rest of my remaining dust.

## *Upon the death of Sir* Albert Morton's *Wife*

He first deceas'd: She for a little tri'd
To live without Him: lik'd it not, and di'd.

UPON THE DEATH OF SIR ALBERT MORTON'S WIFE: Morton's wife was Elizabeth, the daughter of Sir Edward Apsley.

# BENJAMIN JONSON
## 1572–1637

## From *Epigrammes*

### To My Booke

It will be look'd for, booke, when some but see
Thy title, *Epigrammes,* and nam'd of mee,
Thou should'st be bold, licentious, full of gall,
Wormewood, and sulphure, sharpe, and tooth'd withall;
Become a petulant thing, hurle inke, and wit,
As mad-men stones: not caring whom they hit.
Deceive their malice, who could wish it so.
And by thy wiser temper, let men know
Thou are not covetous of least selfe fame,
Made from the hazard of anothers shame:
Much lesse with lewd, prophane, and beastly phrase,
To catch the worlds loose laughter, or vaine gaze.
He that departs with his owne honesty
For vulgar praise, doth it too dearely buy.

### To William Camden

*Camden,* most reverend head, to whom I owe
All that I am in arts, all that I know.
(How nothing's that?) to whom my countrey owes
The great renowne, and name wherewith shee goes.
Then thee the age sees not that thing more grave,
More high, more holy, that shee more would crave.

TO MY BOOKE.
5 *petulant:* making slight attacks on.
13 *departs with:* gives up.

TO WILLIAM CAMDEN: Camden (1551–1633) was Jonson's teacher at Westminster School.
4 *name:* Camden's *Britannia* (1586) rapidly achieved international fame as a work of antiquarian scholarship.

What name, what skill, what faith hast thou in things!
    What sight in searching the most antique springs!
What weight, and what authoritie in thy speech!
    Man scarse can make that doubt, but thou canst teach.
Pardon free truth, and let thy modestie,
    Which conquers all, be once over-come by thee.
Many of thine this better could, then I,
    But for their powers, accept my pietie.

## On My First Daughter

Here lyes to each her parents ruth,
*Mary,* the daughter of their youth:
Yet, all heavens gifts, being heavens due,
It makes the father, lesse, to rue.
At sixe moneths end, shee parted hence
With safetie of her innocence;
Whose soule heavens Queene, (whose name shee beares)
In comfort of her mothers teares,
Hath plac'd amongst her virgin-traine:
Where, while that sever'd doth remaine,
This grave partakes the fleshly birth.
Which cover lightly, gentle earth.

ON MY FIRST DAUGHTER: The date of Mary's death has not been ascertained.
10 *that:* her soul.

## To John Donne

*Donne,* the delight of *Phoebus,* and each *Muse,*
Who, to thy one, all other braines refuse;
Whose every worke, of thy most earely wit,
Came forth example, and remaines so, yet:
Longer a knowing, then most wits doe live.
And which no affection praise enough can give!
To it, thy language, letters, arts, best life,
Which might with halfe mankind maintayne a strife.
All which I meant to praise, and, yet, I would;
But leave, because I cannot as I should!

## On My First Sonne

Farewell, thou child of my right hand, and joy;
My sinne was too much hope of thee, lov'd boy,
Seven yeeres tho' wert lent to me, and I thee pay,
Exacted by thy fate, on the just day.
O, could I loose all father now. For why
Will man lament the state he should envie?
To have so soone scap'd worlds, and fleshes rage,
And, if no other miserie, yet age?
Rest in soft peace, and, ask'd, say here doth lye
*Ben. Jonson* his best piece of *poetrie.*

TO JOHN DONNE.

1–2 *Phoebus . . . refuse:* Apollo and the Muses reject all other brains when compared to Donne's.

7 *To it:* In addition.

ON MY FIRST SONNE: Jonson's son, Benjamin, died in 1603 at the age of six.

5 *loose:* lose.

For whose sake, hence-forth, all his vowes be such,
As what he loves may never like too much.

## On Lucy Countesse of Bedford

This morning, timely rapt with holy fire,
I thought to forme unto my zealous *Muse*,
What kinde of creature I could most desire,
To honor, serve, and love; as *Poets* use.
I meant to make her faire, and free, and wise,
Of greatest bloud, and yet more good then great;
I meant the day-starre should not brighter rise,
Nor lend like influence from his lucent seat.
I meant shee should be curteous, facile, sweet,
Hating that solemne vice of greatnesse, pride;
I meant each softest vertue, there should meet,
Fit in that softer bosome to reside.
Onely a learned, and a manly soule
I purpos'd her; that should, with even powers,
The rock, the spindle, and the sheeres controule
Of destinie, and spin her owne free houres.
Such when I meant to faine, and wish'd to see,
My *Muse* bad, *Bedford* write, and that was shee.

ON LUCY COUNTESSE OF BEDFORD: The Countess of Bedford (d. 1627) was the friend and patron of many authors.

9 *facile:* easy to approach.

15 *rock . . . sheeres:* the emblems of the Fates, Clotho, Lachesis, and Atropos.

## To Lucy, Countesse of Bedford, with Mr. Donnes Satyres

*Lucy,* you brightnesse of our spheare, who are
Life of the *Muses* day, their morning-starre!
If workes (not th'authors) their owne grace should looke,
Whose poems would not wish to be your booke?
But these, desir'd by you, the makers ends
Crowne with their owne. Rare poemes aske rare friends.
Yet, *Satyres,* since the most of mankind bee
Their un-avoided subject, fewest see:
For none ere tooke that pleasure in sinnes sense,
But, when they heard it tax'd, tooke more offence.
They, then, that living where the matter is bred,
Dare for these poemes, yet, both aske, and read,
And like them too; must needfully, though few,
Be of the best: and 'mongst those, best are you.
*Lucy,* you brightnesse of our spheare, who are
The *Muses* evening, as their morning-starre.

## To John Donne

Who shall doubt, *Donne,* where I a *Poet* bee,
When I dare send my *Epigrammes* to thee?
That so alone canst judge, so'alone dost make:
And, in thy censures, evenly, dost take
As free simplicitie, to dis-avow,
As thou hast best authoritie, t'allow.

TO LUCY, COUNTESSE OF BEDFORD.
1 *brightnesse:* The name *Lucy* derives from the Latin *lux,* light.
TO JOHN DONNE.
1 *where:* whether.

Reade all I send: and, if I find but one
    Mark'd by thy hand, and with the better stone,
My title's seal'd. Those that for claps doe write,
    Let pui'nees, porters, players praise delight,
And, till they burst, their backs, like asses load:
    A man should seeke great glorie, and not broad.

## Inviting a Friend to Supper

To night, grave sir, both my poore house, and I
    Doe equally desire your companie:
Not that we thinke us worthy such a ghest,
    But that your worth will dignifie our feast,
With those that come; whose grace may make that seeme
    Something, which, else, could hope for no esteeme.
It is the faire acceptance, Sir, creates
    The entertaynment perfect: not the cates.
Yet shall you have, to rectifie your palate,
    An olive, capers, or some better sallade
Ushring the mutton; with a short-leg'd hen,
    If we can get her, full of egs, and then,
Limons, and wine for sauce: to these, a coney
    Is not to be despair'd of, for our money;
And, though fowle, now, be scarce, yet there are clarkes,
    The skie not falling, thinke we may have larkes.
Ile tell you of more, and lye, so you will come:
    Of partrich, pheasant, wood-cock, of which some
May yet be there; and godwit, if we can:
    Knat, raile, and ruffe too. How so ere, my man

TO JOHN DONNE.

8 *stone:* A white stone was considered to be auspicious by the Romans.

9 *claps:* applause.

10 *pui'nees:* underlings.

INVITING A FRIEND TO SUPPER.

13 *coney:* hare.

19–20 *godwit . . . ruffe:* All four species are edible.

Shall reade a piece of *Virgil, Tacitus,*
*Livie,* or of some better booke to us,
Of which wee'll speake our minds, amidst our meate;
And Ile professe no verses to repeate:
To this, if ought appeare, which I know not of,
That will the pastrie, not my paper, show of.
Digestive cheese, and fruit there sure will bee;
But that, which most doth take my *Muse,* and mee,
Is a pure cup of rich *Canary*-wine,
Which is the *Mermaids,* now, but shall be mine:
Of which had *Horace,* or *Anacreon* tasted,
Their lives, as doe their lines, till now had lasted.
*Tabacco, Nectar,* or the *Thespian* spring,
Are all but *Luthers* beere, to this I sing.
Of this we will sup free, but moderately,
And we will have no *Pooly',* or *Parrot* by;
Nor shall our cups make any guiltie men:
But, at our parting, we will be, as when
We innocently met. No simple word,
That shall be utter'd at our mirthfull boord,
Shall make us sad next morning: or affright
The libertie, that wee'll enjoy to night.

22 *better booke:* probably the Bible, the only book which would outrank the classics in Jonson's humanistic eye.

30 *Mermaids:* the famous London tavern.

34 *Luthers:* i.e. German.

36 *Pooly', or Parrot:* Robert Poley and Henry Parrot were government spies. Poley had been present at Marlowe's death in a tavern brawl. But Jonson is punning on "Polly," the pet name for a "parrot," a bird whose chatter would reveal all the diners' secrets.

## On Gut

*Gut* eates all day, and lechers all the night,
So all his meate he tasteth over, twise:
And, striving so to double his delight,
He makes himselfe a thorough-fare of vice.
Thus, in his belly, can he change a sin
Lust it comes out, that gluttony went in.

## Epitaph on S.P. a Child of Q. El. Chappel

Weepe with me all you that read
This little storie:
And know, for whom a teare you shed,
*Death's* selfe is sorry.
'Twas a child, that so did thrive
In grace, and feature,
As *Heaven* and *Nature* seem'd to strive
Which own'd the creature.
Yeeres he numbred scarse thirteene
When *Fates* turn'd cruell,
Yet three fill'd *Zodiackes* had he beene
The stages jewell;
And did act (what now we mone)
Old men so duely,

EPITAPH ON S.P.: The boy actor whom Jonson celebrates was for long identified as Salathiel Pavy, but modern research has established that his Christian name was Salomon.

11 *three . . . Zodiackes:* three years.

As, sooth, the *Parcae* thought him one,
He plai'd so truely.
So, by error, to his fate
They all consented;
But viewing him since (alas, too late)
They have repented.
And have sought (to give new birth)
In bathes to steepe him;
But, being so much too good for earth,
Heaven vowes to keepe him.

## Epitaph on Elizabeth, L.H.

Would'st thou heare, what man can say
In a little? Reader, stay.
Under-neath this stone doth lye
As much beautie, as could dye:
Which in life did harbour give
To more vertue, then doth live.
If, at all, shee had a fault,
Leave it buryed in this vault.
One name was *Elizabeth*,
Th'other let it sleepe with death:
Fitter, where it dyed, to tell,
Then that it liv'd at all. Farewell.

EPITAPH ON S.P.
15 *Parcae:* Fates.
EPITAPH ON ELIZABETH, L.H.: Elizabeth, L.H. has not been identified.

# From *The Forrest*

## To Penshurst

Thou art not, *Penshurst*, built to envious show,
Of touch, or marble; nor canst boast a row
Of polish'd pillars, or a roofe of gold:
Thou hast no lantherne, whereof tales are told;
Or stayre, or courts; but stand'st an ancient pile,
And these grudg'd at, art reverenc'd the while.
Thou joy'st in better markes, of soyle, of ayre,
Of wood, of water: therein thou art faire.
Thou hast thy walkes for health, as well as sport:
Thy *Mount*, to which the *Dryads* doe resort,
Where *Pan*, and *Bacchus* their high feasts have made,
Beneath the broad beech, and the chest-nut shade;
That taller tree, which of a nut was set,
At his great birth, where all the *Muses* met.
There, in the writhed barke, are cut the names
Of many a *Sylvane*, taken with his flames.
And thence, the ruddy *Satyres* oft provoke
The lighter *Faunes*, to reach thy *Ladies oke*.

FROM THE FORREST: Penshurst was the home of the Sidney family in Kent. Sir Robert Sidney, brother of Sir Philip (d. 1586) was owner of the estate when Jonson wrote.

2 *touch:* black marble or basalt.

4 *lantherne:* glassed-in room at top of house.

6 When other buildings are envied (*grudg'd at*) you are reverenced.

10 *Mount:* elevated ground.

14 *his:* Sir Philip's (November 30, 1554).

16 *taken . . . flames:* Jonson may mean that the country people (*Sylvanes*) were taken with love of Sidney himself; alternatively, they shared the passion which he expressed in his verse.

18 *Ladies oke:* Lady Leicester is reputed to have begun labor pains under an oak tree on the estate.

Thy copp's, too, nam'd of *Gamage,* thou hast there,
    That never failes to serve thee season'd deere,
When thou would'st feast, or exercise thy friends.
    The lower land, that to the river bends,
Thy sheepe, thy bullocks, kine, and calves doe feed:
    The middle grounds thy mares, and horses breed.
Each banke doth yeeld thee coneyes; and the topps
    Fertile of wood, *Ashore,* and *Sydney's* copp's,
To crowne thy open table, doth provide
    The purpled pheasant, with the speckled side:
The painted partrich lyes in every field,
    And, for thy messe, is willing to be kill'd.
And if the high swolne *Medway* faile thy dish,
    Thou hast thy ponds, that pay thee tribute fish,
Fat, aged carps, that runne into thy net.
    And pikes, now weary their owne kinde to eat,
As loth, the second draught, or cast to stay,
    Officiously, at first, themselves betray.
Bright eeles, that emulate them, and leape on land,
    Before the fisher, or into his hand.
Then hath thy orchard fruit, thy garden flowers,
    Fresh as the ayre, and new as are the houres.
The earely cherry, with the later plum,
    Fig, grape, and quince, each in his time doth come:
The blushing apricot, and woolly peach
    Hang on thy walls, that every child may reach.
And though thy walls be of the countrey stone,
    They'are rear'd with no mans ruine, no mans grone,
There's none, that dwell about them, wish them downe;
    But all come in, the farmer, and the clowne:

19 *Gamage:* Barbara Gamage, Sir Robert's wife, fed deer in the copse.
25 *coneyes:* rabbits.
26 *Ashore and Sydney's:* names given to two thickets on the estate.
30 *messe:* table.
31 *Medway:* the river.
35–36 *As loth . . . betray:* Rather than await a second cast and drawing in by the fisherman, they leap into the net at his first effort.
48 *clowne:* peasant.

And no one empty-handed, to salute
 Thy lord, and lady, though they have no sute.
Some bring a capon, some a rurall cake,
 Some nuts, some apples; some that thinke they make
The better cheeses, bring 'hem; or else send
 By their ripe daughters, whom they would commend
This way to husbands; and whose baskets beare
 An embleme of themselves, in plum, or peare.
But what can this (more then expresse their love)
 Adde to thy free provisions, farre above
The neede of such? whose liberall boord doth flow,
 With all, that hospitalitie doth know!
Where comes no guest, but is allow'd to eate,
 Without his feare, and of thy lords owne meate:
Where the same beere, and bread, and selfe-same wine,
 That is his Lordships, shall be also mine.
And I not faine to sit (as some, this day,
 At great mens tables) and yet dine away.
Here no man tells my cups; nor, standing by,
 A waiter, doth my gluttony envy:
But gives me what I call, and lets me eate,
 He knowes, below, he shall finde plentie of meate,
Thy tables hoord not up for the next day,
 Nor, when I take my lodging, need I pray
For fire, or lights, or livorie: all is there;
 As if thou, then, wert mine, or I raign'd here:
There's nothing I can wish, for which I stay.
 That found King *James*, when hunting late, this way,
With his brave sonne, the Prince, they saw thy fires
 Shine bright on every harth as the desires
Of thy *Penates* had beene set on flame,
 To entertayne them; or the countrey came,

50 *sute:* request to make.
67 *tells:* counts.
73 *livorie:* food and drink taken to the bedchamber, as was the Renaissance custom.
77 *Prince:* Henry, Prince of Wales, who died in November 1612.
79 *Penates:* household gods.

With all their zeale, to warme their welcome here.
    What (great, I will not say, but) sodayne cheare
Did'st thou, then, make 'hem! and what praise was heap'd
    On thy good lady, then! who, therein, reap'd
The just reward of her high huswifery;
    To have her linnen, plate, and all things nigh,
When shee was farre: and not a roome, but drest,
    As if it had expected such a guest!
These, *Penshurst*, are thy praise, and yet not all.
    Thy lady's noble, fruitfull, chaste withall.
His children thy great lord may call his owne:
    A fortune, in this age, but rarely knowne.
They are, and have beene taught religion: Thence
    Their gentler spirits have suck'd innocence.
Each morne, and even, they are taught to pray,
    With the whole houshold, and may, every day,
Reade, in their vertuous parents noble parts,
    The mysteries of manners, armes, and arts.
Now, *Penshurst*, they that will proportion thee
    With other edifices, when they see
Those proud, ambitious heaps, and nothing else,
    May say, their lords have built, but thy lord dwells.

82 *sodayne:* impromptu.

# Song

## To Celia

Come my *Celia,* let us prove,
While we may, the sports of love;
Time will not be ours, for ever:
He, at length, our good will sever.
Spend not then his guifts in vaine.
Sunnes, that set, may rise againe:
But if once we loose this light,
'Tis, with us, perpetuall night.
Why should we deferre our joyes?
Fame, and rumor are but toyes.
Cannot we delude the eyes
Of a few poore houshold spyes?
Or his easier eares beguile,
So removed by our wile?
'Tis no sinne, loves fruit to steale,
But the sweet theft to reveale:
To be taken, to be seene,
These have crimes accounted beene.

SONG TO CELIA: From Jonson's *Volpone,* (III.vii.166–83). Celia is the virtuous wife whom Volpone unsuccessfully tries to seduce.

1 *prove:* test, try.

13 *his:* Celia's husband, Corvino.

## To the Same

Kisse me, sweet: The warie lover
Can your favours keepe, and cover,
When the common courting jay
All your bounties will betray.
Kisse againe: no creature comes.
Kisse, and score up wealthy summes
On my lips, thus hardly sundred,
While you breath. First give a hundred,
Then a thousand, then another
Hundred, then unto the tother
Adde a thousand, and so more:
Till you equall with the store,
All the grasse that *Rumney* yeelds,
Or the sands in *Chelsey* fields,
Or the drops in silver *Thames*,
Or the starres, that guild his streames,
In the silent sommer-nights,
When youths ply their stolne delights.
That the curious may not know
How to tell 'hem, as they flow,
And the envious, when they find
What their number is, be pin'd.

TO THE SAME: Lines 19–22 of this song also appear in *Volpone* (III.vii.236–39).
13 *Rumney:* grassy marsh in Kent.
20 *tell:* count.
22 *pin'd:* distressed.

## Song

### To Celia

Drinke to me, onely, with thine eyes,
And I will pledge with mine;
Or leave a kisse but in the cup,
And Ile not looke for wine.
The thirst, that from the soule doth rise,
Doth aske a drinke divine:
But might I of *Jove's Nectar* sup,
I would not change for thine.
I sent thee, late, a rosie wreath,
Not so much honoring thee,
As giving it a hope, that there
It could not withered bee.
But thou thereon did'st onely breath,
And sent'st it backe to mee:
Since when it growes, and smells, I sweare,
Not of it selfe, but thee.

## To Heaven

Good, and great *God,* can I not thinke of thee,
But it must, straight, my melancholy bee?
Is it interpreted in me disease,
That, laden with my sinnes, I seeke for ease?

TO HEAVEN: *To Heaven* is the last poem in the section of Jonson's 1616 *Works* entitled *The Forrest.*

O, be thou witnesse, that the reynes dost know,
And hearts of all, if I be sad for show,
And judge me after: if I dare pretend
To ought but grace, or ayme at other end.
As thou art all, so be thou all to mee,
First, midst, and last, converted one, and three;
My faith, my hope, my love: and in this state,
My judge, my witnesse, and my advocate.
Where have I beene this while exil'd from thee?
And whither rap'd, now thou but stoup'st to mee?
Dwell, dwell here still: O, being every-where,
How can I doubt to finde thee ever, here?
I know my state, both full of shame, and scorne,
Conceiv'd in sinne, and unto labour borne,
Standing with feare, and must with horror fall,
And destin'd unto judgement, after all.
I feele my griefes too, and there scarce is ground,
Upon my flesh t'inflict another wound.
Yet dare I not complaine, or wish for death
With holy *Paul*, lest it be thought the breath
Of discontent; or that these prayers bee
For wearinesse of life, not love of thee.

5 *reynes:* kidneys, conceived of as the seat of the affections.

10 *converted:* appearing as; the allusion in the line is to God's manifestation of himself as either a single being or as the three persons in the Trinity.

14 *rap'd:* rapt, taken away.

24 *Paul:* Cf. Romans 7:24, "O wretched man that I am! who shall deliver me from the body of this death?"

## From *Under-wood*

### A Hymne to God the Father

Heare mee, O God!
  A broken heart,
  Is my best part:
Use still thy rod,
  That I may prove
  Therein, thy Love.

If thou hadst not
  Beene sterne to mee,
  But left me free,
I had forgot
  My selfe and thee.

For, sin's so sweet,
  As minds ill bent
  Rarely repent,
Until they meet
  Their punishment.

Who more can crave
  Then thou hast done:
  That gav'st a Sonne,
To free a slave?
  First made of nought,
  Withall since bought.

A HYMN TO GOD THE FATHER.
5 *prove:* experience.
13 *As:* that.
22 *bought:* redeemed.

Sinne, Death, and Hell,
His glorious Name
Quite overcame,
Yet I rebell,
And slight the same.

But, I'le come in,
Before my losse,
Me farther tosse,
As sure to win
Under his Crosse.

## A Celebration of Charis in Ten Lyrick Peeces

### 1. *His Excuse for loving*

Let it not your wonder move,
Lesse your laughter; that I love.
Though I now write fiftie yeares,
I have had, and have my Peeres;
Poëts, though devine are men:
Some have lov'd as old agen.
And it is not alwayes face,
Clothes, or Fortune gives the grace;
Or the feature, or the youth:
But the Language, and the Truth,

A CELEBRATION OF CHARIS: Charis has never been identified, but her Greek name seems sufficiently explained by its ironic associations with *caritas,* or Love. Jonson apparently did not compose the ten poems as a sequence (number 4 also appears in one of his plays), but there is no reason to doubt that he was responsible for their final arrangement.

*Part 1*

6 *as old agen:* i.e. at the age of one hundred.

9 *feature:* handsomeness.

With the Ardor, and the Passion,
Gives the Lover weight, and fashion.
If you will then read the Storie,
First, prepare you to be sorie,
That you never knew till now,
Either whom to love, or how:
But be glad, as soone with me,
When you know, that this is she,
Of whose Beautie it was sung,
She shall make the old man young.
Keepe the middle age at stay,
And let nothing high decay.
Till she be the reason why,
All the world for love may die.

## 2. *How he saw her*

I Beheld her, on a Day,
When her looke out-flourisht May:
And her dressing did out-brave
All the Pride the fields than have:
Farre I was from being stupid,
For I ran and call'd on *Cupid;*
Love if thou wilt ever see
Marke of glorie, come with me;
Where's thy Quiver? bend thy Bow:
Here's a shaft, thou art to slow!
And (withall) I did untie
Every Cloud about his eye;
But, he had not gain'd his sight
Sooner, then he lost his might,

*Part 2*

10 *to:* too.

11–12: The speaker gives the gift of sight to blind Cupid.

Or his courage; for away
Strait hee ran, and durst not stay,
Letting Bow and Arrow fall,
Nor for any threat, or Call,
Could be brought once back to looke.
I foole-hardie, there up tooke
Both the Arrow he had quit,
And the Bow: with thought to hit
This my object. But she threw
Such a Lightning (as I drew)
At my face, that tooke my sight,
And my motion from me quite;
So that there, I stood a stone,
Mock'd of all: and call'd of one
(Which with griefe and wrath I heard)
*Cupids* Statue with a Beard,
Or else one that plaid his Ape,
In a *Hercules*-his shape.

## 3. *What hee suffered*

After many scornes like these,
Which the prouder Beauties please,
She content was to restore
Eyes and limbes; to hurt me more
And would on Conditions, be
Reconcil'd to Love, and me.
First, that I must kneeling yeeld
Both the Bow, and shaft I held
Unto her; which love might take
At her hand, with oath, to make
Mee, the scope of his next draught.
Armed, with that selfe-same shaft

31–32 *one . . . shape:* one who imitated Cupid in the shape of Hercules.

*Part 3*

9 *love:* Cupid.

11 *scope:* mark; *draught:* shot.

He no sooner heard the Law,
But the Arrow home did draw
And (to gaine her by his Art)
Left it sticking in my heart:
Which when she beheld to bleed,
She repented of the deed,
And would faine have chang'd the fate,
But the Pittie comes too late.
Looser-like, now, all my wreake
Is, that I have leave to speake,
And in either Prose, or Song,
To revenge me with my Tongue,
Which how Dexterously I doe,
Heare and make Example too.

## 4. *Her Triumph*

See the Chariot at hand here of Love
Wherein my Lady rideth!
Each that drawes, is a Swan, or a Dove
And well the Carre Love guideth.
As she goes, all hearts doe duty
Unto her beauty;
And enamour'd, doe wish, so they might
But enjoy such a sight,
That they still were, to run by her side,
Through Swords, through Seas, whether she would ride.

Doe but looke on her eyes, they doe light
All that Loves world compriseth!

21 *Looser-like:* Like a loser; *wreake:* revenge.
26 *make Example:* take as an example.
*Part 4*
9 *still:* always.
10 *whether:* wherever.
11–30 The second and third stanzas of this poem also appeared in Jonson's play, *The Devil Is an Ass* (II.vi.94–113).

Doe but looke on her Haire, it is bright
As Loves starre when it riseth!
Doe but marke her forhead's smoother
Then words that sooth her!
And from her arched browes, such a grace
Sheds it selfe through the face,
As alone there triumphs to the life
All the Gaine, all the Good, of the Elements strife.

Have you seene but a bright Lillie grow,
Before rude hands have touch'd it?
Ha' you mark'd but the fall o' the Snow
Before the soyle hath smutch'd it?
Ha' you felt the wooll of Bever?
Or Swans Downe ever?
Or have smelt o' the bud o' the Brier?
Or the Nard in the fire?
Or have tasted the bag of the Bee?
O so white! O so soft! O so sweet is she!

## 5. *His discourse with Cupid*

Noblest *Charis*, you that are
Both my fortune, and my Starre!
And doe governe more my blood
Then the various Moone the flood!
Heare, what late Discourse of you,
Love, and I have had; and true.
'Mongst my Muses finding me,
Where he chanc't your name to see

14 *Loves starre:* Venus.
20 *Elements strife:* The four elements (earth, air, fire, and water) were imagined as constantly at war.
28 *Nard:* aromatic balsam.
*Part* 5
4 *various:* varying.

Set, and to this softer straine;
Sure, said he, if I have Braine,
This here sung, can be no other
By description, but my Mother!
So hath *Homer* prais'd her haire;
So, *Anacreon* drawne the Ayre
Of her face, and made to rise
Just about her sparkling eyes,
Both her Browes, bent like my Bow.
By her lookes I doe her know,
Which you call my Shafts. And see!
Such my Mothers blushes be,
As the Bath your verse discloses
In her cheekes, of Milke, and Roses;
Such as oft I wanton in.
And, above her even chin,
Have you plac'd the banke of kisses,
Where you say, men gather blisses,
Rip'ned with a breath more sweet,
Then when flowers, and West-winds meet,
Nay her white and polished neck,
With the Lace that doth it deck,
Is my Mothers! Hearts of slaine
Lovers, made into a Chaine!
And betweene each rising breast,
Lyes the Valley, cal'd my nest,
Where I sit and proyn my wings
After flight; and put new stings
To my shafts! Her very Name,
With my Mothers is the same.

12 *Mother:* Venus.

14 *Anacreon:* Anacreon of Teos (born about 550 B.C.) whose light and graceful lyrics were often imitated (as by Jonson himself here). *Ayre:* attitude.

16 *about:* above.

35 *proyn:* preen.

38 *the same:* Vulcan's wife is called "Charis" in the *Iliad* and "Venus" in the *Odyssey*.

I confesse all, I replide,
And the Glasse hangs by her side,
And the Girdle 'bout her waste,
All is *Venus:* save unchaste.
But alas, thou feelst the least
Of her good, who is the best
Of her Sex; But could'st thou *Love,*
Call to mind the formes, that strove
For the Apple, and those three
Make in one, the same were shee.
For this Beauty yet doth hide,
Something more then thou hast spi'd.
Outward Grace weake love beguiles:
Shee is *Venus,* when she smiles,
But shee's *Juno,* when she walkes,
And *Minerva,* when she talkes.

## 6. *Clayming a second kisse by Desert*

*Charis* guesse, and doe not misse,
Since I drew a Morning kisse
From your lips, and suck'd an ayre
Thence, as sweet, as you are faire,
What my Muse and I have done:
Whether we have lost, or wonne,
If by us, the oddes were laid,
That the Bride (allow'd a Maid)
Look'd not halfe so fresh, and faire,
With th' advantage of her haire,
And her Jewels, to the view
Of th' Assembly, as did you!
Or, that did you sit, or walke,
You were more the eye, and talke

47 *Apple:* Minerva, Juno, and Venus contended for this prize in a contest judged by Paris, with Venus winning.

Of the Court, to day, then all
Else that glister'd in *White-hall;*
So, as those that had your sight,
Wisht the Bride were chang'd to night,
And did think, such Rites were due
To no other Grace but you!
   Or, if you did move to night
In the Daunces, with what spight
Of your Peeres, you were beheld,
That at every motion sweld
So to see a Lady tread,
As might all the Graces lead,
And was worthy (being so seene)
To be envi'd of the Queene.
Or if you would yet have stay'd,
Whether any would up-braid
To himself his losse of Time;
Or have charg'd his sight of Crime,
To have left all sight for you:
   Guesse of these, which is the true;
And, if such a verse as this,
May not claime another kisse.

## 7. *Begging another, on colour of mending the former*

For *Loves*-sake, kisse me once againe,
   I long, and should not beg in vaine,
      Here's none to spie, or see;
         Why doe you doubt, or stay?

*Part 6*
16 *White-hall:* royal palace at Westminster.
17 *had . . . sight:* saw you.
22 *spight:* envy.
32 *charg'd:* accused.
*Part 7*
*Title: colour:* pretence.

I'le taste as lightly as the Bee,
That doth but touch his flower, and flies away.
Once more, and (faith) I will be gone:
Can he that loves, aske lesse then one?
Nay, you may erre in this,
And all your bountie wrong:
This could be call'd but halfe a kisse.
What w'are but once to doe, we should doe long:
I will but mend the last, and tell
Where, how it would have relish'd well;
Joyne lip to lip, and try:
Each suck others breath.
And whilst our tongues perplexed lie,
Let who will thinke us dead, or wish our death.

## 8. *Urging her of a promise*

*Charis* one day in discourse
Had of Love, and of his force,
Lightly promis'd, she would tell
What a man she could love well:
And that promise set on fire
All that heard her, with desire.
With the rest, I long expected,
When the worke would be effected:
But we find that cold delay,
And excuse spun every day,
As, untill she tell her one,
We all feare, she loveth none.
Therefore, *Charis*, you must do't,
For I will so urge you to't
You shall neither eat nor sleepe,
No, nor forth your window peepe,

*Part 8*
4 *What:* what kind of.
7 *expected:* awaited.

With your emissarie eye,
To fetch in the Formes goe by:
And pronounce, which band or lace,
Better fits him, then his face;
Nay I will not let you sit
'Fore your Idoll Glasse a whit,
To say over every purle
There; or to reforme a curle;
Or with Secretarie *Sis*
To consult, if *Fucus* this
Be as good, as was the last:
All your sweet of life is past,
Make accompt unlesse you can,
(And that quickly) speake your Man.

## 9. *Her man described by her owne Dictamen*

Of your Trouble, *Ben,* to ease me,
I will tell what Man would please me.
I would have him if I could,
Noble; or of greater Blood:
Titles, I confesse, doe take me;
And a woman God did make me,
French to boote, at least in fashion,
And his Manners of that Nation.
    Young Il'd have him to, and faire,
Yet a man; with crisped haire

17 *emissarie:* questing for sights or news.
18 *Formes:* shapes of men who.
22 *Idoll:* Jonson puns on *idle.*
23 *purle:* lacy loop.
25 *Secretarie Sis:* confidential companion named Cis.
26 *Fucus this:* this particular cosmetic.
30 *speake:* describe, reveal.

*Part* 9
*Title: Dictamen:* pronouncement.
10 *crisped:* curly.

Cast in thousand snares, and rings
For *Loves* fingers, and his wings:
Chestnut colour, or more slack
Gold, upon a ground of black.
*Venus*, and *Minerva's* eyes
For he must looke wanton-wise.
    Eye-brows bent like *Cupids* bow,
Front, an ample field of snow;
Even nose, and cheeke (withall)
Smooth as is the Billiard Ball:
Chin, as woolly as the Peach;
And his lip should kissing teach,
Till he cherish'd too much beard,
And make *Love* or me afeard.
    He would have a hand as soft
As the Downe, and shew it oft;
Skin as smooth as any rush,
And so thin to see a blush
Rising through it e're it came;
All his blood should be a flame
Quickly fir'd as in beginners
In loves schoole, and yet no sinners.
    'Twere to long to speake of all,
What we harmonie doe call
In a body should be there.
Well he should his clothes to weare;
Yet no Taylor help to make him
Drest, you still for man should take him;
And not thinke h' had eat a stake,
Or were set up in a Brake.

13 *more slack:* duller.
14 *ground:* background or basic color.
18 *Front:* Forehead.
37 *Yet:* Even if.
39 *h'had . . . stake:* was too stiff.
40 *Brake:* framework.

Valiant he should be as fire,
Shewing danger more then ire.
Bounteous as the clouds to earth;
And as honest as his Birth.
All his actions to be such,
As to doe nothing too much.
Nor o're-praise, nor yet condemne;
Nor out-valew, nor contemne;
Nor doe wrongs, nor wrongs receave;
Nor tie knots, nor knots unweave;
And from basenesse to be free,
As he durst love Truth and me.
Such a man, with every part,
I could give my very heart;
But of one, if short he came,
I can rest me where I am.

## 10. *Another Ladyes exception present at the hearing*

For his Mind, I doe not care,
That's a Toy, that I could spare:
Let his Title be but great,
His Clothes rich, and band sit neat,
Himselfe young, and face be good,
All I wish is understood.
What you please, you parts may call,
'Tis one good part I'ld lie withall.

42 *danger:* dominion.

*Part 10*

4 *band:* collar or ruff.

8 *part . . . lie:* Jonson puns on the bawdy senses of both words.

## A Song

Oh doe not wanton with those eyes,
    Lest I be sick with seeing;
Nor cast them downe, but let them rise,
    Lest shame destroy their being:
O, be not angry with those fires,
    For then their threats will kill me;
Nor looke too kind on my desires,
    For then my hopes will spill me;
O, doe not steepe them in thy Teares,
    For so will sorrow slay me;
Nor spread them as distract with feares,
    Mine owne enough betray me.

## My Picture Left in Scotland

I now thinke, Love is rather deafe, then blind,
    For else it could not be,
        That she,
Whom I adore so much, should so slight me,
    And cast my love behind:
I'm sure my language to her, was as sweet,
        And every close did meet
    In sentence, of as subtile feet,

A SONG.
8 *spill:* destroy.
11 *spread:* open wide.

MY PICTURE LEFT IN SCOTLAND: Jonson's famous walk to Scotland occurred in 1619.
7 *close:* final phrase (a musical term).
7–8 *meet . . . sentence:* harmonize in meaning.

As hath the youngest Hee,
That sits in shadow of *Apollo's* tree.
Oh, but my conscious feares,
That flie my thoughts betweene,
Tell me that she hath seene
My hundreds of gray haires,
Told seven and fortie yeares.
Read so much wast, as she cannot imbrace
My mountaine belly, and my rockie face,
And all these through her eyes, have stopt her eares.

## An Ode. To Himselfe

Where do'st thou carelesse lie
Buried in ease and sloth?
Knowledge, that sleepes, doth die;
And this Securitie,
It is the common Moath,
That eats on wits, and Arts, and destroyes them both.

Are all th'*Aonian* springs
Dri'd up? lyes *Thespia* wast?
Doth *Clarius* Harp want strings,
That not a Nymph now sings!
Or droop they as disgrac't,
To see their Seats and Bowers by chattring Pies defac't?

MY PICTURE LEFT IN SCOTLAND.
10 *Apollo's:* the patron of poetry.
16 *wast:* waist, with a pun on *waste.*
17 *rockie:* pock-marked or pimply.

AN ODE. TO HIMSELF.
7–8 *Aonian . . . Thespia:* Mount Helicon and the Thespian spring, both sacred to the Muses.
9 *Clarius:* Apollo's. The god had an oracle at Claros.
12 *Pies:* magpies.

If hence thy silence be,
As 'tis too just a cause;
Let this thought quicken thee,
Minds that are great and free,
Should not on fortune pause,
'Tis crowne enough to vertue still, her owne applause.

What though the greedie Frie
Be taken with false Baytes
Of worded Balladrie,
And thinke it Poësie?
They die with their conceits,
And only pitious scorne, upon their folly waites.

Then take in hand thy Lyre,
Strike in thy proper straine,
With *Japhets* lyne, aspire
*Sols* Chariot for new fire,
To give the world againe:
Who aided him, will thee, the issue of *Joves* braine.

And since our Daintie age,
Cannot indure reproofe.
Make not thy selfe a Page,
To that strumpet the Stage,
But sing high and aloofe,
Safe from the wolves black jaw, and the dull Asses hoofe.

19 *Frie:* younglings.
21 *worded:* wordy.
27 *Japhets lyne:* Prometheus, son of Japhet; *aspire:* aspire to.
30 *issue:* Minerva, who sprang from the head of Zeus.

## A Sonnet, to the Noble Lady, the Lady Mary Worth

I that have beene a lover, and could shew it,
    Though not in these, in rithmes not wholly dumbe,
    Since I exscribe your Sonnets, am become
A better lover, and much better Poët.
Nor is my Muse, or I asham'd to owe it
    To those true numerous Graces; whereof some,
    But charme the Senses, others over-come
Both braines and hearts; and mine now best doe know it:

For in your verse all *Cupids* Armorie,
    His flames, his shafts, his Quiver, and his Bow,
    His very eyes are yours to overthrow.
But then his Mothers sweets you so apply,
    Her joyes, her smiles, her loves, as readers take
    For *Venus Ceston*, every line you make.

## A Fit of Rime against Rime

Rime the rack of finest wits,
That expresseth but by fits,
        True Conceipt.

A SONNET: Lady Mary Worth was the daughter of Sir Robert Sidney, for whom see the notes on "To Penshurst." This poem is Jonson's only sonnet.
2 *these:* i.e. in the rhyme scheme and metrics of the sonnet form.
3 *exscribe:* copy out.
9 *your verse:* Lady Mary's poems were published in 1621.
13 *as:* that.
14 *Ceston:* girdle.

A FIT OF RIME AGAINST RIME.
2 *by fits:* fitfully, with a pun on the idea of *fitting* like sounds together.
3 *Conceipt:* conception, imagination.

Spoyling Senses of their Treasure,
Cosening Judgement with a measure,
But false weight.
Wresting words, from their true calling;
Propping Verse, for feare of falling
To the ground.
Joynting Syllabes, drowning Letters,
Fastning Vowells, as with fetters
They were bound!
Soon as lazie thou wert knowne,
All good Poëtrie hence was flowne,
And Art banish'd.
For a thousand yeares together,
All *Pernassus* Greene did wither,
And wit vanish'd.
*Pegasus* did flie away,
At the Wells no Muse did stay,
But bewail'd,
So to see the Fountaine drie,
And *Apollo's* Musique die,
All light failed!
Starveling rimes did fill the Stage,
Not a Poët in an Age,
Worth crowning.
Not a worke deserving Baies,
Nor a lyne deserving praise,
*Pallas* frowning;
Greeke was free from Rimes infection,
Happy Greeke by this protection!
Was not spoyled.

5 *Cosening:* Cheating; *measure:* rhythm.
10 *Joynting:* disjointing.
14 *Poëtrie,* etc.: Classical (Greek and Latin) poetry did not use rhyme.
17 *Pernassus Greene:* everything that flourished on Mount Parnassus, sacred to the Muses.
19 *Pegasus:* winged horse of the Muses.
20 *Wells:* the sacred poetic springs on Mount Helicon.
28 *Baies:* the laureate crown.

Whilst the Latin, Queene of Tongues,
Is not yet free from Rimes wrongs,
But rests foiled.
Scarce the hill againe doth flourish,
Scarce the world a Wit doth nourish,
To restore,
*Phœbus* to his Crowne againe;
And the Muses to their braine;
As before.
Vulgar Languages that want
Words, and sweetnesse, and be scant
Of true measure,
*Tyran* Rime hath so abused,
That they long since have refused,
Other ceasure;
He that first invented thee,
May his joynts tormented bee,
Cramp'd for ever;
Still may Syllabes jarre with time,
Stil may reason warre with rime,
Resting never.
May his Sense when it would meet,
The cold tumor in his feet,
Grow unsounder.
And his Title be long foole,
That in rearing such a Schoole,
Was the founder.

35 *Rimes wrongs:* Post-classical Latin verse was often rhymed.
43 *Vulgar:* Vernacular.
45 *measure:* quantity.
46 *Tyran:* tyrannical.
48 *ceasure:* caesura.

# An Elegie

'Tis true, I'm broke! Vowes, Oathes, and all I had
 Of Credit lost. And I am now run madde,
Or doe upon my selfe some desperate ill;
 This sadnesse makes no approaches, but to kill.
It is a Darknesse hath blockt up my sense,
 And drives it in to eat on my offence,
Or there to sterve it. Helpe O you that may
 Alone lend succours, and this furie stay,
Offended Mistris; you are yet so faire,
 As light breakes from you, that affrights despaire,
And fills my powers with perswading joy,
 That you should be too noble to destroy.
There may some face or menace of a storme
 Looke forth, but cannot last in such a forme.
If there be nothing worthy you can see
 Of Graces, or your mercie here in me,
Spare your owne goodnesse yet; and be not great
 In will and power, only to defeat.
God, and the good, know to forgive, and save.
 The ignorant, and fooles, no pittie have.
I will not stand to justifie my fault,
 Or lay the excuse upon the Vintners vault;
Or in confessing of the Crime be nice,
 Or goe about to countenance the vice,
By naming in what companie 'twas in,
 As I would urge Authoritie for sinne.

AN ELEGIE: This poem can be profitably compared with Donne's *Elegies,* one of which was printed after it in *Under-wood.*

7 *sterve:* kill.

18 *defeat:* undo.

22 *Vintners vault:* The speaker, while drunk, seems to have revealed a secret of his mistress.

23 *nice:* reluctant.

No, I will stand arraign'd, and cast, to be
The Subject of your Grace in pardoning me,
And (Stil'd your mercies Creature) will live more
Your honour now, then your disgrace before.
Thinke it was frailtie, Mistris, thinke me man;
Thinke that your selfe like heaven forgive me can;
Where weaknesse doth offend, and vertue grieve,
There greatnesse takes a glorie to relieve.
Thinke that I once was yours, or may be now;
Nothing is vile, that is a part of you:
Errour and folly in me may have crost
Your just commands; yet those, not I be lost.
I am regenerate now, become the child
Of your compassion; Parents should be mild:
There is no Father that for one demerit,
Or two, or three, a Sonne will dis-inherit:
That as the last of punishments is meant;
No man inflicts that paine, till hope be spent:
An ill-affected limbe (what e're it aile)
We cut not off, till all Cures else doe faile:
And then with pause; for sever'd once, that's gone,
Would live his glory that could keepe it on:
Doe not despaire my mending; to distrust
Before you prove a medicine, is unjust.
You may so place me, and in such an ayre
As not alone the Cure, but scarre be faire.
That is, if still your Favours you apply,
And not the bounties you ha'done, deny.
Could you demand the gifts you gave, againe!
Why was't? did e're the Cloudes aske back their raine?
The Sunne his heat, and light, the ayre his dew?
Or winds the Spirit, by which the flower so grew?

27 *cast:* found guilty.
48 *Would:* It would.
50 *prove:* test.
52 *faire:* beautiful.

That were to wither all, and make a Grave
  Of that wise Nature would a Cradle have.
Her order is to cherish, and preserve,
  Consumptions nature to destroy, and sterve.
But to exact againe what once is given,
  Is natures meere obliquitie! as Heaven
Should aske the blood, and spirits he hath infus'd
  In man, because man hath the flesh abus'd.
O may your wisdome take example hence,
  God lightens not at mans each fraile offence,
He pardons slips, goes by a world of ills,
  And then his thunder frights more, then it kills.
He cannot angrie be, but all must quake,
  It shakes even him, that all things else doth shake.
And how more faire, and lovely lookes the world
  In a calme skie; then when the heaven is horl'd
About in Cloudes, and wrapt in raging weather,
  As all with storme and tempest ran together.
O imitate that sweet Serenitie
  That makes us live, not that which calls to die.
In darke, and sullen mornes, doe we not say
  This looketh like an Execution day?
And with the vulgar doth it not obtaine
  The name of Cruell weather, storme, and raine?
Be not affected with these markes too much
  Of crueltie, lest they doe make you such.
But view the mildnesse of your Makers state,
  As I the penitents here emulate:
He when he sees a sorrow such as this,
  Streight puts off all his Anger, and doth kisse
The contrite Soule, who hath no thought to win
  Upon the hope to have another sin

60 *that:* that which.
64 *obliquitie:* fault; *as:* as if.
65 *he:* God.
68 *lightens:* hurls forth lightning.
74 *horl'd:* hurled.

Forgiven him; And in that lyne stand I,
  Rather then once displease you more, to die,
To suffer tortures, scorne, and Infamie,
  What Fooles, and all their Parasites can apply;
The wit of Ale, and *Genius* of the Malt
  Can pumpe for; or a Libell without salt
Produce; though threatning with a coale, or chalke
  On every wall, and sung where e're I walke.
I number these as being of the Chore
  Of Contumelie, and urge a good man more
Then sword, or fire, or what is of the race
  To carry noble danger in the face:
There is not any punishment, or paine,
  A man should flie from, as he would disdaine.
Then Mistress here, here let your rigour end,
  And let your mercie make me asham'd t'offend.
I will no more abuse my vowes to you,
  Then I will studie falshood, to be true.
O, that you could but by dissection see
  How much you are the better part of me;
How all my Fibres by your Spirit doe move,
  And that there is no life in me, but love.
You would be then most confident, that tho
  Publike affaires command me now to goe
Out of your eyes, and be awhile away,
  Absence, or Distance, shall not breed decay.
Your forme shines here, here fixed in my heart;
  I may dilate my selfe, but not depart.
Others by common Stars their courses run:
  When I see you, then I doe see my Sun;
Till then 'tis all but darknesse, that I have;
  Rather then want your light, I wish a grave.

96 *pumpe:* work; *salt:* wit.
99 *Chore:* common chorus.
101 *the race:* that kind.
102 *carry:* confront.
104 *disdaine:* from the disdain (of others).
108 *Then:* Than.
118 *dilate:* extend.

# An Execration upon Vulcan

And why to me this, thou lame Lord of fire,
  What had I done that might call on thine ire?
Or urge thy Greedie flame, thus to devoure
  So many my Yeares-labours in an houre?
I ne're attempted, *Vulcan*, 'gainst thy life;
  Nor made least line of love to thy loose Wife;
Or in remembrance of thy afront, and scorne
  With Clownes, and Tradesmen, kept thee clos'd in horne.
'Twas *Jupiter* that hurl'd thee headlong downe,
  And *Mars*, that gave thee a Lanthorne for a Crowne:
Was it because thou wert of old denied
  By *Jove* to have *Minerva* for thy Bride,
That since thou tak'st all envious care and paine,
  To ruine any issue of the braine?
Had I wrote treason there, or heresie,
  Imposture, witchcraft, charmes, or blasphemie,
I had deserv'd then, thy consuming lookes,
  Perhaps, to have beene burned with my bookes.
But, on thy malice, tell me, didst thou spie
  Any, least loose, or scurrile paper, lie
Conceal'd, or kept there, that was fit to be,
  By thy owne vote, a sacrifice to thee?
Did I there wound the honours of the Crowne?
  Or taxe the Glories of the Church, and Gowne?

AN EXECRATION UPON VULCAN.

1 *this:* the fire that destroyed Jonson's house in November 1623.

6 *Wife:* Venus.

7 *scorne:* Vulcan was scorned by the other Olympians.

8 *horne:* i.e. in a lantern.

10 *Lanthorne:* Mars gave Vulcan his "horns" by cuckolding him.

12 *Minerva:* Wisdom, who issued from Jove's brain (see line 14), was denied to Vulcan. He takes his revenge by attacking anything that comes from the brain.

20 *least:* in the least way.

24 *Gowne:* legal profession.

Itch to defame the State? or brand the Times?
  And my selfe most, in some selfe-boasting Rimes?
If none of these, then why this fire? Or find
  A cause before; or leave me one behind.
Had I compil'd from *Amadis de Gaule,*
  Th'*Esplandians, Arthur's, Palmerins,* and all
The learned Librarie of *Don Quixote,*
  And so some goodlier monster had begot,
Or spun out Riddles, and weav'd fiftie tomes
  Of *Logogriphes,* and curious *Palindromes,*
Or pomp'd for those hard trifles *Anagrams,*
  Or *Eteostichs,* or those finer flammes
Of Egges, and Halberds, Cradles, and a Herse,
  A paire of Scisars, and a Combe in verse;
*Acrostichs,* and *Telestichs,* on jumpe names,
  Thou then hadst had some colour for thy flames,
On such my serious follies; But, thou'lt say,
  There were some pieces of as base allay,
And as false stampe there; parcels of a Play,
  Fitter to see the fire-light, then the day;
Adulterate moneys, such as might not goe:
  Thou should'st have stay'd, till publike fame said so.
Shee is the Judge, Thou Executioner,
  Or if thou needs would'st trench upon her power,
Thou mightst have yet enjoy'd thy crueltie
  With some more thrift, and more varietie:

29–30 *Amadis . . . Palmerins:* popular romances, many of which found a place in Don Quixote's library.

34 *Logogriphes:* verbal puzzles.

35 *pomp'd:* worked.

36 *Eteostichs:* chronograms; *flammes:* fanciful compositions. The list that follows refers to the Renaissance fashion of shaping poems so that their printed form represented their subject matter.

39 *Acrostichs:* acrostics; *Telestichs:* verses in which the last letters of each line spell out a name; *jumpe:* exactly corresponding.

42 *allay:* alloy (and hence counterfeit).

48 *trench:* encroach.

Thou mightst have had me perish, piece by piece,
To light Tobacco, or save roasted Geese,
Sindge Capons, or poore Pigges, dropping their eyes;
Condemn'd me to the Ovens with the pies;
And so, have kept me dying a whole age,
Not ravish'd all hence in a minutes rage.
But that's a marke, wherof thy Rites doe boast,
To make consumption, ever where thou go'st;
Had I fore-knowne of this thy least desire
T'have held a Triumph, or a feast of fire,
Especially in paper; that, that steame
Had tickled your large Nosthrill: many a Reame
To redeeme mine, I had sent in; enough,
Thou should'st have cry'd, and all beene proper stuffe.
The *Talmud,* and the *Alcoran* had come,
With pieces of the *Legend;* The whole summe
Of errant Knight-hood, with the Dames, and Dwarfes;
The charmed Boates, and the inchanted Wharfes;
The *Tristram's, Lanc'lots, Turpins,* and the *Peer's,*
All the madde *Rolands,* and sweet *Oliveer's;*
To *Merlins* Marvailes, and his *Caballs* losse,
With the Chimæra of the *Rosie-Crosse,*
Their Seales, their Characters, Hermetique rings,
Their Jemme of Riches, and bright Stone, that brings
Invisibilitie, and strength, and tongues:
The art of kindling the true Coale, by lungs,

51 ff. *Thou mightst,* etc.: Scrap paper was put to all these uses in Jonson's day.
53 *dropping their eyes:* i.e. as they roasted on the spit.
65 *Talmud:* Jewish book of the law; *Alcoran:* the Koran.
66 *Legend:* the *Golden Legend,* or *Lives of the Saints.*
66 ff. *The whole summe,* etc.: In the following lines Jonson lists a series of characters and themes from various types of medieval romance.
69 *Turpins:* a hero at the battle of Roncesvalles; *Peer's:* the twelve paladins who fought with Charlemagne.
71 *Caballs losse:* the failure of Merlin's intrigues in Arthurian romance.
72 *Rosie-Crosse:* the secret society of the Rosicrucians, founded in the fifteenth century.
75 *tongues:* the gift of tongues.
76 *lungs:* name often given to an alchemist's assistant.

With *Nicholas Pasquill's,* Meddle with your match,
And the strong lines, that so the times doe catch,
Or Captaine *Pamplets* horse, and foot; that sallie
Upon th'Exchange, still out of Popes-head-Alley.
The weekly Corrants, with *Pauls* Seale; and all
Th'admir'd discourses of the Prophet *Ball:*
These, had'st thou pleas'd either to dine, or sup,
Had made a meale for *Vulcan* to lick up.
But in my Deske, what was there to accite
So ravenous, and vast an appetite?
I dare not say a body, but some parts
There were of search, and mastry in the Arts.
All the old *Venusine,* in *Poëtrie,*
And lighted by the *Stagerite,* could spie,
Was there made English: with the Grammar too,
To teach some that, their Nurses could not doe,
The puritie of Language; and among
The rest, my journey into *Scotland* song,
With all th'adventures; Three bookes not afraid
To speake the Fate of the *Sicilian* Maid
To our owne Ladyes; and in storie there
Of our fift *Henry,* eight of his nine yeare;

77 *Nicholas Pasquill's:* alluding to Nicholas Breton's pasquinade pamphlets; "Meddle with your match" is perhaps a punning title for one of them.

78 *strong lines:* a phrase often used in the seventeenth century to characterize the style of the metaphysical poets.

79 *Captaine Pamplets:* military pamphlets by the soldier Thomas Gainsford, which issued from the publishers in "Popes-head-Alley."

81 *Corrants:* news letters, published in St. Paul's Churchyard.

82 *Ball:* tentatively identified as a tailor given to publishing prophecies.

85 *accite:* arouse.

89 *Venusine:* Horace, whose *Art of Poetry* Jonson translated. Two versions of it were published in 1640. The next line presumably alludes to a (now lost) commentary on it in which Aristotle's view of the art was also discussed.

91 *Grammar:* Jonson's *English Grammar,* published in 1640.

94 *song:* sung. This poem is not extant.

96 *Sicilian Maid:* a translation into English of John Barclay's Latin romance, *Argenis.*

97 *storie:* prose history.

Wherein was oyle, beside the succour spent,
  Which noble *Carew, Cotton, Selden* lent:
And twice-twelve-yeares stor'd up humanitie,
  With humble Gleanings in Divinitie,
After the Fathers, and those wiser Guides
  Whom Faction had not drawne to studie sides.
How in these ruines *Vulcan,* thou dost lurke,
  All soote, and embers! odious, as thy worke!
I now begin to doubt, if ever Grace,
  Or Goddesse, could be patient of thy face.
Thou woo *Minerva!* or to wit aspire!
  'Cause thou canst halt, with us in Arts, and Fire!
Sonne of the Wind! for so thy mother gone
  With lust conceiv'd thee; Father thou hadst none.
When thou wert borne, and that thou look'st at best,
  She durst not kisse, but flung thee from her brest.
And so did *Jove,* who ne're meant thee his Cup:
  No mar'le the Clownes of *Lemnos* tooke thee up.
For none but Smiths would have made thee a God.
  Some alchimist there may be yet, or odde
Squire of the Squibs, against the Pageant day,
  May to thy name a *Vulcanale* say;

100 *Carew . . . Selden:* Three famous English antiquarians: Richard Carew (1555–1620), Sir Robert Cotton (1571–1631), and John Selden (1584–1654), the latter an especially close friend of Jonson.

101 *humanitie:* Jonson's notes on twenty-four years of reading in liberal arts subjects.

103 *wiser Guides:* authorities who wrote before the Reformation.

110 *halt:* limp (Vulcan was crippled when Jove threw him from heaven; see lines 115–16 below); *Arts:* of metal work.

112 *Father . . . none:* Juno was Vulcan's mother but ancient myth did not give him a father.

113 *that . . . best:* you looked best when you were first born.

115 *who . . . Cup:* never intended to have you as his cupbearer. In the *Iliad,* Book I, Vulcan is assigned this role.

116 *mar'le:* marvel; *Clownes:* peasants who helped Vulcan after his fall onto Lemnos.

119 *Squibs:* fireworks (fired off at the Lord Mayor's annual show).

120 *Vulcanale:* hymn to the god.

And for it lose his eyes with Gun-powder,
    As th'other may his braines with Quicksilver.
Well-fare the Wise-men yet, on the *Banckside*,
    My friends, the Watermen! They could provide
Against thy furie, when to serve their needs,
    They made a *Vulcan* of a sheafe of Reedes,
Whom they durst handle in their holy-day coates,
    And safely trust to dresse, not burne their Boates.
But, O those Reeds! thy meere disdaine of them,
    Made thee beget that cruell Stratagem,
(Which, some are pleas'd to stile but thy madde pranck)
    Against the *Globe*, the Glory of the *Banke*.
Which, though it were the Fort of the whole Parish,
    Flanck'd with a Ditch, and forc'd out of a Marish,
I saw with two poore Chambers taken in
    And raz'd; e're thought could urge, this might have been!
See the Worlds Ruines! nothing but the piles
    Left! and wit since to cover it with Tiles.
The Brethren, they streight nois'd it out for Newes,
    'Twas verily some Relique of the Stewes.
And this a Sparkle of that fire let loose
    That was lock'd up in the *Winchestrian* Goose
Bred on the *Banck*, in time of Poperie,
    When *Venus* there maintain'd the Misterie.

122 *th'other:* the alchemist of line 118.
123 *Banckside:* the south bank of the Thames.
124 *Watermen:* ferrymen.
126 *Vulcan:* torch.
132 *Globe:* the famous theater, destroyed by fire on June 29, 1613, when cannon were shot off during a performance of Shakespeare's *Henry VIII*.
134 *Marish:* marsh.
135 *Chambers:* small cannon.
137 *Worlds:* the Globe's.
138 *cover . . . Tiles:* when it was rebuilt in 1614.
139 *Brethren:* probably the Puritans, who had always opposed the theaters.
140 *Stewes:* whorehouses, which were also located on the Bankside—on land belonging to the Bishop of Winchester (see line 142).
142 *Winchestrian Goose:* venereal disease.
144 *Misterie:* trade.

But, others fell, with that conceipt by the eares,
And cry'd, it was a threatning to the beares;
And that accursed ground, the *Parish-Garden:*
Nay, sigh'd, ah Sister 'twas the Nun, *Kate Arden*
Kindled the fire! But, then did one returne,
No Foole would his owne harvest spoile, or burne!
If that were so, thou rather would'st advance
The place, that was thy Wives inheritance.
O no, cry'd all. *Fortune,* for being a whore,
Scap'd not his Justice any jot the more.
He burnt that Idoll of the *Revels* too:
Nay, let *White-Hall* with Revels have to doe,
Though but in daunces, it shall know his power;
There was a Judgement shew'n too in an houre.
Hee is true *Vulcan* still! He did not spare
*Troy,* though it were so much his *Venus* care.
Foole, wilt thou let that in example come?
Did not she save from thence, to build a *Rome?*
And what hast thou done in these pettie spights,
More then advanc'd the houses, and their rites?

145 *fell . . . eares:* didn't believe that story.

146 *the beares:* the Bear-Garden, where the animals were baited for sport; also known as Paris Garden.

148 *Kate Arden:* a famous London slut. Her patrons were often frequenters of theaters.

149 *returne:* answer.

152 *Wives inheritance:* her dowry. For Kate to burn down the Globe would be like a husband burning down the property (his "harvest") of his wife—which became his when he married her.

153 *Fortune:* another theater, destroyed by fire in December 1621.

155 *Idoll . . . Revels:* playhouse (the Fortune).

156 *White-Hall:* the banqueting house in Whitehall Palace, burned in January 1618.

160 *Venus care:* Vulcan's wife helped the Trojans in the Trojan War.

162 *Did . . . Rome:* Venus protected Aeneas, who founded Rome.

164 *rites:* honors. Houses destroyed by fires (each fire "petty" in comparison to the one that destroyed Troy) have been rebuilt more nobly (as Troy was rebuilt in Rome).

I will not argue thee, from those of guilt,
   For they were burnt, but to be better built.
'Tis true, that in thy wish they were destroy'd,
   Which thou hast only vented, not enjoy'd.
So would'st th'have run upon the *Rolls* by stealth,
   And didst invade part of the Common-wealth,
In those Records, which were all Chroniclers gone,
   Will be remembred by *Six Clerkes,* to one.
But, say all sixe, Good Men, what answer yee?
   Lyes there no Writ, out of the *Chancerie*
Against this *Vulcan?* No Injunction?
   No Order? No Decree? Though we be gone
At *Common-Law:* Me thinkes in his despight
   A Court of *Equitie* should doe us right.
But to confine him to the Brew-houses,
   The Glasse-house, Dye-fats, and their Fornaces;
To live in Sea-coale, and goe forth in smoake;
   Or lest that vapour might the Citie choake,
Condemne him to the Brick-kills, or some Hill-
   foot (out in *Sussex*) to an iron Mill;
Or in small Fagots have him blaze about
   Vile Tavernes, and the Drunkards pisse him out;
Or in the *Bell*-Mans Lanthorne like a spie,
   Burne to a snuffe, and then stinke out, and die:

165 *argue:* dissuade; *guilt:* gilded (with a pun on guilty).

168 *vented:* uttered. The antecedent of "Which" in this line is "wish" in line 167. Vulcan never really enjoyed the fulfillment of his wish when he destroyed the Rolls office (in 1621) because the Clerks there remembered everything in the records which were burned.

172 *Six Clerkes:* The six clerks of Chancery. Their house in Chancery Lane was once a brewhouse but had been rebuilt in the late sixteenth century. It stood across the street from the Rolls office.

176 *we be gone:* our case be lost.

178 *Court of Equitie:* a court, like the Court of Conscience, which could correct the inequities of the Common Law.

180 *Dye-fats:* dyeing vats.

181 *Sea-coale:* common coal, and hence smoky.

183 *Brick-kills:* kilns for brickmaking.

187 *Bell-Mans:* night watchman's.

I could invent a sentence, yet were worse;
But I'le conclude all in a civill curse.
Pox on your flameship, *Vulcan;* if it be
To all as fatall as't hath beene to me,
And to *Pauls-Steeple;* which was unto us
'Bove all your Fire-workes, had at *Ephesus,*
Or *Alexandria;* and though a Divine
Losse remaines yet, as unrepair'd as mine.
Would you had kept your Forge at *Ætna* still,
And there made Swords, Bills, Glaves, and Armes your fill.
Maintain'd the trade at *Bilbo;* or else-where;
Strooke in at *Millan* with the Cutlers there;
Or stay'd but where the Fryar, and you first met,
Who from the Divels-Arse did Guns beget;
Or fixt in the *Low-Countrey's,* where you might
On both sides doe your mischiefes with delight;
Blow up, and ruine, myne, and countermyne,
Make your Petards, and Granats, all your fine
Engines of Murder, and receive the praise
Of massacring Man-kind so many wayes.
We aske your absence here, we all love peace,
And pray the fruites thereof, and the increase;
So doth the *King,* and most of the *Kings men*
That have good places: therefore once agen,
Pox on thee *Vulcan,* thy *Pandora's* pox,
And all the Evils that flew out of her box

193 *Pauls-Steeple:* burned in June 1561.
194 *Ephesus:* where Herostratus burned Diana's temple in 356 B.C.
195 *Alexandria:* This city's famous library was burned in A.D. 640.
198 *Glaves:* halberds.
199 *Bilbo:* Bilboa, in Spain, famous for the quality of its steel weapons.
200 *Millan:* Fine swords were made at Milan.
201 *Fryar:* Roger Bacon (1214?–1294), supposedly the inventor of guns.
203 *Low-Countrey's:* at war with Spain through most of this period.
206 *Petards:* artillery used to break down doors and walls; *Granats:* grenades.
213 *Pandora's pox:* Vulcan had created Pandora at Jove's command. Her box contained all the evils in the world. Jonson uses *pox* to mean both *curse* and *venereal disease.*

Light on thee: Or if those plagues will not doo,
Thy Wives pox on thee, and *B.B.'s* too.

## An Epistle Answering to One That Asked to Be Sealed of the Tribe of Ben

Men that are safe, and sure, in all they doe,
Care not what trials they are put unto;
They meet the fire, the Test, as Martyrs would;
And though Opinion stampe them not, are gold.
I could say more of such, but that I flie
To speake my selfe out too ambitiously,
And shewing so weake an Act to vulgar eyes,
Put conscience and my right to comprimise.
Let those that meerely talke, and never thinke,
That live in the wild Anarchie of Drinke,
Subject to quarrell only; or else such
As make it their proficiencie, how much
They'ave glutted in, and letcher'd out that weeke,
That never yet did friend, or friendship seeke
But for a Sealing: let these men protest.
Or th'other on their borders, that will jeast
On all Soules that are absent; even the dead
Like flies, or wormes, with mans corrupt parts fed:
That to speake well, thinke it above all sinne,
Of any Companie but that they are in,

216 *B.B.'s:* Bess Broughton's, a famous whore.

AN EPISTLE: The "Tribe of Ben" included all of Jonson's poetic disciples. Jonson's title here echoes *Revelation* 7:8, "of the tribe of Benjamin were sealed (assured) twelve thousand."

5–6 *flie . . . speake:* refrain from bragging about myself.

8 *comprimise:* i.e. compromise myself by boasting too much.

16 *on . . . borders:* like them.

Call every night to Supper in these fitts,
  And are receiv'd for the Covey of Witts;
That censure all the Towne, and all th'affaires,
  And know whose ignorance is more then theirs;
Let these men have their wayes, and take their times
  To vent their Libels, and to issue rimes,
I have no portion in them, nor their deale
  Of newes they get, to strew out the long meale,
I studie other friendships, and more one,
  Then these can ever be; or else wish none.
What is't to me whether the French Designe
  Be, or be not, to get the *Val-telline*?
Or the States Ships sent forth belike to meet
  Some hopes of *Spaine* in their West-Indian Fleet?
Whether the Dispensation yet be sent,
  Or that the Match from *Spaine* was ever meant?
I wish all well, and pray high heaven conspire
  My Princes safetie, and my Kings desire.
But if for honour, we must draw the Sword,
  And force back that, which will not be restor'd,
I have a body, yet, that spirit drawes
  To live, or fall, a Carkasse in the cause.
So farre without inquirie what the States,
  *Brunsfield,* and *Mansfield* doe this yeare, my fates
Shall carry me at Call; and I'le be well,
  Though I doe neither heare these newes, nor tell
Of *Spaine* or *France;* or were not prick'd down one
  Of the late Mysterie of reception;

22 *receiv'd for:* accepted as.

32 *Val-telline:* valley between Lake Como and the Tyrol, recently captured by the French.

33 *States:* belonging to the Low Countries.

35 *Dispensation:* for Prince Charles to marry the Infanta of Spain (1623).

40 *that:* presumably the forces of Catholic Spain.

44 *Brunsfield:* Christian of Brunswick, in the service of Frederick, the Elector Palatine; *Mansfield:* commander of the Bohemian and Palatine armies.

47 *prick'd down:* listed as.

48 *Mysterie of reception:* the reception committee for the visit of the Infanta.

Although my Fame, to his, not under-heares,
  That guides the Motions, and directs the beares.
But that's a blow, by which in time I may
  Lose all my credit with my Christmas Clay,
And animated *Porc'lane* of the Court,
  I, and for this neglect, the courser sort
Of earthen Jarres, there may molest me too:
  Well, with mine owne fraile Pitcher, what to doe
I have decreed; keepe it from waves, and presse;
  Lest it be justled, crack'd, made nought, or lesse:
Live to that point I will; for which I am man,
  And dwell as in my Center, as I can,
Still looking too, and ever loving heaven;
  With reverence using all the gifts thence given.
'Mongst which, if I have any friendships sent
  Such as are square, wel-tagde, and permanent,
Not built with Canvasse, paper, and false lights
  As are the Glorious Scenes, at the great sights;
And that there be no fev'ry heats, nor colds,
  Oylie Expansions, or shrunke durtie folds,
But all so cleare, and led by reasons flame,
  As but to stumble in her sight were shame;
These I will honour, love, embrace, and serve:
  And free it from all question to preserve.
So short you read my Character, and theirs
  I would call mine, to which not many Staires
Are asked to climbe. First give me faith, who know
  My selfe a little. I will take you so,
As you have writ your selfe. Now stand, and then,
  Sir, you are Sealed of the Tribe of *Ben*.

49 *not under-heares:* is not inferior. Jonson alludes to Inigo Jones, the designer, in this and the following line.
50 *Motions:* puppets.
54 *I:* Ay. Jonson is worried about losing his position at court.
57 *presse:* crowds.
64 *wel-tagde:* well-knit.
65 *Canvasse . . . lights:* used by Jones in his scenery for masques.
68 *Oylie Expansions:* of the canvas after it is painted.
72 *it:* friendship.

# To the Immortall Memorie, and Friendship of That Noble Paire, Sir Lucius Cary, and Sir H. Morison

## *The Turne*

Brave Infant of *Saguntum,* cleare
Thy comming forth in that great yeare,
When the Prodigious *Hannibal* did crowne
His rage, with razing your immortall Towne.

Thou, looking then about,
E're thou wert halfe got out,
Wise child, did'st hastily returne,
And mad'st thy Mothers wombe thine urne.
How summ'd a circle didst thou leave man-kind
Of deepest lore, could we the Center find!

## *The Counter-turne*

Did wiser Nature draw thee back,
From out the horrour of that sack,
Where shame, faith, honour, and regard of right
Lay trampled on; the deeds of death, and night,
Urg'd, hurried forth, and horld
Upon th'affrighted world:

TO THE IMMORTAL MEMORIE: Sir Lucius Cary (1610?–1643), Viscount Falkland; Sir Henry Morison (1608?–29). Cary later married Morison's sister. Jonson uses the terms "Turne," "Counter-turne," and "Stand" as literal translations of the Greek *strophe, antistrophe,* and *epode.*

1 *Infant:* Pliny tells the story of a newly-born child who, when he saw Saguntum destroyed by Hannibal in 219 B.C., returned to the womb.

3 *Prodigious:* like a prodigy.

Sword, fire, and famine, with fell fury met;
And all on utmost ruine set;
As, could they but lifes miseries fore-see,
No doubt all Infants would returne like thee?

## *The Stand*

For, what is life, if measur'd by the space,
Not by the act?
Or masked man, if valu'd by his face,
Above his fact?
Here's one out-liv'd his Peeres,
And told forth fourescore yeares;
He vexed time, and busied the whole State;
Troubled both foes, and friends;
But ever to no ends:
What did this Stirrer, but die late?
How well at twentie had he falne, or stood!
For three of his foure-score, he did no good.

## *The Turne*

Hee entred well, by vertuous parts,
Got up and thriv'd with honest arts:
He purchas'd friends, and fame, and honours then,
And had his noble name advanc'd with men:
But weary of that flight,
Hee stoop'd in all mens sight
To sordid flatteries, acts of strife,
And sunke in that dead sea of life
So deep, as he did then death's waters sup;
But that the Corke of Title boy'd him up.

21 *the space:* its duration.
22 *act:* deed.
24 *fact:* actions.

## *The Counter-turne*

Alas, but *Morison* fell young:
Hee never fell, thou fall'st, my tongue.
Hee stood, a Souldier to the last right end,
A perfect Patriot, and a noble friend,
But most a vertuous Sonne.
All Offices were done
By him, so ample, full, and round,
In weight, in measure, number, sound,
As though his age imperfect might appeare,
His life was of Humanitie the Spheare.

## *The Stand*

Goe now, and tell out dayes summ'd up with feares,
And make them yeares;
Produce thy masse of miseries on the Stage,
To swell thine age;
Repeat of things a throng,
To shew thou hast beene long,
Not liv'd; for life doth her great actions spell,
By what was done and wrought
In season, and so brought
To light: her measures are, how well
Each syllab'e answer'd, and was form'd, how faire;
These make the lines of life, and that's her ayre.

51 *As though:* And even if.
52 *Spheare:* the perfect figure.

## *The Turne*

It is not growing like a tree
In bulke, doth make man better bee;
Or standing long an Oake, three hundred yeare,
To fall a logge, at last, dry, bald, and seare:
A Lillie of a Day,
Is fairer farre, in May,
Although it fall, and die that night;
It was the Plant, and flowre of light.
In small proportions, we just beauties see:
And in short measures, life may perfect bee.

## *The Counter-turne*

Call, noble *Lucius,* then for Wine,
And let thy lookes with gladnesse shine:
Accept this garland, plant it on thy head,
And thinke, nay know, thy *Morison's* not dead.
Hee leap'd the present age,
Possest with holy rage,
To see that bright eternall Day:
Of which we *Priests,* and *Poëts* say
Such truths, as we expect for happy men,
And there he lives with memorie; and *Ben*

## *The Stand*

*Johnson,* who sung this of him, e're he went
Himselfe to rest,
Or taste a part of that full joy he meant
To have exprest,

In this bright *Asterisme:*
Where it were friendships schisme,
(Were not his *Lucius* long with us to tarry)
To separate these twi-
Lights, the *Dioscuri;*
And keepe the one halfe from his *Harry.*
But fate doth so alternate the designe,
Whilst that in heav'n, this light on earth must shine.

## *The Turne*

And shine as you exalted are;
Two names of friendship, but one Starre:
Of hearts the union. And those not by chance
Made, or indentur'd, or leas'd out t'advance
The profits for a time.
No pleasures vaine did chime,
Of rimes, or ryots, at your feasts,
Orgies of drinke, or fain'd protests:
But simple love of greatnesse, and of good;
That knits brave minds, and manners, more then blood.

## *The Counter-turne*

This made you first to know the Why
You lik'd, then after, to apply
That liking; and approach so one the tother,
Till either grew a portion of the other:
Each stiled by his end,
The Copie of his friend.

89 *Asterisme:* constellation.
93 *Dioscuri:* Castor and Pollux.
111 *end:* intention.

You liv'd to be the great surnames,
And titles, by which all made claimes
Unto the Vertue. Nothing perfect done,
But as a *Cary*, or a *Morison.*

## *The Stand*

And such a force the faire example had,
As they that saw
The good, and durst not practise it, were glad
That such a Law
Was left yet to Man-kind;
Where they might read, and find
*Friendship*, in deed, was written, not in words:
And with the heart, not pen,
Of two so early men,
Whose lines her rowles were, and records.
Who, e're the first downe bloomed on the chin,
Had sow'd these fruits, and got the harvest in.

# From Uncollected Poetry

## Song

Slow, slow, fresh fount, keepe time with my salt teares;
Yet slower, yet, ô faintly gentle springs:
List to the heavy part the musique beares,
"Woe weepes out her division, when shee sings.

125 *so early:* such young.
SONG: The song is from *Cynthia's Revels*, I.ii (1600), where it is sung by Echo.
4 *division:* breaking up of slow notes into quick ones.

Droupe hearbs, and flowers,
Fall griefe in showers;
"Our beauties are not ours:
O, I could still
(Like melting snow upon some craggie hill,)
drop, drop, drop, drop,
Since natures pride is, now, a wither'd Daffodill.

## Hymne

*Queene* and *Huntresse*, chaste, and faire,
Now the *Sunne* is laid to sleepe,
Seated, in thy silver chaire,
State in wonted manner keepe:
*Hesperus* intreats thy light,
Goddesse, excellently bright.

Earth, let not thy envious shade
Dare it selfe to interpose;
*Cynthias* shining orbe was made
Heaven to cleere, when day did close:
Blesse us then with wished sight,
Goddesse, excellently bright.

Lay thy bow of pearle apart,
And thy cristall-shining quiver;
Give unto the flying hart
Space to breathe, how short soever:
Thou, that mak'st a day of night,
Goddesse, excellently bright.

HYMNE: from *Cynthia's Revels,* v.vi.
5 *Hesperus:* the evening star.

## Song

If I freely may discover,
What would please me in my lover:
    I would have her faire, and wittie,
    Savouring more of court, then cittie;
    A little proud, but full of pittie:
    Light and humorous in her toying.
    Oft building hopes, and soone destroying,
    Long, but sweet in the enjoying,
Neither too easie, nor too hard:
All extreames I would have bard.

Shee should be allowed her passions,
So they were but us'd as fashions;
    Sometimes froward, and then frowning,
    Sometimes sickish, and then swowning,
    Every fit, with change, still crowning.
    Purely Jelous, I would have her,
    Then onely constant when I crave her.
    'Tis a vertue should not save her.
Thus, nor her delicates would cloy me,
Neither her peevishnesse annoy me.

SONG: from *Poetaster,* II.ii (1601).
19 *delicates:* pleasure-giving parts.

## Song

Fooles, they are the onely nation
Worth mens envy, or admiration;
Free from care, or sorrow-taking,
Selves, and others merry-making:
All they speake, or doe, is sterling.
Your Foole, he is your great mans dearling,
And your ladies sport, and pleasure;
Tongue, and bable are his treasure.
Eene his face begetteth laughter,
And he speakes truth, free from slaughter;
Hee's the grace of every feast,
And, sometimes, the chiefest guest:
Hath his trencher, and his stoole,
When wit waites upon the foole,
        O, who would not bee
        Hee, hee, hee?

## Song

Still to be neat, still to be drest,
As you were going to a feast;
Still to be pou'dred, still perfum'd:
Lady, it is to be presum'd,
Though arts hid causes are not found,
All is not sweet, all is not sound.

SONG: from *Volpone,* I.II (1605).
SONG: from *The Silent Woman,* I.i (1609).
  2 *As:* as if.

Give me a looke, give me a face,
That makes simplicitie a grace;
Robes loosely flowing, haire as free:
Such sweet neglect more taketh me,
Then all th'adulteries of art.
They strike mine eyes, but not my heart.

## To the Memory of My Beloved, the Author Mr. William Shakespeare: and What He Hath Left Us

To draw no envy (*Shakespeare*) on thy name,
   Am I thus ample to thy Booke, and Fame:
While I confesse thy writings to be such,
   As neither *Man*, nor *Muse*, can praise too much.
'Tis true, and all mens suffrage. But these wayes
   Were not the paths I meant unto thy praise:
For seeliest Ignorance on these may light,
   Which, when it sounds at best, but eccho's right;
Or blinde Affection, which doth ne're advance
   The truth, but gropes, and urgeth all by chance;
Or crafty Malice, might pretend this praise,
   And thinke to ruine, where it seem'd to raise.
These are, as some infamous Baud, or Whore,
   Should praise a Matron. What could hurt her more?

TO THE MEMORY OF MY BELOVED: Published in the Shakespeare first folio (1623).

2 *ample:* i.e. in the length of my poem.
5 *mens suffrage:* men grant it.
7 *seeliest:* simplest.
13 *as:* as if.

But thou art proofe against them, and indeed
  Above th'ill fortune of them, or the need.
I, therefore will begin. Soule of the Age!
  The applause! delight! the wonder of our Stage!
My *Shakespeare*, rise; I will not lodge thee by
  *Chaucer*, or *Spenser*, or bid *Beaumont* lye
A little further, to make thee a roome:
  Thou art a Moniment, without a tombe,
And art alive still, while thy Booke doth live,
  And we have wits to read, and praise to give.
That I not mixe thee so, my braine excuses;
  I meane with great, but disproportion'd *Muses:*
For, if I thought my judgement were of yeeres,
  I should commit thee surely with thy peeres,
And tell, how farre thou didst our *Lily* out-shine,
  Or sporting *Kid*, or *Marlowes* mighty line.
And though thou hadst small *Latine*, and lesse *Greeke*,
  From thence to honour thee, I would not seeke
For names; but call forth thund'ring *Æschilus*,
  *Euripides*, and *Sophocles* to us,
*Paccuvius*, *Accius*, him of *Cordova* dead,
  To life againe, to heare thy Buskin tread,
And shake a Stage: Or, when thy Sockes were on,
  Leave thee alone, for the comparison
Of all, that insolent *Greece*, or haughtie *Rome*

20 *Chaucer . . . Beaumont:* All three poets were buried in Westminster Abbey.

27 *of yeeres:* i.e. one which would compare thee with all other poets.

28 *commit:* connect.

29 *Lily:* John Lyly (1554?–1606), author of *Euphues* and of several romantic prose comedies.

30 *Kid:* Thomas Kyd (1557?–1595?), whose *Spanish Tragedy* was the prototype for Elizabethan revenge plays. "Sporting" both refers to Kyd's somewhat reckless career and puns on his name. *Marlowes . . . line:* perhaps especially in *Tamburlaine,* where Marlowe first showed his power in rhetorical verse.

35 *Paccuvius . . . Cordova:* Roman tragic writers; only Seneca's (Cordova was his birthplace) have survived.

36 *Buskin:* worn by tragic actors in the classical period.

37 *Sockes:* the comic sock.

Sent forth, or since did from their ashes come.
Triúmph, my *Britaine,* thou hast one to showe,
To whom all Scenes of *Europe* homage owe.
He was not of an age, but for all time!
And all the *Muses* still were in their prime,
When like *Apollo* he came forth to warme
Our eares, or like a *Mercury* to charme!
Nature her selfe was proud of his designes,
And joy'd to weare the dressing of his lines!
Which were so richly spun, and woven so fit,
As, since, she will vouchsafe no other Wit.
The merry *Greeke,* tart *Aristophanes,*
Neat *Terence,* witty *Plautus,* now not please;
But antiquated, and deserted lye
As they were not of Natures family.
Yet must I not give Nature all: Thy Art,
My gentle *Shakespeare,* must enjoy a part.
For though the *Poets* matter, Nature be,
His Art doth give the fashion. And, that he,
Who casts to write a living line, must sweat,
(Such as thine are) and strike the second heat
Upon the *Muses* anvile: turne the same,
(And himselfe with it) that he thinkes to frame;
Or for the lawrell, he may gaine a scorne,
For a good *Poet's* made, as well as borne.
And such wert thou. Looke how the fathers face
Lives in his issue, even so, the race
Of *Shakespeares* minde, and manners brightly shines
In his well torned, and true-filed lines:
In each of which, he seemes to shake a Lance,
As brandish't at the eyes of Ignorance.
Sweet Swan of *Avon!* what a sight it were
To see thee in our waters yet appeare,
And make those flights upon the bankes of *Thames,*
That so did take *Eliza,* and our *James!*
But stay, I see thee in the *Hemisphere*

59 *casts:* strives.
69 *shake a Lance:* punning on "Shakespeare."

Advanc'd, and made a Constellation there!
Shine forth, thou Starre of *Poets,* and with rage,
Or influence, chide, or cheere the drooping Stage;
Which, since thy flight from hence, hath mourn'd like night,
And despaires day, but for thy Volumes light.

BEN: JONSON.

## [It was a beauty that I saw]

It was a beauty that I saw
So pure, so perfect, as the frame
Of all the universe was lame,
To that one figure, could I draw,
Or give least line of it a law!

A skeine of silke without a knot!
A fair march made without a halt!
A curious forme without a fault!
A printed booke without a blot!
All beauty, and without a spot!

## Ode To Himselfe

Come leave the loathed Stage,
And the more loathsome Age,
Where pride and impudence in faction knit,
Usurpe the Chaire of wit:
Inditing and arraigning every day,
Something they call a Play.

76 *Constellation:* Cygnus, or the Swan.

[IT WAS A BEAUTY THAT I SAW].
This song is taken from *The New Inn,* IV.iv (1629).

8 *curious:* beautifully made.

ODE TO HIMSELFE: Written after the failure of *The New Inn.* Carew replied to this poem in his "To Ben. Johnson," *q.v.*

Let their fastidious vaine
Commission of the braine,
Runne on, and rage, sweat, censure, and condemn:
They were not made for thee, lesse thou for them.

Say that thou pour'st'hem wheat,
And they would Akornes eat:
'Twere simple fury, still thy selfe to wast
On such as have no taste:
To offer them a surfeit of pure bread,
Whose appetites are dead:
No, give them Graines their fill,
Huskes, Draffe to drinke, and swill:
If they love Lees, and leave the lusty Wine,
Envy them not, their pallat's with the Swine.

No doubt a mouldy Tale,
Like Pericles, and stale
As the Shrives crusts, and nasty as his Fish,
Scraps out of every Dish,
Throwne forth and rak'd into the common Tub,
May keep up the Play Club.
Broomes sweepings doe as well
There, as his Masters meale:
For who the relish of these guests will fit,
Needs set them but the Almes-basket of wit.

And much good do't yee then,
Brave Plush and Velvet men

13 *simple:* foolish.
17 *Graines:* malt refuse.
18 *Draffe:* dregs.
22 *Pericles:* Shakespeare's late romance (1609).
23 *Shrives:* Sheriff's (crusts given to prisoners).
25 *common Tub:* containing refuse for the poor.
27 *Broomes:* Richard Brome, Jonson's servant who had turned playwright.

Can feed on Orts; and safe in your scoene cloaths,
Dare quit upon your Oathes
The Stagers, and the stage-writes too; your Peers,
Of stuffing your large eares
With rage of Commicke socks,
Wrought upon twenty Blocks;
Which, if they're torne, and foule, and patch'd enough,
The Gamsters share your gilt, and you their stuffe.

Leave things so prostitute,
And take th'Alcaike Lute;
Or thine owne Horace, or Anacreons Lyre;
Warme thee by Pindars fire:
And though thy Nerves be shrunke, and blood be cold,
Ere years have made thee old,
Strike that disdainfull heat
Throughout, to their defeat:
As curious fooles, and envious of thy straine,
May blushing sweare, no Palsi's in thy braine.

But when they heare thee sing
The glories of thy King;
His zeale to God, and his just awe of men,
They may be blood-shaken, then
Feele such a flesh-quake to possesse their powers,
That no tun'd Harpe like ours,
In sound of Peace or Warres,
Shall truely hit the Starres
When they shall read the Acts of *Charles* his Reigne,
And see his Chariot triumph 'bove his *Waine*.

33 *Orts:* scraps; *scoene cloaths:* clothes worn at the scene, when the courtiers perhaps sat on the stage.

34 *quit . . . Oathes:* revenge by swearing (at them).

38 *Blocks:* Jonson puns on "moulds" and "blockheads," as he does on "gilded" and "guilt" in line 40.

42 *Alcaike:* Alcaeus, the early Greek lyric poet.

45 *Nerves:* sinews.

50 *Palsi:* Jonson had had a stroke in 1628.

60 *Waine:* Charles's Wagon, or the Big Dipper.

# *Masques*

## *Pans* Anniversarie; or, The Shepherds Holy-day. The Scene, *Arcadia.*

As it was presented at Court before
King JAMES. 1620.

The Inventors,
*Inigo Jones. Ben Jonson.*

---

The first presentation is of three Nymphs strewing severall sorts of flowers, followed by an old Shepherd with a Censer and perfumes.

### NYMPH I

*Thus, thus, begin the yearly rites*
*Are due to PAN on these bright nights;*
*His Morne now riseth, and invites*
*To sports, to dances, and delights:*

MASQUES: *1620:* The 1640 folio has, erroneously, 1625. The masque was probably written for James I's birthday on June 19.

*All Envious, and Prophane away,*
*This is the Shepherds Holy-day.*

## NYMPH II

*Strew, strew, the glad and smiling ground*
*With every flower, yet not confound*
*The Prime-rose drop, the Springs owne spouse,*
*Bright Dayes-eyes, and the lips of Cowes,*
*The Garden-star, the Queene of May,*
*The Rose, to crowne the Holy-day.*

## NYMPH III

*Drop, drop you Violets, change your hues,*
*Now red, now pale, as Lovers use,*
*And in your death goe out as well,*
*As when you liv'd unto the smell:*
*That from your odour all may say,*
*This is the Shepherds Holy-day.*

## SHEPHERD

*Well done, my pretty ones, raine Roses still,*
*Untill the last be drapt: Then hence: and fill*
*Your fragrant prickles for a second shower,*
*Bring Corn-flag, Tulips, and Adonis flower,*

27 *drapt:* dropped.
28 *prickles:* wicker baskets.
29 *Corn-flag:* gladiolus; *Adonis flower:* the anemone.

*Faire Oxe-eye, Goldy-locks, and Columbine,*
*Pinkes, Goulands, King-cups, and sweet Sops-in-wine,*
*Blew Harebells, Pagles, Pansies, Calaminth,*
*Flower-gentle, and the faire-hair'd Hyacinth,*
*Bring rich Carnations, Floure-de-luces, Lillies,*
*The chequ'd, and purple-ringed Daffodillies,*
*Bright Crowne-imperiall, Kings-speare, Holy-hocks,*
*Sweet* Venus *Navill, and soft Lady-smocks,*
*Bring too, some branches forth of* Daphnes *haire,*
*And gladdest myrtle for these postes to weare*
*With Spikenard weav'd, and Marjoram betweene,*
*And star'd with yellow-golds, and Meadowes Queene,*
*That when the Altar, as it ought, is drest,*
*More odour come not from the Phoenix nest;*
*The breath thereof* Panchaia *may envie,*
*The colours* China, *and the light the skye.*

## LOUD MUSIQUE

*The* Scene *opens, and in it are the Masquers discover'd sitting about the Fountaine of light. The Musicians attyr'd like the Priests of* Pan *standing in the worke beneath them, when entreth to the old Shepherd.*

30 *Oxe-eye:* a species of marigold; *Goldy-locks:* buttercups or golden maidenhair.

31 *Goulands:* another type of golden flower, in the crowfoot family; *King-cups:* another species of buttercup; *Sops-in-wine:* gillyflowers.

32 *Pagles:* cowslips.

33 *Flower-gentle:* amaranthus.

34 *Floure-de-luces:* white irises.

36 *Crowne-imperiall:* species of fritillary; *Kings-speare:* yellow asphodel.

37 *Venus Navill:* the pennywort; *Lady-smocks:* cuckoo flowers.

38 *Daphnes haire:* the laurel.

41 *yellow-golds:* corn marigolds; *Meadowes Queene:* the meadowsweet.

44 *Panchaia:* fabulous city on the Erythraean Sea, east of Arabia.

## A Fencer *flourishing*

Roome for an old Trophie of Time; a Sonne of the sword, a Servant of *Mars,* the Minion of the Muses, and a Master of Fence. One that hath showne his quarters, and plaid his prizes at all the games of *Greece* in his time; as Fencing, Wrestling, Leaping, Dauncing, what not? And hath now usher'd hither by the light of my long-sword certaine bold Boyes of *Boeotia,* who are come to challenge the Arcadians at their owne sports, call them forth on their owne holy-day, and Daunce them down on their owne Greene-swarth.

### SHEPHERD

'Tis boldly attempted, and must be a *Boeotian* enterprise by the face of it, from all the parts of *Greece* else, especially at this time when the best, and bravest spirits of *Arcadia,* called together by the excellent *Arcas,* are yonder sitting about the Fountaine of light, in consultation of what honours they may doe the great *Pan* by encrease of anniversarie rites fitted to the Musique of his peace.

### FENCER

Peace to thy *Pan,* and mum to thy Musique, Swaine;
There is a Tinker of *Thebes* a comming, called *Epam,*
with his kettle will make all *Arcadia* ring of him;
What are your sports for the purpose? say, if singing,

54–55 *showne . . . quarters:* manifested his abilities.
55 *plaid his prizes:* played his part.
58 *Boeotia:* famed for the stupidity of its inhabitants (in contrast to Athens).
67 *Arcas:* King of Arcadia.

you shall be sung downe, if dauncing, daunc'd downe. There is no more to be done with you, but know what; which it is; and you are in smoke, gone, vapour'd, vanish'd, blowne, and (as a man would say) in a word of two sillables, Nothing.

SHEPHERD

This is short, though not so sweet. Surely the better part of the solemnitie here will be dauncing.

FENCER

Enough; They shall be met with instantly in their owne sphere, the sphere of their owne activitie, a daunce. But by whom, expect: No Cynaetheian, nor Satyres; but (as I said) Boyes of *Boeotia;* thinges of *Thebes,* (the Towne is ours, Shepheard) mad merry Greekes, Lads of life, that have no gall in us, but all ayre and sweetnesse. A Tooth-drawer is our Foreman, that if there be but a bitter tooth in the company, it may bee called out at a twitch; he doth command any mans teeth out of his head upon the point of his Poynard; or tickles them forth with his ryding rod: Hee drawes teeth a horse-backe in full speed, yet hee will daunce a foot, he hath given his word: He is yeoman of the mouth to the whole Brotherhood, and is charged to see their gummes bee cleane, and their breath sweet, at a minutes warning. Then comes my learned *Theban*, the Tinker I told you of, with his kettle Drum (before and after) a Master of Musique, and a man of mettall; He

87 *Cynaetheian:* from the extreme north of Arcadia.

beates the march to the tune of Tickle-foot, *Pam, pam, pam,* brave *Epam* with a *nondas.* That's the straine.

SHEPHERD

A high one.

FENCER

Which is followed by the trace, and tract of an excellent Juggler, that can juggle with every joynt about him, from head to heele. He can doe tricks with his toes, wind silke, and thred Pearle with them, as nimble a fine fellow of his feet, as his hands: For there is a noble Corne-cutter his companion, hath so pared, and finified them—. Indeed, he hath taken it into his care, to reforme the feet of all, and fit all their footing to a forme; onely one splay-foot in the company, and he is a Bellowes-mender, allow'd, who hath the looking to all their lungs by patent, and by his place is to set that leg afore still, and with his puffes keepes them in breath during pleasure; A Tinder-box-man to strike new fire into them at every turne, and where he spies any brave sparke that is in danger to goe out, plie him with a match presently.

SHEPHERD

A most politique provision.

104 *Epam . . . nondas:* Punning on Epaminondas (d. 362 B.C.), famed Theban general.
114 *finified:* adorned.
117 *allow'd:* licensed.

## FENCER

Nay, we have made our provisions beyond example, I hope. For to these there is annexed a Clock-keeper, a grave person, as *Time* himselfe, who is to see that they all keepe time to a nick, and move every elbow in order, every knee in compasse. He is to wind them up, and draw them downe, as he sees cause; Then is there a subtile shrewd-bearded Sir, that hath beene a Politician, but is now a maker of Mouse-traps, a great Inginer yet; and he is to catch the Ladyes favours in the Daunce with certaine cringes he is to make; and to baite their benevolence. Nor can wee doubt of the successe, for we have a Prophet amongst us of that peremptorie pate, a Taylour, or master Fashioner, that hath found it out in a painted cloth, or some old hanging (for those are his Librarie) that we must conquer in such a time, and such a halfe time, therefore bids us goe on crosse-leg'd, or however thred the needles of our owne happiness, goe through-stitch with all, unwind the clew of our cares, he hath taken measure of our mindes, and will fit our fortune to our footing. And to better assure us; at his owne charge, brings his Philosopher with him, a great Clerke, who (they say) can write, and it is shrewdly suspected but he can read too: And he is to take the whole Daunces from the foot by Brachygraphie, and so make a memoriall, if not a map of the businesse. Come forth, lads, and doe your owne turnes.

132 *in compasse:* in time (to the music).
151 *Brachygraphie:* shorthand.

*The Antimasque is Daunced*
*After which*

FENCER

How like you this, Shepheard? was not this geare gotten on a holy-day?

SHEPHERD

Faith, your folly may deserve pardon, because it hath delighted: But, beware of presuming, or how you offer comparison with persons so neere Deities. Behold where they are, that have now forgiven you, whom should you provoke againe with the like, they will justly punish that with anger, which they now dismisse with contempt. Away.

*And come you prime Arcadians forth, that taught*
*By PAN the rites of true societie,*
*From his loud Musicke, all your manners wraught*
*And made your Common-wealth a harmonie,*
*Commending so to all posteritie*
*Your innocence from that faire Fount of light,*
*As still you sit without the injurie*
*Of any rudenesse, Folly can, or spight:*
*Daunce from the top of the Lycaean mountaine*
*Downe to this valley, and with neerer eye*
*Enjoy, what long in that illumin'd Fountaine*
*You did farre of, but yet with wonder spye.*

157 *geare gotten:* device conceived.
174 *Lycaean:* Mount Lycaea, in Arcadia.

## HYMNE I

1. *Of* Pan *we sing, the best of Singers,* Pan,
*That taught us swaines, how first to tune our layes,*
*And on the pipe more aires then* Phoebus *can.*
CHO. *Heare, O you groves, and hills, resound his praise.*
2. *Of* Pan *we sing, the best of Leaders,* Pan,
*That leads the Nayad's, and the Dryad's forth;*
*And to their daunces more then* Hermes *can.*
CHO. *Heare, O you groves, and hills, resound his worth.*
3. *Of* Pan *we sing, the best of Hunters,* Pan,
*That drives the Hart to seeke unused wayes,*
*And in the chace more then* Sylvanus *can.*
CHO. *Heare, O you groves, and hills, resound his praise.*
4. *Of* Pan *we sing, the best of Shepherds,* Pan,
*That keepes our flocks, and us, and both leads forth*
*To better pastures then great* Pales *can.*
CHO. *Heare, O you groves, and hills, resound his worth.*
*And while his powers, and praises thus we sing,*
*And Valleys let rebound, and all the rivers ring.*

The *Masquers* descend, and dance their Entrie.

## HYMNE II

Pan *is our All, by him we breath, wee live,*
*Wee move, we are; 'Tis he our lambes doth reare,*
*Our flocks doth blesse, and from the store doth give*
*The warme and finer fleeces that we weare.*
*He keepes away all heates, and colds,*
*Drives all diseases from our folds:*
*Makes every where the spring to dwell,*
*The Ewes to feed, their udders swell;*

199 *All:* the literal meaning of *Pan* in Greek.

*But if he frowne, the sheepe (alas)*
*The Shepheards wither, and the grasse.*
*Strive, strive, to please him then by still increasing thus*
*The rites are due to him, who doth all right for us.*

## *The Maine Daunce*

### HYMNE III

*If yet, if yet*
Pans *orgies you will further fit,*
*See where the silver-footed Fayes doe sit,*
*The Nymphes of wood and water,*
*Each trees, and Fountaines daughter.*
*Goe take them forth, it will be good*
*To see some wave it like a wood,*
*And others wind it like a flood;*
*In springs,*
*And rings,*
*Till the applause it brings,*
*Wakes Eccho from her seate,*
*The closes to repeate.*
(ECH. *The closes to repeate*)
*Eccho, the truest Oracle on ground,*
*Though nothing but a sound.*
(ECH. *Though nothing but a sound.*)
*Belov'd of* Pan, *the Vall⟨e⟩yes Queene*
(ECH. *The Valleyes Queene*)
*And often heard, though never seene,*
(ECH. *Though never seene.*)

225 *closes:* conclusions of musical phrases.

# Revells

FENCER

Roome, roome there: where are you, Shepheard? I am come againe with my second part of my bold Bloods, the brave Gamesters: who assure you by me, that they perceive no such wonder in all is done here, but that they dare adventure another tryall. They looke for some sheepish devises here in *Arcadia*, not these, and therefore a hall, a hall they demand.

SHEPHERD

Nay, then they are past pittie, let them come, and not expect the anger of a Deitie to pursue them, but meet them. They have their punishment with their fact. They shall be sheepe.

FENCER

O spare me, by the law of Nations, I am but their Ambassadour.

SHEPHERD

You speake in time, Sir.

246 *fact:* deed.

## 2. Antimasque

### SHEPHERD

Now let them returne with their solide heads, and carry their stupiditie into *Boeotia,* whence they brought it, with an embleme of themselves, and their Countrey. This is too pure an aire for so grosse Braines.

*End you the rites, and so be eas'd*
*Of these, and then great* Pan *is pleas'd.*

### HYMNE IIII

*Great* Pan, *the Father of our peace, and pleasure,*
*Who giv'st us all this leasure,*
*Heare what thy hallowd troope of Herdsmen pray*
*For this their Holy-day,*
*And how their vowes to Thee, they in* Lycaeum *pay.*

*So may our Ewes receive the mounting Rammes,*
*And wee bring thee the earliest of our Lambes:*
*So may the first of all our fells be thine,*
*And both the beestning of our Goates, and Kine:*
*As thou our folds dost still secure,*
*And keep'st our fountaines sweet and pure,*
*Driv'st hence the Wolfe, the Tode, the Brock,*
*Or other vermine from the flock.*

269 *fells:* fleeces.
270 *beestning:* first milk drawn from goat or cow after parturition.
273 *Tode . . . Brock:* fox . . . badger.

*That wee preserv'd by Thee, and thou observ'd by us,*
*May both live safe in shade of thy lov'd* Maenalus.

## SHEPHERD

*Now each returne unto his Charge,*
*And though to day you have liv'd at large,*
*And well your flocks have fed their fill,*
*Yet doe not trust your hirelings still.*
*See, yond' they goe, and timely doe*
*The office you have put them to,*
*But if you often give this leave,*
*Your sheepe, and you they will deceave.*

The End.

276 *Maenalus:* shepherd in Virgil's *Eclogues* (VIII.21 f.), who "listens to the shepherds' loves and to Pan."

# Pleasure Reconciled to Vertue

*A Masque*

As it was Presented at Court before King James 1619

---

## The Scene was the Mountaine

### ATLAS

*Who had his top ending in the figure of an old man, his head and beard all hoary, and frost, as if his shoulders were covered with snow; the rest Wood, and Rocke.* A Grove of Ivie *at his feet; out of which, to a wilde* Musicke *of* Cymbals, Flutes, *and* Tabers *is brought forth,* COMUS *the* God *of* Cheere, *or the* Belly, *riding in Triumph, his head crownd with* Roses, *and other flowers, his haire curled: They that waite upon him crownd with* Ivie, *their Javelins done about with it; one of them going with* Hercules *his* Boule *bare before him, while the rest presented him with this* Hymne.

PLEASURE RECONCILED TO VERTUE.
10 *done about:* decorated.
11 *boule:* bowl, drinking cup.

Roome, roome, make roome for the bouncing bellie,
First father of sauce, and deviser of jellie;
Prime master of Arts, and the giver of wit,
That found out the excellent Engine, the spit;
The plough, and the flaile, the mill, and the hopper,
The hutch, and the boulter, the furnace and copper,
The oven, the baven, the mawkin, the peele,
The harth, and the range, the dogge, and the wheele,
He, he first invented the hogshead and tun,
The gimlet and vice too, and taught 'em to run,
And since with the funnell, an *Hippocras* bag,
H'as made of himselfe, that now he cries swag;
Which showes though the pleasure be but of foure inches,
Yet he is a Weesell, the gullet that pinches
Of any delight, and not spares from his backe,
What ever to make of the bellie a sacke!
Haile, haile plump paunch, ô the founder of taste,
For fresh-meats, or powlder'd, or pickle, or paste,
Devourer of broyl'd, back'd, roasted, or sod;
And emptier of cups, be they even or odd;
All which have now made thee so wide i'the waste,
As scarce with no pudding thou art to be lac'd,
But eating and drinking untill thou dost nod,
Thou break'st all thy girdles, and breakst forth a god.

17 *hopper:* through which grain passed into the corn-mill.

18 *hutch:* rabbits' hutch; *boulter:* flour sifter; *copper:* large copper cooking vessel.

19 *baven:* brushwood used to heat oven; *mawkin:* mop used to clean oven; *peele:* a baker's shovel for taking loaves from the oven.

20 *dogge:* firedog, andiron; *wheele:* for turning the spit.

23–24 *an Hippocras . . . himselfe:* Hippocras was a heavily spiced wine. The belly has turned itself into a strainer (bag).

24 *swag:* A "swag-bellied" fellow had a great protruding abdomen.

26–27 *Weesell . . . delight:* a weasel who takes any delight by the throat.

27 *his:* The 1640 folio reads *this,* the Devonshire manuscript *the.*

28 *sacke:* with a pun on the wine, sherry-sack.

30 *powlder'd:* powdered.

31 *sod:* boiled.

## *To this the Boule-bearer*

Doe you heare my friends? to whom did you sing all this now? pardon me onely that I aske you, for I doe not looke for an answere; Ile answer my selfe, I know it is now such a time as the *Saturnalls* for all the World, that every man stands under the eaves of his own hat, and sings what please him; that's the right, and the liberty of it. Now you sing of god *Comus* here the bellie-god; I say it is well, and I say it is not well: It is well as it is a ballad, and the bellie worthie of it; I must needes say, and 'twere forty yards of ballad more, as much ballad as tripe. But when the bellie is not edyfied by it, it is not well; for where did you ever read or heare, that the bellie had any eares? Come never pumpe for an answer, for you are defeated; Our fellow *Hunger* there that was as ancient a reteiner to the bellie as any of us, was turned away for being unseasonable, not unreasonable, but unseasonable; and now is he poore thin-gut, faine to get his living with teaching of *Starlings, Mag-pies, Parrots, and Jacke-dawes,* those things he would have taught the bellie. Beware of dealing with the bellie, the bellie will not bee talk'd too, especially when he is full; then there is no venturing upon *Venter,* he will blow you all up, he will thunder indeed-la: Some in dirision call him the father of farts; but I say he was the first inventor of great Ordnance, and taught us to discharge them on Festivall dayes, would we had a fit feast for him y'faith, to shew his activity; I would have something now fetcht in to please his five sences, the throat, or the two sences the eyes: Pardon mee for my two sences, for I that carry *Hercules* Boule i' the service, may see double by my place; for I have drunke like a frog to day: I would have a Tun now brought in to dance, and so many bottles

41 *Saturnalls:* Roman holiday held in December.
46 *tripe:* intestines.
57 *Venter:* A pun on the Latin *venter* (belly).
59 *Ordnance:* cannon.
60 *y'faith:* in truth.

about him. Ha! you looke as if you would make a probleme of this; doe you see? do you see? a probleme: why bottles? and why a tun? and why a tun? and why bottles to dance? I say that men that drinke hard, and serve the bellie in any place of qualitie (as the *joviall Tinkers,* or the *lusty kindred*) are living measures of drinke, and can transforme themselves, and doe every day to bottles, or tuns when they please: And when they ha' done all they can, they are as I say againe, (for I thinke I said somewhat like it afore) but moving measures of drink, and there is a peece i'the Cellar can hold more than all they. This will I make good, if it please our new god but to give a nod, for the bellie doe's all by signes; and I am all for the bellie, the truest clocke i'the world to goe by.

## *Here the first* Anti-maske, *after which*

### HERCULES

What Rites are these? breeds earth more monsters yet?
*Antaeus* scarce is cold: what can beget
This store? (and stay) such contraries upon her,
Is earth so fruitfull of her owne dishonour?
Or 'cause his vice was inhumanitie,
Hopes she by vicious hospitalitie
To worke an expiation first? and then
(Helpe vertue) these are sponges, and not men:
Bottles? meere vessels? halfe a tun of paunch?
How? and the other halfe thrust forth in haunch?
Whose feast? the bellies? *Comus?* and my cup
Brought in to fill the drunken Orgies up?
And here abus'd? that was the crownd reward,
Of thirstie *Heroes,* after labour hard?

69–70 *joviall Tinkers . . . lusty kindred:* names of popular ballads.
81 *Antaeus:* the son of Neptune and Earth, invincible while he touched the ground. Hercules overcame him by lifting him in the air and strangling him.

Burdens, and shames of nature, perish, die;
(For yet you never liv'd) but in the stie
Of vice have wallow'd, and in that swines strife
Beene buried under the offence of life:
Goe reele and fall under the load you make,
Till your swollen bowells burst with what you take.
Can this be pleasure, to extinguish man?
Or so quite change him in his figure? can
The bellie love his paine? and be content
With no delight but what's a punishment?
These monsters plague themselves, and fitly too,
For they doe suffer; what, and all they doe,
But here must be no shelter, nor no shrowd
For such: Sincke *Grove,* or vanish into cloud.

*At this the whole* Grove *vanished, and the whole* Musicke *was discovered, sitting at the foot of the* Mountaine, *with* Pleasure, *and* Vertue *seated above them. The* Quire *invited* Hercules *to rest with this Song*

Great friend and servant of the good,
Let coole a while thy heated blood,
And from thy mighty labour cease.
Lie downe, lie downe,
And give thy troubled spirits peace,
Whilst vertue, for whose sake
Thou dost this god-like travaile take,
May of the choysest herbage make
(Here on this Mountaine bred,)
A crowne, a crowne
For thy immortall head.

108 *whole Musicke:* all the musicians and singers.

## *Here* Hercules *being layd down at their feet, the second* Anti-mask *which was of* Pigmies, *appeared*

### 1. PIGMIE

*Antaeus* dead! and *Hercules* yet live!
Where is this *Hercules*? what would I give
To meet him now? meet him? nay, three such other,
If they had hand in murther of our brother?
With three? with foure? with ten? nay with as many
As the name yeelds? pray anger there be any
Whereon to feed my just revenge, and soone:
How shall I kill him? hurle him 'gainst the Moone,
And breake him in small portions? give to Greece
His braine? and every tract of earth a peece.
  2 PIG. He is yonder.
  1 Where?
  3 At the hill foot, asleepe.
  1 Let one goe steale his club.
  2 My charge, Ile creepe.
  4 He's ours.
  1 Yes, peace.
  3 Triumph, we have him boy.
  4 Sure, sure, he is sure.
  1 Come, let us dance for joy.

130–31 *with . . . yeelds:* The cult of Hercules was adopted, in ancient times, by several cities.

*At the end of their dance they thought to surprise him, when suddenly being awak'd by the musicke, he rowsed himselfe, they all runne into holes.*

## *Song*

Wake *Hercules,* awake; but heave up thy blacke eye,
'Tis onely ask'd from thee to looke, and these will die,
Or flie:
Already they are fled,
Whom scorne had else left dead.

*At which* Mercury *descended from the hill, with a garland of* Poplar *to crowne him*

### MERCURY

Rest still thou active friend of vertue; These
Should not disturbe the peace of *Hercules.*
Earths wormes, and Honors dwarfes (at too great ods)
Prove, or provoke the issue of the gods.
See, here a *Crowne* the aged *Hill* hath sent thee,
My Grand-sire *Atlas,* he that did present thee
With the best sheepe that in his fold were found,
Or golden fruit in the *Hesperian* ground,
For rescuing his faire Daughters, then the prey
Of a rude Pirate as thou cam'st this way;
And taught thee all the learning of the Sphere,
And how like him thou might'st the heavens up-beare;
As that thy labours vertuous recompence
He, though a Mountaine now, hath yet the sence

Of thanking thee for more, thou being still
Constant to goodnesse, guardian of the hill;
*Antaeus* by thee suffocated here,
And the voluptuous *Comus* god of cheere
Beate from his Grove, and that defac'd, but now
The time's arriv'd that *Atlas* told thee of, how
B' unalterd law, and working of the Stars,
There should be a cessation of all jars,
Twixt *Vertue* and her noted opposite
*Pleasure;* that both should meet here in the sight
Of *Hesperus,* the glory of the West,
The brightest starre that from his burning crest
Lights all on this side the *Atlanticke-Seas,*
As farre as to thy Pillars, *Hercules,*
See where he shines, *Justice,* and *Wisedome* plac'd
About his throne, and those with honour grac'd
*Beauty,* and *Love:* It is not with his Brother
Bearing the world, but ruling such another
Is his renowne. *Pleasure,* for his delight
Is reconcil'd to *Vertue,* and this night
*Vertue* brings forth, twelve Princes have beene bred
In this rough mountaine, and neere *Atlas* head
The hill of knowledge; one, and chiefe of whom
Of the bright race of *Hesperus* is come,
Who shall in time, the same that he is be,
And now is onely a lesse light then he;
These now she trusts with *Pleasure,* and to these
She gives an entrance to the *Hesperides*
Faire beauties garden; neither can she feare
They should grow soft, or waxe effeminate here;
Since in her fight, and by her charge all's done,
*Pleasure* the servant, *Vertue* looking on.

178 *B'unalterd:* By unaltered.
194 *one:* This part was played by Prince Charles, later Charles I.

*Here the whole* Quire *of* Musicke *call'd the twelve Maskers forth from the lap of the* Mountaine, *which then opened with this*

## *Song*

*OPE aged* Atlas, *open then thy lappe,*
*And from thy beamy bosome strike a light,*
*That men may read in the mysterious mappe*
*All lines*
*And signes*
*Of royall education, and the right,*
*See how they come and show,*
*That are but borne to know.*
*Descend*
*Descend*
*Though pleasure lead,*
*Feare not to follow:*
*They who are bred*
*Within the Hill*
*Of skill,*
*May safely tread*
*What path they will,*
*No ground of good is hollow.*

205 *lap:* The folio text reads *top.*
208 *beamy:* radiant.

*In their descent from the* Hill, Daedalus *came downe before them, of whom* Hercules *questioned* Mercury

HERCULES

BUT *Hermes* stay, a little let me pause,
Who's this that leads? MER. A guide that gives them lawes
To all their motions, *Dedalus* the wise;
  HER. And doth in sacred harmonie comprise
His precepts? MER. Yes. HER. they may securely prove
Then any laborinth, though it be of love.

*Here while they put themselves in forme,* Dedalus *had his first Song*

*Come on, come on; and where you go,*
  *so interweave the curious knot,*
*As ev'n th' observer scarce may know*
  *which lines are Pleasures, and which not:*
*First figure out the doubtfull way,*
  *at which a while all youth should stay,*
*Where she and Vertue did contend,*
  *which should have* Hercules *to friend.*
*Then as all actions of mankinde,*
  *are but a laborinth, or maze:*
*So let your Dances be entwin'd,*
  *yet not perplex men unto gaze;*

225 *Daedalus:* Daedalus, the cunning artisan of Greek myth. He built the Cretan labyrinth (below, lines 233 ff.).
232 *securely prove:* safely explore.
234 *put . . . forme:* assumed their positions.

*But measur'd, and so numerous too,*
*as men may read each act they doe;*
*And when they see the graces meet,*
*admire the wisedome of your feet:*
*For dancing is an exercise,*
*not onely showes the movers wit,*
*But maketh the beholders wise,*
*as he hath power to rise to it.*

## The first Dance

## After which *Dedalus* againe

### *Song 2*

*O more, and more, this was so well,*
*As praise wants halfe his voyce to tell,*
*Againe your selves compose,*
*And now put all the aptnesse on,*
*Of figure, that proportion,*
*or colour can disclose.*
*That if those silent Arts were lost,*
*Designe, and picture, they might boast,*
*from you a newer ground,*
*Instructed by the heightning sence*
*Of dignitie and reverence,*
*in their true motions found.*
*Begin, begin; for looke, the faire*
*Do longing, listen to what ayre*
*you forme your second touch;*
*That they may vent their murmuring hymnes,*
*Just to the tune you move your limbs,*
*and wish their owne were such.*

248 *numerous:* rhythmical.
267 *ground:* foundation.

*Make haste, make hast, for this*
*The laborinth of beautie is.*

## The second Dance

## That ended. *Dedalus*

## *Song 3*

*It followes now you are to prove*
*The subt'lest maze of all, that's Love.*
*and if you stay too long,*
*The faire will thinke you do'em wrong:*
*Goe choose among—But with a minde*
*as gentle as the stroaking winde*
*runs ore the gentler flowers.*
*And so let all your actions smile,*
*As if they meant not to beguile,*
*the Ladies but the houres.*
*Grace, laughter, and discourse may meet,*
*and yet the beauty not goe lesse:*
*For what is noble should be sweet,*
*But not dissolv'd in wantonesse.*
*Will you that I give the law*
*to all your sport and some-it,*
*It should be such should envie draw,*
*but ever overcome it.*

296 *Will you:* Do you wish?
297 *some-it:* sum it up, crown it.

Here they Danced with the Ladies, and the whole Revells followed; which ended, *Mercury* cald to him in this following speech: which was after repeated in Song by two *Trebles,* two *Tennors,* a *Base,* and the whole *Chorus*

## *Song 4*

*An eye of looking backe were well,*
*Or any murmure that would tell*
*Your thoughts, how you were sent,*
*and went*
*To walke with Pleasure, not to dwell.*
*These, these are houres by vertue spar'd*
*Her selfe, she being her owne reward:*
*But she will have you know,*
*that though*
*Her sports be soft, her life is hard:*
*You must returne unto the Hill*
*and their advance*
*With labour, and inhabit still*
*that height and Crowne,*
*From whence you ever may looke downe*
*upon triumphed chance.*
*She, she it is in darknesse shines,*
*'Tis she that still her selfe refines,*
*by her owne light to every eye:*
*More seene, more knowne when vice stands by.*

322 *triumphed:* conquered.

*And though a stranger here on earth,*
*In Heaven she hath her right of birth:*
*There, there is Vertues seate,*
*Strive to keepe her your own,*
*Tis onely she can make you great,*
*Though place here make you knowne.*

After which, they Danced their last Dance, returned into the *Scene,* which closed, and was a *Mountaine* againe as before

## *The End*

*This pleas'd the KING so well, as he would see it againe, when it was presented with these additions.*

332 *place:* social position.

# GEORGE SANDYS
# 1578–1644

# Ovid's
# Metamorphosis
# The Sixth Booke

## The Argument

Pallas *an old-wife. Haughtie thoughts o're-throw*
Haemus *and* Rhodope, *who Mountaines grow.*
*The* Pigmy, *a Crane.* Antigone *becomes*
*A Storke. A Statue* Cyneras *intombs:*
*His impious daughters, Stones. In various shapes*
*The Gods commit adulteries and rapes.*
Arachne, *a Spider.* Niobe *yet drownes*
*Her marble cheeks in teares. Uncivill Clownes*
*Are curst to Frogs. From teares cleere* Marsyas *flowes.*
*His ivory shoulder new-made* Pelops *showes.*
Progne, *a Swallow; sign'd with murders staines.*
*Sad* Philomel *to secret might complaines.*
*Rage to a Lapwing turnes th'*Odrysian *king.*
Calais *and* Zetes *native feathers wing.*

*Tritonia* to the Muse attention lends:
Who both her Verse, and just revenge commends.
Then said t' her selfe: To praise is of no worth:
Let our revengefull Powre our praise set forth.

OVID'S METAMORPHOSIS.

In the notes which follow, Sandys' marginal glosses are printed in italics. Many names which Sandys does not gloss in the margins are fully explicated in the Commentary which he appends to each book. A specimen passage from the latter is given at the end of this selection.

*The Argument,* 5–6 In various . . . rapes: cf. Marlowe, *Hero and Leander,* 143–44: "There might you see the gods in sundry shapes, / Committing heady riots, incest, rapes."

1 *Tritonia: Pallas: of the Lake Triton, or of Tritogenia, her excellent wisdome.*

Intends *Arachnes* ruine. She, she heard,
Before her curious webs, her owne preferr'd.
Nor dwelling, nor her nation fame impart
Unto the Damsell, but excelling Art.
Deriv'd from *Colophonian Idmons* side;
Who thirstie Wooll in *Phocian* purple dide:
Her mother (who had paid her debt to fate)
Was also meane, and equall to her mate.
Yet through the *Lydian* townes her praise was spred;
Though poore her birth, in poore *Hypaepa* bred.
The Nymphs of *Tmolus* oft their Vines forsooke;
The sleeke *Pactolian* Nymphs their streames; to looke
On her rare workes: nor more delight in viewing
The done (done with such grace) then when adoing.
Whether she orbe-like roule the ruder wooll;
Or, finely finger'd, the selected cull;
Or draw it into clowd-resembling flakes;
Or equall twine with swift-turn'd spindle makes;
Or with her lively-painting needle wrought:
You might perceive she was by *Pallas* taught.
Yet such a Mistresse her proud thoughts disclame:
Let her with me contend; if foyld, no shame
(Said she) nor punishment will I refuse.
*Pallas,* forth-with, an old-wives shape indues:
Her haire all white; her limbs, appearing weake,
A staffe supports: who thus began to speake.
  Old Age hath something which we need nor shun:
Experience by long tract of time is won.

5 *She* refers to Arachne, *she* to Pallas.

9 *Idmons:* [Arachne was] *The daughter of Idmon; dwelling in Colophon, a cittie of Ionia.*

10 *Phocian:* Not Phoenician, but "from Phocis, a country in Greece between Boeotia and Aetolia." *dide:* dyed.

14 *Hypaepa: A little towne at the foot of the mountain Tmolus* [i.e. Timolus], *from whence it taketh that name.*

26 *foyld:* if I am defeated.

28 *indues:* assumes, puts on.

31 *need nor shun:* need and do not shun.

Scorne not advice: with dames of humane race
Contend for fame, but give a Goddesse place.
Crave pardon, and she will thy crime remit.
  With eyes confessing rage, and eye-brows knit,
(Her labour-leaving hands scarce held from strokes)
She, masked *Pallas* with these words provokes.
  Old foole, that dot'st with age; to whom long-life
Is now a curse: thy daughter, or sonnes wife,
(If thou hast either) taught be they by this:
My wisdome, for my selfe, sufficient is.
And least thy counsell should an intrest clame
In my diversion, I abide the same.
Why comes she not? why tryall thus delayes?
  She comes, said *Pallas,* and her selfe displayes.
Nymphs, and *Mygdonian* dames the Powre adore:
Onely the maid herselfe undaunted bore:
And yet she blusht; against her will the red
Flusht in her cheeks, and thence as swiftly fled.
Even so the purple Morning paints the skyes:
And so they whiten at the Suns uprise.
Who now, as desperately obstinate,
Praise ill affecting, runs on her owne fate.
No more *Joves* daughter labours to disswade;
No more refuseth; nor the strife delayde.
Both settle to their taskes apart: both spread
At once their warps, consisting of fine thread,
Ty'd to their beames: a reed the thred divides,
Through which the quick-returning shuttle glides,
Shot by swift hands. The combs inserted tooth
Betweene the warp suppress the rising woofe:
Strife less'ning toyle. With skirts tuckt to their waste,
Both move their cunning armes with nimble haste.

38 *masked:* disguised.

47 *Mygdonian: Phrygian: for the Mygdonians, a people of Macedon, planted divers Colonies in Phrygia. Others read Moeonian, of Moeonia, an ancient name of Lydia.*

Her crimson, dyde in *Tyrian* brasse, they weave:
The scarce distinguisht shadowes sight deceave.
So watry clowds, guilt by *Apollo,* showe;
The vast sky painted with a mighty Bowe:
Where though a thousand severall colours shine,
No eye their close transition can define:
The next, the same so neerely represents;
As by degrees, scarce sensible, dissents.
Through-out imbellished with ductil gold:
And both reviv'd antiquities unfold.
*Pallas,* in *Athens, Marse's* Rock doth frame:
And that old strife about the Citties name.
Twice six Coelestialls sit inthron'd on hie,
Repleat with awe-infusing gravitie:
*Jove* in the midst. The suted figures tooke
Their lively formes: *Jove* had a royall looke.
The Sea-god stood, and with his Trident strake
The cleaving rock, from whence a fountaine brake:
Whereon he grounds his claime. With speare and shield
Herselfe she armes: her head a murrion steild:
Her brest her *Aegis* guards. Her lance the ground
Appeares to strike; and from that pregnant wound
The hoary olive, charg'd with fruit, ascends.
The Gods admire: with victory she ends.
Yet she, to show the Rivall of her prayse
What hopes to cherish for such bold assayes,

65 *crimson: The purple Fish that yeelded the best scarlet was taken about the Coasts of Tyrus.*

67 *The Sun-beames beating on a dropping clowd beget the Raine-bowe.*

69 *severall:* distinct, separate.

75 *Athens: Areopagus (the street or court of Mars) where the Areopagites the Athenian Magistrates sate in judgement.* Ovid himself here confused the Acropolis with the Areopagus.

81 *strake:* struck.

82 *fountaine: Divers say a Horse: reading Ferum for Fretum, alleadging Virgils authority: but the other, both by the history, and condition of Athens, as famous in navall fights, as in the acts of Peace, appeares to bee the meaning of the Author.*

84 *murrion steild:* A helmet of steel protected her head.

Add's foure contentions in the utmost bounds
Of every angle, wrought in little Rounds.
One, *Thracian Rhodope* and *Haemus* showes,
Now mountaines, topt with never melting snowes,
Once humane bodies: who durst emulate
The blest Coelestialls both instile and state.
The next containes the miserable doome
Of that *Pygmaean* matron, over-come
By *Juno;* made a Crane, and forc't to jar
With her owne nation in perpetuall war.
A third presents *Antigone*, who strove
For unmatcht beautie with the wife of *Jove.*
Not *Ilium,* nor *Laomedon* her sire,
Prevail'd with violent *Saturnia's* ire.
Turn'd to a Storke; who, with white pinions rais'd,
Is ever by her creaking bill selfe-prais'd.
In the last circle *Cynaras* was plac't;
Who, charg'd with griefe, the temples staires imbrac't;
(Of late his daughters by their pride o're-throwne)
Appeares to weepe, and grovel on the stone.
The web a wreathe of peacefull Olive bounds:
And her owne tree her worke both ends and crownes.
*Arachne* weaves *Europa's* rape by *Jove:*
The Bull appeares to live, the Sea to move.
Back to the shore she casts a heavy eye;
To her distracted damsels seemes to cry:
And from the sprinkling waves, that skip to meet
With such a burden, shrinks her trembling feet.
*Asteria* there a strugling Eagle prest:
A Swan here spreds his wings o're *Leda's* brest.

92 *Rounds:* Each corner of Pallas' tapestry contained a little scene in a circular frame.

103 *Laomedon: King of Ilium or Troy.*

104 *Saturnia: Juno: the daughter of Saturne.*

107 *Cynaras: King of Assyria.*

111 *Olive: The symbol of Peace; and dedicated to Pallas, in that Peace is the end for which war is made. Or expressing her virginity; since Oyle will neither corrupt, nor mingle with any other liquor.*

*Jove*, Satyr-like, *Antiope* compels;
Whose fruitfull womb with double issue swels:
*Amphytrio* for *Alcmena's* love became:
A showre for *Danaë;* for *Aegina* flame:
For beautifull *Mnemosyne* he takes
A shepheards forme; for *Deois* a snakes.
Thee also, *Neptune*, like a lustfull Stere,
She makes the faire *Aeolian* Virgin beare:
And get th'*Aloides* in *Enipe's* shape:
Now turn'd t'a Ram in sad *Bisaltis* rape.
The gold-haird mother of life-strengthning seed,
The snake-hair'd mother of the winged Steed,
Found thee a Stallion: *thee Melanthe* findes
A Delphin. She to every forme assignes
Life-equall lookes; to every place the same
Aspect. A Heard-man *Phoebus* here became;
A Lyon now; now falcons wings displayes:
*Macarean Issa* shepheard-like betrayes.
*Liber*, a grape, *Erigone* comprest:
And *Saturne*, horse-like, *Chiron* gets, halfe-beast.
About her web a curious traile designes:
Flowres intermixt with clasping ivy twines.
Not *Pallas* this, not Envy this reproves:
Her faire successe the vext Virago moves;
Who teares the web, with crimes coelestiall fraught:
With shuttle from *Cytorian* mountaines brought,

126 *Deois: Proserpina* [daughter of Deo].
127 *Stere:* steer, a young bull.
128 *Aeolian Virgin:* Arne, the daughter of Aeolus.
129 *Aloides: Othus and Ephialtes, the supposed sonnes of Alous.*
130 *Bisaltis: Theophane, the daughter of Bisaltus.*
131 *mother: Ceres.*
132 *mother: Medusa, the mother of Pegasus.*
134 *Delphin:* dolphin.
138 *Macarean Issa: The daughter of Macarius.*
139 *Liber: Bacchus. comprest:* embraced sexually.
141–42: *Well suting with the wanton Argument: Lasciviousnesse Hieroglyphically presented by Ivy.*
143 *reproves:* finds fault with. The *Virago* in the next line is Pallas.
146 *Cytorian: Cytorus is a mountaine of Papalagonia, abounding with Box.*

*Arachne* thrice upon the fore-head smote.
  Her great heart brookes it not. About her throte
A halter knits. Remorsefull *Pallas* stayd
Her falling waight; Live wretch, yet hang, she said.
This curse (least of succeeding times secure)
Still to thy issue, and their race, indure.
Sprinkled with *Hecat's* banefull weeds, her haire
She forthwith sheds: her nose and eares impaire;
Her head growes little; her whole body so;
Her thighs and legs to spiny fingers grow:
The rest all belly. Whence a thred she sends:
And now, a Spider, her old webs extends.
  All *Lydia* stormes; the fame through *Phrygia* rung:
And gave an argument to every tongue.
Her, *Niobe* had knowne; when she, a maid,
In *Sipylus,* and in *Moeonia* staid.
Yet slights that home example: still rebells
Against the Gods; and with proud language swels.
Much made her haughty. Yet *Amphion's* towne,
Their high descents; nor glory of a crowne,
So pleas'd her (though she pleas'd her selfe in all)
As her faire race. We *Niobe* might call
The happiest mother that yet ever brought
Life unto light; had not herselfe so thought.
*Tiresian Manto,* in presages skild,
The streets, inspir'd by holy fury, fild

148 In each case *her* refers to Arachne, who tries to hang herself in despair.
151 *least . . . secure:* lest you hope to be better off in the future.
153 *Hecat's: Who first found out the use of Magicall Simples.*
154 *impaire:* decay.
158 *Spider: Called by the Grecians Arachne.*
162 *Sipylus: Siphilus is a citty of Phrygia and Moeonia is the same with Lydia; both under the subjection of her father Tantalus.*
165 *Amphion's towne: Thebes.*
166 *Their:* i.e. Niobe's and her husband's.
168 *race:* children.
171 *Manto: The Theban Prophetesse, daughter to Tiresias. presages:* prophecy.

With these exhorts: *Ismenides,* prepare:
To great *Latona,* and her Twins, with prayer
Mix sweet perfumes; your browes with Laurell bind:
By me *Latona* bids. The *Thebans* wind
About their temples the commanded Bay:
And sacred fires, with incense feeding, pray.
Behold, the Queene in height of state appeares:
A *Phrygian* mantle, weav'd with gold, she weares:
Her face, as much as rage would suffer, faire.
She stops; and shaking her disheveled haire,
The godly troope with haughty eyes survaies.
What madnesse is it Unseene Gods (she sayes)
Before the seene Coelestialls to prefer?
Or while I Altars want, to worship her?
Me *Tantalus* (alone allowed to feast
In heaven) begot; my mother not the least
*Pleïas;* greatest *Atlas* sire to those,
On whose high shoulders all the stars repose.
*Jove* is my other Grandfather; and he
My father in law: a double grace to me.
Me *Phrygia, Cadmus* kingdomes me obay:
My husbands harp-rais'd walls we joyntly sway.
Through out my Court behold in every place
Infinite riches! adde to this, a face
Worthy a Goddesse. Then, to crowne my joyes,
Seven beauteous daughters, and as many boyes:
All these by marriage to be multiply'd.
Behold, have we not reason for our pride?

173 *exhorts:* exhortations. *Ismenides: Thebans: of Ismenus a river of Boeotia.*
174 *Twins: Apollo, and Diana.*
179 *the Queene:* i.e. Niobe herself.
188 *mother: Tageta: one of the Pleiades, daughters to Atlas & Pleione.*
191 *Jove: Both Tantalus her father, & her husband Amphion, were the sonnes of Jupiter.*
193 *Phrygia: Boeotia.*
194 *walls: Thebes; immured by Amphion, of this else where.*

Dare you *Latona* then, by *Coeus* got,
Before me place? to whom a little spot
The ample Earth deny'd t'unlade her wombe?
Heaven, Earth, nor Seas, afford your Goddesse roome:
A Vagabond, till *Delos* harbour gave.
Thou wandrest on the land, I on the wave,
It said; and graunted an unstable place.
She brought forth two; the seaventh part of my race,
I happy am: who doubts? So will abide:
Or who doubts that? with plentie fortifi'd.
My state too great for fortune to bereave:
Though much she ravish, she much more must leave.
My blessings are above low feare. Suppose
Some of my hopefull sonnes this people lose,
They cannot be reduced to so few.
Off with your bayes; these idle Rites eschew.
They put them off; the sacrifice forbore:
And yet *Latona* silently adore.
  As much as free from barrennesse, so much
Disdaine and griefe th' inraged Goddesse touch.
Who on the top of *Cynthus* thus beginnes
To vent her passion to her sacred Twins.
Lo I, your mother, proud in you alone;
(Excepting *Juno*, second unto none)
Am question'd if a Goddesse: and must loose,
If you assist not, all religious dews.
Nor is this all: that curst *Tantalian* Seede
Adds foule reproaches to her impious deed.
She dares her children before you prefer;
And calls me childlesse: may it light on her!

201 *Coeus: The Giant: the word Giant signifying the sonne of the Earth: base-borne and ignoble.*
203 *unlade her wombe:* bring forth her children.
205 *Delos: An Iland of the Ægean Sea which formerly floted.*
221 *Cynthus: A mountaine of Delos.*
225 *loose:* lose.
226 *dews:* rites due me.
227 *Tantalian Seede: Niobe.*

Whose wicked words her fathers tongue declare.
  About to second her report with prayer;
Peace, *Phoebus* said, complaint too long delayes
Conceav'd revenge: the same vext *Phoebe* sayes.
Then swiftly through the yeelding ayre they glide
To *Cadmus* towres; in clouds their glories hide.
A spacious plaine before the city lyes,
Made dusty with the daily exercise
Of trampling hooves; by strifefull Chariots trackt.
Part of *Amphions* active sons here backt
High-bounding steeds; whose rich caparison
With scarlet blusht, with gold their bridles shone.
*Ismenus*, from her womb who first did spring,
As with his ready horse he beats a ring,
And checks his fomy jawes; ay me! out cryes;
While through his groaning brest an arrow flyes:
His bridle slackning with his dying force,
He leasurely sinks side-long from his horse.
Next, *Siphilus* from clashing quiver flies
With slackned raignes: as when a Pilot spies
A growing storme; and, least the gentle gaile
Should scape besides him, claps on all his saile.
His haste th'unevitable bowe o're-took,
And through his throat the deadly arrow strook.
Who, by the horses mane and speedy thighes
Drops headlong, and the earth in purple dies.
Now *Phoedimus;* and *Tantalus,* the heire
T' his Grand-sires name; that labour done, prepare

231 *fathers: Who being called to the Festivals and Counsells of the Gods, revealed their secrets.*

234 *Phoebe:* Diana.

236 *Cadmus towres: Thebes: first erected by Cadmus.*

240 *backt:* rode on the backs of.

241 *caparison:* trappings.

244 *beats a ring:* rides in a circle.

249 *from clashing quiver:* i.e. as he hears the sound of the rattling quiver.

250 *raignes:* reins.

253 *unevitable:* inevitable.

258 *that labour done:* The Latin has only *ut solito finem inposuere labori,* "when they had finished their usual tasks."

To wrastle. Whilst with oyled limbs they prest
Each others power, close grasping brest to brest;
A shaft, which from th'impulsive bow-string flew,
Them, in that sad Conjunction joyntly slew.
Both grone at once, at once their bodies bend
With bitter pangs, at once to earth descend:
Their rowling eyes together set in death:
Together they expire their parting breath.
In rusht *Alphenor* (bleeding in their harmes)
And raised their heatlesse corses in his armes:
But in that pious dutie fell. The threds
Of life, his heart-strings wrathfull *Delius* shreds.
Part of his lungs clave to th'extracted head:
And with his blood his troubled spirit fled.
But unshorne *Damasichthon* slaughtred lies
Not by a single wound: shot where the thighes
Knit with the ham-strings in the knotty joint.
Striving from thence to tug the fatall point,
Another at his neck the bow directs.
Thick-gushing blood the piercing shaft ejects;
Which spinning upward cleft the passive ayre.
Last *Ilioneus*, with succeslesse prayer,
His hands up-heaves: You Gods in generall
Said he (and ignorantly pray'd to all)
O pitty me! The Archer had remorce;
But now irrevocable was that force:
And yet his life a little wound dispatcht,
His heart but onely with the arrow scratcht.
  Ill newes, the peoples griefe, her housholds teares
Present their ruine to their mothers eares:
Who wonders how the Gods their lives durst touch;
And swels with anger that their powre was such.
For sad *Amphion*, wounding his owne brest,
Had now his sorrow, with his soule releast.

268 *corses:* bodies.
270 *Delius: Apollo; of Delos, where hee was borne, and had his Temple.*
271 *head:* i.e. the head of the arrow with which Apollo had pierced him.
283 *Archer: Apollo.*

How different is this *Niobe* from that!
Who great *Latona's* Rites supprest of late,
And proudly pac't the streets; envi'd by those
That were her friends; now pittied by her foes!
Frantick she doth on their cold corses fall,
And her last kisses distributes to all.
From whom, to heaven erecting her bruz'd armes:
  Cruell *Latona*, feast thee with our harmes:
Feast, feast, she said, thy salvage stomack cloy;
Cloy thy wild rage, and in our sorrow joy:
Seaven times, upon seaven Herses borne, I dy.
Triumph, triumph, victorious foe. But why
Victorious? haplesse I have not so few:
Who, after all these funeralls, subdew.
  This said, the bow-string twangs. Pale terror chils
All hearts save *Niobes;* obdur'd by ills.
The sisters, in long mourning robes array'd,
About their herses stood, with haire display'd.
One drawes an arrow from her brothers side;
And joyning her pale lips to his, so dide.
Another striving to asswage the woes
That rackt her mother, forth-with speechlesse growes:
And bowing with the wound, which inly bled,
Shuts her fixt teeth; the soule already fled.
This, flying falls: that, her dead sister makes
Her bed of death: this, hides herselfe: that quakes.
Six slaine by sundry wounds; to shield the last,
Her mother, over her, her body cast,
This one, she cryes, and that the least, ô save!
The least of many, and but one, I crave!
Whilst thus she sues, the su'd-for *Delia* hits.
Shee, by her husband, sons, and daughters, sits

301 *salvage:* savage.

305–06 The literal sense of the Latin here is "In my misery I still have more than you in your felicity. After so many deaths, I triumph still." In Sandys' version the implied object of "subdew" is Apollo; the antecedent of "Who" is I (Niobe) in line 305.

308 *obdur'd:* hardened.

323 *Delia: Diana: of the Iland Delos, where she was borne.*

A childlesse widdow; waxing stiffe with woes.
The winde wags not one haire; the ruddy rose
Forsakes her cheeke: in her declining head
Her eye-balls fix: through-out appearing dead.
Her tongue, and pallat rob'd of inward heat
At once congeale: her pulse forbeares to beat:
Her neck wants power to turne, her feet to goe,
Her armes to move: her very bowels grow
Into a stone. She yet retaines her teares.
Whom straight a whirle-winde to her country beares
And fixes on the summit of a hill.
Now from that mourning marble teares distill.
  Th'exemplary revenge struck all with feare:
Who offerings to *Latona's* altars beare
With doubled zeale. When, one as oft befalls,
By present accidents the past recalls.
  In fruitfull *Lycia* once, said he, there dwelt
A sort of Pesants, who her vengeance felt.
'Twas of no note, in that the men were base:
Yet wonderfull. I saw the poole, and place,
Fam'd by the prodigie. My father, spent
Almost with age, ill brooking travell, sent
Me thither for choice Steeres: and for my Guide
A native gave. Those pastures searcht, we spy'd
An ancient Altar, black with cinders, plac't
Amidst a Lake, with shivering reeds imbrac't.
O favour me! he, softly murmuring, said:
O favour me! I, softly murmuring, praid:
Then askt, if Nymph, or Faune therein reside;
Or rurall God. The *Lycian* thus reply'd.
  O youth, no mountaine Powres this altar hold:
She calls it hers, to whom *Joves* wife, of old,

329 *pallat rob'd:* palate robbed.

335 *a hill: Siphylus: so fained, because the marble of that Mountaine is much given to sweat through the moisture of the aire.*

339 *one: Of the Thebans, which sacrificed to Latona.*

348 *A native: A Lycian.*

356 *She: Latona.*

Earth interdicted: scarce that floting Ile,
Wave-wandering *Delos*, finisht her exile.
Where, coucht on Palmes and Olives, she in spight
Of fretfull *Juno*, brought her Twins to light.
Thence also, frighted from her painfull bed,
With her two infant Deities she fled.
Now in *Chimaera*-breeding *Lycia* (fir'd
By burning beames) and with long travell tyr'd,
Heat raising thirst the Goddesse sore opprest:
By their exhausting of her milke increast.
By fortune, in a dale, with longing eyes
A Lake of shallow water she descries:
Where Clownes were then a gathering picked weeds,
With shrubby Osiers, and plash-loving reeds.
Approacht; *Titania* kneeles upon the brinke:
And of the cooling liquor stoops to drinke.
The Clownes with-stood. Why hinder you, said she,
The use of water, that to all is free?
The Sun, aire, water, Nature did not frame
Peculiar; a publick gift I clame.
Yet humbly I intreat it: not to drench
My weary lims, but killing thirst to quench.
My tongue wants moisture, and my jawes are drie:
Scarce is there way for speech. For drink I die.
Water to me were Nectar. If I live,
'Tis by your favour: life with water give.
Pitty these babes: for pitty they advance
Their little armes! their armes they stretcht by chance.
  With whom would not such gentle words prevaile?
But they, persisting to prohibit, raile;

360 *Twins:* Apollo and Diana.

363 *Chimaera: A Monster, with the head of a Lyon, the body of a Gote, and the taile of a Serpent. Of this hereafter.*

369 *Clownes:* peasants.

370 *plash-loving reeds:* reeds that liked to grow in marshy ponds.

371 *Titania: Latona: daughter to Coeus, one of the Titans.*

376 *Peculiar:* as private property.

The place with threats command her to forsake.
Then with their hands and feet disturbe the lake:
And leaping with malicious motion, move
The troubled mud; which rising, flotes above.
Rage quencht her thirst: no more *Latona* sues
To such base-slaves: but Goddesse-like doth use
Her dreadfull tongue; which thus their fates imply'd:
May you for ever in this lake reside!
Her wish succeeds. In loved lakes they strive;
Now sprawle above, now under water dive;
Oft hop upon the banke, as oft againe
Back to the water: nor can yet restraine
Their brawling tongues; but setting shame aside,
Though hid in water, under water chide.
Their voyces still are hoarce: the breath they fetch
Swels their wide throtes; their jawes with railing stretch:
Their heads their shoulders touch; no neck betweene,
As intercepted. All the back is greene:
Their bellies (every part o're-sizing) white.
Who now, new Frogs, in slimy pooles delight.
  Thus much, I know not by what *Theban*, said:
An other mention of a Satyre made,
By *Phoebus*, with *Tritonia's* reede, o're-come:
Who for presuming felt a heavy doome.
Me from my selfe, ah why doe you distract?
(Oh!) I repent, he cry'd: Alas! this fact
Deserves not such a vengeance! Whilst he cry'd;
*Apollo* from his body stript his hide.
His body was one wound, blood every way
Streames from all parts: his sinewes naked lay.
His bare veines pant: his heart you might behold;
And all the fivers in his brest have told.

405 *o're-sizing:* becoming larger than (every other part).

409 *Tritonia's reede: Minerva's Pipe, whereon Marsyas the Satyre played. See the comment.*

411 *me,* etc.: *The words of Marsyas.*

412 *fact:* deed.

418 *fivers:* fibers; *told:* counted.

For him the Faunes, that in the forrests keepe;
For him the Nymphs, and brother Satyres weepe:
His end, *Olympus* (famous then) bewailes:
With all the shepherds of those hills and dales.
The pregnant Earth conceiveth with their teares;
Which in her penetrated womb she beares,
Till big with waters: then discharg'd her fraught.
This purest *Phrygian* Streame a way out sought
By down-falls, till to toyling seas he came:
Now called *Marsyas* of the Satyres name.
  The Vulgar, these examples told, returne
Unto the present: for *Amphion* mourne,
And his lost issue. All the mother hate.
*Pelops* alone laments his sisters fate.
While with torne garments he presents his woes,
The ivory peece on his left shoulder showes.
This once was flesh, and coloured like the right.
Slaine by his Sire, the Gods his lims unite:
His scattered parts all sound; save that alone
Which interpos'd the neck and shoulder bone.
They then with ivory supply'd th'unfound:
And thus restored *Pelops* was made sound.
  The neighbouring princes met: the Cities neare
Intreat their kings the desolate to cheare.
Renown'd *Mycenae, Sparta,* th'*Argive* State;
And *Calydon,* no yet in *Dian's* hate;
Fertill *Orchomenos; Corinthus,* fam'd
For high-priz'd brasse; *Messene,* never tam'd;

421 *Olympus: An excellent Piper remembred by Plato, and beloved of Marsyas, of whom that mountaine in Mysia was so called.*

425 *fraught:* freight, load.

432 *Pelops: The son of Tantalus, and brother to Niobe.*

438 *interpos'd:* came between.

442 *the desolate to cheare: To condole with Pelops for the death of his sister, and the Theban Princes.*

444 *not yet: For Oeneus their king had not yet by his neglect provoked Diana. Whereof in the 8 booke.*

*Cleonae; Patrae; Pylos, Nelius* crowne;
And *Troezen,* not as then *Pittheus* towne;
With all that two-sea'd *Isthmos* Streights include:
And all without, by two-sea'd *Isthmos* view'd.
*Athens* alone (who would beleev't?) with-held:
Thee, from that civill office, war compeld.
Th'inhabitants about the *Pontick* coast
Had then besieg'd thee with a barbarous hoast:
Whom *Thracian Tereus,* with his Aids, o'rethrew;
And by that victorie renowned grew.
Powerfull in wealth, and people; from the loynes
Of *Mars* deriv'd: *Pandion Progne* joynes
To him in marriage. This, nor *Juno* blest;
Nor *Hymen,* nor the Graces grac't that feast.
The snake-haird furies held the sputtering light
From funeralls snatcht, and made the bed that Night.
Th'ill boading Owle upon the roofe was set.
*Progne* and *Tereus* with these omens met:
Thus parents grew. The *Thracians* yet rejoyce;
And thanke the Gods with one united voyce.
The marriage day, and that of *Itys* birth,
They consecrate to universall mirth.
So lyes the good unseene. By this the Sun,
Conducting Time, had through five Autums run:
When flattering *Progne* thus allures her Lord.
If I have any grace with thee, afford
This favour, that I may my sister see:
Send me to her, or bring thou her to me.
Promise my father that with swiftest speede
She shall returne. If this attempt succeede,
The summe of all my wishes I obtaine.
He bids them lanch his ships into the maine:

448 *Pittheus: The father of Aethera (mother to Theseus) who after raigned in Troezen.*

449 *two-sea'd Isthmos: The streights of Corinth: an Isthmos being a neck of land betweene two Seas.*

458 *Pandion: King of Athens.*

Then make th'*Athenian* port with sailes and ores;
And lands upon the wisht *Piraean* shores.
Brought to *Pandion's* presence, they salute.
The King with bad presage begins his sute.
For loe, as he his wifes command recites,
And for her quick returne his promise plights,
Bright *Philomela* came in rich array;
More rich in beauty. So they use to say
The stately *Naiades,* and *Dryad's* goe
In Sylvan shades; were they apparel'd so.
This sight in *Tereus* such a burning breeds,
As when we fire a heap of hoary reeds;
Or catching flames to Sun-dry'd stubble thrust.
Her face was excellent: but in-bred lust
Inrag'd his blood; to which those Climes are prone:
Stung by his countries fury, and his owne.
He streight intends her women to intice,
And bribe her Nurse to prosecute his vice;
Herselfe to tempt with gifts; his crowne to spend:
Or ravish, and by warre his rape defend.
What dares he not, thrust on by wilde desire?
Nor can his brest containe so great a fire.
Rackt with delay, he *Progne's* sute renewes:
And for himselfe, that but pretended sues.
Love made him eloquent. As oft as he
Exceeded, he would say. Thus charged she.
And moving teares (as she had sent them) sheds.
You Gods! how dark a blindnesse over-spreds
The soules of men! whilst to his sin he climes,
They thinke him good; and praise him for his crimes.
Even *Philomela* wisht the same! now she
Hangs on her fathers neck: and what would be

480 *Piraean: Piraeus was the Haven to Athens; so called of the adjoyning promontory.*

487 *Naiades . . . Dryad's: Nymphs of fountaines and woods.*

493 *those Climes: The Thracians, a warlike people, were much addicted to Venus; and gloried in the multitude of their wives, as recorded by Mela and Solinus.*

Her utter ruine, as her safety prest:
While *Tereus* by beholding pre-possest.
Her kisses and imbraces heat his blood:
And all afford his fire and fury food.
And wisht, as oft as she her Sire imbrac't,
Him-selfe her Sire: nor would have beene more chast.
He, by their importunities is wrought.
She, over-joy'd, her father thankes: and thought
Her selfe and sister in that fortunate,
Which drew on both a lamentable fate.
The labour of the Day now neere an end,
From steepe *Olympus Phoebus* steeds descend.
The boards are princely serv'd: *Lyaeus* flowes
In burnish't gold. Then take their soft repose.
And yet th'*Odrysian* King, though parted, fries:
Her face and graces ever in his eyes.
Who parts unseene unto his fancy faines;
And feeds his fires: Sleep flies his troubled braines.
Day rose: *Pandion* his departing son
Wrings by the hand; and weeping, thus begun.
  Deare Son, since Piety this due requires;
With her, receave both your and their desires.
By faith, aliance, by the Gods above,
I charge you guard her with a fathers love:
And suddenly send back (for all delay
To me is death) my ages onely stay.
And Daughter ('tis enough thy sister's gone)
For pitty leave me not too long alone.
As he impos'd this charge, he kist with-all:
And drops of teares at every accent fall.
The pledges then of promis'd faith demands
(Which mutually they give) their plighted hands.

522 *Olympus: Heaven: of the hight of that Mountaine, ever in the Sun-shine.*
523 *Lyaeus: A name of Bacchus: here taken for wine.*
525 *Odrysian King: Tereus: of Odrysa, a Citty of Thrace.*
527 Tereus imagines [fains] what he cannot see.
533 *aliance:* kinship.

To *Progne,* and her little boy, said he,
My love remember, and salute from me.
Scarce could he bid farewell: sobs so ingage
His troubled speech; who dreads his soules presage.
  As soone as shipt; as soone as active ores
Had mov'd the surges, and remov'd the shores;
She's ours! with me my wish I beare! he cryes.
Exults; and barbarous, scarce defers his joyes:
His eyes fast fixt. As when *Joves* eagle beares
A Hare t'her Ayery, truss't in rapefull seares:
And to the trembling prisoner leaves no way
For hoped flight; but still beholds her pray.
The voyage made; on his owne land he treads:
And to a Lodge *Pandions* daughter leads;
Obscur'd with woods: pale, trembling full of feares;
And for her sister asking now with teares.
There mues her up; his foule intent makes knowne:
Inforc't her; a weake virgin, and but one.
Helpe father! sister helpe! in her distresse
She cries; and on the Gods, with like successe.
She trembles like a lambe, snatcht from the phangs
Of some fell wolfe; that dreads her former pangs:
Or as a dove, who on her feathers beares
Her bloods fresh staines, and late-felt talants feares.
Restor'd unto her mind, her rufled haire,
As at a wofull funerall she tare;
Her armes with her owne fury bloody made:
Who, wringing her up-heaved hands, thus said.
  O monster! barbarous in thy horrid lust!
Trecherous Tyrant! whom my fathers trust,

552 *Ayery:* aerie, nest; *seares:* talons.
556 *Pandions daughter: Philomela.*
559 *mues:* mews, locks.
563 *phangs:* fangs.
564 *that . . . pangs:* The Latin has *nondum sibi tuta videtur,* "she cannot yet believe that she is safe."
566 *talants:* claws.
568 *tare:* tore.

Impos'd with holy teares; my sisters love;
My virgin state; nor nuptiall ties, could move!
O what a wild confusion hast thou bred!
I, an adultresse to my sisters bed:
Thou, husband to us both; my only hate;
And to expect a miserable fate.
Why mak'st thou not thy villanies compleat;
By forcing life from her abhorred seat?
O would thou hadst, e're I my honour lost!
Then had I parted with a spotlesse ghost.
Yet, if the Gods have eyes; if their Powers be
Not meerely names; nor all decay with me;
Thou shalt not scape due vengeance. Sense of shame
I will abandon; and thy crime proclaime:
To men, if free; if not, my voice shall breake
Through these thick walls; and teach the woods to speake:
Hard rockes resolve to ruth. Let heaven this heare;
And Heaven-thron'd Gods: if there be any there!
  These words the salvage Tyrant moves to wroth:
Nor lesse his feare: a like provok't by both.
Who drawes his sword: his cruell hands he winds
In her loose haire: her arms behind her binds.
Her throte glad *Philomela* ready made:
Conceiving hope of death from his drawne blade.
Whilst she reviles, invokes her father; sought
To vent her spleene; her tongue in pincers caught,
His sword devideth from the panting root:
Which, trembling, murmurs curses at his foot.
And as a serpents taile, dissever'd, Leaps:
Even so her tongue: and dying sought her steps.
After this fact (if we may rumor trust)
He oft abus'd her body with his lust.

582 *ghost:* soul, spirit.
589 *ruth:* pity.
591 *salvage:* savage; *wroth:* wrath.
603 *fact:* deed.

Yet to his wife, even after this, retires:
Who for her sister hastily inquires.
He funeralls belyes, with fained griefe:
And by instructed teares begets beliefe.
*Progne* her royall ornaments rejects;
And puts on black: an empty tombe erects;
To her imagin'd Ghost oblations burnes:
Her sisters fate, not as she should, she mournes.
Now through twelve Signes the sun had borne his light.
What should sad *Philomela* doe? her flight
A barbarous guard restrain'd; the walls were strong;
Her mouth had lost the Index of her wrong.
The wit that misery begets is great:
Great sorrow addes a quicknesse to conceit.
A woofe upon a *Thracian* loome she spreds;
And inter-weaves the white with crimson threds;
That character her wrong. The closely wrought,
Gave to a servant, by her looks besought
To beare it to her Mistresse: who presents
The Queene therewith; not knowing the contents.
The wife to that dire Tyrant this unfolds:
And in a wofull verse her state beholds.
She held her peace: 'twas strange! griefe struck her mute.
No language could with such a passion sute.
Nor had she time to weepe. Right, wrong, were mixt
In her fell thoughts: her soule on vengeance fixt.
It was that time; when, in a wild disguise,
*Sithonian* matrons use to solemnise

607 *funeralls belyes:* Tereus made up a false story about Philomela's death.
610 *empty tombe: As they anciently used for the absent: in some sort observed by Princes at this day.*
612 *not as she should: As dead, and not as dishonoured.*
618 *conceit:* imagination.
621 *character:* depict.
622 *looks: By signes.*
623 *Mistresse: Progne.*
625 *to:* of.
626 *verse:* story.
632 *Sithonian: Thracian; of Sithonia a province of Thrace.*

*Lyoeus* three-yeares Feast. Night spreds her wings:
By night high *Rhodope* with timbrels rings.
By night th'impatient Queene a javelin takes,
And now a Bacchanal, the Court forsakes.
Vines shade her browes: the rough hide of a Deare
Shogs at her side: her shoulder beare a speare.
Hurried through woods, with her attendant froes,
Terrible *Progne,* frantick with her woes,
Thy farre more sober fury, *Bacchus,* strives
To counterfeit. Now at the lodge arrives:
Howles; *Evohe,* cries: breakes ope the doores, and tooke
Her sister thence: with ivy hides her looke:
In habit of a Bacchanal arrayd:
And to her Citty the amaz'd convayd.
That hated roofe when *Philomela* knew;
The poore soule shooke; her visage bloodlesse grew.
*Progne* with-drawes; the sacred weeds unlos'd;
Her wofull sisters bashfull face disclos'd:
Falls on her neck. The other durst not raise
Her downe-cast eyes: her sisters wrong survayes
In her dishonour. As she strove t'have sworne
With up-raisd lookes; and call the Gods t'have borne
Her pure thoughts witnesse, how she was compeld
To that loth'd fact; she hands, for speech, upheld.
Sterne *Progne* broiles; her bosome hardly beares
So vast a rage: who chides her sisters teares.
  No teares, said she, our lost condition needs:
But steele; or if thou hast what steele exceeds.

633 *Lyoeus: Trieterica Bacchi [the triennial feast of Bacchus].*

634 *Rhodope: A mountaine of Thrace.*

638 *Shogs:* jogs, shakes.

639 *froes:* The word means literally a "Dutchwoman" [frow] but in the Renaissance it often was used to designate, as here, the Maenads or Bacchantes.

642 *counterfeit:* imitate. The words "farre more sober" in the preceding line are Sandys' addition to the original Latin.

643 *Evohe: An acclamation in use with the Bacchides: signifying, wee wish thee well.*

I, for all horrid practises, am fit:
To wrap this roofe in flame, and him in it:
His eyes, his tongue, or what did thee inforce,
T'extirp; or with a thousand wounds, divorce
His guilty soule. The deede I intend, is great:
But what, as yet, I know not. In this heat
Came *Itys* in, and taught her what to doe.
Beheld with cruell eyes; Ah, how I view;
In thee, said shee, thy father! then intends
Her tragick Scene: Rage in her lookes ascends.
But when her sonne saluted her, and clung
Unto her neck; mixt kisses, as he hung,
With childish blandishments; her high-wrought blood
Began to calme, and rage distracted stood.
Teares trickl'd from her eyes by strong constraint.
But when she found her resolution faint
With too much pittie; her sad sister viewes,
And said, while both, her eyes by turnes peruse.
Why flatters he? why tonguelesse weepes the other?
Why sister calls not she, whom he calls mother?
Degenerate! thinke whose daughter; to whom wed:
All piety is sinne to *Tereus* bed.
Then *Itys* trailes: as when by *Ganges* floods
A Tigresse drags a Fawne through silent woods.
Retiring to the most sequestred roome:
While he, with hands up-heav'd, fore-sees his doome,
Clings to her bosome; mother! mother! cry'd;
She stabs him: nor once turn'd her face aside.
His throte was cut by *Philomela's* knife:
Although one wound suffic'd to vanquish life.
His yet quick lims, ere all his soule could passe,
She peece-meale teares. Some boyle in hollow brasse,
Some hisse on spits. The pavements blusht with blood.
*Progne* invites her husband to this food:

669–70 *intends . . . Scene:* her tragic scene takes shape in her mind.
676 *she:* he *1632.*
683 *Then Itys trailes:* she drags Itys away.

And faines her Countries Rite; which would afford
No servant, nor companion, but her Lord.
Now *Tereus,* mounted on his Grand-sires throne,
With his sonnes carved entrailes stuffes his owne:
And bids her (so Soule-blinded!) call his boy.
*Progne* could not disguise her cruell joy:
In full fruition of her horrid ire,
Thou hast, said she, within thee thy desire.
He lookes about: asks where. And while againe
He asks, and calls: all bloody with the slaine,
Forth like a Fury, *Philomela* flew;
And at his face the head of *Itys* threw.
Nor ever more then now desir'd a tongue;
T'expresse the joy of her revenged wrong.
He, with lowd out-cryes, doth the boord repell;
And calls the Furies from the depth of hell.
Now teares his brest, and strives from thence in vaine
To pull th'abhorred food: now weepes amaine.
And calls himselfe his sonnes unhappy tombe.
Then drawes his sword; and through the guilty roome
Pursues the Sisters; who appeare with wings
To cut the ayre: and so they did. One sings
In woods; the other neare the house remaines:
And on her brest yet beares her murders staines.
He, swift with griefe and fury, in that space
His person chang'd. Long tufts of feathers grace
His shining crowne; his sword a bill became;
His face all arm'd: whom we a Lapwing name.
This killing newes, ere halfe his age was spent,
*Pandion* to th'infernall Shadowes sent.
*Erichtheus* his throne and scepter held:
Who, both in justice, and bold armes exceld.
To him his wife foure sonnes, all hopefull, bare:
As many daughters: two, surpassing faire.

716 *One: Philomela a Nightingall.*
717 *other: Progne a Swallow.*
725 Erichtheus inherited Pandion's throne.
728 *two: Orithya and Procris.*

Thee, *Cephalus*, thy *Procris* happy made:
But *Thrace* and *Tereus, Boreas* nuptiall stayed.
The God belov'd *Orithya* wanted long;
While he put off his powre, to use his tongue.
His sute rejected; horridly inclin'd
To anger (too familiar with that Wind.)
  I justly suffer this indignity:
For why said he, have I my armes laid by?
Strength, violence, high rage and awfull threats.
'Tis my dishonour to have us'd intreats.
Force me befits. With this, thick clouds I drive;
Tosse the blew billowes, knotty Okes up-rive;
Congeale soft snow, and beat the earth with haile.
When I my brethren in the ayre assaile,
(For that's our field) we meete with such a shock,
That thundring skyes with our incounters rock,
And clowd-struck lightning flashes from on high.
When through the crannies of the earth I fly,
And force her in her hollow caves, I make
The Ghosts to tremble and the ground to quake.
Thus should I have woo'd; with these my match have made:
*Erichtheus* should have beene compeld, not pray'd.
Thus *Boreas* chafes; or no lesse storming, shooke
His horrid wings; whose ayery motion strooke
The earth with blasts, and made the Ocean rore.
Trailing his dusky mantle on the flore,
He hid himselfe in clouds of dust, and caught
Belov'd *Orythia,* with her feare distraught.
Flying, his agitated fires increast:
Nor of his ayery race the raignes supprest

730 *But . . . stayd: For the Rape of Philomela.* Boreas (the wind god) lived in the North and thus, like Tereus and the Thracians, was hated by the Athenians.

732 Boreas at first preferred to woo rather than to use force.

738 *intreats:* supplications.

742 *brethren: The winds were fained to be the sonnes of the Gyant Astraeus and Aurora. Of this in* [on 1632] *the first booke.*

Till to the walled *Cicones* he came.
Two goodly Twins th'espous'd *Athenian* Dame
Gave to the Icie author of her rape:
Who had their fathers wings and mothers shape.
Yet not so borne. Before their faces bare
The manly ensignes of their yellow haire,
*Calaïs* and *Zetes* both unplumed were.
But as the downe did on their chins appeare;
So, foule-like, from their sides soft feathers bud.
When youth to action had inflam'd their blood;
In the first vessell, with the flowre of *Greece,*
Through unknowne seas, they sought the Golden Fleece.

## Sandys' Commentary on the Philomela Legend

But the *Furies* kindled the nuptiall torches with funerall fires at this wedding of *Tereus* and *Progne;* the ominous Owle screeching sad presages; confirmed by the sequel: *Tereus* ravishing *Philomela,* and revengefull *Progne* feasting her husband with the flesh of her owne son; as he before had contaminated his table with the flesh of others. *Astyages* so served his favorite *Harpalus:* who having suffered him to glut himselfe with his misfortunes, produced their heads, and askt him how he likt his viands: who replied, that *all feasts were pleasant with a King.* An answer which set him in the highway to safety: as it would have done to revenge, had he so intended. Nor doth the former story lesse agree with the truth, but only in the transformations: the two sisters fained to have been changed into birds, for their speedy flight unto *Athens,* by which they escaped the revenge of *Tereus. Philomela* into a Nightingall, and *Progne* into a Swallow; in that no Nightingalls are seene in

759 *Cicones: A People of Thrace.*
761 *Icie author: Boreas.*
765 *unplumed:* wingless.
767 *foule-like:* birdlike.

*Thrace,* as hating the country of *Tereus;* nor Swallow ever builds there; as is observed by *Pausanias*. Such also fained for their mournfull songs and seeming lamentations. The Nightingall chanting in the solitary woods; deservedly called *Philomela,* or a lover of musicke, in that no bird hath so sweet a voice among all the silvan musitians: singing fifteene dayes and nights together, when the leaves begin to afford her a shelter, with little or no intermission. So shrill a voice in so little a body, and a breath so long extended, is worthy admiration; shee alone in her songs expressing the exact art of Musicke in infinite variety. Neither have all the same tunes and divisions, which shewes their skill to be more then naturall. They strive among themselves in fervent contention: the vanquished not sildome ending her life with her song, through griefe, or over-straining. The young ones heare with attention: practise, and repeat their lesson, which the old correct; and being perfect in that, proceed to a new. The spring neere an end, they surcease, as satiated, or weary: and in the summer, in that neither heard nor seene, are said to change both their voice and colour: the latter disproved by such as are kept in cages. Perhaps she sleepes, or lies senselesse all the winter; as her sister the Swallow. For Swallowes, when the cold comes in, and flyes, their only sustenance faile them; creepe into clefts of rocks, and sinke to the bottome of waters: insomuch as no extraordinary thing in *Germany* to drag them among fishes out of their ponds: these, seeming dead, when brought into their Stoves, or laid by the fire, will after a while revive with the heat, and betake them to their wings. As the other the woods, so these frequent houses; building their nests under arches, and in the cornishes of windowes, with wonderfull architecture, (which to robb, or pull downe, was held not only unfortunate, but sacrilegious) recording their complaints on the tops of chimnies. Yet surely birds rather sing for delight then sorrow.

# RICHARD CORBETT
## 1582–1635

# A
# *Proper New* Ballad
# Intituled
# *The* Faeryes Farewell:
# *Or* God-A-Mercy Will:
## *To be sung or whistled to the Tune of the* Meddow Brow *by the Learned; by the unLearned; To the Tune of FORTUNE*

Farewell, Rewards & *Faeries,*
  Good Houswives now may say;
For now foule Slutts in Daries
  Doe fare as well as they;
And though they sweepe theyr Hearths no less
  Then Maydes were wont to doe,
Yet who of late for Cleaneliness
  Finds *sixe-pence* in her Shoe?

Lament, lament, old Abbies,
  The *Faries* lost Command:
They did but change Priests *Babies,*
  But some have changd your *Land;*
And all your Children sprung from thence
  Are now growne *Puritanes:*
Who live as *Changelings* ever since
  For love of your Demaines.

A PROPER NEW BALLAD: Corbett's ballad has become well-known since it was printed by Percy in his *Reliques of Antient English Poetry* (1765). Seventeenth-century Protestant writers often connected the rule of the fairies with the old religion (Roman Catholicism).

16 *Demaines:* estates. The monasteries were dissolved by Henry VIII and their lands distributed.

At Morning & at Evening both
  You merry were & glad,
So little Care of Sleepe or Sloth
  These Prettie ladies had.
When *Tom* came home from labour,
  Or *Ciss* to Milking rose,
Then merrily went theyre Tabor,
  And nimbly went theyre Toes.

Wittness those Rings & Roundelayes
  Of theirs, which yet remaine,
Were footed in Queene *Maries* dayes
  On many a Grassy Playne;
But, since of late *Elizabeth*,
  And later *James*, came in,
They never daunc'd on any heath
  As *when the Time hath bin.*

By which wee note the *Faries*
  Were of the old Profession;
Theyre Songs were *Ave Maryes*,
  Theyre Daunces were *Procession.*
But now, alas, they all are dead,
  Or gone beyond the Seas,
Or Farther for Religion fled,
  Or elce they take theyre Ease.

A Tell-tale in theyre Company
  They never could endure,
And whoe so kept not secretly
  Theyre Mirth, was punisht sure.
It was a just & Christian Deed
  To pinch such blacke & blew.
O, how the Common welth doth need
  Such Justices as you!

Now they have left our Quarters
  A *Register* they have,
Who looketh to theyre Charters,
  A Man both *Wise* & *Grave;*
An hundred of theyre merry Prancks
  By one that I could name
Are kept in Store, conn twenty Thanks
  To *William* for the same.

I marvell who his Cloake would turne
  When *Puck* had led him round,
Or where those Walking Fires would burne,
  Where *Cureton* would be found;
How *Broker* would appeare to be,
  For whom this Age doth mourne;
But that theyre Spiritts live in Thee,
  In Thee, old *William Chourne.*

To *William Chourne* of Stafford Shire
  Give Laud & Prayses due,
Who every Meale can mend your Cheare
  With Tales both old & true.
To *William* all give Audience,
  And pray yee for his Noddle,
For all the *Faries* Evidence
  Were lost, if that were Addle.

50 *Register:* registrar.
55 *conn:* offer.
56 *William:* William Chourne, the servant of Corbett's friend, Doctor Leonard Hutten.
59 *Walking Fires:* will-o'-the-wisps.
60–61 *Cureton . . . Broker:* Presumably the names of former Staffordshire residents whom Chourne could conjure up.

# An Elegie

## Upon the death of his owne Father

*Vincent Corbet*, farther knowne
By *Poynters* name, then by his owne,
Here lyes ingaged till the Day
Of raising bones, and quickning clay.
Nor wonder, Reader, that he hath
Two Surnames in his Epitaph,
For this one did comprehend
All that two Familyes could lend.
And if to know more Arts then any
Could multiply one into many,
Here a *Colony* lyes then,
Both of *qualityes* and *men.*
Yeares he liv'd well nigh fourscore,
But, count his vertues, he liv'd more;
And, number him by doeing good,
He liv'd the age before the Flood.
Should wee undertake his Story,
*Truth* would seeme *fain'd,* and plainesse, *glory.*
Beside, this Tablet were to small;
Add to the pillers and the wall.
Yet of this Volume much is found,
Written in many a fertill ground;
Where the Printer thee affords
Earth for paper, Trees for words.

AN ELEGIE: The poet's father was a well-known gardener who died on April 29, 1619. Ben Jonson wrote an epitaph for him. For some reason he had assumed the surname "Poynter."

7 *one:* i.e. this one man.

He was natures Factour here,
And Legier lay for every Sheire,
To supply the ingenious wants
Of soone-sprung fruites, and forraigne plants,
Simple he was, and wise withall;
His purse nor base, nor prodigall;
Poorer in substance, then in freinds;
Future and publicke were his endes;
His conscience, like his dyett, such
As neither tooke, nor left too much:
Soe that made Lawes were uselesse growne
To him, he needed but his owne.
Did he his Neighbours bid, like those
That feast them only to enclose?
Or with their rost meate racke their rents,
And cozen them with their consents?
Noe; the free meetings at his boord
Did but one litterall sence afforde;
Noe *Close* or *Aker* understood,
But only *love* and *neighbourhood*.
His Almes were such as *Paul* defines;
Not Causes to be sav'd, but signes;
Which Almes, by faith, hope, love laid downe,
Layd up, what now he weares, a Crowne.
Besides his fame, his goods, his life,
He left a greiv'd Sonne, and a wife.
Straunge Sorrow, not to be beleiv'd,
When the Sonne and Heire is greiv'd.

25 *Factour:* agent.
26 *Legier lay:* a secular nuncio or commissioner.
27 *ingenious:* indigenous.
38 *enclose:* alluding to the enclosing of arable land for pasturage.
39 *racke:* raise to an excessive price.
40 *cozen:* cheat.
43 *Aker:* acre.
45 *Paul:* I Corinthians 13, on charity as the greatest of virtues.
50 *wife:* Corbett's mother did not die until 1634.

*Reade* then, and *mourne*, whate're thou art
That doost hope to have a part
In honest Epitaphs; least, being dead,
Thy life bee *written*, and not *read.*

# Upon Faireford Windowes

Tell mee, you Anti-Saintes, why glasse
With you is longer liv'd then brasse?
And why the Saintes have scap't their falls
Better from Windowes, then from Walles?
Is it because the Brethrens fires
Maintaine a Glass-house at Blackfryars?
Next which the Church stands North and South,
And East and West the Preachers mouth.
Or is't because such painted ware
Resembles something that you are,
Soe py'de, soe seeming, soe unsound
In manners, and in doctrine, found,
That, out of Emblematick witt,
You spare your selves in sparing it?
If it be soe, then, Faireford, boast
Thy Church hath kept, what all have lost;

UPON FAIREFORD WINDOWES: The stained glass windows of Fairford church in Gloucestershire were fortunate enough to escape destruction during the Civil War. Corbett, writing about 1630, seems to have anticipated the threat which the Puritans would make against them.

1 *Anti-Saintes:* ironically used of the Puritan sects, who prided themselves on their holiness.

6 *Blackfryars:* A glass factory there was a center for extreme Puritan preaching.

11 *py'de:* parti-colored (black and white).

And is preserved from the bane
Of either warr, or Puritane:
Whose life is colour'd in thy paint,
The Inside drosse, the Outside Saint.

## *To his sonne* Vincent Corbett

What I shall leave thee none can tell,
But all shall say I wish thee well:
I wish thee (*Vin*), before all wealth,
Both bodily and ghostly health.
Nor too much wealth, nor wit, come to thee:
Too much of either may undoe thee.
I wish thee learning, not for show,
But truly to instruct and know:
Not such as Gentlemen require,
To prate at Table, or at Fire.
I wish thee all thy mothers graces,
Thy fathers fortunes, and his places.
I wish thee friends, and one at Court,
Not to build up, but to support:
To keepe thee, not in doing many
Oppressions, but from suffering any.
I wish thee peace in all thy wayes,
Nor lazy nor contentious dayes;
And when thy soule and body part,
As innocent as now thou art.

TO HIS SONNE VINCENT CORBETT: Corbett's son was born in 1627; he did not live up to his father's hopes for him.

4 *ghostly:* spiritual.

## *An Epitaph on Doctor* Donne, *Deane of Pauls*

Hee that would write an Epitaph for thee,
And do it well, must first beginne to be
Such as thou wert; for, none can truly know
Thy worth, thy life, but he that hath liv'd so;
He must have wit to spare, and to hurle downe:
Enough, to keepe the gallants of the towne.
He must have learning plenty; both the Lawes,
Civill, and Common, to judge any cause;
Divinity great store, above the rest;
Not of the last Edition, but the best.
Hee must have language, travaile, all the Arts;
Judgement to use, or else he wants thy parts.
He must have friends the highest, able to do;
Such as *Mecaenas*, and *Augustus* too.
He must have such a sicknesse, such a death;
Or else his vaine descriptions come beneath;
Who then shall write an Epitaph for thee,
He must be dead first, let' it alone for mee.

AN EPITAPH ON DOCTOR DONNE: First printed in the 1633 edition of Donne's poems, from which the text given here is taken. Donne died on March 31, 1631.

10 *last:* latest, probably alluding to Puritan theology.

# Certain true Woords spoken concerning one Benet Corbett after her death; she dyed October the Second Anno 1634

Here, or not many feet from hence
The virtue lies call'd Patience.
Sickness and Death did do her honour
By loosing paine and feare upon her.
Tis true they forst her to a grave,
That's all the triumph that they have,—
A silly one; retreat o'er night
Proves conquest in a morning fight.
She will rise up against them both;
All sleep, believe it, is not sloth.
   And thou that read'st her elegie,
Take something of her historie:
She had one husband and one sonne;
Ask who they were, and thou hast done.

CERTAIN TRUE WORDS SPOKEN: Benet Corbett was Richard's mother.

# LORD HERBERT OF CHERBURY
# 1583–1648

## *A Description*

I sing her worth and praises hy,
Of whom a Poet cannot ly,
The little World the Great shall blaze;
Sea, Earth, her Body; Heaven, her Face;
Her Hair, Sun-beams; whose every part
Lightens, enflames, each Lover's Heart:
That thus you prove the Axiom true,
Whilst the Sun help'd Nature in you.
  Her Front, the White and Azure Sky,
In Light and Glory raised hy,
Being o'recast by a Cloudy frown,
All Hearts and Eyes dejecteth down.
  Her each Brow a Coelestial Bow,
Which through this Sky her Light doth show,
Which doubled, if it strange appear,
The Sun's likewise is doubled there.
  Her either Cheek a Blushing Morn,
Which, on the Wings of Beauty born,
Doth never set, but only fair
Shineth, exalted in her hair.
  Within her Mouth, Heavens Heav'n reside,
Her Words, the Soul's there Glorifi'd.
  Her Nose th'*AEquator* of this Globe,
Where Nakedness, Beauties best Robe,
Presents a form all Hearts to win.
  Last Nature made that dainty Chin;

A DESCRIPTION: Some of the poems given here have no titles in the 1665 edition. These have been supplied from G. C. Moore Smith's edition (Oxford, 1923).

1 *hy:* Here, and in lines 10 and 69, the 1665 edition reads *ey.*

3–4: The 1665 edition adds the Greek words *microcosmos* and *macrocosmos* in the margin.

7 *That:* So that; *Axiom:* The 1665 edition adds *sol et homo generant hominem* (The sun and man generate man) in the margin. The proposition comes from Aristotle's *Physics* 194b.

18 *born:* borne.

Which that it might in every fashion
Answer the rest, a Constellation,
Like to a Desk, she there did place,
To write the Wonders of her Face.
  In this Coelestial Frontispiece,
Where Happiness eternal lies;
First aranged stand three Senses,
This Heavens Intelligences.
Whose several Motions, sweet combin'd,
Come from the first Mover, her Mind.
  The weight of this harmonique Sphere,
The *Atlas* of her Neck doth bear;
Whose Favours Day to Us imparts,
When Frowns make Night in Lovers Hearts.
  Two foming Billows are her Breasts,
That carry, rais'd upon their Crests,
The *Tyrian* Fish: More white's their Fome,
Then that, whence *Venus* once did come:
  Here take her by the Hand, my Muse,
With that sweet Foe, to make my Truce,
To compact Manna, best compar'd,
Whose dewy inside's not full hard.
  Her Waste's an envers'd Pyramis,
Upon whose Cone Love's Trophee is:
  Her Belly is that Magazine,
At whose peep Nature did resigne
That pretious Mould, by which alone,
There can be framed such a One:
  At th' entrance of which hidden Treasure,
Happy making above measure,
Two Alabaster Pillars stand,
To warn all passage from that Land;

34 *Intelligences:* spirits which govern the celestial spheres.

36 *first Mover:* The motion of the spheres came from the *primum mobile,* the unmoved first sphere.

43 *Tyrian Fish:* the *murex,* a purple fish.

49 *envers'd Pyramis:* inverted pyramid.

At foot whereof engraved is,
The sad *Non Ultra* of Mans Bliss:
The Back of this most pretious Frame
Holds up in Majesty the same:
Where, to make Musick to all Hearts,
Love bound the descant of her parts:
Though all this Beauties Temple be,
There's known within no Deity
Save Vertues, shrin'd within her Will:
As I began, so say I still,
I sing her Worth and Praises hy,
Of whom a Poet cannot ly.

## *Loves End*

Thus ends my Love, but this doth grieve me most,
That so it ends, but that ends too, this yet,
Besides the Wishes, hopes and time I lost,
Troubles my mind awhile, that I am set
Free, worse then deny'd: I can neither boast
Choice nor success, as my Case is, nor get
Pardon from my self, that I loved not
A better Mistress, or her worse; this Debt
Only's her due, still, that she be forgot
Ere chang'd, lest I love none; this done, the taint
Of foul Inconstancy is clear'd at least
In me, there only rests but to unpaint
Her form in my mind, that so dispossest
It be a Temple, but without a Saint.

60 *Non Ultra:* nothing beyond.
64 *descant:* melodious accompaniment.
LOVES END: This is the fourth and last of a short sequence of sonnets. The first three poems are addressed "To her face," "To her Body," and "To her Mind."
12 *rests:* remains.

## *Ditty in imitation of the Spanish*

Entre tanto que L'Avril

Now that the *April* of your youth adorns
 The Garden of your face,
Now that for you each knowing Lover mourns,
 And all seek to your Grace:
Do not repay affection with Scorns.

What though you may a matchless Beauty vaunt,
 And that all Hearts can move,
By such a power, as seemeth to inchant?
 Yet without help of Love
Beauty no pleasure to it self can grant.

Then think each minute that you lose, a day,
 The longest Youth is short,
The shortest Age is long; time flies away,
 And makes us but his sport;
And that which is not Youth's is Age's prey.

See but the bravest Horse, that prideth most,
 Though he escape the Warr,
Either from Master to the man is lost,
 Or turn'd unto the Carr,
Or else must die with being ridden Post.

Then lose not beauty, Lovers, time, and all,
 Too late your fault you see,
When that in vain you would these dayes recall;
 Nor can you vertuous be,
When without these you have not wherewithall.

DITTY IN IMITATION OF THE SPANISH.

19–20: is either turned into a carriage horse or dies from being ridden (too quickly) as a post horse.

## *Parted Souls*

I must depart, but like to his last breath
That leaves the seat of life, for liberty
I go, but dying, and in this our death,
Where soul and soul is parted, it is I
The deader part that fly away,
While she alas, in whom before
I liv'd, dyes her own death and more,
I feeling mine too much, and her own stay.

But since I must depart, and that our love
Springing at first but in an earthly mould,
Transplanted to our souls, now doth remove
Earthly effects, what time and distance would,
Nothing now can our loves allay,
Though as the better Spirits will
That both love us and know our ill,
We do not either all the good we may.

Thus when our souls that must immortal be,
For our loves cannot dye, nor we, (unless
We dye not both together) shall be free
Unto their open and eternal peace,
Sleep, Death's Embassadour, and best
Image, doth yours often so show,
That I thereby must plainly know,
Death unto us must be freedom and rest.

PARTED SOULS.
5 *that:* The 1665 edition reads *yet.*
8 *I:* possibly an error for *aye* (forever).
13 *allay:* soil.

## *Madrigal*

How should I love my best?
What though my love unto that height be grown,
That taking joy in you alone
I utterly this world detest,
Should I not love it yet as th'only place
Where Beauty hath his perfect grace,
And is possest?

But I beauties despise,
You, universal beauty seem to me,
Giving and shewing form and degree
To all the rest, in your fair eyes,
Yet should I not love them as parts whereon
Your beauty, their perfection
And top, doth rise?

But ev'n my self I hate,
So far my love is from the least delight
That at my very self I spite,
Sensless of any happy state,
Yet may I not with justest reason fear
How hating hers, I truly her
Can celebrate?

Thus unresolved still
Although world, life, nay what is fair beside
I cannot for your sake abide,
Methinks I love not to my fill,
Yet if a greater love you can devise,
In loving you some otherwise,
Believe't, I will.

## *To his Friend* Ben. Johnson, *of his* Horace *made English*

’Twas not enough, *Ben Johnson,* to be thought
Of English Poets best, but to have brought
In greater state, to their acquaintance, one
So equal to himself and thee, that none
Might be thy second, while thy Glory is,
To be the *Horace* of our times and his.

## *Epitaph.* Caecil. Boulstr. *quae post languescentem morbum non sine inquietudine spiritus & conscientiae obiit*

Methinks Death like one laughing lyes,
Shewing his teeth, shutting his eys,
Only thus to have found her here
He did with so much reason fear,
And she despise.

For barring all the gates of sin,
Death’s open wayes to enter in,
She was with a strict siege beset,
To what by force he could not get,
By time to win.

TO HIS FRIEND: Jonson’s translation of Horace, although written at least as early as 1614, was first published in 1640.

EPITAPH: The Latin may be translated as follows: “Epitaph for Cecilia Boulstred who, after a lingering disease, not without vexation of spirit and conscience, died.” She died at the age of twenty-five on August 4, 1609. Cf. Donne’s “Elegy on Mistris Boulstred,” beginning “Death I recant.”

This mighty Warrior was deceived yet,
For what he, muting in her powers, thought
Was but their zeal,
And what by their excess might have been wrought,
Her fasts did heal.

Till that her noble soul, by these, as wings,
Transcending the low pitch of earthly things,
As b'ing reliev'd by God, and set at large,
And grown by this worthy a higher charge,
Triumphing over Death, to Heaven fled,
And did not dye, but left her body dead.

## *In a Glass-Window for Inconstancy*

Love, of this clearest, frailest Glass,
Divide the properties, so as
In the division may appear
Clearness for me, frailty for her.

## A Vision

*A Lady combing her hair.*

Within an *open curled Sea of Gold* — *The hair*
A *Bark of Ivory*, one day, I saw, — *The Comb*
Which striking with his *Oars* did seem to draw — *The teeth of the Comb.*
Tow'rds a fair *Coast*, which I then did behold. — *Her side.*

12 *muting:* mutinying, rebelling.
*Title:* The marginalia explain the riddle of the "vision" which this piece develops.

A Lady held the Stern, while her white hand
  Whiter then either Ivory or *Sail*, *The Cuff or smock sleeve,*
  Over the surging Waves did so prevail,
That she had now approached near the *Land*. *Her shoulder.*

When suddenly, as if she fear'd some wrack,
  And yet the Sky was fair, and Air was clear,
  And neither *Rock*, nor *Monster* did appear, *Wart Lice.*
Doubting the Point, which spi'd, she turned back.

Then with a *Second course* I saw her steer *Combing in another place.*
  As if she meant to reach some other Bay,
  Where being approach'd she likewise turn'd away,
Though in the Bark some *Waves* now entred were. *Hairs in the Comb.*

Thus varying oft her course, at last I found,
  While I in quest of the Adventure go,
  *The Sail took down, and Oars had ceas'd to row,* *She had given over combing.*
*And that the Bark it self was run aground.*

Wherewith *Earths fairest Creature* I beheld, *Her face.*
  For which both *Bark and Sea I gladly lost.* *Her hair put up, and Comb cast away.*
  Let no Philosopher of Knowledge boast,
Unless that he my Vision can unfold.

## *Tears, flow no more*

Tears, flow no more, or if you needs must flow,
    Fall yet more slow,
  Do not the world invade,
From smaller springs then yours rivers have grown,

And they again a Sea have made,
Brackish like you, and which like you hath flown.

Ebb to my heart, and on the burning fires
Of my desires,
O let your torrents fall,
From smaller heate then theirs such sparks arise
As into flame converting all,
This world might be but my love's sacrifice.

Yet if the tempests of my sighs so blow
You both must flow,
And my desires still burn,
Since that in vain all help my love requires,
Why may not yet their rages turn
To dry those tears, and to blow out those fires?

## *Love speaks at last*

I am the first that ever lov'd,
He yet that for the place contends
Against true love so much offends,
That even this way it is prov'd.

For whose affection once is shown,
No longer can the World beguile,
Who see his pennance all the while,
He holds a Torch to make her known.

TEARS, FLOW NO MORE.
9 *O:* omitted in *1665*.
10 *heate:* sparks *1665*.
13 *blow:* slow *1665*.
17 *their:* i.e. those of the tempests.
LOVE SPEAKS AT LAST.
2–4: "He who disputes with me offends against love and proves my assertion." (Moore Smith)

You are the first were ever lov'd,
And who may think this not so true,
So little knows of love or you,
It need not otherwise be prov'd.

For though the more judicious eyes
May know when Diamonds are right,
There is requir'd a greater light
Their estimate and worth to prise.

While they who most for beauty strives,
Can with no Art so lovely grow
As she who doth but only ow
So much as true affection gives.

Thus first of Lovers I appear,
For more appearance makes me none;
And thus are you belov'd alone,
That are pris'd infinitely dear.

Yet as in our Northern Clime
Rare fruits, though late, appear at last;
As we may see, some years b'ing past,
Our Orenge-trees grow ripe with time.

So think not strange, if Love to break
His wonted silence now make bold,
For when a Love is seven years old,
Is it not time to learn to speak?

Then gather in that which doth grow
And ripen to that fairest hand;
'Tis not enough that trees do stand,
If their fruit fall and perish too.

16 *prise:* prize, esteem.
19 *only ow:* possess alone.
31 *when:* omitted in *1665*.

## *Elegy over a Tomb*

Must I then see, alas! eternal night
Sitting upon those fairest eyes,
And closing all those beams, which once did rise
So radiant and bright,
That light and heat in them to us did prove
Knowledge and Love?

Oh, if you did delight no more to stay
Upon this low and earthly stage,
But rather chose an endless heritage,
Tell us at least, we pray,
Where all the beauties that those ashes ow'd
Are now bestow'd?

Doth the Sun now his light with yours renew?
Have Waves the curling of your hair?
Did you restore unto the Sky and Air,
The red, and white, and blew?
Have you vouchsafed to flowrs since your death
That sweetest breath?

Had not Heav'ns Lights else in their houses slept,
Or to some private life retir'd?
Must not the Sky and Air have else conspir'd,
And in the Regions wept?
Must not each flower else the earth could breed
Have been a weed?

ELEGY OVER A TOMB.

11 *ow'd:* possessed.

19 *houses:* the "mansions" of the planets; astrological divisions of the heavens.

But thus enrich'd may we not yield some cause
Why they themselves lament no more?
That must have changed the course they held before,
And broke their proper Laws,
Had not your beauties giv'n this second birth
To Heaven and Earth?

Tell us, for Oracles must still ascend,
For those that crave them at your tomb:
Tell us, where are those beauties now become,
And what they now intend:
Tell us alas, that cannot tell our grief,
Or hope relief.

## *To Mrs.* Diana Cecyll

*Diana Cecyll,* that rare beauty thou dost show
Is not of Milk, or Snow,
Or such as pale and whitely things do ow.
But an illustrious Oriental Bright,
Like to the Diamonds refracted light,
Or early Morning breaking from the Night.

Nor is thy hair and eyes made of that ruddy beam,
Or golden-sanded stream,
Which we find still the vulgar Poets theme,
But reverend black, and such as you would say,
Light did but serve it, and did shew the way,
By which at first night did precede the day.

27 *the:* omitted in *1665.*

TO MRS. DIANA CECYLL: This lady, who died in 1654, was reputed to be the greatest beauty of her day.

3 *ow:* own.

Nor is that symmetry of parts and force divine
Made of one vulgar line,
Of such as any know how to define,
But of proportions new, so well exprest,
That the perfections in each part confest,
Are beauties to themselves, and to the rest.

Wonder of all thy Sex! let none henceforth inquire
Why they so much admire,
Since they that know thee best ascend no higher;
Only be not with common praises woo'd
Since admiration were no longer good,
When men might hope more then they understood.

## *Sonnet of Black Beauty*

Black beauty, which above that common light,
Whose Power can no colours here renew,
But those which darkness can again subdue,
Do'st still remain unvary'd to the sight.

And like an object equal to the view,
And neither chang'd with day, nor hid with night,
When all these colours which the world call bright,
And which old Poetry doth so persue,

Are with the night so perished and gone,
That of their being there remains no mark,
Thou still abidest so intirely one,
That we may know thy blackness is a spark
Of light inaccessible, and alone
Our darkness which can make us think it dark.

## *The first Meeting*

As sometimes with a sable Cloud
We see the Heav'ns bow'd,
And darkning all the aire,
Untill the lab'ring fires they do contain
Break forth again,
Ev'n so from under your black hair
I saw such an unusual blaze
Light'ning and sparkling from your eyes,
And with unused prodigies
Forcing such terrors and amaze,
That I did judge your Empire here
Was not of love alone, but fear.

But as all that is violent
Doth by degrees relent,
So when that sweetest face,
Growing at last to be serene and clear,
Did now appear
With all its wonted heav'nly Grace,
And your appeased eyes did send
A beam from them so soft and mild,
That former terrors were exil'd,
And all that could amaze did end;
Darkness in me was chang'd to light,
Wonder to love, love to delight.

Nor here yet did your goodness cesse
My heart and eyes to bless,
For being past all hope,

THE FIRST MEETING.
3 *aire: 1665* reads *fire.*
25 *cesse:* cease.

That I could now enjoy a better state,
And orient gate
(As if the Heav'ns themselves did ope)
First found in thee, and then disclos'd
So gracious and sweet a smile,
That my soul ravished the while,
And wholly from it self unloos'd,
Seem'd hov'ring in your breath to rise,
To feel an air of Paradise.

Nor here yet did your favours end,
For whil'st I down did bend,
As one who now did miss
Would turn no more,
A soul, which grown much happier then before,
You did bestow on me a Kiss,
And in that Kiss a soul infuse,
Which was so fashion'd by your mind,
And which was so much more refin'd,
Then that I formerly did use,
That if one soul found joys in thee,
The other fram'd them new in me.

But as those bodies which dispense
Their beams, in parting hence
Those beams do recollect,
Until they in themselves resumed have
The forms they gave,
So when your gracious aspect
From me was turned once away,
Neither could I thy soul retain,
Nor you gave mine leave to remain,
To make with you a longer stay,
Or suffer'd ought else to appear
But your hair, nights hemisphere.

Only as we in Loadstones find
Vertue of such a kind,
That what they once do give,
B'ing neither to be chang'd by any Clime,
Or forc'd by time,
Doth ever in its subjects live;
So though I be from you retir'd,
The power you gave yet still abides,
And my soul ever so guides,
By your magnetique touch inspir'd,
That all it moves, or is inclin'd,
Comes from the motions of your mind.

## *The Thought*

*1.*

If you do love, as well as I,
Then every minute from your heart
A thought doth part:
And winged with desire doth fly
Till it hath met in a streight line,
A thought of mine
So like to yours, we cannot know
Whether of both doth come or go,
Till we define
Which of us two that thought doth ow.

61 *Loadstones:* magnets.

THE THOUGHT.

8 *Whether:* which.

10 *Which . . . ow:* Which of us two possess or own that thought.

2.

I say then, that your thoughts which pass,
Are not so much the thoughts you meant,
As those I sent:
For as my image in a Glass
Belongs not to the Glass you see,
But unto me,
So when your fancy is so clear,
That you would think you saw me there,
It needs must be,
That it was I did first appear.

3.

Likewise when I send forth a thought,
My reason tells me, 'tis the same,
Which from you came,
And which your beauteous Image wrought;
Thus while our thoughts by turns do lead
None can precede,
And thus while in each others mind
Such interchanged forms we find,
Our loves may plead
To be of more then vulgar kind.

4.

May you then often think on me,
And by that thinking know 'tis true
I thought on you:
I in the same belief will be,

26 *precede:* take precedence (over the other).

While by this mutual address
We will possess
A love must live, when we do dy,
Which rare and secret property
You will confess,
If you do love as well as I.

## *To a Lady who did sing excellently*

1.

When our rude & unfashion'd words, that long
A being in their elements enjoy'd,
Sensless and void,
Come at last to be formed by thy tongue,
And from thy breath receive that life and place,
And perfect grace,
That now thy power diffus'd through all their parts
Are able to remove
All the obstructions of the hardest hearts,
And teach the most unwilling how to love.

2.

When they again, exalted by thy voice,
Tun'd by thy soul, dismiss'd into the air,
To us repair,
A living, moving, and harmonious noise,
Able to give the love they do create
A second state,
And charm not only all his griefs away,
And his defects restore,
But make him perfect, who, the Poets say,
Made all was ever yet made heretofore.

TO A LADY.
19 *who:* i.e. Love.

3.

When again all these rare perfections meet,
  Composed in the circle of thy face,
    As in their place,
So to make up of all one perfect sweet,
  Who is not then so ravish'd with delight
    Ev'n of thy sight,
That he can be assur'd his sense is true,
    Or that he die, or live,
Or that he do enjoy himself, or you,
  Or only the delights, which you did give?

## *Echo in a Church*

Where shall my troubled soul, at large
        Discharge
The burden of her sins, oh where?
        *Echo* Here.
    Whence comes this voice I hear?
    Who doth this grace afford?
    If it be thou, O Lord,
Say, if thou hear my prayers when I call.
        *Echo* All.
And wilt thou pity grant when I do cry?
        *Echo* I.
Then though I fall,
    Thy Grace will my defects supply,
    But who will keep my soul from ill,

ECHO IN A CHURCH: As has often been remarked, this poem could well have been written by Herbert's brother, George.

1 *Where:* When *1665*.

11 *I:* i.e. *Aye,* yes.

Quench bad desires, reform my Will?
*Echo* I will.

O may that will and voice be blest,
Which yields such comforts unto one distrest,
More blessed yet, would'st thou thy self unmask,
Or tell, at least, who undertakes this task.
*Echo* Ask.

Then quickly speak,
Since now with crying I am grown so weak,
I shall want force even to crave thy name,
O speak before I wholly weary am.
*Echo* I am.

## *To his Mistress for her true Picture*

Death, my lifes Mistress, and the soveraign Queen
Of all that ever breath'd, though yet unseen,
My heart doth love you best, yet I confess,
Your picture I beheld, which doth express
No such eye-taking beauty, you seem lean,
Unless you'r mended since. Sure he did mean
No honour to you, that did draw you so;
Therefore I think it false; Besides, I know
The picture, Nature drew, (which sure's the best)
Doth figure you by sleep and sweetest rest:
Sleep, nurse of our life, care's best reposer,
Natures high'st rapture, and the vision giver:
Sleep, which when it doth seize us, souls go play,
And make Man equal as he was first day.
Yet some will say, Can pictures have more life
Then the original? To end this strife,

22 This line is omitted in *1665*.
26 *I am:* God's definition of himself as given to Moses: "I am who am."

Sweet Mistress come, and shew your self to me,
In your true form, while then I think to see
Some beauty Angelick, that comes t' unlock
My bodies prison, and from life unyoke
My well divorced soul, and set it free,
To liberty eternal: Thus you see,
I find the Painters error, and protect
Your absent beauties, ill drawn, by th'effect:
For grant it were your work, and not the Graves,
Draw Love by Madness then, Tyrants by Slaves,
Because they make men such. Dear Mistress, then
If you would not be seen by owl-ey'd Men,
Appear at noon i' th' Air, with so much light,
The Sun may be a Moon, the Day a Night,
Clear to my Soul, but dark'ning the weak sense
Of those, the other Worlds Cimmeriens,
And in your fatal Robe, imbroidered
With Starr-characters, teaching me to read
The destiny of Mortals, while your clear brow
Presents a Majesty, to instruct me how
To love or dread nought else: May your bright hair,
Which are the threds of life, fair crown'd appear
With that your Crown of Immortality:
In your right hand the Keys of Heaven be;
In th'other those of the Infernal Pit,
Whence none retires, if once he enter it.
And here let me complain, how few are those
Whose souls you shall from earth's vast dungeon lose
To endless happiness? few that attend
You, the true Guide, unto their journeys end:
And if of old Vertue's way narrow were,
'Tis rugged now, having no passenger.

TO HIS MISTRESS.

32 *Cimmeriens:* men living in spiritual darkness. See Homer, *Odyssey, XI.*
44 *lose:* loose.
47 *of:* omitted in *1665*.
48 *passenger:* traveler (upon it).

Our life is but a dark and stormy night,
To which sense yields a weak and glimmering light;
While wandring Man thinks he discerneth all,
By that which makes him but mistake and fall:
He sees enough, who doth his darkness see;
These are great lights, by which less dark'ned be.
Shine then Sun-brighter through my senses vail,
A day-star of the light doth never fail;
Shew me that Goodness which compounds the strife
'Twixt a long sickness and a weary life.
Set forth that Justice which keeps all in aw,
Certain and equal more then any Law.
Figure that happy and eternal Rest,
Which till Man do enjoy, he is not blest.
Come and appear then, dear Soul-ravisher,
Heavens-Light-Usher, Man's deliverer,
And do not think, when I new beauties see,
They can withdraw my settled love from thee.
Flesh-beauty strikes me not at all, I know,
When thou do'st leave them to the grave, they show
Worse, then they now show thee: they shal not move
In me the least part of delight, or love,
But as they teach your power: Be they nut brown,
The loveliest colour which the flesh doth crown:
I'll think it like a Nut, a fair outside,
Within which Worms and rottenness abide:
If fair, then like the Worm it self to be;
If painted, like their slime and sluttery.
If any yet will think their beauties best,
And will, against you, spite of all, contest,
Seize them with Age: so in themselves they'l hate
What they scorn'd in your picture, and too late
See their fault, and the Painters: Yet if this,
Which their great'st plague and wrinkled torture is,

55 *Sun-brighter:* Sun-bright, or *1665; vail:* veil.
64 *Heavens-Light-Usher:* Heav'ns lightest Usher *1665*.
71 *Be they:* Be the *1665*.

Please not, you may to the more wicked sort,
Or such as of your praises make a sport,
Denounce an open warr, send chosen bands
Of Worms, your souldiers, to their fairest hands,
And make them lep'rous-scabb'd: upon their face
Let those your Pioneers, Ring-worms, take their place,
And safely near with strong approaches got
Intrench it round, while their teeths rampire rot
With other Worms, may with a damp inbred
Stink to their senses, which they shall not dead:
And thus may all that e'r they prided in,
Confound them now: As for the parts within,
Send Gut-worms, which may undermine a way
Unto their vital parts, and so display
That your pale Ensign on the walls: then let
Those Worms, your Veteranes, which never yet
Did fail, enter *Pel mel,* and ransack all,
Just as they see the well-rais'd building fall:
While they do this, your Forragers command,
The Caterpillars, to devour their land;
And with them Wasps, your wing'd-worm-horsmen, bring,
To charge, in troop, those Rebels, with their sting:
All this, unless your beauty they confess.

And now, sweet Mistress, let m' a while digress,
T'admire these noble Worms, whom I invoke,
And not the Muses: You that eat through Oak
And bark, will you spare Paper, and my Verse,
Because your praises they do here reherse?

Brave Legions then, sprung from the mighty race
Of Man corrupted, and which hold the place
Of his undoubted Issue; you that are
Brain-born, *Minerva*-like, and like her warr,

85 *Denounce:* Declare.
90 *rampire rot:* rampart rotten.
92 *Stink:* Sink *1665*.

Well-arm'd compleat-mail'd-jointed Souldiers,
Whose force *Herculean* links in pieces tears;
To you the vengeance of all spill-bloods falls,
Beast-eating Men, Men-eating Cannibals.
Death-priviledg'd, were you to sunder smit
You do not lose your life, but double it:
Best framed types of the immortal Soul,
Which in your selves, and in each part are whole:
Last-living Creatures, heirs of all the earth,
For when all men are dead, it is your birth:
When you dy, your brave self-kill'd Generall
(For nothing else can kill him) doth end all.
What vermine-breeding body then thinks scorn,
His flesh should be by your brave fury torn.

Willing, to you, this Carkass I submit,
A gift so free, I do not care for it:
Which yet you shall not take, untill I see
My Mistress first reveal her self to me.

Mean while, Great Mistress, whom my soul admires,
Grant me your true picture, who it desires,
That he your matchless beauty might maintain
'Gainst all men that will quarrels entertain
For a Flesh-Mistress; the worst I can do,
Is but to keep the way that leads to you,
And howsoever the event doth prove,
To have Revenge below, Reward above;
Hear, from my bodies prison, this my Call,
Who from my mouth-grate, and eye-window bawl.

## *Epitaph for himself*

*Reader,*
The Monument which thou beholdest here,
  Presents *Edward* Lord *Herbert,* to thy sight,
A man, who was so free from either hope or fear,
  To have or loose this ordinary light,
That when to elements his body turned were,
  He knew that as those elements would fight,
So his Immortal Soul should find above,
With his Creator, Peace, Joy, Truth, and Love.

## *Elegy for Doctor* Dunn

What though the vulgar and received praise,
With which each common Poet strives to raise
His worthless Patron, seem to give the height
Of a true Excellence; yet as the weight
Forc'd from his Centre, must again recoil,
So every praise, as if it took some foil,
Only because it was not well imploy'd,
Turns to those senseless principles and void,
Which in some broken syllables being couch'd,
Cannot above an Alphabet be vouch'd,
In which dissolved state, they use to rest,
Until some other in new forms invest

EPITAPH FOR HIMSELF.
  5 *loose:* lose.
ELEGY FOR DOCTOR DUNN: Donne's friendship with Herbert's mother and brother are well established; Edward probably knew him from his Oxford days.
  5 *his Centre:* the place at which it (the weight) is naturally at rest.
  8 *Turns:* Returns.

Their easie matter, striving so to fix
Glory with words, and make the parts to mix.
  But since praise that wants truth, like words that want
Their proper meaning, doth it self recant;
Such tearms, however elevate and high,
Are but like Meteors, which the pregnant Sky
Varies in divers figures, till at last
They either be by some dark Cloud o'rcast,
Or wanting inward sustenance do devolve,
And into their first Elements resolve.
  Praises, like Garments, then, if loose and wide,
Are subject to fall off: if gay and py'd,
Make men ridiculous; the just and grave
Are those alone, which men may wear and have.
  How fitting were it then, each had that part
Which is their due: And that no fraudulent art
Could so disguise the truth, but they might own
Their rights, and by that property be known.
  For since praise is publick inheritance,
If any Inter-Commoner do chance
To give or take more praise then doth belong
Unto his part, he doth so great a wrong,
That all who claim an equal interest,
May him implead untill he do devest
His usurpations, and again restore
Unto the publick what was theirs before.
  Praises should then like definitions be
Round, neat, convertible, such as agree
To persons so, that, were their names conceal'd,
Must make them known as well as if reveal'd:
Such as contain the kind and difference,
And all the properties arising thence.
All praises else, as more or less then due,
Will prove, or strongly false, or weakly true.

24 *py'd:* variegated.

32 *Inter-Commoner:* One who shares the common (pasturage) equally with others.

36 *implead:* take legal action against.

Having deliver'd now, what praises are,
It rests that I should to the world declare
Thy praises, *DUNN*, whom I so lov'd alive,
That with my witty *Carew* I should strive
To celebrate thee dead, did I not need
A language by it self, which should exceed
All those which are in use: For while I take
Those common words, which men may even rake
From Dunghil-wits, I find them so defil'd,
Slubber'd and false, as if they had exil'd
Truth and propriety, such as do tell
So little other things, they hardly spell
Their proper meaning, and therefore unfit
To blazon forth thy merits, or thy wit.
Nor will it serve, that thou did'st so refine
Matter with words, that both did seem divine,
When thy breath utter'd them: for thou b'ing gone,
They streight did follow thee: Let therefore none
Hope to find out an Idiom and sence,
Equal to thee, and to thy Eminence,
Unless our Gracious King give words their bound,
Call in false titles, which each where are found,
In Prose and Verse, and as bad Coin and light
Suppress them and their values, till the right
Take place, and do appear, and then in lieu
Of those forg'd Attributes stamp some anew,
Which being currant, and by all allow'd,
In Epitaphs and Tombs might be avow'd
More then their Escocheons. Mean while, because
Nor praise is yet confined to its Laws,

50 *Carew:* His "Elegy on Donne" had appeared in 1633. See below for the text.

69 *light:* not containing the true weight.

70–71 *till . . . place:* until the right words present themselves.

75 *Escocheons:* Escutcheons, tablets bearing the coats of arms of deceased persons.

Nor rayling wants his proper dialect,
Let thy detractors thy late life detect;
And though they term all thy heat, frowardness;
Thy solitude, self-pride; fasts, niggardness,
And on this false supposal would inferr,
They teach not others right, themselves who err;
Yet as men to the adverse part do ply
Those crooked things which they would rectifie,
So would perchance, to loose and wanton Man
Such vice avail more then their vertues can.

## *The Brown Beauty*

*1.*

While the two contraries of Black and White,
In the Brown *Phaie* are so well unite,
That they no longer now seem opposite,
    Who doubts but love, hath this his colour chose,
    Since he therein doth both th' extremes compose,
    And as within their proper Centre close.

2.

Therefore as it presents not to the view
That whitely raw and unconcocted hiew,
Which Beauty Northern Nations think the true;

78 *detractors:* detraction *1665*.
83 *ply:* twist.
THE BROWN BEAUTY.
2 *Phaie:* The name is formed from the Greek φαια, "dusky."
6 *close:* enclose.

So neither hath it that adust aspect,
The *Moor* and *Indian* so much affect,
That for it they all other do reject.

3.

Thus while the White well shadow'd doth appear,
And black doth through his lustre grow so clear,
That each in other equal part doth bear;
All in so rare proportion is combin'd,
That the fair temper, which adorns her mind,
Is even to her outward form confin'd.

4.

*Phaie*, your Sexes honour, then so live,
That when the World shall with contention strive
To whom they would a chief perfection give,
They might the controversie so decide,
As quitting all extreams on either side,
You more then any may be dignify'd.

## *An Ode upon a Question moved, Whether Love should continue for ever?*

Having interr'd her Infant-birth,
The watry ground that late did mourn,
Was strew'd with flow'rs for the return
Of the wish'd Bridegroom of the earth.

10 *adust:* scorched, blackened (by the sun).
AN ODE UPON A QUESTION.
4 *Bridegroom:* i.e. the sun.

The well accorded Birds did sing
  Their hymns unto the pleasant time,
  And in a sweet consorted chime
Did welcom in the chearful Spring.

To which, soft whistles of the Wind,
  And warbling murmurs of a Brook,
  And vari'd notes of leaves that shook,
An harmony of parts did bind.

While doubling joy unto each other,
  All in so rare consent was shown,
  No happiness that came alone,
Nor pleasure that was not another.

When with a love none can express,
  That mutually happy pair,
  *Melander* and *Celinda* fair,
The season with their loves did bless.

Walking thus towards a pleasant Grove,
  Which did, it seem'd, in new delight
  The pleasures of the time unite,
To give a triumph to their love,

They stay'd at last, and on the Grass
  Reposed so, as o'r his breast
  She bow'd her gracious head to rest,
Such a weight as no burden was.

While over eithers compass'd waste
  Their folded arms were so compos'd,
  As if in straitest bonds inclos'd,
They suffer'd for joys they did taste.

14 *consent:* concent, agreement.

19 *Melander:* Herbert has another poem entitled "Melander suppos'd to love Susan." *Melander* means "black" in Greek and Herbert himself was a dark, swarthy man.

Long their fixt eyes to Heaven bent,
  Unchanged, they did never move,
  As if so great and pure a love
No Glass but it could represent.

When with a sweet, though troubled look,
  She first brake silence, saying, Dear friend,
  O that our love might take no end,
Or never had beginning took!

I speak not this with a false heart,
  (Wherewith his hand she gently strain'd)
  Or that would change a love maintain'd
With so much faith on either part.

Nay, I protest, though Death with his
  Worst Counsel should divide us here,
  His terrors could not make me fear,
To come where your lov'd presence is.

Only if loves fire with the breath
  Of life be kindled, I doubt,
  With our last air 'twill be breath'd out,
And quenched with the cold of death.

That if affection be a line,
  Which is clos'd up in our last hour;
  Oh how 'twould grieve me, any pow'r
Could force so dear a love as mine!

She scarce had done, when his shut eyes
  An inward joy did represent,
  To hear *Celinda* thus intent
To a love he so much did prize.

43 *that:* as one who.
50 *doubt:* fear.

Then with a look, it seem'd, deny'd
  All earthly pow'r but hers, yet so,
  As if to her breath he did ow
This borrow'd life, he thus repli'd;

O you, wherein, they say, Souls rest,
  Till they descend pure heavenly fires,
  Shall lustful and corrupt desires
With your immortal seed be blest?

And shall our Love, so far beyond
  That low and dying appetite,
  And which so chast desires unite,
Not hold in an eternal bond?

Is it, because we should decline,
  And wholly from our thoughts exclude
  Objects that may the sense delude,
And study only the Divine?

No sure, for if none can ascend
  Ev'n to the visible degree
  Of things created, how should we
The invisible comprehend?

Or rather since that Pow'r exprest
  His greatness in his works alone,
  B'ing here best in's Creatures known,
Why is he not lov'd in them best?

But is't not true, which you pretend,
  That since our love and knowledge here,
  Only as parts of life appear,
So they with it should take their end?

65–66 *O you . . . fires:* According to Plato's *Timaeus,* souls before birth existed in the stars.

73 *decline:* repudiate.

O no, Belov'd, I am most sure,
Those vertuous habits we acquire,
As being with the Soul intire,
Must with it evermore endure.

For if where sins and vice reside,
We find so foul a guilt remain,
As never dying in his stain,
Still punish'd in the Soul doth bide,

Much more that true and real joy,
Which in a vertuous love is found,
Must be more solid in its ground,
Then Fate or Death can e'r destroy.

Else should our Souls in vain elect,
And vainer yet were Heavens laws,
When to an everlasting Cause
They gave a perishing Effect.

Nor here on earth then, nor above,
Our good affection can impair,
For where God doth admit the fair,
Think you that he excludeth Love?

These eyes again then, eyes shall see,
And hands again these hands enfold,
And all chast pleasures can be told
Shall with us everlasting be.

For if no use of sense remain
When bodies once this life forsake,
Or they could no delight partake,
Why should they ever rise again?

106 *impair:* decay.

And if every imperfect mind
Make love the end of knowledge here,
How perfect will our love be, where
All imperfection is refin'd?

Let then no doubt, *Celinda,* touch,
Much less your fairest mind invade,
Were not our souls immortal made,
Our equal loves can make them such.

So when one wing can make no way,
Two joyned can themselves dilate,
So can two persons propagate,
When singly either would decay.

So when from hence we shall be gone,
And be no more, nor you, nor I,
As one anothers mystery,
Each shall be both, yet both but one.

This said, in her up-lifted face,
Her eyes which did that beauty crown,
Were like two starrs, that having faln down,
Look up again to find their place:

While such a moveless silent peace
Did seize on their becalmed sense,
One would have thought some Influence
Their ravish'd spirits did possess.

## *The Green-Sickness Beauty*

*1.*

Though the pale white within your cheeks compos'd,
  And doubtful light unto your eye confin'd,
Though your short breath not from it self unloos'd,
  And careless motions of your equal mind,
Argue, your beauties are not all disclos'd.

**2.**

Yet as a rising beam, when first 'tis shown,
  Points fairer, then when it ascends more red,
Or as a budding Rose, when first 'tis blown,
  Smells sweeter far, then when it is more spread,
As all things best by principles are known:

**3.**

So in your green and flourishing estate
  A beauty is discern'd more worthy love,
Then that which further doth it self dilate,
  And those degrees of variation prove,
Our vulgar wits so much do celebrate.

THE GREEN-SICKNESS BEAUTY: *Green-Sickness,* or chlorosis, is the name given to an anemic disease which affects young women about the age of puberty.

4.

Thus though your eyes dart not that piercing blaze,
Which doth in busie Lovers looks appear,
It is, because you do not need to gaze,
On other object then your proper sphere,
Nor wander further then to run that maze.

5.

So, if you want that blood which must succeed,
And give at last a tincture to your skin,
It is, because neither in outward deed,
Nor inward thought, you yet admit that sin,
For which your Cheeks a guilty blush should need.

6.

So, if your breath do not so freely flow,
It is because you love not to consume
That vital treasure, which you do bestow
As well to vegetate as to perfume
Your Virgin leaves, as fast as they do grow.

7.

Yet stay not here, Love for his right will call,
You were not born to serve your only will,
Nor can your beauty be perpetual,
'Tis your perfection for to ripen still,
And to be gather'd rather then to fall.

29 *vegetate:* cause to flourish.

## *Platonick Love*

Disconsolate and sad,
So little hope of remedy I find,
That when my matchless Mistress were inclin'd
To pity me, 'twould scarcely make me glad,
The discomposing of so fair a Mind
B'ing that which would to my Afflictions add.

For when she should repent,
This Act of Charity had made her part
With such a precious Jewel as her Heart,
Might she not grieve that e'r she did relent?
And then were it not fit I felt the smart
Untill I grew the greater Penitent.

Nor were't a good excuse,
When she pleas'd to call for her Heart again,
To tell her of my suffering and pain,
Since that I should her Clemency abuse,
While she did see what wrong she did sustain,
In giving what she justly might refuse.

Vex'd thus with me at last,
When from her kind restraint she now were gone,
And I left to the Manacles alone,
Should I not on another Rock be cast?
Since they who have not yet content, do mone
Far less then they whose hope thereof is past.

PLATONICK LOVE.
3 *when:* if.
11 *not:* omitted in *1665*.

Besides I would deserve,
And not live poorly on the alms of Love,
Or claim a favour did not singly move
From my regard: If she her joys reserve
Unto some other, she at length should prove,
Rather then beg her pity I would sterve.

Let her then be serene,
Alike exempt from pity and from hate:
Let her still keep her dignity and state;
Yet from her glories something I shall glean,
For when she doth them every where dilate,
A beam or two to me must intervene.

And this shall me sustain,
For though due merit I cannot express,
Yet she shall know none ever lov'd for less,
Or easier reward: Let her remain
Still Great and Good, and from her happiness
My chief contentment I will entertain.

## October 14. 1644

Enraging Griefs, though you most divers be,
In your first Causes, you may yet agree
To take an equal share within my heart,
Since if each grief strive for the greatest part,
You needs must vex your selves as well as me.

27 *did:* that did.
OCTOBER 14. 1644: *1644* is a conjectural emendation for the impossible *1664* in the 1665 edition.

For your own sakes and mine then make an end,
In vain you do about a Heart contend,
    Which though it seem in greatness to dilate,
    Is but a tumor, which in this its state
The choicest remedies would but offend.

Then storm't at once, I neither feel constraint
Scorning your worst, nor suffer any taint
    Dying by multitudes, though if you strive,
    I fear my heart may thus be kept alive,
Until it under its own burden faint.

What is't not done? Why then, my God, I find,
Would have me use you to reform my mind:
    Since through his help I may from you extract
    An essence pure, so spriteful and compact,
As it will be from grosser parts refin'd.

Which b'ing again converted by his Grace
To godly sorrow, I may both efface
    Those sins first caus'd you, and together have
    Your pow'r to kill turn'd to a power to save,
And bring my Soul to its desired place.

13 *by multitudes:* at the hands of multitudes.
23 *first:* that first.

# AURELIAN TOWNSHEND
?1583–1651?

## *Let Not Thy Beauty*

Let not thy beauty make thee proud
  Though Princes do adore thee,
Since time & sicknes were alow'd
  To mow such flowers before thee.

Nor be not shy to that degree,
  Thy friends may hardly know thee,
Nor yet so comming or so free,
  That every fly may blow thee.

A state in every Princely brow,
  As decent is requir'd,
Much more in thine, to whom they bow
  By Beauties lightnings fir'd.

And yet a state so sweetly mixt
  With an attractive mildnesse,
It may like Vertue sit betwixt
  The extreams of pride and vilenesse.

Then every eye that sees thy face
  Will in thy Beauty glory,
And every tongue that wags will grace
  Thy vertue with a story.

LET NOT THY BEAUTY: There is a tradition that Townshend addressed this poem to his daughter, Mary (1626–1702), who became a much admired beauty at court.

7 *comming:* forward.

8 *blow:* taint (by depositing his eggs upon you).

## To the Countesse of Salisbury

Victorious beauty, though your eyes
  Are able to subdue an hoast,
  And therefore are unlike to boast
The taking of a little prize,
Do not a single heart dispise.

It came alone, but yet so arm'd
  With former love, I durst have sworne
  That where a privy coat was worne,
With characters of beauty charm'd,
Thereby it might have scapt unharm'd.

But neither steele nor stony breast
  Are proofe against those lookes of thine,
  Nor can a Beauty lesse divine
Of any heart be long possest,
Where thou pretend'st an interest.

Thy Conquest in regard of me
  Alasse is small, but in respect
  Of her that did my Love protect,
Were it divulged, deserv'd to be
Recorded for a Victory.

And such a one, as some that view
  Her lovely face perhaps may say,
  Though you have stolen my heart away,
If all your servants prove not true,
May steale a heart or two from you.

TO THE COUNTESS OF SALISBURY: The Countess of Salisbury, Catherine Howard, married William Cecil in 1608. He became second Earl in 1612.

## Youth and Beauty

Thou art so fair, and yong withall,
  Thou kindl'st yong desires in me,
Restoreing life to leaves that fall,
  And sight to Eyes that hardly see
  Halfe those fresh Beauties bloom in thee.

Those, under sev'rall Hearbs and Flowr's
  Disguis'd, were all *Medea* gave,
When she recal'd Times flying howrs,
  And aged *AEson* from his grave,
  For Beauty can both kill and save.

Youth it enflames, but age it cheers,
  I would go back, but not return
To twenty but to twice those yeers;
  Not blaze, but ever constant burn,
  For fear my Cradle prove my Urn.

## A Dialogue Betwixt Time and a Pilgrime

*Pilgr.* Aged man, that mowes these fields.
*Time.* Pilgrime speak, what is thy will?
*Pilgr.* Whose soile is this that such sweet Pasture yields?
  Or who art thou whose Foot stand never still?
    Or where am I? *Time.* In love.
*Pilgr.* His Lordship lies above.
*Time.* Yes and below, and round about
    Where in all sorts of flow'rs are growing
  Which as the early Spring puts out,
    Time fals as fast a mowing.

*Pilgr.* If thou art Time, these Flow'rs have Lives,
And then I fear,
Under some Lilly she I love
May now be growing there.
*Time.* And in some Thistle or some spyre of grasse,
My syth thy stalk before hers come may passe.
*Pilgr.* Wilt thou provide it may. *Time.* No.
*Pilgr.* Alleage the cause.
*Time.* Because Time cannot alter but obey Fates laws.
*Cho.* Then happy those whom Fate, that is the stronger,
Together twists their threads, & yet draws hers the longer.

## Come Not To Me For Scarfs

Come not to me for scarfs, nor plumes,
Nor from the needy look for gould;
Incense wee have, but noe perfumes,
Nor noe such fleece in all our Fold,
As Jason wonn,
But wooll home spunn
To keepe us from the winters cold;
And when our garments should be thinne,
We leave the Fleece and take the skinn;

Which heere we neither pinke, nor race,
Unlesse a bramble or a thorne,
Deriding of the printers place,
Supply his offices in scorne;
Nor yet much lesse
Strive to possesse
Things that might be as well forborne.
What wee can spare, wee never lack;
A sheapheards wardrobe is his back.

COME NOT TO ME.
10 *pinke:* cut holes in (for ornamentation); *race:* cut or slash.
12 *printers:* the clothmaker who "prints" or stamps the garment.

Our roofes are low, our cabins small,
  Our loves, as well as loaves, are browne,
Yet soe contented there withall,
  Wee seeke noe finer in the towne;
        For thach and mudd
        Sometimes have stood,
  When lead and marble weare blowne downe,
And love, they say, as often rests
In sunnburnt, as in snowy breasts.

And by my sheapheards kalander,
  Tis love alone, thou com'st to seeke,
And our predictions seldome erre,
  For though unstudied in the Greeke
        Or Hebrew tongue,
        Sheapheards have sung
  Southsayings, which the learned like,
And I may hitt perhaps on this
Upon a trueth when doctors misse.

The pulcee of love beates in our eyes,
  And when that goes as quick as yours,
Admit the patient seldom dies,
  Experience noe such life assures;
        For as the stone
        Kills not alone,
  But Feavers frequently procures,
Which deaths sadd offices fullfill,
Soe love must cease, or death will kill.

Take but the country aire a while,
  And if thou wilt descend soe lowe,
To please thyne eare, wee'll raise our stile,
  Which soe refind perhaps may grow,

36 *doctors:* learned scholars.
37 *pulcee:* pulse.
41 *stone:* kidney disease.

Thy hearing sence
Shall not stirr hence,
Admit thyne eyes from court doe goe;
For every homely thing we have,
Att least in title, shalbe brave.

A mountaine toppe shalbe thy throne,
Thy Percian carpetts flowry feildes;
Thy cooch with green mosse over growne,
As unshorne velvet, summer yealds;
Thy lamp by night
The constant light,
That glisters, wher the gloworme builds,
Thy sparver a well tufted tree,
Ore heaven itselfe, thy canopy.

A larke shall call thee from thy rest,
And sing thee mattens every day;
The nightingall that warbells best
Shall vespers every evening saye;
The wise ant preach,
And bees shall teach
Us, how to rule, and to obaye;
A crane the watch and ward shall keepe,
And noe lambe bleat, to breake thy sleepe.

And if a Feather of Loves winges,
To slacken and retard his flight,
The goulden-headed shaft he brings,
Impoverishing his quiver quite,
The scarfe fame tyes
About his eyes,
Thy stepps may hitherward invite,
Thou mayst from this tyme forth dispose
Of him and us, and each of those.

62 *sparver:* a canopy for a bed.

Thou needes must thinke, I know full well
  Wher Love resides, that undertake
Without the helpe of charme, or spell,
  Hee shall soe quick appearance make,
      Yet thinke withall
      His power not small,
  That in the plurall number spake,
Though likely to be sick and ill,
Hee is so apt to make his will.

But as the wisest sorte dispose
  Of all they have in perfect health,
Least wayward sicknesse fancy those
  That are unworthy of their wealth,
      So passion free
      Doe I by thee,
  Scorning thou shouldst come in by stealth,
Or watch my weakenesse or a Fit
Of love, and soe inherite itt.

Att court new Fashions are not strange,
  But heere wee ever keepe our old;
There love (they say) consists in change,
  Heere, after one, all ours are told.
      The first is last,
      Because wee cast
  One hand can but another hold;
But they have loves, wee understand,
For every finger of the hand.

Brothers and sisters, cosens, freindes,
  And two scarce parted in the wombe
At court, for their peculiar ends,
  Hard by Loves cradle build their tombe.
      Heere hee survives
      Eyther two lives,

103 *after one:* directed towards one person.
105 *cast:* believe.

Or els Fills up an empty roome;
And after such a league beginns,
Though strangers borne, wee dye like twinns.

And after death the lowly mynde
And humble spirite raysed by grace
A place in glory sooner finde
Than they who vainely seeke a place.
Thou mayst soe caught
Perhapps be brought,
Though slow at first, to mend thy pace,
And cast thy purple roabes away,
To take a scripp and sheapheards grey.

## Pure Simple Love

Hide not thy love and myne shal bee
Open and free;
No mask dooth well upon thy face.
Lett those that meane more hurt provide
Love of a guide,
Or of some close retyring place.
A harmles kisse would make us thinck
Love hath no Nectar else to drinck.

Our loves are not of age to will
Both good and ill,
For thine, alas, is but new borne,
And myne is yett to yonge to speake.
How can they breake
Or hold Loves civill Lawes in skorne?
Wee might go naked if some spie,
Apt to traduce us, stood not by.

126 *scripp:* small bag carried by shepherds.

Had wee been that created paire,
Eve half so faire,
Or Adam lov'd but half so well,
The Serpent could have found no charme
To doe us harme,
Or had so much as tyme to tell
His tale to thee, or I to view
An apple where such cherries grew.

Yett had hee ledd mee to thy brest,
That waye was best
To have seduct mee from thy lipp.
Those apples tempt mee most; They bee
Fruit of that Tree,
That made our first forefathers slipp.
I dare not touch them least I dye
The death thou threatnest with thyne Eye.

Yett hee that meanes not to transgres
Needes fearr the lesse,
For what hath Justice heere to doe
But with her skales? Her sword may lye
As Useles by,
When shee comes downe to Judge us twoe;
For no persuations can infect
Thyne innocence or my respect.

If all the stings of envy laye
Strewde in our waye,
And tongues to tell of all wee did,
As our affection waxeth old,
Shall itt growe cold?
Loves Elementall fire forbid
Such frost and snowe, for past all doubt,
If our sparks dye, his fire will out.

Though thanckfull hands and eyes may prove
Cyphers of love,
Yett, till some figure bee prefixt,
As oos, by thousands or alone,
Stand all for none,
So, till our lookes and smiles bee mixt
With further meaning, they amount
To nothing by a just account.

How golden was that age that lett,
When Couples mett,
Theire lips and hands doe what they woulde,
Left out theire haires and more skinn bare,
Then now they dare;
For libertie misunderstood
Is counted lightnes, and when twoe
Maie doe amise, tis thought they doe.

Yett since there bee some people still,
That meane no ill,
The worlde is not so full of sinne,
Butt that wee maie finde some place yett
Proper and fitt
To act our mutuall friendship in,
And some Spectators to allowe
Of our old loving fashion now.

Then will I lay my cheeke to thyne,
And thou shalt twyne
Thy maiden armes about my neck,
And I will compas in thy waste
With arms as chaste,
And one anothers eyes bedeck
With little babies which shall bee
Our unpolluted progenee.

PURE SIMPLE LOVE.

50 *Cyphers:* symbols. The circle was often conceived of as the perfect figure.

Besides weele doe such childish things,
Though Love have wings,
Hee shal bee lothe to fly awaye;
And restles tyme, as lothe to passe
By with his glase,
Shall offer everie foote to staie;
One spinn, the next draw out our yeeres,
And the third Fate lett fall her sheeres.

If anie Lovers of one sort
Hether resort,
Theyll fitt them with our modest sceanes,
And prompted by a wanton eye
Quicklie discrye
Wee know not what such action meanes,
Butt runn awaye and leave the Stage
To them and this corrupted age.

And if her eyes, clearest and best
Of all the rest,
Surveigh theise Lynes tract with Loves dart,
Presume to ask her, ere you go,
Whether or no
Shee wilbe pleasd to act her part;
Which if shee be ashamd to doe,
Intreat her to excuse mee toe.

## A Paradox

There is no Lover hee or shee,
That ever was or can be false.
Tis passion or symplycitie
Or some Apostacie that calls

85 *glase:* hourglass.
99 *tract:* traced, written.

Those votaries, those dead folke soe;
For if we goe
To vowes, to prayers, to paines, to all
The penuries Monasticall,
No bare foote man,
Rock Hermitt or Carthusian,
Can in a course of life survive
More strict or more contemplative.

For till that sparke of fyre be out,
As holy men are not allow'd
Among the Saints nor goe aboute
To prove them selves in sufferance proud,
Soe was there never Lover found
But under ground;
And if he tooke the style before,
And name uncanonized wore,
People might say,
This Saint hath nere a holliday,
But like a bold, unbidden Guest,
Intrudes uppon anothers feaste.

What desperate challenger is he,
Before he vanish in his flame,
What ere his paines or patience be,
That dares assume a Martyrs name;
For all the way he goes he's none,
Till he be gone.
'Tis death, not dyeing, that must doe
This right to them and Lovers too,
Which they approve,
That make and marr the Lawes of love.
Yet better cheape can none acquire
This Crowne of thornes, this Robe of fire.

A PARADOX.

22 *nere:* never.
32 *right:* rite.
35 *better cheape:* at a cheaper price.

'Tis not a yeare will serve to trye
How weake ones faith is or how strong;
In this austere Societye
Probation lasts a whole life long.
No observation singlie vowd
Is here allow'd.
Two heartes must joyne and then those two
Must both alike beleeve and doe;
But as a twynn,
This colledge takes no fellow in;
At home, abroade, in all affaires,
They live, they dye, they goe, by payres.

And as two Turtells that have pearcht
And interchangd their fervent eyes,
When each in others bosome searcht,
If either Male or Female dyes
And the live Bird survyvith still
To prune and bill,
Not only this that never pynde
Is thought of some forgettfull kynde,
But that's denyde
To be a Turtle true that died;
So fares it here that past all doubt
Th'instinct of Love findes Lovers out.

Hard happ when death cannot assure
What our whole lives have deerely bought,
But we must Relatives procure
To Answer every Loving thought.
'Tis much to dye; 'tis more to fynde
Two of my minde.

49 *Turtells:* turtle doves.

# An Elegie Made by Mr Aurelian Townshend in Remembrance of the Ladie Venetia Digby

What Travellers of matchlesse Venice say,
Is true of thee, admir'd Venetia;
Hee that ner'e saw thee, wants beleife to reach
Halfe those perfections, thy first sight would teach.
Imagination can noe shape create
Aery enough thy forme to imitate;
Nor bedds of Roses, Damask, red, and white,
Render like thee a sweetnes to the sight.
Thou wer't eye-Musike, and no single part,
But beauties concert; Not one onely dart,
But loves whole quiver; no provinciall face,
But universall; Best in every place.
Thow wert not borne, as other women be,
To need the help of heightning Poesie,
But to make Poets. Hee, that could present
Thee like thy glasse, were superexcellent.
Witnesse that Pen which, prompted by thy parts
Of minde and bodie, caught as many heartes
With every line, as thou with every looke;
Which wee conceive was both his baite and hooke.
His Stile before, though it were perfect steele,
Strong, smooth, and sharp, and so could make us feele
His love or anger, Witnesses agree,
Could not attract, till it was toucht by thee.
Magneticke then, Hee was for heighth of style
Suppos'd in heaven; And so he was, the while

AN ELEGIE: The much celebrated Venetia Stanley (1600–1633) had married Sir Kenelm Digby (1603–1665) in 1625. Townshend's poem is the last item in a collection of poems in her honor.

17 *that Pen:* The poet referred to is Ben Jonson, whose "Eupheme" was written in Lady Digby's memory (*Poems*, ed. W. B. Hunter, Jr., pp. 250 ff.).

He sate and drewe thy beauties by the life,
Visible Angell, both as maide and wife.
In which estate thou did'st so little stay,
Thy noone and morning made but halfe a day;
Or halfe a yeare, or halfe of such an age
As thy complexion sweetly did presage,
An houre before those cheerfull beames were sett,
Made all men loosers, to paye Natures debt;
And him the greatest, that had most to doe,
Thy freind, companion, and copartner too,
Whose head since hanging on his pensive brest
Makes him looke just like one had bin possest
Of the whole world, and now hath lost it all.
Doctors to Cordialls, freinds to counsell fall.
Hee that all med'cines can exactly make,
And freely give them, wanting power to take,
Sitts and such Doses howerly doth dispense,
A man unlearn'd may rise a Doctor thence.
I that delight most in unusuall waies,
Seeke to asswage his sorrowe with thy praise,
Which if at first it swell him up with greife,
At last may drawe, and minister releife;
Or at the least, attempting it expresse
For an old debt a freindly thanckfulnesse.
I am no Herald! So ye can expect
From me no Crests or Scutcheons, that reflect
With brave Memorialls on her great Allyes;
Out of my reach that tree would quickly rise.
I onely stryve to doe her Fame som Right,
And walke her Mourner, in this Black and Whight.

# ROBERT HERRICK
1591–1674

## *The Argument of his Book*

I sing of *Brooks*, of *Blossomes, Birds*, and *Bowers:*
Of *April, May*, of *June*, and *July*-Flowers.
I sing of *May-poles, Hock-carts, Wassails, Wakes,*
Of *Bride-grooms, Brides*, and of their *Bridall-cakes.*
I write of *Youth*, of *Love*, and have Accesse
By these, to sing of cleanly-*Wantonnesse.*
I sing of *Dewes*, of *Raines*, and piece by piece
Of *Balme*, of *Oyle*, of *Spice*, and *Amber-Greece.*
I sing of *Times trans-shifting;* and I write
How *Roses* first came *Red*, and *Lillies White.*
I write of *Groves*, of *Twilights*, and I sing
The Court of *Mab*, and of the *Fairie-King.*
I write of *Hell;* I sing (and ever shall)
Of *Heaven*, and hope to have it after all.

## *To his Booke*

To read my Booke the Virgin shie
May blush, (while *Brutus* standeth by:)
But when He's gone, read through what's writ,
And never staine a cheeke for it.

THE ARGUMENT OF HIS BOOK.

3 *Hock-carts:* wagons which carried home the last of the harvest; *Wassails:* healths drunk at festivals.

8 *Amber-Greece:* ambergris.

12 *Mab:* Queen of the fairies, as in Mercutio's speech in *Romeo and Juliet.*

## *Another*

Who with thy leaves shall wipe (at need)
The place, where swelling *Piles* do breed:
May every Ill, that bites, or smarts,
Perplexe him in his hinder-parts.

## *To the soure Reader*

If thou dislik'st the Piece thou light'st on first;
Thinke that of All, that I have writ, the worst:
But if thou read'st my Booke unto the end,
And still do'st this, and that verse, reprehend:
O Perverse man! If All disgustfull be,
The Extreame Scabbe take thee, and thine, for me.

## *To* Perilla

Ah my Perilla! do'st thou grieve to see
Me, day by day, to steale away from thee?
Age cals me hence, and my gray haires bid come,
And haste away to mine eternal home;
'Twill not be long (*Perilla*) after this,
That I must give thee the *supremest* kisse:
Dead when I am, first cast in salt, and bring
Part of the creame from that *Religious Spring;*

TO THE SOURE READER.
6 *Scabbe:* ringworm or eczema.

TO PERILLA
8 *Religious Spring:* i.e. the "holy fountain" from which her tears will flow.

With which (*Perilla*) wash my hands and feet;
That done, then wind me in that very sheet
Which wrapt thy smooth limbs (when thou didst implore
The Gods protection, but the night before)
Follow me weeping to my Turfe, and there
Let fall a *Primrose,* and with it a teare:
Then lastly, let some weekly-strewings be
Devoted to the memory of me:
Then shall my *Ghost* not walk about, but keep
Still in the coole, and silent shades of sleep.

## *No Loathsomnesse in love*

What I fancy, I approve,
*No Dislike there is in love:*
Be my Mistresse short or tall,
And distorted there-withall:
Be she likewise one of those,
That an *Acre* hath of Nose:
Be her forehead, and her eyes
Full of incongruities:
Be her cheeks so shallow too,
As to shew her *Tongue* wag through:
Be her lips ill hung, or set,
And her grinders black as jet;
Ha's she thinne haire, hath she none,
She's to me a *Paragon.*

## *Love what it is*

Love is a circle that doth restlesse move
In the same sweet eternity of love.

TO PERILLA.
15 *weekly-strewings:* of flowers over his grave.
NO LOATHSOMNESSE.
12 *grinders:* teeth.

## *Upon the losse of his Mistresses*

I have lost, and lately, these
Many dainty Mistresses:
Stately *Julia*, prime of all;
*Sapho* next, a principall:
Smooth *Anthea*, for a skin
White, and Heaven-like Chrystalline:
Sweet *Electra*, and the choice
*Myrha*, for the Lute, and Voice.
Next, *Corinna*, for her wit,
And the graceful use of it:
With *Perilla:* All are gone;
Onely *Herrick's* left alone,
For to number sorrow by
Their departures hence, and die.

## *Discontents in Devon*

More discontents I never had
  Since I was born, then here;
Where I have been, and still am sad,
  In this dull *Devon-shire:*
Yet justly too I must confesse;
  I ne'r invented such
Ennobled numbers for the Presse,
  Then where I loath'd so much.

# TO THE KING,

## Upon his comming with his Army into the West

Welcome, most welcome to our Vowes and us,
Most great, and universall *Genius!*
The Drooping West, which hitherto has stood
As one, in long-lamented-widow-hood;
Looks like a Bride now, or a bed of flowers,
Newly refresh't, both by the Sun, and showers.
War, which before was horrid, now appears
Lovely in you, brave Prince of Cavaliers!
A deale of courage in each bosome springs
By your accesse; (*O you the best of Kings!*)
Ride on with all white *Omens;* so, that where
Your Standard's up, we fix a Conquest there.

TO THE KING: Charles I was at Exeter in the summer of 1644.
2 *Genius:* Guardian spirit of the place.
9 *deale:* large amount.
11 *white:* i.e. auspicious.

## *To the reverend shade of his religious Father*

That for seven *Lusters* I did never come
To doe the *Rites* to thy Religious Tombe:
That neither haire was cut, or true teares shed
By me, o'r thee, (*as justments to the dead*)
Forgive, forgive me; since I did not know
Whether thy bones had here their Rest, or no.
But now 'tis known, Behold; behold, I bring
Unto thy Ghost, th'Effused Offering:
And look, what Smallage, Night-shade, Cypresse, Yew,
Unto the shades have been, or now are due,
Here I devote; And something more then so;
I come to pay a Debt of Birth I owe.
Thou gav'st me life, (but Mortall;) For that one
Favour, Ile make full satisfaction;
For my life mortall, Rise from out thy Herse,
And take a life immortall from my Verse.

TO THE REVEREND: Herrick's father died on November 9, 1592, after falling out of a window of his house. The poet was then only fourteen months old.

1 *Lusters:* periods of five years. If literally accurate, this would place the composition of the poem in 1627.

4 *justments:* appropriate ceremonies.

9 *Smallage:* celery or parsley.

## *Delight in Disorder*

A Sweet disorder in the dresse
Kindles in cloathes a wantonnesse:
A Lawne about the shoulders thrown
Into a fine distraction:
An erring Lace, which here and there
Enthralls the Crimson Stomacher:
A Cuffe neglectfull, and thereby
Ribbands to flow confusedly:
A winning wave (deserving Note)
In the tempestuous petticote:
A carelesse shooe-string, in whose tye
I see a wilde civility:
Doe more bewitch me, then when Art
Is too precise in every part.

## *To* Dean-bourn, *a rude River in* Devon, *by which sometimes he lived*

*Dean-Bourn*, farewell; I never look to see
*Deane*, or thy warty incivility.
Thy rockie bottome, that doth teare thy streams,
And makes them frantick, ev'n to all extreames;
To my content, I never sho'd behold,
Were thy streames silver, or thy rocks all gold.
Rockie thou art; and rockie we discover
Thy men; and rockie are thy wayes all over.

DELIGHT IN DISORDER: For another treatment of this theme, see Jonson's song, "Still to be neat."

3 *Lawne:* piece of fine linen.

6 *Stomacher:* an ornamental covering worn under the lacing of the bodice.

O men, O manners; Now, and ever knowne
To be *A Rockie Generation!*
A people currish; churlish as the seas;
And rude (almost) as rudest Salvages
With whom I did, and may re-sojourne when
Rockes turn to Rivers, Rivers turn to Men.

## *Upon* Fone *a School-master. Epigram*

*Fone* sayes, those mighty whiskers he do's weare,
Are twigs of Birch, and willow, growing there:
If so, we'll think too, (when he do's condemne
Boyes to the lash) that he do's whip with them.

## *Upon* Scobble. *Epigram*

*Scobble* for Whoredome whips his wife; and cryes,
He'll slit her nose; But blubb'ring, she replyes,
Good Sir, make no more cuts i' th' outward skin,
One slit's enough to let Adultry in.

TO DEAN-BOURN.

9 *O men, O manners:* echoing Cicero's invective against Catiline, *O tempora, O mores.*

10 *Rockie Generation:* Jeremiah 5:3, "they have made their faces harder than a rock."

12 *Salvages:* savages.

# *His fare-well to Sack*

Farewell thou Thing, time-past so knowne, so deare
To me, as blood to life and spirit: Neare,
Nay, thou more neare then kindred, friend, man, wife,
Male to the female, soule to body: Life
To quick action, or the warme soft side
Of the resigning, yet resisting Bride.
The kisse of Virgins; First-fruits of the bed;
Soft speech, smooth touch, the lips, the Maiden-head:
These, and a thousand sweets, co'd never be
So neare, or deare, as thou wast once to me.
O thou the drink of Gods, and Angels! Wine
That scatter'st Spirit and Lust; whose purest shine,
More radiant then the Summers Sun-beams shows;
Each way illustrious, brave; and like to those
Comets we see by night; whose shagg'd portents
Fore-tell the comming of some dire events:
Or some full flame, which with a pride aspires,
Throwing about his wild, and active fires.
'Tis thou, above Nectar, O Divinest soule!
(Eternall in thy self) that canst controule
That, which subverts whole nature, grief and care;
Vexation of the mind, and damn'd Despaire.
'Tis thou, alone, who with thy Mistick Fan,
Work'st more then Wisdome, Art, or Nature can,
To rouze the sacred madnesse; and awake
The frost-bound-blood, and spirits; and to make
Them frantick with thy raptures, flashing through
The soule, like lightning, and as active too.

HIS FARE-WELL TO SACK.

12 *scatter'st:* disperses through the veins.

15 *shagg'd:* hairy.

23 *Mistick Fan:* used to winnow grain and carried in ceremonies honoring Bacchus.

'Tis not *Apollo* can, or those thrice three
*Castalian* Sisters, sing, if wanting thee.
*Horace, Anacreon* both had lost their fame,
Had'st thou not fill'd them with thy fire and flame.
*Phœbean* splendour! and thou *Thespian* spring!
Of which, sweet Swans must drink, before they sing
Their true-pac'd-Numbers, and their Holy-Layes,
Which makes them worthy *Cedar*, and the *Bayes*.
But why? why longer doe I gaze upon
Thee with the eye of admiration?
Since I must leave thee; and enforc'd, must say
To all thy witching beauties, Goe, Away.
But if thy whimpring looks doe ask me why?
Then know, that Nature bids thee goe, not I.
'Tis her erroneous self has made a braine
Uncapable of such a Soveraigne,
As is thy powerfull selfe. Prethee not smile;
Or smile more inly; lest thy looks beguile
My vowes denounc'd in zeale, which thus much show thee,
That I have sworn, but by thy looks to know thee.
Let others drink thee freely; and desire
Thee and their lips espous'd; while I admire,
And love thee; but not taste thee. Let my Muse
Faile of thy former helps; and onely use
Her inadult'rate strength: what's done by me
Hereafter, shall smell of the Lamp, not thee.

30 *Sisters:* the Nine Muses.
32 *Phoebean:* Apollo's (god of poetry); *Thespian:* Thespis was the reputed founder of Greek drama.
36 *Cedar:* oil of cedar was used to preserve manuscripts.
47 *denounc'd:* proclaimed.
53 *inadult'rate:* unadulterated.

# *Upon* Gryll

*Gryll* eates, but ne're sayes Grace; To speak the troth,
*Gryll* either keeps his breath to coole his broth;
Or else because *Grill's* roste do's burn his Spit,
*Gryll* will not therefore say a Grace for it.

# *The Vision*

Sitting alone (as one forsook)
Close by a Silver-shedding Brook;
With hands held up to Love, I wept;
And after sorrowes spent, I slept:
Then in a Vision I did see
A glorious forme appeare to me:
A Virgins face she had; her dresse
Was like a sprightly *Spartanesse*.
A silver bow with green silk strung,
Down from her comely shoulders hung:
And as she stood, the wanton Aire
Dandled the ringlets of her haire.
Her legs were such *Diana* shows,
When tuckt up she a hunting goes;
With Buskins shortned to descrie
The happy dawning of her thigh:
Which when I saw, I made accesse
To kisse that tempting nakednesse:

UPON GRYLL.

1 *Gryll:* In addition to the pun on "grill," Herrick perhaps employs the name as an echo of Spenser, *Faerie Queene,* II.xii,87: "Let Gryll be Gryll, and have his hoggish minde."

THE VISION

6 *forme:* Venus, as in Virgil's *Aeneid* I.315–20.

But she forbad me, with a wand
Of Mirtle she had in her hand:
And chiding me, said, Hence, Remove,
*Herrick,* thou art too coorse to love.

## Julia's *Petticoat*

Thy Azure Robe, I did behold,
As ayrie as the leaves of gold;
Which erring here, and wandring there,
Pleas'd with transgression ev'ry where:
Sometimes 'two'd pant, and sigh, and heave,
As if to stir it scarce had leave:
But having got it; thereupon,
'Two'd make a brave expansion.
And pounc't with Stars, it shew'd to me
Like a *Celestiall Canopie.*
Sometimes 'two'd blaze, and then abate,
Like to a flame growne moderate:
Sometimes away 'two'd wildly fling;
Then to thy thighs so closely cling,
That some conceit did melt me downe,
As Lovers fall into a swoone:
And all confus'd, I there did lie
Drown'd in Delights; but co'd not die.
That Leading Cloud, I follow'd still,
Hoping t'ave seene of it my fill;
But ah! I co'd not: sho'd it move
To Life Eternal, I co'd love.

JULIA'S PETTICOAT.

2 *leaves of gold:* presumably these were attached to the blue skirt.
9 *pounc't:* powdered.
15 *conceit:* fancy.

## Corinna's *going a Maying*

Get up, get up for shame, the Blooming Morne
Upon her wings presents the god unshorne.
See how *Aurora* throwes her faire
Fresh-quilted colours through the aire:
Get up, sweet-Slug-a-bed, and see
The Dew-bespangling Herbe and Tree.
Each Flower has wept, and bow'd toward the East,
Above an houre since; yet you not drest,
Nay! not so much as out of bed?
When all the Birds have Mattens seyd,
And sung their thankfull Hymnes: 'tis sin,
Nay, profanation to keep in,
When as a thousand Virgins on this day,
Spring, sooner then the Lark, to fetch in May.

Rise; and put on your Foliage, and be seene
To come forth, like the Spring-time, fresh and greene;
And sweet as *Flora*. Take no care
For Jewels for your Gowne, or Haire:
Feare not; the leaves will strew
Gemms in abundance upon you:
Besides, the childhood of the Day has kept,
Against you come, some *Orient Pearls* unwept:
Come, and receive them while the light
Hangs on the Dew-locks of the night:
And *Titan* on the Eastern hill
Retires himselfe, or else stands still

CORINNA'S GOING A MAYING.

2 *god unshorne:* Apollo, whose strength, like Samson's, is greatest when his fertile locks are uncut.

25 *Titan:* the sun-god.

Till you come forth. Wash, dresse, be briefe in praying:
Few Beads are best, when once we goe a Maying.

Come, my *Corinna*, come; and comming, marke
How each field turns a street; each street a Parke
Made green, and trimm'd with trees: see how
Devotion gives each House a Bough,
Or Branch: Each Porch, each doore, ere this,
An Arke a Tabernacle is
Made up of white-thorn neatly enterwove;
As if here were those cooler shades of love.
Can such delights be in the street,
And open fields, and we not see't?
Come, we'll abroad; and let's obay
The Proclamation made for May:
And sin no more, as we have done, by staying;
But my *Corinna*, come, let's goe a Maying.

There's not a budding Boy, or Girle, this day,
But is got up, and gone to bring in May.
A deale of Youth, ere this, is come
Back, and with *White-thorn* laden home.
Some have dispatcht their Cakes and Creame,
Before that we have left to dreame:
And some have wept, and woo'd, and plighted Troth,
And chose their Priest, ere we can cast off sloth:
Many a green-gown has been given;
Many a kisse, both odde and even:
Many a glance too has been sent
From out the eye, Loves Firmament:
Many a jest told of the Keyes betraying
This night, and Locks pickt, yet w'are not a Maying.

Come, let us goe, while we are in our prime;
And take the harmlesse follie of the time.

28 *Beads:* prayers.
45 *deale:* great many.

We shall grow old apace, and die
Before we know our liberty.
Our life is short; and our dayes run
As fast away as do's the Sunne:
And as a vapour, or a drop of raine
Once lost, can ne'r be found againe:
So when or you or I are made
A fable, song, or fleeting shade;
All love, all liking, all delight
Lies drown'd with us in endlesse night.
Then while time serves, and we are but decaying;
Come, my *Corinna*, come, let's goe a Maying.

## *Upon* Batt

*Batt* he gets children, not for love to reare 'em;
But out of hope his wife might die to beare 'em.

## *How Lillies came white*

White though ye be; yet, Lillies, know,
From the first ye were not so:
But Ile tell ye
What befell ye;
*Cupid* and his Mother lay
In a Cloud; while both did play,
He with his pretty finger prest
The rubie niplet of her breast;
Out of the which, the creame of light,
Like to a Dew,
Fell downe on you,
And made ye white.

## *The Lilly in a Christal*

You have beheld a smiling *Rose*
When Virgins hands have drawn
O'r it a Cobweb-Lawne:
And here, you see, this Lilly shows,
Tomb'd in a *Christal* stone,
More faire in this transparent case,
Then when it grew alone;
And had but single grace.

You see how *Creame* but naked is;
Nor daunces in the eye
Without a Strawberrie:
Or some fine tincture, like to this,
Which draws the sight thereto,
More by that wantoning with it;
Then when the paler hieu
No mixture did admit.

You see how *Amber* through the streams
More gently stroaks the sight,
With some conceal'd delight;
Then when he darts his radiant beams
Into the boundlesse aire:
Where either too much light his worth
Doth all at once impaire,
Or set it little forth.

Put Purple Grapes, or Cherries in-
To Glasse, and they will send
More beauty to commend
Them, from that cleane and subtile skin,

THE LILLY.
15 *hieu:* hue.

Then if they naked stood,
And had no other pride at all,
But their own flesh and blood,
And tinctures naturall.

Thus Lillie, Rose, Grape, Cherry, Creame,
And Straw-berry do stir
More love, when they transfer
A weak, a soft, a broken beame;
Then if they sho'd discover
At full their proper excellence;
Without some Scean cast over,
To juggle with the sense.

Thus let this *Christal'd Lillie* be
A Rule, how far to teach,
Your nakednesse must reach:
And that, no further, then we see
Those glaring colours laid
By Arts wise hand, but to this end
They sho'd obey a shade;
Lest they too far extend.

So though y'are white as Swan, or Snow,
And have the power to move
A world of men to love:
Yet, when your Lawns and Silks shal flow;
And that white cloud divide
Into a doubtful Twi-light; then,
Then will your hidden Pride
Raise greater fires in men.

39 *Scean:* veil.

## *Upon some women*

Thou who wilt not love, doe this;
Learne of me what Woman is.
Something made of thred and thrumme;
A meere Botch of all and some.
Pieces, patches, ropes of haire;
In-laid Garbage ev'ry where.
Out-side silk, and out-side Lawne;
Sceanes to cheat us neatly drawne.
False in legs, and false in thighes;
False in breast, teeth, haire, and eyes:
False in head, and false enough;
Onely true in shreds and stuffe.

## *The Welcome to Sack*

So soft streams meet, so springs with gladder smiles
Meet after long divorcement by the Iles:
When Love (the child of likenesse) urgeth on
Their Christal natures to an union.
So meet stolne kisses, when the Moonie nights
Call forth fierce Lovers to their wisht Delights:
So *Kings and Queens* meet, when Desire convinces
All thoughts, but such as aime at getting Princes,
A[s] I meet thee. Soule of my life, and fame!
Eternall Lamp of Love! whose radiant flame

UPON SOME WOMEN.
3 *thrumme:* a piece of waste yarn.
8 *Sceanes:* veils.

THE WELCOME TO SACK.
7 *convinces:* conquers.

Out-glares the Heav'ns *Osiris;* and thy gleams
Out-shine the splendour of his mid-day beams.
Welcome, O welcome my illustrious Spouse;
Welcome as are the ends unto my Vowes:
I! far more welcome then the happy soile,
The Sea-scourg'd Merchant, after all his toile,
Salutes with tears of joy; when fires betray
The smoakie chimneys of his *Ithaca.*
Where hast thou been so long from my embraces,
Poore pittyed Exile? Tell me, did thy Graces
Flie discontented hence, and for a time
Did rather choose to blesse another clime?
Or went'st thou to this end, the more to move me,
By thy short absence, to desire and love thee?
Why frowns my Sweet? Why won't my Saint confer
Favours on me, her fierce Idolater?
Why are Those Looks, Those Looks the which have been
Time-past so fragrant, sickly now drawn in
Like a dull Twi-light? Tell me; and the fault
Ile expiate with Sulphur, Haire, and Salt:
And with the Christal humour of the spring,
Purge hence the guilt, and kill this quarrelling.
Wo't thou not smile, or tell me what's amisse?
Have I been cold to hug thee, too remisse,
Too temp'rate in embracing? Tell me, ha's desire
To thee-ward dy'd i'th'embers, and no fire
Left in this rak't-up Ash-heap, as a mark
To testifie the glowing of a spark?
Have I divorc't thee onely to combine
In hot Adult'ry with another Wine?
True, I confesse I left thee, and appeale
'Twas done by me, more to confirme my zeale,

11 *Heav'ns Osiris:* the sun (Herrick's note).
18 *Ithaca:* Ulysses' kingdom, to which he returned after twenty years of wandering.
31 *Christal humour:* water.
41 *I left thee:* See above, "His fare-well to Sack."

And double my affection on thee; as doe those,
Whose love growes more enflam'd, by being Foes.
But to forsake thee ever, co'd there be
A thought of such like possibilitie?
When thou thy selfe dar'st say, thy Iles shall lack
Grapes, before *Herrick* leaves Canarie Sack.
Thou mak'st me ayrie, active to be born,
Like *Iphyclus,* upon the tops of Corn.
Thou mak'st me nimble, as the winged howers,
To dance and caper on the heads of flowers,
And ride the Sun-beams. Can there be a thing
Under the heavenly *Isis,* that can bring
More love unto my life, or can present
My *Genius* with a fuller blandishment?
Illustrious Idoll! co'd th'*AEgyptians* seek
Help from the *Garlick, Onyon,* and the *Leek,*
And pay no vowes to thee? who wast their best
God, and far more transcendent then the rest?
Had *Cassius,* that weak Water-drinker, known
Thee in thy Vine, or had but tasted one
Small Chalice of thy frantick liquor; He
As the wise *Cato* had approv'd of thee.
Had not *Joves* son, that brave *Tyrinthian* Swain,
(Invited to the *Thesbian* banquet) ta'ne
Full goblets of thy gen'rous blood; his spright
Ne'r had kept heat for fifty Maids that night.
Come, come and kisse me; Love and lust commends
Thee, and thy beauties; kisse, we will be friends
Too strong for Fate to break us: Look upon
Me, with that full pride of complexion,

50 *Iphyclus:* a Greek hero, so fleet a runner that he skimmed over the fields.

51 *howers:* goddesses of the seasons.

54 *Isis:* the moon (Herrick's note).

61 *Cassius:* Brutus' co-conspirator against Caesar.

64 *Cato:* Cato the Censor (234–149 B.C.), who wrote a treatise on grape-growing and winemaking.

65 *Joves son:* Hercules, whose father ruled Tiryนthus, in Argolis. Thespius had fifty daughters.

As *Queenes,* meet *Queenes;* or come thou unto me,
As *Cleopatra* came to *Anthonie;*
When her high carriage did at once present
To the *Triumvir,* Love and Wonderment.
Swell up my nerves with spirit; let my blood
Run through my veines, like to a hasty flood.
Fill each part full of fire, active to doe
What thy commanding soule shall put it to.
And till I turne Apostate to thy love,
Which here I vow to serve, doe not remove
Thy Fiers from me; but *Apollo's* curse
Blast these-like actions, or a thing that's worse;
When these Circumstants shall but live to see
The time that I prevaricate from thee.
Call me *The sonne of Beere,* and then confine
Me to the Tap, the Tost, the Turfe; Let Wine
Ne'r shine upon me; May my Numbers all
Run to a sudden Death, and Funerall.
And last, when thee (deare Spouse) I disavow,
Ne'r may Prophetique *Daphne* crown my Brow.

## *To live merrily, and to trust to Good Verses*

Now is the time for mirth,
    Nor cheek, or tongue be dumbe:
For with the flowrie earth,
    The golden pomp is come.

85 *Circumstants:* bystanders.
88 *Tost:* bread dipped in beer; *Turfe:* He will be earthbound without wine.
92 *Daphne:* the laurel, into which Apollo transformed her. Poets were crowned with laurel wreaths.

The golden Pomp is come;
  For now each tree do's weare
(Made of her Pap and Gum)
  Rich beads of *Amber* here.

Now raignes the *Rose,* and now
  Th'*Arabian* Dew besmears
My uncontrolled brow,
  And my retorted haires.

*Homer,* this Health to thee,
  In Sack of such a kind,
That it wo'd make thee see,
  Though thou wert ne'r so blind.

Next, *Virgil,* Ile call forth,
  To pledge this second Health
In Wine, whose each cup's worth
  An Indian Common-wealth.

A Goblet next Ile drink
  To *Ovid;* and suppose,
Made he the pledge, he'd think
  The world had all *one Nose.*

Then this immensive cup
  Of *Aromatike* wine,
*Catullus,* I quaffe up
  To that Terce Muse of thine.

Wild I am now with heat;
  O *Bacchus!* coole thy Raies!
Or frantick I shall eate
  Thy *Thyrse,* and bite the *Bayes.*

TO LIVE MERRILY.

12 *retorted:* bent backwards.
24 *Nose:* a pun on Ovid's full name, Publius Ovidius Naso.
32 *Thyrse:* Bacchus' rod.

Round, round, the roof do's run;
  And being ravisht thus,
Come, I will drink a Tun
  To my *Propertius.*

Now, to *Tibullus,* next,
  This flood I drink to thee:
But stay; I see a Text,
  That this presents to me.

Behold, *Tibullus* lies
  Here burnt, whose smal return
Of ashes, scarce suffice
  To fill a little Urne.

Trust to good Verses then;
  They onely will aspire,
When Pyramids, as men,
  Are lost, i' th' funerall fire.

And when all Bodies meet
  In *Lethe* to be drown'd;
Then onely Numbers sweet,
  With endless life are crown'd.

## *To the Virgins, to make much of Time*

1. Gather ye Rose-buds while ye may,
  Old Time is still a flying:
And this same flower that smiles today,
  To morrow will be dying.

39 *Text:* two lines from Ovid (*Amores* III.9.39–40), which are translated in the next stanza.

2. The glorious Lamp of Heaven, the Sun,
   The higher he's a getting;
The sooner will his Race be run,
   And neerer he's to Setting.

3. That Age is best, which is the first,
   When Youth and Blood are warmer;
But being spent, the worse, and worst
   Times, still succeed the former.

4. Then be not coy, but use your time;
   And while ye may, goe marry:
For having lost but once your prime,
   You may for ever tarry.

## *His Poetrie his Pillar*

1. Onely a little more
   I have to write,
   Then Ile give o're,
And bid the world Good-night.

2. 'Tis but a flying minute,
   That I must stay,
   Or linger in it;
And then I must away.

3. O time that cut'st down all!
   And scarce leav'st here
   Memoriall
Of any men that were.

4. How many lye forgot
   In Vaults beneath?
   And piece-meale rot
Without a fame in death?

5. Behold this living stone,
   I reare for me,
   Ne'r to be thrown
Downe, envious Time by thee.

6. Pillars let some set up,
   (If so they please)
   Here is my hope,
And my *Pyramides.*

## *Upon* Sudds *a Laundresse*

*Sudds* Launders Bands in pisse; and starches them
Both with her Husband's, and her own tough fleame.

## *The Hock-cart,* or *Harvest home: To the Right Honourable,* Mildmay, *Earle of* Westmoreland

Come Sons of Summer, by whose toile,
We are the Lords of Wine and Oile:
By whose tough labours, and rough hands,
We rip up first, then reap our lands.
Crown'd with the eares of corne, now come,
And, to the Pipe, sing Harvest home.
Come forth, my Lord, and see the Cart
Drest up with all the Country Art.

UPON SUDDS A LAUNDRESSE.
1 *Bands:* collars.
2 *fleame:* phlegm.

See, here a *Maukin*, there a sheet,
As spotlesse pure, as it is sweet:
The Horses, Mares, and frisking Fillies,
(Clad, all, in Linnen, white as Lillies.)
The Harvest Swaines, and Wenches bound
For joy, to see the *Hock-cart* crown'd.
About the Cart, heare, how the Rout
Of Rurall Younglings raise the shout;
Pressing before, some coming after,
Those with a shout, and these with laughter.
Some blesse the Cart; some kisse the sheaves;
Some prank them up with Oaken leaves:
Some crosse the Fill-horse; some with great
Devotion, stroak the home-borne wheat:
While other Rusticks, lesse attent
To Prayers, then to Merryment,
Run after with their breeches rent.
Well, on, brave boyes, to your Lords Hearth,
Glitt'ring with fire; where, for your mirth,
Ye shall see first the large and cheefe
Foundation of your Feast, Fat Beefe:
With Upper Stories, Mutton, Veale
And Bacon, (which makes full the meale)
With sev'rall dishes standing by,
As here a Custard, there a Pie,
And here all tempting Frumentie.
And for to make the merry cheere,
If smirking Wine be wanting here,
There's that, which drowns all care, stout Beere;
Which freely drink to your Lords health,
Then to the Plough, (the Common-wealth)

THE HOCK-CART: Mildmay Fane, second Earl of Westmoreland (d. 1666).
9 *Maukin:* scarecrow or other grotesque effigy.
21 *crosse the Fill-horse:* sit on the shaft horse.
34 *Frumentie:* sweet pudding made of wheat and milk.

Next to your Flailes, your Fanes, your Fatts;
Then to the Maids with Wheaten Hats:
To the rough Sickle, and crookt Sythe,
Drink frollick boyes, till all be blythe.
Feed, and grow fat; and as ye eat,
Be mindfull, that the lab'ring Neat
(As you) may have their fill of meat.
And know, besides, ye must revoke
The patient Oxe unto the Yoke,
And all goe back unto the Plough
And Harrow, (though they'r hang'd up now.)
And, you must know, your Lords word's true,
Feed him ye must, whose food fils you.
And that this pleasure is like raine,
Not sent ye for to drowne your paine,
But for to make it spring againe.

## *To Primroses fill'd with morning-dew*

1. Why doe ye weep, sweet Babes? can Tears
Speak griefe in you,
Who were but borne
Just as the modest Morne
Teem'd her refreshing dew?
Alas you have not known that shower,
That marres a flower;
Nor felt th'unkind
Breath of a blasting wind;
Nor are ye worne with yeares;
Or warpt, as we,
Who think it strange to see,

40 *Fanes:* fans for winnowing grain; *Fatts:* vats, barrels.
45 *Neat:* cattle.
47 *revoke:* call back.

Such pretty flowers, (like to Orphans young)
To speak by Teares, before ye have a Tongue.

2. Speak, whimp'ring Younglings, and make known
The reason, why
Ye droop, and weep;
Is it for want of sleep?
Or childish Lullabie?
Or that ye have not seen as yet
The *Violet?*
Or brought a kisse
From that Sweet-heart, to this?
No, no, this sorrow shown
By your teares shed,
Wo'd have this Lecture read,
That things of greatest, so of meanest worth,
Conceiv'd with grief are, and with teares brought forth.

## *To* Anthea, *who may command him any thing*

1. Bid me to live, and I will live
Thy Protestant to be:
Or bid me love, and I will give
A loving heart to thee.

2. A heart as soft, a heart as kind,
A heart as sound and free,
As in the whole world thou canst find,
That heart Ile give to thee.

TO ANTHEA.
2 *Protestant:* suitor, who solemnly proclaims his love.

3. Bid that heart stay, and it will stay,
To honour thy Decree:
Or bid it languish quite away,
And't shall doe so for thee.

4. Bid me to weep, and I will weep,
While I have eyes to see:
And having none, yet I will keep
A heart to weep for thee.

5. Bid me despaire, and Ile despaire,
Under that *Cypresse* tree:
Or bid me die, and I will dare
E'en Death, to die for thee.

6. Thou art my life, my love, my heart,
The very eyes of me:
And hast command of every part,
To live and die for thee.

## *To Daffadills*

1. Faire Daffadills, we weep to see
You haste away so soone:
As yet the early-rising Sun
Has not attain'd his Noone.
Stay, stay,
Untill the hasting day
Has run
But to the Even-song;
And, having pray'd together, we
Will goe with you along.

2. We have short time to stay, as you,
We have as short a Spring;
As quick a growth to meet Decay,
As you, or any thing.
We die,
As your hours doe, and drie
Away,
Like to the Summers raine;
Or as the pearles of Mornings dew
Ne'r to be found againe.

## *To* Dianeme

Shew me thy feet; shew me thy legs, thy thighes;
Shew me Those *Fleshie Principalities;*
Shew me that Hill (where smiling Love doth sit)
Having a living Fountain under it.
Shew me thy waste; Then let me there withall,
By the *Assention* of thy Lawn, see All.

## *Upon Parson* Beanes

Old Parson *Beanes* hunts six dayes of the week,
And on the seaventh, he has his Notes to seek.
Six dayes he hollows so much breath away,
That on the seaventh, he can nor preach, or pray.

TO DIANEME.

6 *Assention:* Herrick puns on "assent" and "ascension."

UPON PARSON BEANES

3 *hollows:* halloos (in the hunt), with a play upon "hallows" (makes holy).

## *To the Water Nymphs, drinking at the Fountain*

1. Reach, with your whiter hands, to me,
Some Christall of the Spring;
And I, about the Cup shall see
Fresh Lillies flourishing.

2. Or else sweet Nimphs do you but this;
To'th' Glasse your lips encline;
And I shall see by that one kisse,
The Water turn'd to Wine.

## *Upon* Jack *and* Jill. *Epigram*

When *Jill* complaines to *Jack* for want of meate;
*Jack* kisses *Jill,* and bids her freely eate:
*Jill* sayes, of what? sayes *Jack,* on that sweet kisse,
Which full of Nectar and Ambrosia is,
The food of Poets; so I thought sayes *Jill,*
That makes them looke so lanke, so Ghost-like still.
Let Poets feed on aire, or what they will;
Let me feed full, till that I fart, sayes *Jill.*

TO THE WATER NYMPHS: For the meter and the theme, cf. Jonson's "Drinke to me, onely, with thine eyes."

## *Art above Nature, to* Julia

When I behold a Forrest spread
With silken trees upon thy head;
And when I see that other Dresse
Of flowers set in comlinesse:
When I behold another grace
In the ascent of curious Lace,
Which like a Pinacle doth shew
The top, and the top-gallant too.
Then, when I see thy Tresses bound
Into an Ovall, square, or round;
And knit in knots far more then I
Can tell by tongue; or true-love tie:
Next, when those Lawnie Filmes I see
Play with a wild civility:
And all those airie silks to flow,
Alluring me, and tempting so:
I must confesse, mine eye and heart
Dotes less on Nature, then on Art.

ART ABOVE NATURE.
8 *top . . . top-gallant:* shows the platforms at the top of the highest and second highest masts.

## *The Apparition of his Mistresse calling him to* Elizium

*Desunt nonnulla*——

Come then, and like two Doves with silv'rie wings,
Let our soules flie to' th' shades, where ever springs
Sit smiling in the Meads; where Balme and Oile,
Roses and Cassia crown the untill'd soyle.
Where no disease raignes, or infection comes
To blast the Aire, but *Amber-greece* and *Gums*.
This, that, and ev'ry Thicket doth transpire
More sweet, then *Storax* from the hallowed fire:
Where ev'ry tree a wealthy issue beares
Of fragrant Apples, blushing Plums, or Peares:
And all the shrubs, with sparkling spangles, shew
Like Morning-Sun-shine tinsilling the dew.
Here in green Meddowes sits eternall May,
Purfling the Margents, while perpetuall Day
So double gilds the Aire, as that no night
Can ever rust th'Enamel of the light.
Here, naked Younglings, handsome Striplings run
Their Goales for Virgins kisses; which when done,
Then unto Dancing forth the learned Round
Commixt they meet, with endlesse Roses crown'd.
And here we'l sit on Primrose-banks, and see
Love's *Chorus* led by *Cupid;* and we'l be

THE APPARITION: *Desunt nonnulla,* i.e. some things are lacking; the poem is not complete.

8 *Storax:* gum from a Syrian tree.

14 *Purfling:* adorning; *Margents:* edges.

Two loving followers too unto the Grove,
Where Poets sing the stories of our love.
There thou shalt hear Divine *Musæus* sing
Of *Hero,* and *Leander;* then Ile bring
Thee to the Stand, where honour'd *Homer* reades
His *Odisees,* and his high *Iliades.*
About whose Throne the crowd of Poets throng
To heare the incantation of his tongue:
To *Linus,* then to *Pindar;* and that done,
Ile bring thee *Herrick* to *Anacreon,*
Quaffing his full-crown'd bowles of burning Wine,
And in his Raptures speaking Lines of Thine,
Like to His subject; and as his Frantick-
Looks, shew him truly *Bacchanalian* like,
Besmear'd with Grapes; welcome he shall thee thither,
Where both may rage, both drink and dance together.
Then stately *Virgil,* witty *Ovid,* by
Whom faire *Corinna* sits, and doth comply
With Yvorie wrists, his Laureat head, and steeps
His eye in dew of kisses, while he sleeps.
Then soft *Catullus,* sharp-fang'd *Martial,*
And towring *Lucan, Horace, Juvenal,*
And Snakie *Perseus,* these, and those, whom Rage
(Dropt from the jarres of heaven) fill'd t'engage
All times unto their frenzies; Thou shalt there
Behold them in a spacious Theater.
Among which glories, (crown'd with sacred Bayes,
And flatt'ring Ivie) Two recite their Plaies,
*Beumont* and *Fletcher,* Swans, to whom all eares
Listen, while they (like Syrens in their Spheres)

25–26: Cf. Marlowe, *Hero and Leander,* lines 51–52: "Amorous Leander, beautiful and young, / (Whose tragedy divine Musaeus sung)."

31 *Linus:* the reputed inventor of Greek verse.

40 *comply:* embrace.

45 *Snakie:* tortuous.

52 *Syrens:* musical guardians of the celestial spheres.

Sing their *Evadne;* and still more for thee
There yet remaines to know, then thou can'st see
By glim'ring of a fancie: Doe but come,
And there Ile shew thee that capacious roome
In which thy Father *Johnson* now is plac't,
As in a Globe of Radiant fire, and grac't
To be in that Orbe crown'd (that doth include
Those Prophets of the former Magnitude)
And he one chiefe; But harke, I heare the Cock,
(The Bell-man of the night) proclaime the clock
Of late struck one; and now I see the prime
Of Day break from the pregnant East, 'tis time
I vanish; more I had to say;
But Night determines here, Away.

## *His Prayer to* Ben. Johnson

1. When I a Verse shall make,
Know I have praid thee,
For old *Religions* sake,
Saint *Ben* to aide me.

2. Make the way smooth for me,
When I, thy *Herrick*,
Honouring thee, on my knee
Offer my *Lyrick*.

3. Candles Ile give to thee,
And a new Altar;
And thou Saint *Ben*, shalt be
Writ in my *Psalter*.

53 *Evadne:* heroine in Beaumont and Fletcher's *The Maid's Tragedy.*
57 *Johnson:* here, as elsewhere, Herrick views himself as a "Son of Ben."
HIS PRAYER TO BEN. JOHNSON.
3 *old Religions sake:* Herrick's phrase both presents an ideal of classical *pietas*, or duty, and whimsically apologizes for the many echoes of Roman Catholicism (England's "old Religion") which permeate his little prayer.

## *The bad season makes the Poet sad*

Dull to my selfe, and almost dead to these
My many fresh and fragrant Mistresses:
Lost to all Musick now; since every thing
Puts on the semblance here of sorrowing.
Sick is the Land to'th'heart; and doth endure
More dangerous faintings by her desp'rate cure.
But if that golden Age wo'd come again,
And *Charles* here Rule, as he before did Raign;
If smooth and unperplext the Seasons were,
As when the *Sweet Maria* lived here:
I sho'd delight to have my Curles halfe drown'd
In *Tyrian Dewes*, and Head with Roses crown'd.
And once more yet (ere I am laid out dead)
*Knock at a Starre with my exalted Head.*

## *The Night-piece, to* Julia

1. Her Eyes the Glow-worme lend thee,
The Shooting Starres attend thee;
And the Elves also,
Whose little eyes glow,
Like the sparks of fire, befriend thee.

2. No *Will-o'th'-Wispe* mis-light thee;
Nor Snake, or Slow-worme bite thee:

THE BAD SEASON MAKES THE POET SAD.

14 *Knock . . . Head:* Directly echoing Horace *Odes* I.i, "sublimi feriam sidera vertice." *Maria* in line 10 is Henrietta Maria, Queen of Charles I.

THE NIGHT-PIECE, TO JULIA.

7 *Slow-worme:* harmless lizard or blindworm, but the older meaning, *adder,* is probably intended.

But on, on thy way
Not making a stay,
Since Ghost ther's none to affright thee.

3. Let not the darke thee cumber;
What though the Moon do's slumber?
The Starres of the night
Will lend thee their light,
Like Tapers cleare without number.

4. Then *Julia* let me wooe thee,
Thus, thus to come unto me:
And when I shall meet
Thy silv'ry feet,
My soule Ile poure into thee.

## *Upon* Jone *and* Jane

*Jone* is a wench that's painted;
*Jone* is a Girle that's tainted;
Yet *Jone* she goes
Like one of those
Whom purity had Sainted.

*Jane* is a Girle that's prittie;
*Jane* is a wench that's wittie;
Yet, who wo'd think,
Her breath do's stinke,
As so it doth? that's pittie.

## *To* Master Denham, *on his Prospective Poem*

Or lookt I back unto the Times hence flown,
To praise those Muses, and dislike our own?
Or did I walk those *Pean*-Gardens through,
To kick the Flow'rs, and scorn their odours too?
I might (and justly) be reputed (here)
One nicely mad, or peevishly severe.
But by *Apollo!* as I worship wit,
(Where I have cause to burn perfumes to it:)
So, I confesse, 'tis somwhat to do well
In our high art, although we can't excell,
Like thee; or dare the Buskins to unloose
Of thy brave, bold, and sweet *Maronian* Muse.
But since I'm cal'd (rare *Denham*) to be gone,
Take from thy *Herrick* this conclusion:
'Tis dignity in others, if they be
Crown'd Poets; yet live Princes under thee:
The while their wreaths and Purple Robes do shine,
Lesse by their own jemms, then those beams of thine.

TO MASTER DENHAM, ON HIS PROSPECTIVE POEM: Denham's *Cooper's Hill* was first published in 1642.

1 *Or:* Either.

3 *Pean-Gardens:* Either gardens in which black earth is powdered with yellow flowers (an heraldic allusion) or *Paean* as a song of Apollo, appropriate in the *Hesperides,* which form a kind of garden sacred to the god of poetry.

6 *nicely:* quaintly. The poet would be an odd kind of madman if he disliked both past and present verse.

12 *Maronian:* Virgilian.

## *The Funerall Rites of the Rose*

The Rose was sick, and smiling di'd;
And (being to be sanctifi'd)
About the Bed, there sighing stood
The sweet, and flowrie Sisterhood.
Some hung the head, while some did bring
(To wash her) water from the Spring.
Some laid her forth, while other wept,
But all a solemne Fast there kept.
The holy Sisters some among
The sacred *Dirge* and *Trentall* sung.
But ah! what sweets smelt every where,
As Heaven had spent all perfumes there.
At last, when prayers for the dead,
And Rites were all accomplished;
They, weeping, spread a Lawnie Loome,
And clos'd her up, as in a Tombe.

## *His returne to London*

From the dull confines of the drooping West,
To see the day spring from the pregnant East,
Ravisht in spirit, I come, nay more, I flie
To thee, blest place of my Nativitie!
Thus, thus with hallowed foot I touch the ground,
With thousand blessings by thy Fortune crown'd.
O fruitfull Genius! that bestowest here
An everlasting plenty, yeere by yeere.

THE FUNERALL RITES OF THE ROSE.

10 *Dirge:* funeral song; *Trentall:* originally, a series of thirty masses said for the repose of the soul. Herrick uses the word to mean *elegy* or funeral hymn.

O *Place!* O *People!* Manners! fram'd to please
All *Nations, Customes, Kindreds, Languages!*
I am a free-born *Roman;* suffer then,
That I amongst you live a Citizen.
London my home is: though by hard fate sent
Into a long and irksome banishment;
Yet since cal'd back; henceforward let me be,
O native countrey, repossest by thee!
For, rather then I'le to the West return,
I'le beg of thee first here to have mine Urn.
Weak I am grown, and must in short time fall;
Give thou my sacred Reliques Buriall.

## *His Grange, or private wealth*

Though Clock,
To tell how night drawes hence, I've none,
A Cock,
I have, to sing how day drawes on.
I have
A maid (my *Prew*) by good luck sent,
To save
That little, Fates me gave or lent.
A Hen
I keep, which creeking day by day,
Tells when
She goes her long white egg to lay.
A goose
I have, which, with a jealous eare,
Lets loose
Her tongue, to tell what danger's neare.
A Lamb
I keep (tame) with my morsells fed,
Whose Dam
An Orphan left him (lately dead.)

HIS GRANGE, OR PRIVATE WEALTH: Herrick's *grange* was his country residence, the vicarage at Dean Prior.

A Cat
I keep, that playes about my House,
Grown fat,
With eating many a miching Mouse.
To these
A *Trasy* I do keep, whereby
I please
The more my rurall privacie:
Which are
But toyes, to give my heart some ease:
Where care
None is, slight things do lightly please.

## *Love dislikes nothing*

Whatsoever thing I see,
Rich or poore although it be;
'Tis a Mistresse unto mee.

Be my Girle, or faire or browne,
Do's she smile, or do's she frowne:
Still I write a Sweet-heart downe.

Be she rough, or smooth of skin;
When I touch, I then begin
For to let Affection in.

Be she bald, or do's she weare
Locks incurl'd of other haire;
I shall find enchantment there.

24 *miching:* thieving.
26 *Trasy:* as Herrick notes, his spaniel.
32 *lightly:* easily.

Be she whole, or be she rent,
So my fancie be content,
She's to me most excellent.

Be she fat, or be she leane,
Be she sluttish, be she cleane,
I'm a man for ev'ry Sceane.

## *Upon* Julia's *Clothes*

When as in silks my *Julia* goes,
Then, then (me thinks) how sweetly flowes
That liquefaction of her clothes.

Next, when I cast mine eyes and see
That brave Vibration each way free;
O how that glittering taketh me!

## *Ceremonies for Christmasse*

Come, bring with a noise,
My merrie merrie boyes,
The Christmas Log to the firing;
While my good Dame, she
Bids ye all be free;
And drink to your hearts desiring.

With the last yeeres brand
Light the new block, And
For good successe in his spending,

CEREMONIES FOR CHRISTMASSE.
9 *spending:* consuming.

On your Psaltries play,
That sweet luck may
Come while the Log is a teending.

Drink now the strong Beere,
Cut the white loafe here,
The while the meat is a shredding;
For the rare Mince-Pie
And the Plums stand by
To fill the Paste that's a kneading.

## *An Ode for him*

Ah *Ben!*
Say how, or when
Shall we thy Guests
Meet at those *Lyrick* Feasts,
Made at the *Sun,*
The *Dog,* the triple *Tunne?*
Where we such clusters had,
As made us nobly wild, not mad;
And yet each Verse of thine
Out-did the meate, out-did the frolick wine.

My *Ben*
Or come agen:
Or send to us,
Thy wits great over-plus;
But teach us yet
Wisely to husband it;

10 *Psaltries:* harplike instruments.
12 *teending:* kindling.
AN ODE FOR HIM: *him* is Ben Jonson.
5–6 *Sun . . . Tunne:* the names of London taverns.

Lest we that Tallent spend:
And having once brought to an end
That precious stock; the store
Of such a wit the world sho'd have no more.

## TO THE KING,

## *Upon his welcome to* Hampton-Court

*Set and Sung.*

Welcome, *Great Cesar,* welcome now you are,
As dearest Peace, after destructive Warre:
Welcome as slumbers; or as beds of ease
After our long, and peevish sicknesses.
O *Pompe of Glory!* Welcome now, and come
To re-possess once more your long'd-for home.
A thousand Altars smoake; a thousand thighes
Of Beeves here ready stand for Sacrifice.
Enter and prosper, while our eyes doe waite
For an *Ascendent* throughly *Auspicate:*
Under which signe we may the former stone
Lay of our safeties new foundation:
That done; *O Cesar,* live, and be to us,
Our *Fate,* our *Fortune,* and our *Genius;*
To whose free knees we may our temples tye
As to a still protecting Deitie.

TO THE KING: Charles I, the army's prisoner, was moved to Hampton Court on August 24, 1647. He still hoped to gain a favorable settlement which would restore him to power. There is no extant evidence to verify the statement that Herrick's poem was "Set and Sung."

10 *Ascendent . . . Auspicate:* a zodiacal sign that would be completely auspicious.

That sho'd you stirre, we and our Altars too
May (*Great Augustus*) *goe along with You.*
*Chor.* Long live the King; and to accomplish this,
We'l from our owne, adde far more years to his.

## *The pillar of Fame*

Fames pillar here, at last, we set,
Out-during *Marble, Brasse,* or *Jet,*
Charm'd and enchanted so,
As to withstand the blow
Of overthrow:
Nor shall the seas,
Or OUTRAGES
Of storms orebear
What we up-rear,
Tho Kingdoms fal,
This pillar never shall
Decline or waste at all;
But stand for ever by his owne
Firme and well fixt foundation.

To his Book's end this last line he'd have plac't,
*Jocond his Muse was; but his Life was chast.*

THE PILLAR OF FAME.

2 *Out-during:* outlasting. This poem and the following couplet are the last two poems in the *Hesperides*. The remaining selections are from Herrick's companion volume, *Noble Numbers.*

## *His Prayer for Absolution*

For Those my unbaptized Rhimes,
Writ in my wild unhallowed Times;
For every sentence, clause and word,
That's not inlaid with Thee, (my Lord)
Forgive me God, and blot each Line
Out of my Book, that is not Thine.
But if, 'mongst all, thou find'st here one
Worthy thy Benediction;
That One of all the rest, shall be
The Glory of my Work, and Me.

## *His Letanie, to the Holy Spirit*

1. In the houre of my distresse,
When temptations me oppresse,
And when I my sins confesse,
Sweet Spirit comfort me!

2. When I lie within my bed,
Sick in heart, and sick in head,
And with doubts discomforted,
Sweet Spirit comfort me!

3. When the house doth sigh and weep,
And the world is drown'd in sleep,
Yet mine eyes the watch do keep;
Sweet Spirit comfort me!

4. When the artlesse Doctor sees
No one hope, but of his Fees,
And his skill runs on the lees;
Sweet Spirit comfort me!

5. When his Potion and his Pill,
His, or none, or little skill,
Meet for nothing, but to kill;
Sweet Spirit comfort me!

6. When the passing-bell doth tole,
And the Furies in a shole
Come to fright a parting soule;
Sweet Spirit comfort me!

7. When the tapers now burne blew,
And the comforters are few,
And that number more then true;
Sweet Spirit comfort me!

8. When the Priest his last hath praid,
And I nod to what is said,
'Cause my speech is now decaid;
Sweet Spirit comfort me!

9. When (God knowes) I'm tost about,
Either with despaire, or doubt;
Yet before the glasse be out,
Sweet Spirit comfort me!

10. When the Tempter me pursu'th
With the sins of all my youth,
And halfe damns me with untruth;
Sweet Spirit comfort me!

HIS LETANIE, TO THE HOLY SPIRIT.
15 *runs . . . lees:* is almost exhausted.
25 *tapers . . . blewe:* a sign of the presence of evil spirits.

11. When the flames and hellish cries
Fright mine eares, and fright mine eyes,
And all terrors me surprize;
Sweet Spirit comfort me!

12. When the Judgment is reveal'd,
And that open'd which was seal'd,
When to Thee I have appeal'd;
Sweet Spirit comfort me!

## *A Thanksgiving to God, for his House*

Lord, Thou hast given me a cell
Wherein to dwell;
And little house, whose humble Roof
Is weather-proof;
Under the sparres of which I lie
Both soft, and drie;
Where Thou my chamber for to ward
Hast set a Guard
Of harmlesse thoughts, to watch and keep
Me, while I sleep.
Low is my porch, as is my Fate,
Both void of state;
And yet the threshold of my doore
Is worn by th' poore,
Who thither come, and freely get
Good words, or meat:
Like as my Parlour, so my Hall
And Kitchin's small:
A little Butterie, and therein
A little Byn,
Which keeps my little loafe of Bread
Unchipt, unflead:

A THANKSGIVING TO GOD.
22 *unflead:* unaffected by mice or mould.

Some brittle sticks of Thorne or Briar
Make me a fire,
Close by whose living coale I sit,
And glow like it.
Lord, I confesse too, when I dine,
The Pulse is Thine,
And all those other Bits, that bee
There plac'd by Thee;
The Worts, the Purslain, and the Messe
Of Water-cresse,
Which of Thy kindnesse Thou hast sent;
And my content
Makes those, and my beloved Beet,
To be more sweet.
'Tis thou that crown'st my glittering Hearth
With guiltlesse mirth;
And giv'st me Wassaile Bowles to drink,
Spic'd to the brink.
Lord, 'tis thy plenty-dropping hand,
That soiles my land;
And giv'st me, for my Bushell sowne,
Twice ten for one:
Thou mak'st my teeming Hen to lay
Her egg each day:
Besides my healthfull Ewes to beare
Me twins each yeare:
The while the conduits of my Kine
Run Creame, (for Wine.)
All these, and better Thou dost send
Me, to this end,
That I should render, for my part,
A thankfull heart;
Which, fir'd with incense, I resigne,
As wholly Thine;
But the acceptance, that must be,
My Christ, by Thee.

28 *Pulse:* peas, beans, lentils.
31 *Worts:* cabbages; *Purslain:* herb used in salad.

## *To his ever-loving God*

Can I not come to Thee, my God, for these
So very-many-meeting hindrances,
That slack my pace; but yet not make me stay?
Who slowly goes, rids (in the end) his way.
Cleere Thou my paths, or shorten Thou my miles,
Remove the barrs, or lift me o're the stiles:
Since rough the way is, help me when I call,
And take me up; or els prevent the fall.
I kenn my home; and it affords some ease,
To see far off the smoaking Villages.
Fain would I rest; yet covet not to die,
For feare of future-biting penurie:
No, no, (my God) Thou know'st my wishes be
To leave this life, not loving it, but Thee.

## *To his Conscience*

Can I not sin, but thou wilt be
My private *Protonotarie?*
Can I not wooe thee to passe by
A short and sweet iniquity?
I'le cast a mist and cloud, upon
My delicate transgression,
So utter dark, as that no eye
Shall see the hug'd impietie:

TO HIS EVER-LOVING GOD.
1 *for:* because of.
4 *rids:* i.e. rids of encumbrances.

TO HIS CONSCIENCE.
2 *Protonotarie:* chief recording clerk in a court.
8 *hug'd:* cherished.

*Gifts blind the wise,* and bribes do please,
And winde all other witnesses:
And wilt not thou, with gold, be ti'd
To lay thy pen and ink aside?
That in the mirk and tonguelesse night,
Wanton I may, and thou not write?
It will not be: And, therefore, now,
For times to come, I'le make this Vow,
From aberrations to live free;
So I'le not feare the Judge, or thee.

## *Another Grace for a Child*

Here a little child I stand,
Heaving up my either hand;
Cold as Paddocks though they be,
Here I lift them up to Thee,
For a Benizon to fall
On our meat, and on us all. *Amen.*

## *His wish to God*

I would to God, that mine old age might have
Before my last, but here a living grave,
Some one poore Almes-house; there to lie, or stir,
Ghost-like, as in my meaner sepulcher;

9 *Gifts . . . wise:* Deuteronomy 16:19.
10 *winde:* pervert.
13 *mirk:* murky.

ANOTHER GRACE FOR A CHILD.
3 *Paddocks:* toads.
5 *Benizon:* blessing.

HIS WISH TO GOD.
2 *last:* i.e. before my final grave.

A little piggin, and a pipkin by,
To hold things fitting my necessity;
Which, rightly us'd, both in their time and place,
Might me excite to fore, and after-grace.
Thy Crosse, my *Christ,* fixt 'fore mine eyes sho'd be,
Not to adore that, but to worship Thee.
So, here the remnant of my dayes I'd spend,
Reading Thy Bible, and my Book; *so end.*

## *The white Island: or place of the Blest*

In this world (the *Isle of Dreames*)
While we sit by sorrowes streames,
Teares and terrors are our theames
Reciting:

But when once from hence we flie,
More and more approaching nigh
Unto young Eternitie
Uniting:

In that *whiter Island,* where
Things are evermore sincere;
Candor here, and lustre there
Delighting:

There no monstrous fancies shall
Out of hell an horrour call,
To create (or cause at all)
Affrighting.

HIS WISH TO GOD.
5 *piggin:* small pail; *pipkin:* small pot.

There in calm and cooling sleep
We our eyes shall never steep;
But eternall watch shall keep,
Attending

Pleasures, such as shall pursue
Me immortaliz'd, and you;
And fresh joyes, as never too
Have ending.

## *To keep a true Lent*

1 Is this a Fast, to keep
The Larder leane?
And cleane
From fat of Veales, and Sheep?

2 Is it to quit the dish
Of Flesh, yet still
To fill
The platter high with Fish?

3 Is it to fast an houre,
Or rag'd to go,
Or show
A down-cast look, and sowre?

4 No: 'tis a Fast, to dole
Thy sheaf of wheat,
And meat,
Unto the hungry Soule.

TO KEEP A TRUE LENT.
10 *rag'd:* ragged.

5 It is to fast from strife,
From old debate,
And hate;
To circumcise thy life.

6 To shew a heart grief-rent;
To sterve thy sin,
Not Bin;
And that's to keep thy Lent.

## *To God*

Come to me God; but do not come
To me, as to the gen'rall Doome,
In power; or come Thou in that state,
When Thou Thy Lawes didst promulgate,
When as the Mountaine quak'd for dread,
And sullen clouds bound up his head.
No, lay thy stately terrours by,
To talke with me familiarly;
For if Thy thunder-claps I heare,
I shall lesse swoone, then die for feare.
Speake thou of love and I'le reply
By way of *Epithalamie*,
Or sing of *mercy*, and I'le suit
To it my Violl and my Lute:
Thus let Thy lips but love distill,
Then come my God, and hap what will.

TO GOD.
6 *his:* its.

# HENRY KING
1592–1669

# POEMS, ELEGIES, PARADOXES, and SONNETS.

*LONDON,*

Printed by *J.G.* for *Rich: Marriot* and *Hon: Herringman*, and sold in St. *Dunstans* Churchyard *Fleet-street*, and at the *New-Exchange*.
1657.

1.

## Sonnet

### *The Double Rock*

Since thou hast view'd some Gorgon, and art grown
A solid stone:
To bring again to softness thy hard heart
Is past my art.
Ice may relent to water in a thaw;
But stone made flesh Loves Chymistry ne're saw.

Therefore by thinking on thy hardness, I
Will petrify;
And so within our double Quarryes Wombe,
Dig our Loves Tombe.
Thus strangely will our difference agree;
And, with our selves, amaze the world, to see
How both Revenge and Sympathy consent
To make two Rocks each others Monument.

## *Sonnet*

Tell me no more how fair she is,
I have no minde to hear
The story of that distant bliss
I never shall come near:
By sad experience I have found
That her perfection is my wound.

THE DOUBLE ROCK.
1 *Gorgon:* Medusa, the daughter of Phorcus, whose look turned men to stone. She was slain by Perseus.

And tell me not how fond I am
  To tempt a daring Fate,
From whence no triumph ever came,
  But to repent too late:
There is some hope ere long I may
In silence dote my self away.

I ask no pity (Love) from thee,
  Nor will thy justice blame,
So that thou wilt not envy mee
  The glory of my flame:
Which crowns my heart when ere it dyes,
In that it falls her sacrifice.

## *The Retreat*

Pursue no more (my thoughts!) that false unkind,
You may as soon imprison the North-wind;
Or catch the Lightning as it leaps; or reach
The leading billow first ran down the breach;
Or undertake the flying clouds to track
In the same path they yesterday did rack.
  Then, like a Torch turn'd downward, let the same
  Desire which nourisht it, put out your flame.

Loe thus I doe divorce thee from my brest,
False to thy vow, and traitour to my rest!
Henceforth thy tears shall be (though thou repent)
Like pardons after execution sent.
Nor shalt thou ever my loves story read,
But as some Epitaph of what is dead.
  So may my hope on future blessings dwell,
  As 'tis my firm resolve and last farewell.

SONNET.
*7 fond:* foolish.

## *Sonnet*

When I entreat, either thou wilt not hear,
Or else my suit arriving at thy ear
Cools and dies there. A strange extremitie
To freeze 'ith Sun, and in the shade to frie.
Whil'st all my blasted hopes decline so soon,
Tis Evening with me, though at high Noon.

For pity to thy self, if not to me
Think time will ravish, what I lose, from thee.
If my scorcht heart wither through thy delay,
Thy beauty withers too. And swift decay
Arrests thy Youth. So thou whil'st I am slighted
Wilt be too soon with age or sorrow nighted.

## *The Surrender*

My once dear Love; hapless that I no more
Must call thee so: the rich affections store
That fed our hopes, lies now exhaust and spent,
Like summes of treasure unto Bankrupts lent.

We that did nothing study but the way
To love each other, with which thoughts the day
Rose with delight to us, and with them set,
Must learn the hateful Art how to forget.

We that did nothing wish that Heav'n could give
Beyond our selves, nor did desire to live
Beyond that wish, all these now cancell must
As if not writ in faith, but words and dust.

Yet witness those cleer vowes which Lovers make,
Witness the chast desires that never brake
Into unruly heats; witness that brest
Which in thy bosom anchor'd his whole rest,
Tis no default in us, I dare acquite
Thy Maiden faith, thy purpose fair and white
As thy pure self. Cross Planets did envie
Us to each other, and Heaven did untie
Faster then vowes could binde. O that the Starres,
When Lovers meet, should stand oppos'd in warres!

Since then some higher Destinies command,
Let us not strive nor labour to withstand
What is past help. The longest date of grief
Can never yield a hope of our relief;
And though we waste our selves in moist laments,
Tears may drown us but not our discontents.

Fold back our arms, take home our fruitless loves,
That must new fortunes trie, like Turtle Doves
Dislodged from their haunts. We must in tears
Unwind a love knit up in many years.
In this last kiss I here surrender thee
Back to thy self, so thou again art free.
Thou in another, sad as that, resend
The truest heart that Lover ere did lend.

Now turn from each. So fare our sever'd hearts
As the divorc't soul from her body parts.

## *The Legacy*

My dearest Love! when thou and I must part,
And th'icy hand of death shall seize that heart
Which is all thine; within some spacious will
Ile leave no blanks for Legacies to fill:

Tis my ambition to die one of those
Who but himself hath nothing to dispose.

And since that is already thine, what need
I to re-give it by some newer deed?
Yet take it once again. Free circumstance
Does oft the value of mean things advance;
Who thus repeats what he bequeath'd before,
Proclaims his bounty richer then his store.

But let me not upon my love bestow
What is not worth the giving. I do ow
Somwhat to dust: my bodies pamper'd care
Hungry corruption and the worm will share.
That mouldring relick which in earth must lie
Would prove a gift of horrour to thine eie.

With this cast ragge of my mortalitie
Let all my faults and errours buried be.
And as my sear-cloth rots, so may kind fate
Those worst acts of my live incinerate.
He shall in story fill a glorious room
Whose ashes and whose sins sleep in one Tomb.

If now to my cold hearse thou deign to bring
Some melting sighs as thy last offering,
My peaceful exequies are crown'd. Nor shall
I ask more honour at my Funerall.
Thou wilt more richly balm me with thy tears
Then all the Nard fragrant Arabia bears.

THE LEGACY.
6 *but:* except for.
19 *cast:* cast off.
21 *sear-cloth:* waxed cloth used as a shroud.
22 *live:* life.

And as the Paphian Queen by her griefs show'r
Brought up her dead Loves Spirit in a flow'r:
So by those precious drops rain'd from thine eies
Out of my dust, O may some vertue rise!
  And like thy better Genius thee attend,
  Till thou in my dark Period shalt end.

Lastly, my constant truth let me commend
To him thou choosest next to be thy friend.
For (witness all things good) I would not have
Thy Youth and Beauty married to my grave,
  'Twould shew thou didst repent the style of wife
  Should'st thou relapse into a single life.

They with preposterous grief the world delude
Who mourn for their lost Mates in solitude;
Since Widdowhood more strongly doth enforce
The much lamented lot of their divorce.
  Themselves then of their losses guilty are
  Who may, yet will not suffer a repaire.

Those were Barbarian wives that did invent
Weeping to death at th' Husbands Monument,
But in more civil Rites She doth approve
Her first, who ventures on a second Love;
  For else it may be thought, if She refrain,
  She sped so ill Shee durst not trie again.

Up then my Love, and choose some worthier one
Who may supply my room when I am gone;
So will the stock of our affection thrive
No less in death, then were I still alive.
  And in my urne I shall rejoyce, that I
  Am both Testatour thus and Legacie.

31 *Paphian Queen:* Venus. Her lament for Adonis is alluded to.
52 *Her:* Herself.

## *To his unconstant Friend*

But say thou very woman, why to me
This fit of weakness and inconstancie?
What forfeit have I made of word or vow,
That I am rack't on thy displeasure now?
If I have done a fault I do not shame
To cite it from thy lips, give it a name:
I ask the banes, stand forth, and tell me why
We should not in our wonted loves comply?
Did thy cloy'd appetite urge thee to trie
If any other man could love as I?
I see friends are like clothes, laid up whil'st new,
But after wearing cast, though nere so true.
Or did thy fierce ambition long to make
Some Lover turn a martyr for thy sake?
Thinking thy beauty had deserv'd no name
Unless some one do perish in that flame:
Upon whose loving dust this sentence lies,
Here's one was murther'd by his Mistriss eyes.

Or was't because my love to thee was such,
I could not choose but blab it? swear how much
I was thy slave, and doting let thee know,
I better could my self then thee forgo.

Hearken ye men that ere shall love like me,
Ile give you counsel gratis: if you be
Possest of what you like, let your fair friend
Lodge in your bosom, but no secrets send
To seek their lodging in a female brest;
For so much is abated of your rest.

TO HIS UNCONSTANT FRIEND.
7 *banes:* bans, read in church before the celebration of a wedding.
11 *laid:* The 1657 edition reads *lad.*

The Steed that comes to understand his strength
Growes wild, and casts his manager at length:
And that tame Lover who unlocks his heart
Unto his Mistriss, teaches her an art
To plague himself; shews her the secret way
How She may tyrannize another day.

And now my fair unkindness, thus to thee;
Mark how wise Passion and I agree:
Hear and be sorry for't. I will not die
To expiate thy crime of levitie:
I walk (not cross-arm'd neither) eat, and live,
Yea live to pity thy neglect, not grieve
That thou art from thy faith and promise gone,
Nor envy him who by my loss hath won.
Thou shalt perceive thy changing Moon-like fits
Have not infected me, or turn'd my wits
To Lunacie. I do not mean to weep
When I should eat, or sigh when I should sleep;
I will not fall upon my pointed quill,
Bleed ink and Poems, or invention spill
To contrive Ballads, or weave Elegies
For Nurses wearing when the infant cries.
Nor like th'enamour'd Tristrams of the time,
Despair in prose, and hang my self in rhime.
Nor thither run upon my verses feet,
Where I shall none but fools or mad-men meet,
Who mid'st the silent shades, and Myrtle walks,
Pule and do penance for their Mistress faults.
I'm none of those poetick male-contents
Born to make paper dear with my laments:
Or wild Orlando that will rail and vex,
And for thy sake fall out with all the sex.

50 *wearing:* wearing themselves out.
56 *Pule:* Whimper.
59 *Orlando:* alluding to Ariosto's *Orlando Furioso.*

No, I will love again, and seek a prize
That shall redeem me from thy poor despise.
Ile court my fortune now in such a shape
That will no faint die, nor starv'd colour take.

Thus launch I off with triumph from thy shore,
To which my last farewell; for never more
Will I touch there. I put to Sea again
Blown with the churlish wind of thy disdain.
Nor will I stop this course till I have found
A Coast that yields safe harbour, and firm ground.

Smile ye Love-Starres; wing'd with desire I fly
To make my wishes full discovery:
Nor doubt I but for one that proves like you,
I shall find ten as fair, and yet more true.

## *The Exequy*

Accept thou Shrine of my dead Saint,
Insteed of Dirges this complaint;
And for sweet flowres to crown thy hearse,
Receive a strew of weeping verse
From thy griev'd friend, whom thou might'st see
Quite melted into tears for thee.

Dear loss! since thy untimely fate
My task hath been to meditate
On thee, on thee: thou art the book,
The library whereon I look
Though almost blind. For thee (lov'd clay)
I languish out not live the day,

THE EXEQUY: Written after the death of King's wife, Anne. She was buried on January 5, 1624. The word "exequy" means "funeral rites," but King's poem has led to the development of the meaning "funeral ode." A manuscript version has the subtitle: "To his matchless never to be forgotten friend."

Using no other exercise
But what I practise with mine eyes:
By which wet glasses I find out
How lazily time creeps about
To one that mourns: this, onely this
My exercise and bus'ness is:
So I compute the weary houres
With sighs dissolved into showres.

Nor wonder if my time go thus
Backward and most preposterous;
Thou hast benighted me, thy set
This Eve of blackness did beget,
Who was't my day, (though overcast
Before thou had'st thy Noon-tide past)
And I remember must in tears,
Thou scarce had'st seen so many years
As Day tells houres. By thy cleer Sun
My love and fortune first did run;
But thou wilt never more appear
Folded within my Hemisphear,
Since both thy light and motion
Like a fled Star is fall'n and gon,
And twixt me and my soules dear wish
The earth now interposed is,
Which such a strange eclipse doth make
As ne're was read in Almanake.

I could allow thee for a time
To darken me and my sad Clime,
Were it a month, a year, or ten,
I would thy exile live till then;
And all that space my mirth adjourn,
So thou wouldst promise to return;
And putting off thy ashy shrowd
At length disperse this sorrows cloud.

23 *set:* setting (as in "sunset").
26 *Before . . . past:* Anne was only about twenty-four when she died.

But woe is me! the longest date
Too narrow is to calculate
These empty hopes: never shall I
Be so much blest as to descry
A glimpse of thee, till that day come
Which shall the earth to cinders doome,
And a fierce Feaver must calcine
The body of this world like thine,
(My Little World!) that fit of fire
Once off, our bodies shall aspire
To our soules bliss: then we shall rise,
And view our selves with cleerer eyes
In that calm Region, where no night
Can hide us from each others sight.

Mean time, thou hast her earth: much good
May my harm do thee. Since it stood
With Heavens will I might not call
Her longer mine, I give thee all
My short-liv'd right and interest
In her, whom living I lov'd best:
With a most free and bounteous grief,
I give thee what I could not keep.
Be kind to her, and prethee look
Thou write into thy Dooms-day book
Each parcell of this Rarity
Which in thy Casket shrin'd doth ly:
See that thou make thy reck'ning streight,
And yield her back again by weight;
For thou must audit on thy trust
Each graine and atome of this dust,
As thou wilt answer *Him* that lent,
Not gave thee my dear Monument.

So close the ground, and 'bout her shade
Black curtains draw, my *Bride* is laid.

53 *calcine:* burn to dust.
69 *prethee:* I pray thee.

Sleep on my *Love* in thy cold bed
Never to be disquieted!
My last good night! Thou wilt not wake
Till I thy fate shall overtake:
Till age, or grief, or sickness must
Marry my body to that dust
It so much loves; and fill the room
My heart keeps empty in thy Tomb.
Stay for me there; I will not faile
To meet thee in that hallow Vale.
And think not much of my delay;
I am already on the way,
And follow thee with all the speed
Desire can make, or sorrows breed.
Each minute is a short degree,
And ev'ry houre a step towards thee.
At night when I betake to rest,
Next morn I rise neerer my West
Of life, almost by eight houres saile,
Then when sleep breath'd his drowsie gale.

Thus from the Sun my Bottom stears,
And my dayes Compass downward bears:
Nor labour I to stemme the tide
Through which to *Thee* I swiftly glide.

'Tis true, with shame and grief I yield,
Thou like the *Vann* first took'st the field,
And gotten hast the victory
In thus adventuring to dy
Before me, whose more years might crave
A just precedence in the grave.
But heark! My pulse like a soft Drum
Beats my approch, tells *Thee* I come;
And slow howere my marches be,
I shall at last sit down by *Thee*.

90 *hallow:* hollow.
113 *howere:* however.

The thought of this bids me go on,
And wait my dissolution
With hope and comfort. *Dear* (forgive
The crime) I am content to live
Divided, with but half a heart,
Till we shall meet and never part.

## *To my dead friend Ben: Johnson*

I see that wreath which doth the wearer arm
'Gainst the quick strokes of thunder, is no charm
To keep off deaths pale dart. For, *Johnson* then
Thou hadst been number'd still with living men.
Times sithe had fear'd thy Lawrel to invade,
Nor thee this subject of our sorrow made.

Amongst those many votaries who come
To offer up their Garlands at thy Tombe;
Whil'st some more lofty pens in their bright verse
(Like glorious Tapers flaming on thy herse)
Shall light the dull and thankless world to see,
How great a maim it suffers wanting thee;
Let not thy learned shadow scorn, that I
Pay meaner Rites unto thy memory;
And since I nought can adde, but in desire
Restore some sparks which leapt from thine own fire.

What ends soever others quills invite,
I can protest, it was no itch to write,
Nor any vain ambition to be read,
But meerly Love and Justice to the dead

TO MY DEAD FRIEND BEN: JOHNSON: Jonson died on August 6, 1637.

1–2 *wreath . . . thunder:* The laurel wreath was supposed to protect its wearer from lightning and thunder.

9 *more lofty pens:* King's elegy was published along with thirty-two poems by other writers in *Jonsonus Virbius* (1638).

Which rais'd my fameless Muse; and caus'd her bring
These drops, as tribute thrown into that spring,
To whose most rich and fruitful head we ow
The purest streams of language which can flow.

For 'tis but truth, thou taught'st the ruder age
To speake by Grammar, and reform'dst the Stage:
Thy Comick Sock induc'd such purged sence,
A *Lucrece* might have heard without offence.
Amongst those soaring wits that did dilate
Our English, and advance it to the rate
And value it now holds, thy self was one
Helpt lift it up to such proportion.
That thus refin'd and roab'd, it shall not spare
With the full *Greek* or *Latine* to compare.
For what tongue ever durst, but ours, translate
Great *Tully's* Eloquence, or *Homers* State?
Both which in their unblemisht lustre shine,
From *Chapmans* pen, and from thy *Catiline.*
All I would ask for thee, in recompence
Of thy successful toyl and times expence,
Is onely this poor Boon: that those who can
Perhaps read *French,* or talk *Italian,*
Or do the lofty *Spaniard* affect;
To shew their skill in Forrein Dialect,
Prove not themselves so unnaturally wise,
They therefore should their *Mother-tongue* despise.
(As if her Poets both for style and wit
Not equall'd, or not pass'd their best that writ)
Untill by studying *Johnson* they have known
The height and strength and plenty of their own.

29 *dilate:* expand, enrich.
36 *Tully's:* Cicero's.
38 *Chapmans:* George Chapman (1559?–1634), the translator of Homer; *Catiline:* Jonson's play, which drew heavily on Cicero, was first acted in 1611.

Thus in what low earth or neglected room
Soere thou sleep'st, *thy book* shall be thy tomb.
Thou wilt go down a happy Coarse, bestrew'd
With thine own Flowres; and feel thy self renew'd,
Whil'st thy immortal never-with'ring Bayes
Shall yearly flourish in thy Readers praise.
And when more spreading Titles are forgot,
Or spight of all their Lead and Sear-cloth rot,
Thou wrapt and Shrin'd in *thine own sheets*, wilt ly
A Relick fam'd by all Posterity.

## *An Elegy*

### *Upon S. W. R.*

I will not weep, for 'twere as great a sin
To shed a tear for thee, as to have bin
An Actor in thy death. Thy life and age
Was but a various Scene on fortunes Stage,
With whom thou tugg'st & strov'st ev'n out of breath
In thy long toil: nere master'd till thy death;
And then despight of trains and cruell wit,
Thou did'st at once subdue malice and it.

I dare not then so blast thy memory
As say I do lament or pity thee.
Were I to choose a subject to bestow
My pity on, he should be one as low
In spirit as desert. That durst not dy
But rather were content by slavery

53 *Coarse:* corpse.

*Title:* Sir Walter Raleigh was executed on October 29, 1618. King's opening lines seem to echo Raleigh's short poem, "What is our life? A play of passion."

AN ELEGY.

7 *trains:* plots, intrigues.

To purchase life: or I would pity those
Thy most industrious and friendly foes:
Who when they thought to make thee scandals story
Lent thee a swifter flight to Heav'n and glory.
That thought by cutting off some wither'd dayes,
(Which thou could'st spare them) to eclipse thy praise;
Yet gave it brighter foil, made thy ag'd fame
Appear more white and fair, then foul their shame:
And did promote an Execution
Which (but for them) Nature and Age had done.
  Such worthless things as these were onely born
To live on Pities almes (too mean for scorn.)
Thou dy'dst an envious wonder, whose high fate
The world must still admire, scarce imitate.

## *Upon the death of my ever desired friend Doctor Donne Dean of Pauls*

To have liv'd eminent in a degree
Beyond our lofty'st flights, that is like thee;
Or t'have had too much merit is not safe;
For such excesses find no Epitaph.
At common graves we have Poetick eyes
Can melt themselves in easie Elegies;
Each quill can drop his tributary verse,
And pin it with the Hatchments, to the Herse:
But at thine, Poem or inscription
(Rich Soul of wit and language:) we have none;
Indeed a silence does that Tomb befit
Where is no Herald left to blazon it.

UPON THE DEATH: Donne's death occurred on March 31, 1631. King's elegy, which had first appeared in the 1632 edition of Donne's sermon, "Death's Duel," was the opening poem in the group of elegies included in the 1633 edition of *Poems by J. D.*

8 *Hatchments:* plaques bearing the coat of arms of the deceased.

Widdow'd invention justly doth forbear
To come abroad knowing thou art not here,
Late her great Patron; whose prerogative
Maintain'd and cloth'd her so, as none alive
Must now presume to keep her at thy rate,
Though he the Indies for her dowre estate:
Or else that awful fire, which once did burn
In thy clear brain, now fall'n into thy Urn.
Lives there to fright rude Empericks from thence,
Which might profane thee by their ignorance:
Who ever writes of thee, and in a style
Unworthy such a Theme, does but revile
Thy precious dust, and wake a learned spirit
Which may revenge his rapes upon thy merit.
For all a low-pitcht fancie can devise,
Will prove at best but hallow'd injuries.

Thou, like the dying Swan, didst lately sing
Thy mournful Dirge in audience of the King;
When pale looks, and faint accents of thy breath,
Presented so to life that piece of death,
That it was fear'd and prophesi'd by all
Thou thither cam'st to preach thy Funerall.
O! hadst thou in an Elegiack knell
Rung out unto the world thine own farewell;
And in thy high victorious numbers beat
The solemn measure of thy griev'd retreat:
Thou might'st the Poets service now have mist,
As well as then thou didst prevent the Priest:
And never to the world beholden be,
So much as for an Epitaph for thee.

18 *for . . . estate:* furnish as her dowry.
21 *Empericks:* pretenders, charlatans.
30 *Dirge:* Donne's last sermon, "Death's Duel," preached before Charles I in January 1631.

I do not like the office. Nor is't fit
Thou, who didst lend our age such summes of wit,
Should'st now reborrow from her Bankrupt Mine
That Ore to bury thee, which once was thine.
Rather still leave us in thy debt; and know
(Exalted Soul!) More glory 'tis to ow
Unto thy Herse what we can never pay,
Then with embased coin those Rites defray.

Commit we then Thee to Thy self: nor blame
Our drooping loves, which thus to thine own fame
Leave Thee Executour: since but thy own
No pen could do Thee Justice, nor Bayes crown
Thy vast desert; save that we nothing can
Depute to be thy ashes Guardian.

So Jewellers no Art or Metal trust
To form the Diamond, but the Diamonds dust.

## *To my honoured Friend Mr.* George Sandys

It is, Sir, a confest intrusion here
That I before your labours do appear,
Which no loud Herald need, that may proclaim
Or seek acceptance, but the Authors fame.
Much less that should this happy work commend,
Whose subject is its licence, and doth send
It to the world to be receiv'd and read,
Far as the glorious beams of truth are spread.

Nor let it be imagin'd that I look
Onely with Customes eye upon your book;
Or in this service that 'twas my intent
T'exclude your person from your argument:

I shall profess much of the love I ow,
Doth from the root of our extraction grow;
To which though I can little contribute,
Yet with a naturall joy I must impute
To our Tribes honour, what by you is done
Worthy the title of a *Prelates* son.

And scarcely have two brothers farther borne
A Fathers name, or with more value worne
Their own, then two of you; whose pens and feet
Have made the distant Points of Heav'n to meet;
He by exact discoveries of the West,
Your self by painful travels in the East.

Some more like you might pow'rfully confute
Th'opposers of Priests marriage by the fruit.
And (since tis known for all their streight vow'd life,
They like the sex in any style but wife)
Cause them to change their Cloyster for that State
Which keeps men chaste by vowes legitimate:
Nor shame to father their relations,
Or under Nephews names disguise their sons.
This Child of yours born without spurious blot,
And fairly Midwiv'd as it was begot,
Doth so much of the Parents goodness wear,
You may be proud to own it for your Heir.
Whose choice acquits you from the common sin
Of such, who finish worse then they begin:

TO MY HONOURED FRIEND: King's poem first appeared in the 1638 edition of Sandys' *Paraphrase upon the Divine Poems.* Carew and Waller also contributed eulogies to this volume.

14 *our extraction:* Both Sandys and King were the sons of bishops.

23 *He:* Sir Edwin Sandys (1561–1629), George's brother, whose *View or Survey of the State of Religion in the Western Parts of the World* was published in 1629.

24 *Your self:* George Sandys' *The Relation of a Journey* [to *Turkey, Egypt, etc.*] first appeared in 1615.

You mend upon your self, and your last strain
Does of your first the start in judgment gain;
Since what in curious travel was begun,
You here conclude in a devotion.

Where in delightful raptures we descry
As in a Map, *Sions Chorography*
Laid out in so direct and smooth a line,
Men need not go about through Palestine:
Who seek Christ here will the streight Rode prefer,
As neerer much then by the Sepulchre.
For not a limb growes here, but is a path;
Which in Gods City the blest Center hath:
And doth so sweetly on each passion strike,
The most fantastick taste will somewhat like.
To the unquiet soul *Job* still from hence
Pleads in th'example of his patience.
The mortify'd may hear the wise King preach,
When his repentance made him fit to teach.
Nor shall the singing Sisters be content
To chant at home the Act of Parliament,
Turn'd out of reason into rhime by one
Free of his trade, though not of Helicon,
Who did in his Poetick zeal contend
Others edition by a worse to mend.
Here are choice Hymnes and Carolls for the glad,
With melancholy Dirges for the sad:
And *David* (as he could his skill transfer)
Speaks like himself by an interpreter.
Your Muse rekindled hath the Prophets fire,
And tun'd the strings of his neglected Lyre;
Making the Note and Ditty so agree,
They now become a perfect harmonie.

44 *Chorography:* geography and topography.

55 *wise King:* Solomon, the reputed author of Ecclesiastes.

58 *Act of Parliament:* In this and the following lines King alludes to H. Dod's *The Act of Parliament for publick Thanksgiving on the fifth of Novemb.*, which was appended to a 1620 edition of the Psalms in the old version of Sternhold and Hopkins.

I must confess, I have long wisht to see
The Psalmes reduc'd to this conformity:
Grieving the songs of Sion should be sung
In phrase not diff'ring from a barbarous tongue.
As if, by custome warranted, we may
Sing that to God we would be loth to say.
Far be it from my purpose to upbraid
Their honest meaning, who first offer made
That book in Meeter to compile, which you
Have mended in the form, and built anew:
And it was well, considering the time,
Which hardly could distinguish verse and rhime.
But now the language, like the Church, hath won
More lustre since the Reformation;
None can condemn the wish or labour spent
Good matter in good words to represent.

Yet in this jealous age some such there be,
So without cause afraid of novelty,
They would not (were it in their pow'r to choose)
An old ill practise for a better lose.
Men who a rustick plainnesse so affect,
They think God served best by their neglect.
Holding the cause would be profan'd by it,
Were they at charge of learning or of wit.
And therefore bluntly (what comes next) they bring
Course and unstudy'd stuffs for offering;
Which like th'old Tabernacles cov'ring are,
Made up of Badgers skins, and of Goats haire.
But these are Paradoxes they must use
Their sloth and bolder ignorance t'excuse.
Who would not laugh at one will naked go,
'Cause in old hangings truth is pictur'd so?
Though plainness be reputed honours note,
They mantles use to beautify the coat;
So that a curious (unaffected) dress
Addes much unto the bodies comeliness:

105 *curious:* careful.

And wheresoere the subjects best, the sence
Is better'd by the speakers eloquence.

But, Sir, to you I shall no trophee raise
From other mens detraction or dispraise:
That Jewel never had inherent worth,
Which askt such foils as these to set it forth.
If any quarrel your attempt or style,
Forgive them; their own folly they revile.
Since, 'gainst themselves, their factious envy shall
Allow this work of yours Canonicall.
Nor may you fear the Poets common lot,
Read, and commended, and then quite forgot:
The brazen Mines and Marble Rocks shall wast,
When your foundation will unshaken last.
'Tis fames best pay, that you your labours see
By their immortal subject crowned be.
For nere was writer in oblivion hid
Who firm'd his name on such a Pyramid.

## *Sic Vita*

Like to the falling of a Starre;
Or as the flights of Eagles are;
Or like the fresh springs gawdy hew;
Or silver drops of morning dew;
Or like a wind that chafes the flood;
Or bubbles which on water stood;
Even such is man, whose borrow'd light
Is streight call'd in, and paid to night.

*The Wind blowes out; the Bubble dies;*
*The Spring entomb'd in Autumn lies;*
*The Dew dries up; the Starre is shot;*
*The Flight is past; and Man forgot.*

SIC VITA: "Such is Life."

# An Elegy Upon My Best Friend

*L. K. C.*

Should we our Sorrows in this Method range,
Oft as Misfortune doth their Subjects change,
And to the sev'ral Losses which befall,
Pay diff'rent Rites at ev'ry Funeral;
Like narrow Springs drain'd by dispersed Streams,
We must want Tears to wail such various Themes,
And prove defective in Deaths mournfull Laws,
Not having Words proportion'd to each Cause.
In your Dear loss my much afflicted Sense,
Discerns this Truth by sad experience,
Who never Look'd my Verses should survive,
As wet Records, That you are not Alive;
And less desir'd to make that Promise due,
Which pass'd from Me in jest, when urg'd by You.
How close and slily doth our Frailty work!
How undiscover'd in the Body lurk!
That Those who this Day did salute you well,
Before the Next were frighted by your Knell.
O wherefore since we must in Order rise,
Should we not Fall in equal Obsequies?
But bear th'Assaults of an uneven Fate,
Like Feavers which their Hour anticipate;

AN ELEGY: L. K. C. was Lady Katherine Cholmondeley, who died on June 15, 1657.

2 *Oft . . . change:* This poem is the last (cf. line 35) of eighteen elegies written by King. No poem of his can be dated after 1657.

Had this Rule constant been, my long wish'd End
Might render you a Mourner for your Friend:
As He for you, whose most deplor'd surprise
Imprints your Death on all my Faculties;
That hardly my dark Phant'sie or Discourse,
This final Duty from the Pen inforce:
  Such Influence hath your Eclipsed Light,
It doth my Reason like my Self benight.
  Let me, with Luckless Gamesters, then think best
(After I have Set up and Lost my Rest,)
Grow'n desp'rate through mischance, to Venture last
My whole remaining Stock upon a Cast,
And flinging from me my now Loathed Pen,
Resolve for your Sake nev'r to write agen:
For whilst Successive days their Light renew,
I must no Subject hope to Equal you,
In whose Heroick Brest as in their Sphear,
All Graces of your Sex concentred were.
  Thus take I my long Farewell of that Art,
Fit only glorious Actions to impart;
That Art wherewith our Crosses we beguile,
And make them in Harmonious numbers smile:
Since you are gone, This holds no further use,
Whose Virtue and Desert inspir'd my Muse.
O may She in your Ashes Buried be,
Whilst I my Self become the Elegie.
  And as it is observ'd when Princes Dye,
  In honour of that sad Solemnity,
The now unoffic'd Servants crack their Staves,
And throw them down into their Masters Graves:
So this last Office of my broken Verse,
I solemnly resign upon your Hearse;
And my Brains moisture, all that is unspent,
Shall melt to nothing at the Monument.

27 *hardly:* with difficulty.
32 *Rest:* wager.

Thus in moist Weather when the Marble weeps,
You'l think it only his Tears reck'ning keeps,
Who doth for ever to his Thoughts bequeath
The Legacy of your lamented Death.

# THOMAS CAREW
1594/95–1639

# POEMS.

By

THOMAS CAREVV

Esquire.

One of the Gentlemen of the Privie-Chamber, and Sewer in Ordinary to His Majesty.

LONDON,

Printed by *I. D.* for *Thomas Walkley*, and are to be sold at the signe of the flying Horse, between Brittains Burse, and York-House.

1640.

## *The Spring*

Now that the winter's gone, the earth hath lost
Her snow-white robes, and now no more the frost
Candies the grasse, or castes an ycie creame
Upon the silver Lake, or Chrystall streame:
But the warme Sunne thawes the benummed Earth,
And makes it tender, gives a sacred birth
To the dead Swallow; wakes in hollow tree
The drowzie Cuckow, and the Humble-Bee.
Now doe a quire of chirping Minstrels bring
In tryumph to the world, the youthfull Spring.
The Vallies, hills, and woods, in rich araye,
Welcome the comming of the long'd for May.
Now all things smile; onely my *Love* doth lowre:
Nor hath the scalding Noon-day-Sunne the power,
To melt that marble yce, which still doth hold
Her heart congeald, and makes her pittie cold.
The Oxe which lately did for shelter flie
Into the stall, doth now securely lie
In open fields; and love no more is made
By the fire side; but in the cooler shade
*Amyntas* now doth with his *Cloris* sleepe
Under a Sycamoure, and all things keepe
Time with the season, only shee doth carry
*June* in her eyes, in her heart *January*.

## To *A. L.*
## *Perswasions to love*

Thinke not cause men flatt'ring say,
Y' are fresh as Aprill sweet as May,
Bright as is the morning starre,
That you are so, or though you are

TO A. L.: The lady A.L. has not been identified.

Be not therefore proud, and deeme
All men unworthy your esteeme.
For being so, you loose the pleasure
Of being faire, since that rich treasure
Of rare beauty, and sweet feature
Was bestow'd on you by nature
To be enjoy'd, and 'twere a sinne,
There to be scarce, where shee hath bin
So prodigall of her best graces;
Thus common beauties, and meane faces
Shall have more pastime, and enjoy
The sport you loose by being coy.
Did the thing for which I sue
Onely concerne my selfe not you,
Were men so fram'd as they alone
Reap'd all the pleasure, women none,
Then had you reason to be scant;
But 'twere a madnesse not to grant
That which affords (if you consent)
To you the giver, more content
Then me the beggar; Oh then bee
Kinde to your selfe if not to mee;
Starve not your selfe, because you may
Thereby make me pine away;
Nor let brittle beautie make
You your wiser thoughts forsake:
For that lovely face will faile,
Beautie's sweet, but beautie's fraile;
'Tis sooner past, 'tis sooner done
Then Summers raine, or winters Sun:
Most fleeting when it is most deare,
'Tis gone while wee but say 'tis here.
These curious locks so aptly twind,
Whose every haire a soule doth bind,

7 *loose:* lose.

Will change their abroun hue, and grow
White, and cold as winters snow.
That eye which now is *Cupids* nest
Will prove his grave, and all the rest
Will follow; in the cheeke, chin, nose
Nor lilly shall be found nor rose.
And what will then become of all
Those, whom now you servants call?
Like swallowes when your summers done,
They'le flye and seeke some warmer Sun.
Then wisely chuse one to your friend,
Whose love may, when your beauties end,
Remaine still firme: be provident
And thinke before the summers spent
Of following winter; like the Ant
In plenty hoord for time of scant.
Cull out amongst the multitude
Of lovers, that seeke to intrude
Into your favour, one that may
Love for an age, not for a day;
One that will quench your youthfull fires,
And feed in age your hot desires.
For when the stormes of time have mov'd
Waves on that cheeke which was belov'd,
When a faire Ladies face is pin'd
And yellow spred, where red once shin'd,
When beauty, youth, and all sweets leave her,
Love may returne, but lover never:
And old folkes say there are no paynes
Like itch of love in aged vaines.
Oh love me then, and now begin it,
Let us not loose this present minute:
For time and age will worke that wrack
Which time or age shall ne're call backe.
The snake each yeare fresh skin resumes,
And Eagles change their aged plumes;

39 *abroun:* auburn.

The faded Rose each spring, receives
A fresh red tincture on her leaves:
But if your beauties once decay,
You never know a second *May*.
Oh, then be wise, and whilst your season
Affords you dayes for sport doe reason;
Spend not in vaine your lives short houre,
But crop in time your beauties flower:
Which will away, and doth together
Both bud, and fade, both blow and wither.

## *A divine Mistris*

In natures peeces still I see
Some errour, that might mended bee;
Something my wish could still remove,
Alter or adde; but my faire love
Was fram'd by hands farre more divine;
For she hath every beauteous line:
Yet I had beene farre happier,
Had Nature that made me, made her;
Then likenes, might (that love creates)
Have made her love what now she hates:
Yet I confesse I cannot spare,
From her just shape the smallest haire;
Nor need I beg from all the store
Of heaven, for her one beautie more:
Shee hath too much divinity for mee,
You Gods teach her some more humanitie.

## *A cruell Mistris*

Wee read of Kings and Gods that kindly tooke,
A pitcher fil'd with water from the brooke;
But I have dayly tendred without thankes
Rivers of teares that overflow their bankes.
A slaughter'd bull will appease angry *Jove,*
A horse the Sun, a Lambe the God of love,
But shee disdaines the spotlesse sacrifice
Of a pure heart that at her altar lyes.
*Vesta* is not displeas'd if her chast urne
Doe with repayred fuell ever burne;
But my Saint frownes though to her honour'd name,
I consecrate a never dying flame.
Th'Assyrian King did none i'th' furnace throw,
But those that to his Image did not bow;
With bended knees I daily worship her,
Yet she consumes her owne Idolater.
Of such a Goddesse no times leave record,
That burnt the temple where she was ador'd.

A CRUELL MISTRIS.

1 *Kings and Gods:* Perhaps an allusion to the story told by Plutarch of King Artaxerxes, who richly rewarded a peasant when the latter, having nothing else to give, presented the king with a handful of water from a brook.

10 *repayred:* mended, replenished.

13 *Assyrian King:* Nebuchadnezzar. See the third chapter of the Book of Daniel.

## *Song.*
## *Murdring beautie*

*Ile gaze no more on her bewitching face,*
*Since ruine harbours there in every place:*
*For my enchanted soule alike shee drownes*
*With calmes and tempests of her smiles and frownes.*
*I'le love no more those cruell eyes of hers,*
*Which pleas'd or anger'd still are murderers:*
*For if she dart (like lightning) through the ayre*
*Her beames of wrath, she kils me with despaire.*
*If shee behold me with a pleasing eye,*
*I surfet with excesse of joy, and dye.*

## *Secresie protested*

Feare not (deare Love) that I'le reveale
Those houres of pleasure we two steale;
No eye shall see, nor yet the Sun
Descry, what thou and I have done;
No eare shall heare our love, but wee
Silent as the night will bee.
The God of love himselfe (whose dart
Did first wound mine, and then thy heart)
Shall never know, that we can tell
What sweets in stolne embraces dwell.
This only meanes may find it out,
If when I dye, Physicians doubt

SECRESIE PROTESTED.

12 *If when I dye,* etc.: Cf. Donne, "The Dampe," "When I am dead, and Doctors know not why, / And my friends curiositie / Will have me cut up to survay each part, / When they shall finde your Picture in my heart, etc."

What caus'd my death, and there to view
Of all their judgements which was true,
Rip up my heart, Oh then I feare
The world will see thy picture there.

## *A prayer to the Wind*

Goe thou gentle whispering wind,
Beare this sigh; and if thou find
Where my cruell faire doth rest,
Cast it in her snowie brest,
So, enflamed by my desire,
It may set her heart a-fire.
Those sweet kisses thou shalt gaine,
Will reward thee for thy paine:
Boldly light upon her lip,
There suck odours, and thence skip
To her bosome; lastly fall
Downe, and wander over all:
Range about those Ivorie hills,
From whose every part distills
Amber deaw; there spices grow,
There pure streames of Nectar flow;
There perfume thy selfe, and bring
All those sweets upon thy wing:
As thou return'st, change by thy power,
Every weed into a flower;
Turne each Thistle to a Vine,
Make the Bramble Eglantine.
For so rich a bootie made,
Doe but this, and I am payd.
Thou canst with thy powerfull blast,
Heat apace, and coole as fast:
Thou canst kindle hidden flame,
And ag'en destroy the same;

Then for pittie, either stir
Up the fire of love in her,
That alike both flames may shine,
Or else quite extinguish mine.

## *Mediocritie in love rejected.*
## *Song*

*Give me more love, or more disdaine;*
*The Torrid, or the frozen Zone,*
*Bring equall ease unto my paine;*
*The temperate affords me none:*
*Either extreame, of love, or hate,*
*Is sweeter than a calme estate.*

*Give me a storme; if it be love,*
*Like* Danae *in that golden showre*
*I swimme in pleasure; if it prove*
*Disdaine, that torrent will devoure*
*My Vulture-hopes; and he's possest*
*Of Heaven, that's but from Hell releast;*
*Then crowne my joyes, or cure my paine;*
*Give me more love, or more disdaine.*

MEDIOCRITIE IN LOVE REJECTED.
8 *Danae:* The mother of Perseus. Zeus made love to her in the form of a shower of gold.

# *Good counsel to a young Maid.*
## *Song*

*Gaze not on thy beauties pride,*
*Tender Maid, in the false tide,*
*That from Lovers eyes doth slide.*

*Let thy faithfull Crystall show,*
*How thy colours come, and goe,*
*Beautie takes a foyle from woe.*

*Love, that in those smooth streames lyes,*
*Under pitties faire disguise,*
*Will thy melting heart surprize.*

*Netts, of passions finest thred,*
*Snaring Poems, will be spred,*
*All, to catch thy maiden-head.*

*Then beware, for those that cure*
*Loves disease, themselves endure*
*For reward, a Calenture.*

*Rather let the Lover pine,*
*Then his pale cheeke, should assigne*
*A perpetuall blush to thine.*

GOOD COUNSEL TO A YOUNG MAID.
10 *passions:* The 1640 edition reads *passion.*
15 *Calenture:* a raging fever.

## *To my Mistris sitting by a Rivers side. An Eddy*

Marke how yond Eddy steales away,
From the rude streame into the Bay,
There lockt up safe, she doth divorce
Her waters from the chanels course,
And scornes the Torrent, that did bring
Her headlong from her native spring.
Now doth she with her new love play,
Whilst he runs murmuring away.
Marke how she courts the bankes, whilst they
As amorously their armes display,
T'embrace, and clip her silver waves:
See how she strokes their sides, and craves
An entrance there, which they deny;
Whereat she frownes, threatning to flye
Home to her streame, and 'gins to swim
Backward, but from the chanels brim,
Smiling, returnes into the creeke,
With thousand dimples on her cheeke.
  Be thou this Eddy, and I'le make
My breast thy shore, where thou shalt take
Secure repose, and never dreame
Of the quite forsaken streame:
Let him to the wide Ocean hast,
There lose his colour, name, and tast;
Thou shalt save all, and safe from him,
Within these armes for ever swim.

TO MY MISTRIS.

1 f.: Carew's conceit is based directly on Donne's elegy, "Natures lay Ideot," lines 21–34.

## *Song.*
## *To my inconstant Mistris*

*When thou, poore excommunicate*
*From all the joyes of love, shalt see*
*The full reward, and glorious fate,*
*Which my strong faith shall purchase me,*
*Then curse thine owne inconstancie.*

*A fayrer hand then thine, shall cure*
*That heart, which thy false oathes did wound;*
*And to my soule, a soule more pure*
*Than thine, shall by Loves hand be bound,*
*And both with equall glory crown'd.*

*Then shalt thou weepe, entreat, complaine*
*To Love, as I did once to thee;*
*When all thy teares shall be as vaine*
*As mine were then, for thou shalt bee*
*Damn'd for thy false Apostasie.*

## *Song.*
## *Perswasions to enjoy*

*If the quick spirits in your eye*
*Now languish, and anon must dye;*
*If every sweet, and every grace,*
*Must fly from that forsaken face:*

SONG. PERSWASIONS TO ENJOY.

1 *spirits:* the "vital spirit" of medieval and Renaissance physiology, which originated in the heart and flowed through the veins, animating the body.

*Then* (Celia) *let us reape our joyes,*
*E're time such goodly fruit destroyes.*

*Or, if that golden fleece must grow*
*For ever, free from aged snow:*
*If those bright Suns must know no shade,*
*Nor your fresh beauties ever fade;*
*Then feare not* (Celia) *to bestow,*
*What still being gather'd, still must grow.*
*Thus, either* Time *his Sickle brings*
*In vaine, or else in vaine his wings.*

## *A deposition from Love*

I was foretold, your rebell sex,
Nor love, nor pitty knew;
And with what scorne, you use to vex
Poore hearts, that humbly sue;
Yet I believ'd, to crowne our paine,
Could we the fortresse win,
The happy lover sure should gaine,
A Paradise within:
I thought loves plagues, like Dragons sate,
Only to fright us at the gate.

But I did enter, and enjoy,
What happy lovers prove;
For I could kisse, and sport, and toy,
And tast those sweets of love;
Which had they but a lasting state,
Or if in *Celia's* brest,
The force of love might not abate,
*Jove* were too meane a guest.

A DEPOSITION FROM LOVE.
12 *prove:* experience.
17 *not:* The 1640 edition has *nor.*

But now her breach of faith, far more
Afflicts, then did her scorne before.

Hard fate! to have been once possest
As victor, of a heart,
Atchiev'd with labour, and unrest,
And then forc'd to depart.
If the stout Foe will not resigne,
When I besiege a Towne,
I lose, but what was never mine;
But he that is cast downe
From enjoy'd beautie, feeles a woe,
Onely deposed Kings can know.

## *Ingratefull beauty threatned*

Know *Celia,* (since thou art so proud,)
'Twas I that gave thee thy renowne:
Thou hadst, in the forgotten crowd
Of common beauties, liv'd unknowne,
Had not my verse exhal'd thy name,
And with it, ympt the wings of fame.

That killing power is none of thine,
I gave it to thy voyce, and eyes:
Thy sweets, thy graces, all are mine;
Thou art my starre, shin'st in my skies;
Then dart not from thy borrowed sphere
Lightning on him, that fixt thee there.

Tempt me with such affrights no more,
Lest what I made, I uncreate;
Let fooles thy mystique formes adore,
I'le know thee in thy mortall state:

INGRATEFULL BEAUTY THREATNED.
6 *ympt:* grafted feathers onto.

Wise Poets that wrap't Truth in tales,
Knew her themselves, through all her vailes.

## *To my Mistresse in absence*

Though I must live here, and by force
Of your command suffer divorce;
Though I am parted, yet my mind,
(That's more my selfe) still stayes behind;
I breath in you, you keepe my heart;
'Twas but a carkasse that did part.
Then though our bodyes are dis-joynd,
As things that are to place confin'd;
Yet let our boundlesse spirits meet,
And in loves spheare each other greet;
There let us worke a mystique wreath,
Unknowne unto the world beneath;
There let us claspt loves sweetly twin;
There let our secret thoughts unseen,
Like nets be weav'd, and inter-twin'd,
Wherewith wee'le catch each others mind:
There whilst our soules doe sit and kisse,
Tasting a sweet, and subtle blisse,
(Such as grosse lovers cannot know,
Whose hands, and lips, meet here below;)
Let us looke downe, and marke what paine
Our absent bodyes here sustaine,
And smile to see how farre away
The one, doth from the other stray;
Yet burne, and languish with desire
To joyne, and quench their mutuall fire.
There let us joy to see from farre,
Our emulous flames at loving warre,

TO MY MISTRESSE.

1 ff.: This poem can be profitably compared and contrasted with Donne's "Extasie" and, for lines 23–24, "A Valediction forbidding mourning."

Whilst both with equall luster shine,
Mine bright as yours, yours bright as mine.
There seated in those heavenly bowers,
Wee'le cheat the lag, and lingring houres,
Making our bitter absence sweet,
Till soules, and bodyes both, may meet.

## Celia *bleeding, to the Surgeon*

Fond man, that canst beleeve her blood
  Will from those purple chanels flow;
Or that the pure untainted flood,
  Can any foule distemper know;
Or that thy weake steele can incize
The Crystall case, wherein it lyes.

Know; her quick blood, proud of his seat,
  Runs dauncing through her azure veines;
Whose harmony no cold, nor heat
  Disturbs, whose hue no tincture staines;
And the hard rock wherein it dwells,
The keenest darts of Love repels.

But thou reply'st, behold she bleeds;
  Foole, thou'rt deceivd; and dost not know
The mystique knot whence this proceeds,
  How Lovers in each other grow;
Thou struckst her arme, but 'twas my heart
Shed all the blood, felt all the smart.

## *To* T. H. *a Lady resembling my Mistresse*

Fayre copie of my *Celia's* face,
Twin of my soule, thy perfect grace
Claymes in my love an equall place.

Disdaine not a divided heart,
Though all be hers, you shall have part;
Love is not tyde to rules of art.

For as my soule first to her flew,
Yet stay'd with me; so now 'tis true
It dwells with her, though fled to you.

Then entertaine this wandring guest,
And if not love, allow it rest;
It left not, but mistooke the nest.

Nor thinke my love, or your faire eyes
Cheaper, 'cause from the sympathise
You hold with her, these flames arise.

To Lead, or Brasse, or some such bad
Mettall, a Princes stamp may adde
That valew, which it never had.

But to the pure refined Ore,
The stamp of Kings imparts no more
Worth, then the mettall held before.

TO T. H.

14 *sympathise:* sympathies, community of feeling.

16–27: Dunlap (*Poems*) compares Donne's elegy, "Image of her whom I love," lines 1–6, and "The Second Anniversary," lines 223–25.

Only the Image gives the rate
To Subjects; in a forraine State
'Tis priz'd as much for its owne waight.

So though all other hearts resigne
To your pure worth, yet you have mine
Only because you are her coyne.

## *To Saxham*

Though frost, and snow, lockt from mine eyes
That beautie which without dore lyes;
Thy gardens, orchards, walkes, that so
I might not all thy pleasures know;
Yet (*Saxham*) thou within thy gate,
Art of thy selfe so delicate;
So full of native sweets, that blesse
Thy roofe with inward happinesse;
As neither from, nor to thy store
Winter takes ought, or Spring addes more.
The cold and frozen ayre had sterv'd
Much poore, if not by thee preserv'd;
Whose prayers have made thy Table blest
With plenty, far above the rest.
The season hardly did afford
Course cates unto thy neighbours board,
Yet thou hadst daintyes, as the skie
Had only been thy Volarie;

TO SAXHAM: Little Saxham, near Bury, was the estate of Sir John Crofts (1563–1628), with whose family Carew was quite intimate. Jonson had provided Carew with a model for this country-house poem in "To Penshurst."

11 *sterv'd:* caused to die.
16 *Course:* Coarse, rude.
18 *Volarie:* aviary.

Or else the birds, fearing the snow
Might to another deluge grow:
The Pheasant, Partiridge, and the Larke,
Flew to thy house, as to the Arke.
The willing Oxe, of himselfe came
Home to the slaughter, with the Lambe,
And every beast did thither bring
Himselfe, to be an offering.
The scalie herd, more pleasure tooke,
Bath'd in thy dish, then in the brooke:
Water, Earth, Ayre, did all conspire,
To pay their tributes to thy fire,
Whose cherishing flames themselves divide
Through every roome, where they deride
The night, and cold abroad; whilst they
Like suns within, keepe endlesse day.
Those chearfull beames send forth their light,
To all that wander in the night,
And seeme to becken from aloofe,
The weary Pilgrim to thy roofe;
Where if refresh't, he will away,
Hee's fairly welcome, or if stay
Farre more, which he shall hearty find,
Both from the Master, and the Hinde.
The strangers welcome, each man there
Stamp'd on his chearfull brow, doth weare;
Nor doth this welcome, or his cheere
Grow lesse, 'cause he staies longer here.
There's none observes (much lesse repines)
How often this man sups or dines.
Thou hast no Porter at the doore
T'examine, or keep back the poore;
Nor locks, nor bolts; thy gates have bin
Made onely to let strangers in;

37 *from aloofe:* at a distance.
42 *Hinde:* servant.

Untaught to shut, they doe not feare
To stand wide open all the yeare;
Carelesse who enters, for they know,
Thou never didst deserve a foe;
And as for theeves, thy bountie's such;
They cannot steale, thou giv'st so much.

## *Upon a Ribband*

This silken wreath, which circles in mine arme,
Is but an Emblem of that mystique charme,
Wherewith the magique of your beauties binds
My captive soule, and round about it winds
Fetters of lasting love; This hath entwind
My flesh alone, That hath empalde my mind:
Time may weare out These soft weak bands; but Those
Strong chaines of brasse, Fate shall not discompose.
This holy relique may preserve my wrist,
But my whole frame doth by That power subsist:
To That my prayers and sacrifice, to This
I onely pay a superstitious kisse:
This but the Idoll, That's the Deitie,
Religion there is due; Here ceremonie.
That I receive by faith, This but in trust;
Here I may tender dutie, There I must.
This order as a Layman I may beare,
But I become Loves Priest when That I weare.
This moves like ayre; That as the Center stands:
That knot your vertue tide: This but your hands:
That Nature fram'd, but This was made by Art;
This makes my arme your prisoner, That my heart.

UPON A RIBBAND.

1 ff.: For the image, cf. Donne, "The Funerall," line 3: "That subtile wreath of haire, which crowns my arme."

6 *empalde:* shut in, hedged about.

19 *Center:* the earth.

## *Song.*

## To my Mistris, I burning in love

*I burne, and cruell you, in vaine*
*Hope to quench me with disdaine;*
*If from your eyes, those sparkles came,*
*That have kindled all this flame,*
*What bootes it me, though now you shrowde*
*Those fierce Comets in a cloude?*
*Since all the flames that I have felt,*
*Could your snow yet never melt,*
*Nor, can your snow (though you should take*
Alpes *into your bosome) slake*
*The heate of my enamour'd heart;*
*But with wonder learne Loves art!*
*No seaes of yce can coole desire,*
*Equall flames must quench Loves fire:*
*Then thinke not that my heat can dye,*
*Till you burne aswell as I.*

## *Song.*

## To her againe, she burning in a Feaver

*Now she burnes as well as I,*
*Yet my heat can never dye;*
*She burnes that never knew desire,*
*She that was yce, she now is fire.*
*Shee whose cold heart, chaste thoughts did arme*
*So, as Loves flames could never warme*
*The frozen bosome where it dwelt,*
*She burnes, and all her beauties melt;*
*She burnes, and cryes, Loves fires are milde;*
*Feavers are Gods, and He's a childe.*
*Love; let her know the difference*
*Twixt the heat of soule, and sence.*
*Touch her with thy flames divine,*
*So shalt thou quench her fire, and mine.*

## *A flye that flew into my Mistris her eye*

When this Flye liv'd, she us'd to play
In the Sun-shine all the day;
Till comming neere my *Celia's* sight,
She found a new, and unknowne light

TO HER AGAINE, SHE BURNING IN A FEAVER.

4 *now is: 1640* reads *that was.*

10 *and: 1640* omits; *childe:* i.e. Cupid, the god of love, to whom the fevers belong.

So full of glory, as it made
The noone-day Sun a gloomy shade;
Then this amorous Flye became
My rivall, and did court my flame.
She did from hand to bosome skip,
And from her breath, her cheeke, and lip,
Suckt all the incense, and the spice,
And grew a bird of Paradise:
At last into her eye she flew,
There scorcht in flames, and drown'd in dew:
Like *Phaeton* from the Suns spheare
She fell, and with her dropt a teare:
Of which a pearle was straight compos'd,
Wherein her ashes lye enclos'd.
Thus she receiv'd from *Celia's* eye,
Funerall flame, tombe, Obsequie.

## *Song.*

## To one that desired to know my Mistris

*Seeke not to know my love, for shee*
*Hath vow'd her constant faith to me;*
*Her milde aspects are mine, and thou*
*Shalt only find a stormy brow:*
*For if her beautie stirre desire*
*In me, her kisses quench the fire.*
*Or, I can to Love's fountaine goe,*
*Or dwell upon her hills of snow.*
*But when thou burn'st, she shall not spare*
*One gentle breath to coole the ayre.* VJ

TO ONE THAT DESIRED TO KNOW MY MISTRIS.
7 *Or:* Either.

*Thou shalt not climbe those* Alpes, *nor spye*
*Where the sweet springs of* Venus *lye;*
*Search hidden Nature, and there find*
*A treasure to inrich thy mind;*
*Discover Arts not yet reveal'd,*
*But let my Mistris live conceal'd;*
*Though men by knowledge wiser grow,*
*Yet here 'tis wisdome not to know.*

## *Boldnesse in love*

Marke how the bashfull morne, in vaine
Courts the amorous Marigold,
With sighing blasts, and weeping raine;
Yet she refuses to unfold.
But when the Planet of the day,
Approacheth with his powerfull ray,
Then she spreads, then she receives
His warmer beames into her virgin leaves.
So shalt thou thrive in love, fond Boy;
If thy teares, and sighes discover
Thy griefe, thou never shalt enjoy
The just reward of a bold lover:
But when with moving accents, thou
Shalt constant faith, and service vow,
Thy *Celia* shall receive those charmes
With open eares, and with unfolded armes.

## A Pastorall Dialogue.
### *Celia.* *Cleon.*

As *Celia* rested in the shade
With *Cleon* by her side;
The swaine thus courted the young Maid,
And thus the Nymph replide.

*CL.*

Sweet! let thy captive, fetters weare
Made of thine armes, and hands;
Till such as thraldome scorne, or feare,
Envie those happy bands.

*CE.*

Then thus my willing armes I winde
About thee, and am so
Thy pris'ner; for my selfe I bind,
Untill I let thee goe.

*CL.*

Happy that slave, whom the faire foe
Tyes in so soft a chaine.
*CE.* Farre happier I, but that I know
Thou wilt breake loose againe.

*CL.*

By thy immortall beauties never.
*CE.* Fraile as thy love's thine oath.
*CL.* Though beautie fade, my faith lasts ever.
*CE.* Time will destroy them both.

*CL.*

I dote not on thy snow-white skin.
*CE.* What then? *CL.* Thy purer mind.
*CE.* It lov'd too soone. *CL.* Thou hadst not bin
So faire, if not so kind.

*CE.*

Oh strange vaine fancie! *CL.* But yet true.
*CE.* Prove it. *CL.* Then make a brade
Of those loose flames, that circle you,
My sunnes, and yet your shade.

*CE.*

'Tis done. *CL.* Now give it me. *CE.* Thus thou
Shalt thine owne errour find,
If these were beauties, I am now
Lesse faire, because more kind.

A PASTORALL DIALOGUE.
26 *brade:* a wreath or bracelet of hair.

*CL.*

You shall confesse you erre; that haire
Shall it not change the hue,
Or leave the golden mountaine bare?
*CE.* Aye me! it is too true.

*CL.*

But this small wreathe, shall ever stay
In its first native prime,
And smiling when the rest decay,
The triumphs sing of time.

*CE.*

Then let me cut from thy faire grove,
One branch, and let that be
An embleme of eternall love,
For such is mine to thee.

*CL.*

Thus are we both redeem'd from time,
I by thy grace. *CE.* And I
Shall live in thy immortall rime,
Untill the Muses dye.

*CL.*

By heaven! *CE.* Sweare not; if I must weepe,
*Jove* shall not smile at me;
This kisse, my heart, and thy faith keepe.
*CL.* This breathes my soule to thee.

Then forth the thicket *Thirsis* rusht,
Where he saw all their play:
The swaine stood still, and smil'd, and blusht,
The Nymph fled fast away.

## A Pastorall Dialogue.

### *Shepherd.* *Nymph.* *Chorus.*

*Shep.* This mossie bank they prest. *Ny.* That aged Oak
Did canopie the happy payre
All night from the dampe ayre.
*Cho.* Here let us sit and sing the words they spoke,
Till the day breaking, their embraces broke.

*Shep.*

See love, the blushes of the morne appeare,
And now she hangs her pearlie store
(Rob'd from the Easterne shore)
I'th' Couslips bell, and Roses eare:
Sweet, I must stay no longer here.

A PASTORALL DIALOGUE.
9 *eare:* The 1640 edition reads *rare.*

*Nymph.*

Those streakes of doubtfull light, usher not day,
But shew my sunne must set; no Morne
Shall shine till thou returne,
The yellow Planets, and the gray
Dawne, shall attend thee on thy way.

*Shep.*

If thine eyes guild my pathes, they may forbeare
Their uselesse shine. *Nymph.* My teares will quite
Extinguish their faint light.
*She.* Those drops will make their beames more cleare,
Loves flames will shine in every teare.

*Cho.*

They kist, and wept, and from their lips, and eyes,
In a mixt dew, of brinie sweet,
Their joyes, and sorrowes meet,
But she cryes out. *Nymp.* Shepherd arise,
The Sun betrayes us else to spies.

*Shep.*

The winged houres flye fast, whilst we embrace,
But when we want their help to meet,
They move with leaden feet.
*Nym.* Then let us pinion *Time,* and chase
The day for ever from this place.

*Shep.*

Harke! *Ny.* Aye me stay! *She.* For ever. *Ny.* No, arise,
Wee must be gone. *Shep.* My nest of spice.
*Nymph.* My soule. *Shep.* My Paradise.
*Cho.* Neither could say farewell, but through their eyes
Griefe, interrupted speach with teares supplyes.

## *Red, and white Roses*

Reade in these Roses, the sad story
Of my hard fate, and your owne glory:
In the White you may discover
The palenesse of a fainting lover:
In the Red, the flames still feeding
On my heart with fresh wounds bleeding.
The White will tell you how I languish,
And the Red expresse my anguish.
The White my innocence displaying,
The Red my martyrdome betraying.
The frownes that on your brow resided,
Have those Roses thus divided.
Oh let your smiles but cleare the weather,
And then they both shall grow together.

## *To my Cousin* (C. R.) *marry-ing my Lady* (A.)

Happy Youth, that shalt possesse
Such a spring-tyde of delight,
As the sated Appetite
Shall enjoying such excesse,
Wish the flood of pleasure lesse:
When the Hymeneall Rite
Is perform'd, invoke the night,
That it may in shadowes dresse
Thy too reall happinesse;
Else (as *Semele*) the bright
Deitie in her full might,
May thy feeble soule oppresse.
Strong perfumes, and glaring light,
Oft destroy both smell, and sight.

## *A Rapture*

I will enjoy thee now my *Celia,* come
And flye with me to Loves Elizium:
The Gyant, Honour, that keepes cowards out,
Is but a Masquer, and the servile rout
Of baser subjects onely, bend in vaine
To the vast Idoll, whilst the nobler traine

TO MY COUSIN: Carew's cousin, a distant relation, was Carew Raleigh (d. 1666), the second son of Sir Walter. He married Philippa, the widow of Sir Anthony Ashley (d. 1627).

10 *Semele:* The daughter of Cadmus, who was destroyed when Jove, at her request, revealed his full majesty to her.

Of valiant Lovers, daily sayle betweene
The huge Collosses legs, and passe unseene
Unto the blissfull shore; be bold, and wise,
And we shall enter, the grim Swisse denies
Only tame fooles a passage, that not know
He is but forme, and onely frights in show
The duller eyes that looke from farre; draw neere,
And thou shalt scorne, what we were wont to feare.
We shall see how the stalking Pageant goes
With borrowed legs, a heavie load to those
That made, and beare him; not as we once thought
The seed of Gods, but a weake modell wrought
By greedy men, that seeke to enclose the common,
And within private armes empale free woman.
  Come then, and mounted on the wings of love
Wee'le cut the flitting ayre, and sore above
The Monsters head, and in the noblest seates
Of those blest shades, quench, and renew our heates.
There, shall the Queene of Love, and Innocence,
Beautie and Nature, banish all offence
From our close Ivy twines, there I'le behold
Thy bared snow, and thy unbraded gold.
There, my enfranchiz'd hand, on every side
Shall o're thy naked polish'd Ivory slide.
No curtaine there, though of transparant lawne,
Shall be before thy virgin-treasure drawne;
But the rich Mine, to the enquiring eye
Expos'd, shall ready still for mintage lye,
And we will coyne young *Cupids*. There, a bed
Of Roses, and fresh Myrtles, shall be spread
Under the cooler shade of Cypresse groves:
Our pillowes, of the downe of *Venus* Doves,

A RAPTURE.

10 *Swisse:* a Swiss-guard, like those at the Vatican in Rome.
11 *tame: 1640* reads *to tame.*
22 *sore:* soar.
25 *Queene: 1640* reads *Queens.*
31 *lawne:* fine linen.

Whereon our panting lims wee'le gently lay
In the faint respites of our active play;
That so our slumbers, may in dreames have leisure,
To tell the nimble fancie our past pleasure;
And so our soules that cannot be embrac'd,
Shall the embraces of our bodyes taste.
Meane while the bubbling streame shall court the shore,
Th'enamoured chirping Wood-quire shall adore
In varied tunes the Deitie of Love;
The gentle blasts of Westerne winds, shall move
The trembling leaves, & through their close bows breath
Still Musick, whilst we rest our selves beneath
Their dancing shade; till a soft murmure, sent
From soules entranc'd in amorous languishment
Rowze us, and shoot into our veines fresh fire,
Till we, in their sweet extasie expire.
  Then, as the empty Bee, that lately bore,
Into the common treasure, all her store,
Flyes 'bout the painted field with nimble wing,
Deflowring the fresh virgins of the Spring;
So will I rifle all the sweets, that dwell
In my delicious Paradise, and swell
My bagge with honey, drawne forth by the power
Of fervent kisses, from each spicie flower.
I'le seize the Rose-buds in their perfum'd bed,
The Violet knots, like curious Mazes spread
O're all the Garden, taste the ripned Cherry,
The warme, firme Apple, tipt with corall berry:
Then will I visit, with a wandring kisse,
The vale of Lillies, and the Bower of blisse:
And where the beauteous Region doth divide
Into two milkie wayes, my lips shall slide
Downe those smooth Allies, wearing as I goe
A tract for lovers on the printed snow;
Thence climbing o're the swelling *Appenine*,
Retire into thy grove of Eglantine;

72 *tract:* trail, path.

Where I will all those ravisht sweets distill
Through Loves Alimbique, and with Chimmique skill
From the mixt masse, one soveraigne Balme derive,
Then bring that great *Elixar* to thy hive.
  Now in more subtile wreathes I will entwine
My sinowie thighes, my legs and armes with thine;
Thou like a sea of milke shalt lye display'd,
Whilst I the smooth, calme Ocean, invade
With such a tempest, as when *Jove* of old
Fell downe on *Danae* in a storme of gold:
Yet my tall Pine, shall in the *Cyprian* straight
Ride safe at Anchor, and unlade her fraight:
My Rudder, with thy bold hand, like a tryde,
And skilfull Pilot, thou shalt steere, and guide
My Bark into Loves channell, where it shall
Dance, as the bounding waves doe rise or fall:
Then shall thy circling armes, embrace and clip
My willing bodie, and thy balmie lip
Bathe me in juyce of kisses, whose perfume
Like a religious incense shall consume,
And send up holy vapours, to those powres
That blesse our loves, and crowne our sportfull houres,
That with such Halcion calmenesse, fix our soules
In steadfast peace, as no affright controules.
There, no rude sounds shake us with sudden starts,
No jealous eares, when we unrip our hearts
Sucke our discourse in, no observing spies
This blush, that glance traduce; no envious eyes
Watch our close meetings, nor are we betrayd
To Rivals, by the bribed chamber-maid.
No wedlock bonds unwreathe our twisted loves;
We seeke no midnight Arbor, no darke groves
To hide our kisses, there, the hated name
Of husband, wife, lust, modest, chaste, or shame,

76 *Alimbique:* vessel used in alchemy for distillation; *Chimmique:* chemical.
85 *Cyprian:* The island of Cyprus was sacred to Venus.

Are vaine and empty words, whose very sound
Was never heard in the Elizian ground.
All things are lawfull there, that may delight
Nature, or unrestrained Appetite;
Like, and enjoy, to will, and act, is one,
We only sinne when Loves rites are not done.
  The Roman *Lucrece* there, reades the divine
Lectures of Loves great master, *Aretine,*
And knowes as well as *Lais,* how to move
Her plyant body in the act of love.
To quench the burning Ravisher, she hurles
Her limbs into a thousand winding curles,
And studies artfull postures, such as be
Carv'd on the barke of every neighbouring tree
By learned hands, that so adorn'd the rinde,
Of those faire Plants, which as they lay entwinde,
Have fann'd their glowing fires. The Grecian Dame,
That in her endlesse webb, toyl'd for a name
As fruitlesse as her worke, doth there display
Her selfe before the Youth of *Ithaca,*
And th'amorous sport of gamesome nights prefer,
Before dull dreams of the lost Traveller.
*Daphne* hath broke her barke, and that swift foot,
Which th'angry Gods had fastned with a root
To the fixt earth, doth now unfetter'd run,
To meet th'embraces of the youthfull Sun:
She hangs upon him, like his Delphique Lyre,
Her kisses blow the old, and breath new fire:
Full of her God, she sings inspired Layes,
Sweet Odes of love, such as deserve the Bayes,

115 *Lucrece:* The chaste matron of Roman legend, who committed suicide after being ravished by Tarquin. In the next line Carew alludes to Pietro Aretino (1492–1556), the notorious Italian satirist, who, in one of his dialogues, had reversed the traditional view of Lucrece.

117 *Lais:* The celebrated prostitute of ancient Corinth.

125 *Grecian Dame:* Penelope, the wife of Ulysses.

131 *Daphne:* Changed into a tree after she refused to submit to Apollo's advances.

Which she her selfe was. Next her, *Laura* lyes
In *Petrarchs* learned armes, drying those eyes
That did in such sweet smooth-pac'd numbers flow,
As made the world enamour'd of his woe.
These, and ten thousand Beauties more, that dy'de
Slave to the Tyrant, now enlarg'd, deride
His cancell'd lawes, and for their time mispent,
Pay into Loves Exchequer double rent.
  Come then my *Celia*, wee'le no more forbeare
To taste our joyes, struck with a Pannique feare,
But will depose from his imperious sway
This proud *Usurper* and walke free, as they
With necks unyoak'd; nor is it just that Hee
Should fetter your soft sex with Chastitie,
Which Nature made unapt for abstinence;
When yet this false Imposter can dispence
With humane Justice, and with sacred right,
And maugre both their lawes command me fight
With Rivals, or with emulous Loves, that dare
Equall with thine, their Mistresse eyes, or haire:
If thou complaine of wrong, and call my sword
To carve out thy revenge, upon that word
He bids me fight and kill, or else he brands
With markes of infamie my coward hands,
And yet religion bids from blood-shed flye,
And damns me for that Act. Then tell me why
This Goblin Honour which the world adores,
Should make men Atheists, and not women Whores.

139 *Laura:* The lady to whom Petrarch (1304–1374) addressed his sonnets.
156 *maugre:* despite.

## *Epitaph on the Lady* Mary Villers

The Lady *Mary Villers* lyes
Under this stone; with weeping eyes
The Parents that first gave her birth,
And their sad Friends, lay'd her in earth:
If any of them (Reader) were
Knowne unto thee, shed a teare,
Or if thyselfe possesse a gemme,
As deare to thee, as this to them;
Though a stranger to this place,
Bewayle in theirs, thine owne hard case;
For thou perhaps at thy returne
Mayest find thy Darling in an Urne.

## *An other*

The purest Soule that e're was sent
Into a clayie tenement
Inform'd this dust, but the weake mold
Could the great guest no longer hold,
The substance was too pure, the flame
Too glorious that thither came;
Ten thousand *Cupids* brought along
A Grace on each wing, that did throng
For place there, till they all opprest
The seat in which they sought to rest;
So the faire Modell broke, for want
Of roome to lodge th'Inhabitant.

EPITAPH ON THE LADY: Mary Villers died on August 4, 1630, aged two and one half years.

AN OTHER.
11 *Modell:* mould, form.

## *An other*

This little Vault, this narrow roome,
Of Love, and Beautie is the tombe,
The dawning beame that 'gan to cleare
Our clouded skie, lyes darkned here,
For ever set to us, by death
Sent to enflame the world beneath;
'Twas but a bud, yet did containe
More sweetnesse then shall spring againe,
A budding starre that might have growne
Into a Sun, when it had blowne.
This hopefull beautie, did create
New life in Loves declining state;
But now his Empire ends, and we
From fire, and wounding darts are free:
His brand, his bow, let no man feare,
The flames, the arrowes, all lye here.

## *Maria Wentworth, Thomae Comitis Cleveland, filia praemortua prima Virgineam animam exhalavit*

*An. Dom. 1632 AEt. suae 18*

And here the precious dust is layd;
Whose purely-tempered Clay was made
So fine, that it the guest betray'd.

Else the soule grew so fast within,
It broke the outward shell of sinne,
And so was hatch'd a Cherubin.

In heigth, it soar'd to God above;
In depth, it did to knowledge move,
And spread in breadth to generall love.

Before, a pious duty shind
To Parents, courtesie behind,
On either side an equall mind,

Good to the Poore, to kindred deare,
To servants kind, to friendship cleare,
To nothing but her selfe, severe.

So though a Virgin, yet a Bride
To every Grace, she justifi'd
A chaste Poligamie, and dy'd.

MARIA WENTWORTH: Maria was the second daughter of Sir Thomas Wentworth and Anne, the daughter of Sir John Crofts of Saxham. Her tomb, at Toddington, Bedfordshire, has Carew's first six stanzas inscribed on it.

Learne from hence (Reader) what small trust
We owe this world, where vertue must
Fraile as our flesh, crumble to dust.

## To Ben. Iohnson.

### *Upon occasion of his Ode of defiance annext to his Play of the new Inne*

Tis true (deare *Ben:*) thy just chastizing hand
Hath fixt upon the sotted Age a brand
To their swolne pride, and empty scribbling due,
It can nor judge, nor write, and yet 'tis true
Thy commique Muse from the exalted line
Toucht by thy *Alchymist,* doth since decline
From that her Zenith, and foretells a red
And blushing evening, when she goes to bed,
Yet such, as shall out-shine the glimmering light
With which all stars shall guild the following night.
Nor thinke it much (since all thy Eaglets may
Endure the Sunnie tryall) if we say
This hath the stronger wing, or that doth shine
Trickt up in fairer plumes, since all are thine;
Who hath his flock of cackling Geese compar'd
With thy tun'd quire of Swans? or else who dar'd
To call thy births deformed? but if thou bind
By Citie-custome, or by *Gavell-kind,*

TO BEN IOHNSON: Jonson's play was hissed when first performed in 1629. When he published it in 1631, he appended the ode, "Come leave the loathed stage."

11–12 *Eaglets . . . tryall:* The eagle tested the legitimacy of her offspring by forcing them to look directly at the sun.

16 *quire:* choir.

18 *Citie-custome:* the estate of a citizen of London was divided into three parts, one to the wife, one to the children, and one to the executors to discharge

In equall shares thy love on all thy race,
We may distinguish of their sexe, and place;
Though one hand form them, & though one brain strike
Soules into all, they are not all alike.
Why should the follies then of this dull age
Draw from thy Pen such an immodest rage
As seemes to blast thy (else-immortall) Bayes,
When thine owne tongue proclaimes thy ytch of praise?
Such thirst will argue drouth. No, let be hurld
Upon thy workes, by the detracting world,
What malice can suggest; let the Rowte say,
The running sands, that (ere thou make a play)
Count the slow minutes, might a *Goodwin* frame
To swallow when th' hast done thy ship-wrackt name.
Let them the deare expence of oyle upbraid
Suckt by thy watchfull Lampe, that hath betray'd
To theft the blood of martyr'd Authors, spilt
Into thy inke, whilst thou growest pale with guilt.
Repine not at the Tapers thriftie waste,
That sleekes thy terser Poems, nor is haste
Prayse, but excuse; and if thou overcome
A knottie writer, bring the bootie home;
Nor thinke it theft, if the rich spoyles so torne
From conquered Authors, be as Trophies worne.
Let others glut on the extorted praise
Of vulgar breath, trust thou to after dayes:
Thy labour'd workes shall live, when Time devoures
Th'abortive off-spring of their hastie houres.
Thou art not of their ranke, the quarrell lyes
Within thine owne Virge, then let this suffice,
The wiser world doth greater Thee confesse
Then all men else, then Thy selfe onely lesse.

---

legacies. *Gavell-kind:* a system of land tenure peculiar to Kent. Under its provisions, directly opposed to primogeniture, an estate was divided up equally among the heirs rather than descending to the oldest alone.

29 *Rowte:* the (vulgar) populace.

31 *Count . . . minutes:* Jonson's slowness in composition was well-known. *Goodwin:* the famous Goodwin Sands, treacherous to sailors.

48 *Virge:* territory, domain.

# An Hymeneall Dialogue.
# Bride and Groome

*Groome.* Tell me (my love) since Hymen ty'de
The holy knot, hast thou not felt
A new infused spirit slide
Into thy brest, whilst thine did melt?

*Bride.* First tell me (sweet) whose words were those?
For though your voyce the ayre did breake,
Yet did my soule the sence compose,
And through your lips my heart did speake.

*Groo.* Then I perceive, when from the flame
Of love, my scorch'd soule did retire,
Your frozen heart in her place came,
And sweetly melted in that fire.

*Bride.* 'Tis true, for when that mutuall change
Of soules, was made with equall gaine,
I straight might feele diffus'd a strange,
But gentle heat through every veine.

*Chorus.* Oh blest dis-union, that doth so
Our bodyes from our soules divide,
As two doe one, and one foure grow,
Each by contraction multiply'de.

*Bride.* Thy bosome then I'le make my nest,
Since there my willing soule doth pearch.
*Groo.* And for my heart in thy chast brest,
I'le make an everlasting search.

*Chorus.* Oh blest disunion, & *c.*

AN HYMENEALL DIALOGUE.
6 *the:* The 1640 edition reads *your.*

## *Obsequies to the Lady*
## Anne Hay

I heard the Virgins sigh, I saw the sleeke
And polisht Courtier, channell his fresh cheeke
With reall teares; the new-betrothed Maid
Smild not that day; the graver Senate layd
Their businesse by; of all the Courtly throng,
Griefe seald the heart, and silence bound the tongue.
I that ne're more of private sorrow knew
Then from my Pen some froward Mistresse drew,
And for the publike woe, had my dull sense
So sear'd with ever adverse influence,
As the invaders sword might have, unfelt,
Pierc'd my dead bosome, yet began to melt:
Griefe's strong instinct, did to my blood suggest
In the unknowne losse peculiar interest.
But when I heard, the noble *Carlil's* Gemme,
The fayrest branch of *Dennye's* ancient stemme
Was from that Casket stolne, from this Trunke torne,
I found just cause, why they, why I should mourne.
  But who shall guide my artlesse Pen, to draw
Those blooming beauties, which I never saw?
How shall posteritie beleeve my story,
If I, her crowded graces, and the glory
Due to her riper vertues, shall relate
Without the knowledge of her mortall state?

OBSEQUIES TO THE LADY: The Lady Anne Hay, a distant cousin of Carew, died on November 17, 1629.

15–16 *Carlil's . . . Dennye's:* Anne was descended from Sir Anthony Denny and James Hay, the first Earl of Carlisle.

Shall I, as once *Apelles,* here a feature,
There steale a Grace, and rifling so whole Nature
Of all the sweets a learned eye can see,
Figure one *Venus,* and say, such was shee?
Shall I her legend fill, with what of old
Hath of the Worthies of her sex beene told,
And what all pens, and times to all dispence,
Restraine to her, by a prophetique sence?
Or shall I, to the Morall, and Divine
Exactest lawes, shape by an even line,
A life so straight, as it should shame the square
Left in the rules of *Katherine,* or *Clare,*
And call it hers, say, so did she begin,
And had she liv'd, such had her progresse been?
These are dull wayes, by which base pens, for hire,
Dawbe glorious vice, and from *Apollo's* quire
Steale holy Dittyes, which prophanely they
Upon the herse of every strumpet lay.
  We will not bathe thy corps with a forc'd teare,
Nor shall thy traine borrow the blacks they weare:
Such vulgar spice, and gums, embalme not thee,
Thou art the Theame of Truth, not Poetrie.
Thou shalt endure a tryall by thy Peeres,
Virgins of equall birth, of equall yeares,
Whose vertues held with thine an emulous strife,
Shall draw thy picture, and record thy life.
One shall enspheare thine eyes, another shall
Impearle thy teeth; a third, thy white and small
Hand, shall besnow; a fourth, incarnadine
Thy rosie cheeke, untill each beauteous line,

25 *Apelles:* This story is told of Zeuxis by Pliny (*Natural History* 35.6), but it was often applied to Apelles.

36 *Katherine:* St. Catherine of Siena (1347–1380), famed for her ascetic discipline; *Clare:* St. Clare (1194–1253) founded the Franciscan order of Poor Clares.

40 *Dawbe . . . vice:* paint vice as if it were glorious, whitewash it.

44 *blacks:* black funeral garments.

Drawne by her hand, in whom that part excells,
Meet in one Center, where all beautie dwells.
Others, in taske shall thy choyce vertues share,
Some shall their birth, some their ripe growth declare,
Though niggard *Time* left much unhach'd by deeds,
They shall relate how thou hadst all the seeds
Of every Vertue, which in the pursuit
Of time, must have brought forth admired fruit.
Thus shalt thou, from the mouth of envy, raise
A glorious journall of thy thrifty dayes,
Like a bright starre, shot from his spheare, whose race
In a continued line of flames, we trace.
This, if survay'd, shall to thy view impart
How little more then late, thou wer't, thou art,
This shall gaine credit with succeeding times,
When nor by bribed pens, nor partiall rimes
Of engag'd kindred, but the sacred truth
Is storied by the partners of thy youth;
Their breath shall Saint thee, and be this thy pride,
Thus even by Rivals to be Deifide.

## An Elegie upon the death of the Deane of Pauls, Dr. John Donne

Can we not force from widdowed Poetry,
Now thou art dead (Great DONNE) one Elegie
To crowne thy Hearse? Why yet dare we not trust
Though with unkneaded dowe-bak't prose thy dust,
Such as the uncisor'd Churchman from the flower
Of fading Rhetorique, short liv'd as his houre,

AN ELEGIE: Donne's death occurred on March 31, 1631; Carew's elegy first appeared in the 1633 edition of Donne's poems, from which the text given here is taken.

5 *uncisor'd:* unscissored, with long hair.

Dry as the sand that measures it, should lay
Upon thy Ashes, on the funerall day?
Have we no voice, no tune? Did'st thou dispense
Through all our language, both the words and sense?
'Tis a sad truth; The Pulpit may her plaine,
And sober Christian precepts still retaine,
Doctrines it may, and wholesome Uses frame,
Grave Homilies, and Lectures, But the flame
Of thy brave Soule, that shot such heat and light,
As burnt our earth, and made our darknesse bright,
Committed holy Rapes upon our Will,
Did through the eye the melting heart distill;
And the deep knowledge of darke truths so teach,
As sense might judge, what phansie could not reach;
Must be desir'd for ever. So the fire,
That fills with spirit and heat the Delphique quire,
Which kindled first by thy Promethean breath,
Glow'd here a while, lies quench't now in thy death;
The Muses garden with Pedantique weedes
O'rspred, was purg'd by thee; The lazie seeds
Of servile imitation throwne away;
And fresh invention planted, Thou didst pay
The debts of our penurious bankrupt age;
Licentious thefts, that make poëtique rage
A Mimique fury, when our soules must bee
Possest, or with Anacreons Extasie,
Or Pindars, not their owne; The subtle cheat
Of slie Exchanges, and the jugling feat
Of two-edg'd words, or whatsoever wrong
By ours was done the Greeke, or Latine tongue,
Thou hast redeem'd, and open'd Us a Mine
Of rich and pregnant phansie, drawne a line

9 *dispense:* Carew uses this word with an echo of its religious sense, i.e. to administer the sacraments. The literal meaning here is "to mete out" or "apportion."

21 *Must be desir'd:* The subject of this verb is *flame* in line 14.

22 *Delphique quire:* the voice of Apollo, as it issued from his oracle at Delphos.

Of masculine expression, which had good
Old Orpheus seene, Or all the ancient Brood
Our superstitious fooles admire, and hold
Their lead more precious, then thy burnish't Gold,
Thou hadst beene their Exchequer, and no more
They each in others dust, had rak'd for Ore.
Thou shalt yield no precedence, but of time,
And the blinde fate of language, whose tun'd chime
More charmes the outward sense; Yet thou maist claime
From so great disadvantage greater fame,
Since to the awe of thy imperious wit
Our stubborne language bends, made only fit
With her tough-thick-rib'd hoopes to gird about
Thy Giant phansie, which had prov'd too stout
For their soft melting Phrases. As in time
They had the start, so did they cull the prime
Buds of invention many a hundred yeare,
And left the rifled fields, besides the feare
To touch their Harvest, yet from those bare lands
Of what is purely thine, thy only hands
(And that thy smallest worke) have gleaned more
Then all those times, and tongues could reape before.
  But thou art gone, and thy strict lawes will be
Too hard for Libertines in Poetrie.
They will repeale the goodly exil'd traine
Of gods and goddesses, which in thy just raigne
Were banish'd nobler Poems, now, with these
The silenc'd tales o'th' Metamorphoses
Shall stuffe their lines, and swell the windy Page,
Till Verse refin'd by thee, in this last Age
Turne ballad rime, Or those old Idolls bee
Ador'd againe, with new apostasie.
  Oh, pardon mee, that breake with untun'd verse
The reverend silence that attends thy herse,

63 *repeale:* call back.
66 *Metamorphoses:* alluding to Ovid's work, recently translated by George Sandys.

Whose awfull solemne murmures were to thee
More then these faint lines, A loud Elegie,
That did proclaime in a dumbe eloquence
The death of all the Arts, whose influence
Growne feeble, in these panting numbers lies
Gasping short winded Accents, and so dies:
So doth the swiftly turning wheele not stand
In th'instant we withdraw the moving hand,
But some small time maintaine a faint weake course
By vertue of the first impulsive force:
And so whil'st I cast on thy funerall pile
Thy crowne of Bayes, Oh, let it crack a while,
And spit disdaine, till the devouring flashes
Suck all the moysture up, then turne to ashes.
  I will not draw the envy to engrosse
All thy perfections, or weepe all our losse;
Those are too numerous for an Elegie,
And this too great, to be express'd by mee.
Though every pen should share a distinct part,
Yet art thou Theme enough to tyre all Art;
Let others carve the rest, it shall suffice
I on thy Tombe this Epitaph incise.
  *Here lies a King, that rul'd as hee thought fit*
  *The universall Monarchy of wit;*
  *Here lie two Flamens, and both those, the best,*
  *Apollo's first, at last, the true Gods Priest.*

92 *tyre:* attire, clothe, with a play on "tire."
97 *Flamens:* high priests.

# *In answer of an Elegiacall Letter upon the death of the King of* Sweden *from* Aurelian Townsend, *inviting me to write on that subject*

Why dost thou sound, my deare *Aurelian*,
In so shrill accents, from thy *Barbican*,
A loude allarum to my drowsie eyes,
Bidding them wake in teares and Elegies
For mightie *Swedens* fall? Alas! how may
My Lyrique feet, that of the smooth soft way
Of Love, and Beautie, onely know the tread,
In dancing paces celebrate the dead
Victorious King, or his Majesticke Hearse
Prophane with th' humble touch of their low verse?
*Virgil*, nor *Lucan*, no, nor *Tasso* more
Then both, not *Donne*, worth all that went before,
With the united labour of their wit
Could a just Poem to this subject fit,
His actions were too mighty to be rais'd
Higher by Verse, let him in prose be prays'd,
In modest faithfull story, which his deedes
Shall turne to Poems: when the next Age reades
Of *Frankfort, Leipsigh, Worsburgh*, or the *Rhyne;*
The *Leck*, the *Danube, Tilly, Wallestein,*
*Bavaria, Papenheim, Lutzenfield,* where Hee
Gain'd after death a posthume Victorie,

IN ANSWER: Gustavus Adolphus died at the battle of Lützen on November 6, 1632. Townshend's poem to Carew was first printed by G. C. Moore Smith in the *Modern Language Review,* 12 (1917), 422. A number of elegies on the king by English poets were published in 1633.

2 *Barbican:* a portion of the parish of St. Giles, Cripplegate, where Townshend lived at the time. Carew puns on the word, which also means "watchtower."

They'le thinke his Acts things rather feign'd then done
Like our Romances of the Knight o'th' Sun.
Leave we him then to the grave Chronicler,
Who though to Annals he can not refer
His too-briefe storie, yet his Journals may
Stand by the *Caesars* yeares, and every day
Cut into minutes, each, shall more containe
Of great designement then an Emperours raigne;
And (since 'twas but his Church-yard) let him have
For his owne ashes now no narrower Grave
Then the whole *German* Continents vast wombe,
Whilst all her Cities doe but make his Tombe.
Let us to supreame providence commit
The fate of Monarchs, which first thought it fit
To rend the Empire from the *Austrian* graspe,
And next from *Swedens,* even when he did claspe
Within his dying armes the Soveraigntie
Of all those Provinces, that men might see
The Divine wisedome would not leave that Land
Subject to any one Kings sole command.
Then let the Germans feare if *Caesar* shall,
Or the United Princes, rise, and fall,
But let us that in myrtle bowers sit
Under secure shades, use the benefit
Of peace and plenty, which the blessed hand
Of our good King gives this obdurate Land,
Let us of Revels sing, and let thy breath
(Which fill'd Fames trumpet with *Gustavus* death,
Blowing his name to heaven) gently inspire
Thy past'rall pipe, till all our swaines admire
Thy song and subject, whilst they both comprise
The beauties of the *SHEPHERDS PARADISE;*

24 *Knight o'th' Sun:* hero of a famous Spanish romance, translated into English in the late sixteenth century.

54 *SHEPHERDS PARADISE:* i.e. Townshend's masque, *Tempe Restord.* In lines 59–88 Carew describes the action of the play.

For who like thee (whose loose discourse is farre
More neate and polisht then our Poems are,
Whose very gate's more gracefull then our dance)
In sweetly-flowing numbers may advance
The glorious night? When, not to act foule rapes,
Like birds, or beasts, but in their Angel-shapes
A troope of Deities came downe to guide
Our steerlesse barkes in passions swelling tide
By vertues Carde, and brought us from above
A patterne of their owne celestiall love.
Nor lay it in darke sullen precepts drown'd
But with rich fancie, and cleare Action crown'd
Through a misterious fable (that was drawne
Like a transparant veyle of purest Lawne
Before their dazelling beauties) the divine
*Venus*, did with her heavenly *Cupid* shine.
The stories curious web, the Masculine stile;
The subtile sence, did Time and sleepe beguile,
Pinnion'd and charm'd they stood to gaze upon
Th'Angellike formes, gestures, and motion,
To heare those ravishing sounds that did dispence
Knowledge and pleasure, to the soule, and sense.
It fill'd us with amazement to behold
Love made all spirit, his corporeall mold
Dissected into Atomes melt away
To empty ayre, and from the grosse allay
Of mixtures, and compounding Accidents
Refin'd to immateriall Elements.
But when the Queene of Beautie did inspire
The ayre with perfumes, and our hearts with fire,
Breathing from her celestiall Organ sweet
Harmonious notes, our soules fell at her feet,
And did with humble reverend dutie, more
Her rare perfections, then high state adore.

63 *Carde:* compass.
83 *Queene of Beautie:* This part was played by Henrietta Maria herself.

These harmelesse pastimes let my *Townsend* sing
To rurall tunes; not that thy Muse wants wing
To soare a loftier pitch, for she hath made
A noble flight, and plac'd th' Heroique shade
Above the reach of our faint flagging ryme;
But these are subjects proper to our clyme.
Tourneyes, Masques, Theaters, better become
Our *Halcyon* dayes; what though the German Drum
Bellow for freedome and revenge, the noyse
Concernes not us, nor should divert our joyes;
Nor ought the thunder of their Carabins
Drowne the sweet Ayres of our tun'd Violins;
Beleeve me friend, if their prevailing powers
Gaine them a calme securitie like ours,
They'le hang their Armes up on the Olive bough,
And dance, and revell then, as we doe now.

## *To a Lady that desired I would love her*

*1.*

Now you have freely given me leave to love,
What will you doe?
Shall I your mirth, or passion move
When I begin to wooe;
Will you torment, or scorne, or love me too?

99 *Carabins:* carbines, short rifles.

2.

Each pettie beautie can disdaine, and I
Spight of your hate
Without your leave can see, and dye;
Dispence a nobler Fate,
'Tis easie to destroy, you may create.

3.

Then give me leave to love, and love me too,
Not with designe
To rayse, as Loves curst Rebells doe,
When puling Poets whine,
Fame to their beautie, from their blubbr'd eyne.

*4.*

Griefe is a puddle, and reflects not cleare
Your beauties rayes,
Joyes are pure streames, your eyes appeare
Sullen in sadder layes,
In chearfull numbers they shine bright with prayse;

5.

Which shall not mention to expresse you fayre
Wounds, flames, and darts,
Stormes in your brow, nets in your haire,
Suborning all your parts,
Or to betray, or torture captive hearts.

*6.*

I'le make your eyes like morning Suns appeare,
As milde, and faire;
Your brow as Crystall smooth, and cleare,
And your dishevell'd hayre
Shall flow like a calme Region of the Ayre.

*7.*

Rich Natures store, (which is the Poets Treasure)
I'le spend to dresse
Your beauties, if your mine of Pleasure
In equall thankfulnesse
You but unlocke, so we each other blesse.

## *To my friend* G. N. *from* Wrest

I breathe (sweet *Ghib:*) the temperate ayre of *Wrest*
Where I no more with raging stormes opprest,
Weare the cold nights out by the bankes of Tweed,
On the bleake Mountains, where fierce tempests breed,
And everlasting Winter dwells; where milde
*Favonius,* and the Vernall windes exilde,
Did never spread their wings: but the wilde North
Brings sterill Fearne, Thistles, and Brambles forth.

TO MY FRIEND: G. N. may perhaps be Gilbert North, like Carew a gentleman of Charles's privy chamber. Wrest Park in Bedfordshire belonged to the de Grey family.

3 *Tweed:* Carew had served, with G. N. (see line 110) on Charles's expedition against the Scots, which reached Berwick-on-Tweed, in May and June of 1639.

6 *Favonius:* the west wind.

Here steep'd in balmie dew, the pregnant Earth,
Sends from her teeming wombe a flowrie birth,
And cherisht with the warme Suns quickning heate,
Her porous bosome doth rich odours sweate;
Whose perfumes through the Ambient ayre diffuse
Such native Aromatiques, as we use
No forraigne Gums, nor essence fetcht from farre,
No Volatile spirits, nor compounds that are
Adulterate, but at Natures cheape expence
With farre more genuine sweetes refresh the sense.
Such pure and uncompounded beauties, blesse
This Mansion with an usefull comelinesse.
Devoide of Art, for here the Architect
Did not with curious skill a Pile erect
Of carved Marble, Touch, or Porpherie,
But built a house for hospitalitie;
No sumptuous Chimney-peece of shining stone
Invites the strangers eye to gaze upon,
And coldly entertaines his sight, but cleare
And cheerefull flames, cherish and warme him here:
No Dorique, nor Corinthian Pillars grace
With Imagery this structures naked face,
The Lord and Lady of this place delight
Rather to be in act, then seeme in sight;
In stead of Statues to adorne their wall
They throng with living men, their merry Hall,
Where at large Tables fill'd with wholsome meates
The servant, Tennant, and kind neighbour eates.
Some of that ranke, spun of a finer thred
Are with the Women, Steward, and Chaplaine fed
With daintier cates; Others of better note
Whom wealth, parts, office, or the Heralds coate
Have sever'd from the common, freely sit
At the Lords Table, whose spread sides admit

21–23: Cf. Jonson, "To Penshurst," lines 1–3.
23 *Touch:* touchstone, black stone used in building.

A large accesse of friends to fill those seates
Of his capacious circle, fill'd with meates
Of choycest rellish, till his Oaken back
Under the load of pil'd-up dishes crack.
Nor thinke, because our Piramids, and high
Exalted Turrets threaten not the skie,
That therefore *Wrest* of narrownesse complaines
Or streightned Walls, for she more numerous traines
Of Noble guests daily receives, and those
Can with farre more conveniencie dispose
Then prouder Piles, where the vaine builder spent
More cost in outward gay Embellishment
Then reall use: which was the sole designe
Of our contriver, who made things not fine,
But fit for service. *Amalthea's* Horne
Of plentie is not in Effigie worne
Without the gate, but she within the dore
Empties her free and unexhausted store.
Nor, croun'd with wheaten wreathes, doth *Ceres* stand
In stone, with a crook'd sickle in her hand:
Nor, on a Marble Tunne, his face besmear'd
With grapes, is curl'd uncizard *Bacchus* rear'd.
We offer not in Emblemes to the eyes,
But to the taste those usefull Deities.
Wee presse the juycie God, and quaffe his blood,
And grinde the Yeallow Goddesse into food.
Yet we decline not, all the worke of Art,
But where more bounteous Nature beares a part
And guides her Hand-maid, if she but dispence
Fit matter, she with care and diligence
Employes her skill, for where the neighbour sourse
Powers forth her waters she directs their course,
And entertaines the flowing streames in deepe
And spacious channells, where they slowly creepe

57 *Amalthea's Horne:* a goat's horn, given to the nymph by Jupiter. It could produce whatever its owner desired.

64 *uncizard:* with hair uncut.

In snakie windings, as the shelving ground
Leades them in circles, till they twice surround
This Island Mansion, which i'th' center plac'd,
Is with a double Crystall heaven embrac'd,
In which our watery constellations floate,
Our Fishes, Swans, our Water-man and Boate,
Envy'd by those above, which wish to slake
Their starre-burnt limbes, in our refreshing lake,
But they stick fast nayl'd to the barren Spheare,
Whilst our encrease in fertile waters here
Disport, and wander freely where they please
Within the circuit of our narrow Seas.
  With various Trees we fringe the waters brinke,
Whose thirstie rootes the soaking moysture drinke,
And whose extended boughes in equall rankes
Yeeld fruit, and shade, and beautie to the bankes.
On this side young *Vertumnus* sits, and courts
His ruddie-cheek'd *Pomona, Zephyre* sports
On th'other, with lov'd *Flora,* yeelding there
Sweetes for the smell, sweetes for the palate here.
But did you taste the high & mighty drinke
Which from that Fountaine flowes, you'ld cleerly think
The God of Wine did his plumpe clusters bring,
And crush the Falerne grape into our spring;
Or else disguis'd in watery Robes did swim
To *Ceres* bed, and make her big of Him,
Begetting so himselfe on Her: for know
Our Vintage here in *March* doth nothing owe
To theirs in Autumne, but our fire boyles here
As lustie liquour as the Sun makes there.
  Thus I enjoy my selfe, and taste the fruit
Of this blest Peace, whilst toyl'd in the pursuit
Of Bucks, and Stags, th'embleme of warre, you strive
To keepe the memory of our Armes alive.

85 *barren Spheare:* the eighth sphere, that of the fixed stars.
93 *Vertumnus:* god of fruits and seasons.

## *To my worthy friend Master* Geo. Sands, *on his translation of the Psalmes*

I presse not to the Quire, nor dare I greet
The holy place with my unhallowed feet;
My unwasht Muse, polutes not things Divine,
Nor mingles her prophaner notes with thine;
Here, humbly at the porch she listning stayes,
And with glad eares sucks in thy sacred layes.
So, devout penitents of Old were wont,
Some without dore, and some beneath the Font,
To stand and heare the Churches Liturgies,
Yet not assist the solemne exercise:
Sufficeth her, that she a lay-place gaine,
To trim thy Vestments, or but beare thy traine;
Though nor in tune, nor wing, she reach thy Larke,
Her Lyrick feet may dance before the Arke.
Who knowes, but that her wandring eyes that run,
Now hunting Glow-wormes, may adore the Sun,
A pure flame may, shot by Almighty power
Into her brest, the earthy flame devoure.
My eyes, in penitentiall dew may steepe
That brine, which they for sensuall love did weepe.
So (though 'gainst Natures course) fire may be quencht
With fire, and water be with water drencht;
Perhaps my restlesse soule, tyr'de with persuit
Of mortall beauty, seeking without fruit
Contentment there, which hath not, when enjoy'd,
Quencht all her thirst, nor satisfi'd, though cloy'd;
Weary of her vaine search below, Above
In the first faire may find th'immortall Love.

TO MY WORTHY FRIEND: First printed in the second edition of Sandys' *A Paraphrase upon the Divine Poems*, 1638.

5 *listning:* omitted in the 1640 edition.

Prompted by thy example then, no more
In moulds of clay will I my God adore;
But teare those Idols from my heart, and write
What his blest Sprit, not fond Love shall indite;
Then, I no more shall court the verdant Bay,
But the dry leavelesse Trunke on *Golgotha;*
And rather strive to gaine from thence one Thorne,
Then all the flourishing wreathes by Laureats worne.

## *The Comparison*

Dearest thy tresses are not threads of gold,
Thy eyes of Diamonds, nor doe I hold
Thy lips for Rubies: Thy faire cheekes to be
Fresh Roses; or thy teeth of Ivorie:
Thy skin that doth thy daintie bodie sheath
Not Alablaster is, nor dost thou breath
*Arabian* odours, those the earth brings forth
Compar'd with which would but impaire thy worth.
Such may be others Mistresses, but mine
Holds nothing earthly, but is all divine.
Thy tresses are those rayes that doe arise
Not from one Sunne, but two; Such are thy eyes:
Thy lips congealed Nectar are, and such
As but a Deitie, there's none dare touch.
The perfect crimson that thy cheeke doth cloath
(But onely that it farre exceeds them both)
*Aurora's* blush resembles, or that redd
That *Iris* struts in when her mantl's spred.
Thy teeth in white doe *Leda's* Swan exceede,
Thy skin's a heavenly and immortall weede,
And when thou breath'st, the winds are readie strait
To filch it from thee, and doe therefore wait

34 *Trunke:* i.e. the cross on which Christ was crucified.

Close at thy lips, and snatching it from thence
Beare it to Heaven, where 'tis *Joves* frankincense.
Faire Goddesse, since thy feature makes thee one,
Yet be not such for these respects alone;
But as you are divine in outward view
So be within as faire, as good, as true.

## A Song

*Aske me no more where* Jove *bestowes,*
*When* June *is past the fading rose:*
*For in your beauties orient deepe,*
*These flowers as in their causes, sleepe.*

*Aske me no more whether doth stray,*
*The golden Atomes of the day:*
*For in pure love heaven did prepare,*
*Those powders to inrich your haire.*

*Aske me no more whether doth hast,*
*The Nightingale when May is past:*
*For in your sweet dividing throat,*
*She winters and keepes warme her note.*

*Aske me no more where those starres light,*
*That downewards fall in dead of night:*
*For in your eyes they sit and there,*
*Fixed become as in their sphere.*

A SONG.

4 *causes:* i.e. her beauty contains that which makes roses roses. Carew is alluding to the philosophical "formal cause."

11 *dividing:* sighing melodiously.

*Aske me no more if East or West,*
*The Phenix builds her spicy nest:*
*For unto you at last shee flies,*
*And in your fragrant bosome dyes.*

## *On a Damaske rose sticking upon a Ladies breast*

Let pride grow big my rose, and let the cleare
And damaske colour of thy leaves appeare.
Let scent and lookes be sweete and blesse that hand,
That did transplant thee to that sacred land.
O happy thou that in that garden rest's,
That Paradice betweene that Ladies breasts.
There's an eternall spring; there shalt thou lie,
Betwixt two lilly mounts, and never die.
There shalt thou spring amongst the fertile valleyes,
By budds like thee that grow in midst of Allyes.
There none dare plucke thee, for that place is such
That but a god devine, there's none dare touch,
If any but approach, straite doth arise
A blushing lightning flash, and blasts his eyes.
There stead of raine shall living fountaines flow,
For wind her fragrant breath for ever blow.
Nor now, as earst, one Sun shall on thee shine,
But those two glorious suns, her eyes devine.
O then what Monarch would not think't a grace,
To leave his Regall throne to have thy place.
My selfe to gaine thy blessed seat do vow,
Would be transformd into a rose as thou.

ON A DAMASKE ROSE.
12 *god:* The 1640 edition reads *good.*

# *Upon a Mole in* Celias *bosome*

That lovely spot which thou dost see
In Celias bosome was a Bee,
Who built her amorous spicy nest
I'th Hyblas of her either breast,
But from close Ivery Hyves, she flew
To suck the Arromattick dew,
Which from the neighbour vale distils,
Which parts those two twin-sister hils.
There feasting on Ambrosiall meat,
A rowling file of Balmy sweat,
(As in soft murmurs before death,
Swan-like she sung) chokt up her breath,
So she in water did expire,
More precious then the Phaenix fire;
  Yet still her shaddow there remaines
Confind to those Elizian plaines;
With this strict Law, that who shall lay
His bold lips on that milky way,
The sweet, and smart, from thence shall bring
Of the Bees Honey, and her sting.

UPON A MOLE: First printed in the 1642 edition of Carew's poems.
4 *Hyblas:* Hybla was a mountain in Sicily abounding in flowers and honey.
5 *close:* secluded.

# To *Celia*, upon Love's Ubiquity

As one that strives, being sick, and sick to death
By changing places, to preserve a breath,
A tedious restlesse breath, removes and tryes
A thousand roomes, a thousand policyes,
To cozen payne, when he thinks to find ease,
At last he finds all change, but his disease,
So (like a Ball with fire and powder fild)
I restles am, yet live, each minute kild,
And with that moving torture must retain
(With change of all things else) a constant payn.
Say I stay with you, presence is to me
Nought but a light, to shew my miserie,
And partings are as Rackes, to plague love on,
The further stretchd, the more affliction.
Goe I to *Holland, France,* or furthest *Inde,*
I change but onely Countreys not my mind.
And though I passe through ayr and water free,
Despair and hopelesse fate still follow me.
Whilest in the bosome of the waves I reel
My heart I'le liken to the tottering keel,
The sea to my own troubled fate, the wind
To your disdayn, sent from a soul unkind:
But when I lift my sad lookes to the skyes,
Then shall I think I see my *Celia's* eyes,
And when a Cloud or storm appeares between,
I shall remember what her frownes have been.
Thus, whatsoever course my fates allow,
All things but make me mind my busines, you.

TO CELIA: First printed in the 1651 edition of Carew's poems.
5 *cozen:* cheat.

The good things that I meet I think streames be
From you the fountain, but when bad I see
How vile and cursed is that thing thinke I,
That to such goodnes is so contrary?
My whole life is bout you, the Center starre,
But a perpetuall Motion Circular:
I am the dyalls hand, still walking round,
You are the Compasse, and I never sound
Beyond your Circle, neyther can I shew
Ought, but what first expressed is in you.
That wheresoever my teares doe cause me move
My fate still keepes me bounded with your love;
Which ere it dye, or be extinct in me,
Time shall stand still, and moist waves flaming be.
Yet, being gon, think not on me, I am
A thing too wretched for thy thoughts to name;
But when I dye, and wish all comforts given,
Ile think on you, and by you think on heaven.

# THOMAS RANDOLPH
## 1605–1635

## *A gratulatory to M^r^ Ben Johnson for his adopting of him to be his Son*

I was not borne to *Helicon,* nor dare
Presume to thinke my selfe a Muses heire.
I have no title to *Parnassus* hill,
Nor any acre of it by the will
Of a dead Ancestour, nor could I bee
Ought but a tenant unto Poëtrie.
But thy Adoption quits me of all feare,
And makes me challenge a childs portion there.
I am a kinne to *Hero's* being thine,
And part of my alliance is divine.
*Orpheus, Musaeus, Homer* too; beside
Thy Brothers by the *Roman* Mothers side;
As *Ovid, Virgil,* and the *Latine Lyre,*
That is so like thy Horace; the whole quire
Of Poets are by thy Adoption, all
My uncles; thou hast given me pow'r to call
*Phoebus* himselfe my grandsire; by this graunt
Each Sister of the nine is made my Aunt.
Go you that reckon from a large descent
Your lineall Honours, and are well content
To glory in the age of your great name,
Though on a Herralds faith you build the same:
I do not envy you, nor thinke you blest
Though you may beare a Gorgon on your Crest
By direct line from *Perseus;* I will boast
No farther than my Father; that's the most
I can, or should be proud of; and I were
Unworthy his adoption, if that here
I should be dully modest; boast I must
Being sonne of his Adoption, not his lust.

A GRATULATORY: This "adoption" probably occurred about 1630.

And to say truth, that which is best in mee
May call you father, 'twas begot by thee.
Have I a sparke of that coelestiall flame
Within me, I confesse I stole the same
*Prometheus* like, from thee; and may I feed
His vulture, when I dare deny the deed.
Many more moones thou hast, that shine by night,
All Bankrups, wer't not for a borrow'd light;
Yet can forsweare it; I the debt confesse,
And thinke my reputation ne're the lesse.
For Father let me be resolv'd by you;
Is't a disparagement from rich *Peru*
To ravish gold; or theft, for wealthy Ore
To ransack *Tagus,* or *Pactolus* shore?
Or does he wrong *Alcinous,* that for want
Doth take from him a sprig or two, to plant
A lesser Orchard? sure it cannot bee:
Nor is it theft to steale some flames from thee.
Grant this, and I'le cry guilty, as I am,
And pay a filiall reverence to thy name.
For when my Muse upon obedient knees,
Askes not a Fathers blessing, let her leese
The fame of this Adoption; 'tis a curse
I wish her 'cause I cannot thinke a worse.
And here, as Piety bids me, I intreat
*Phoebus* to lend thee some of his own heat,
To cure thy Palsie; else I will complaine
He has no skill in hearbs; Poets in vaine
Make him the God of Physicke; 'twere his praise
To make thee as immortall as thy Baies;
As his own *Daphne;* 'twere a shame to see
The God, not love his Preist, more then his Tree.
    But if heaven take thee, envying us thy Lyre,
    'Tis to pen Anthems for an Angels quire.

44 *Tagus, or Pactolus:* Spanish and Lydian rivers, famed for their golden sands.
52 *leese:* lose.
59 *Physicke:* medicine.

## *Upon the losse of his little finger*

Arithmetique nine digits, and no more
Admits of, then I still have all my store.
For what mischance hath tane from my left hand,
It seemes did only for a Cipher stand.
But this I'le say for thee departed joynt,
Thou wert not given to steale, nor pick, not point
At any in disgrace; but thou didst go
Untimely to thy Death only to show
The other members what they once must doe;
Hand, arme, legge, thigh, and all must follow too.
Oft didst thou scan my verse, where if I misse
Henceforth I will impute the cause to this.
A fingers losse (I speake it not in sport)
Will make a verse a Foot too short.
Farewell deare finger, much I greive to see
How soone mischance hath made a Hand of thee.

## *An Ode to Mr* Anthony Stafford *to hasten him into the country*

Come spurre away,
I have no patience for a longer stay;
But must goe downe,
And leave the chargeable noise of this great Towne.
I will the country see,
Where old simplicity,

UPON THE LOSSE: Randolph's finger was cut off in a tavern brawl. He is said to have composed these verses immediately after that event.
6 *pick:* i.e. pick pockets.
AN ODE: Anthony Stafford (1587–1645), scholar and author.
4 *chargeable:* burdensome.

Though hid in gray
Doth looke more gay
Then foppery in plush and scarlat clad.
Farewell you City-wits that are
Almost at Civill warre;
'Tis time that I grow wise, when all the world grows mad.

More of my dayes
I will not spend to gaine an Idiots praise;
Or to make sport
For some slight Punie of the Innes of Court.
Then worthy *Stafford* say
How shall we spend the day.
With what delights
Shorten the nights?
When from this tumult we are got secure;
Where mirth with all her freedome goes
Yet shall no finger loose;
Where every word is thought, and every thought is pure.

There from the tree
Wee'l cherries plucke, and pick the strawbery.
And every day
Go see the wholesome Country Girles make hay.
Whose browne hath lovlier grace,
Then any painted face,
That I doe know
*Hide-Parke* can show.
Where I had rather gaine a kisse then meet
Though some of them in greater state
Might court my love with plate
The beauties of the *Cheape,* and wives of *Lumbardstreet.*

16 *Punie:* newly admitted law student.

But thinke upon
Some other pleasures, these to me are none,
Why doe I prate
Of woemen, that are things against my fate?
I never meane to wed,
That torture to my bed.
My Muse is shee
My Love shall bee.
Let Clownes get wealth, and heires; when I am gone
And the great Bugbeare grisly death
Shall take this idle breath
If I a Poem leave, that Poem is my Sonne.

Of this, no more;
Wee'l rather tast the bright *Pomona's* store.
No fruit shall scape
Our pallats, from the damsen, to the grape.
Then full we'l seek a shade,
And heare what musique's made;
How Philomell
Her tale doth tell:
And how the other Birds doe fill the quire;
The Thrush and Blackbird lend their throats
Warbling melodious notes;
Wee will all sports enjoy, which others but desire.

Ours is the skie,
Where at what fowle we please our Hauke shall flye;
Nor will we spare
To hunt the crafty foxe, or timorous hare;
But let our hounds runne loose
In any ground they'l choose,
The Bucke shall fall,
The stagge and all:
Our pleasures must from their owne warrants bee,
For to my *Muse*, if not to mee,
I'me sure all game is free;
Heaven, Earth, are all but parts of her great Royalty.

And when we meane
To tast of *Bacchus* blessings now and then,
And drinke by stealth
A cup or two to noble *Barkleys* health.
I'le take my pipe and try
The *Phrygian* melody;
Which he that heares
Lets through his eares
A madnesse to distemper all the braine.
Then I another pipe will take
And *Dorique* musique make,
To Civilize with graver notes our wits againe.

## *On the Death of a Nightingale*

Goe solitary wood, and henceforth be
Acquainted with no other Harmonie,
Then the Pyes chattering, or the shreeking note
Of bodeing Owles, and fatall Ravens throate.
Thy sweetest Chanters dead, that warbled forth
Layes, that might tempests calme, and still the North;
And call downe Angels from their glorious Spheare
To heare her Songs, and learne new Anthems there.
That soule is fled, and to *Elisium* gone;
Thou a poore desert left; goe then and runne,
Begge there to stand a grove, and if shee please
To sing againe beneath thy shadowy Trees;
The soules of happy Lovers crown'd with blisses
Shall flock about thee, and keepe time with kisses.

76 *Barkleys:* George Berkeley, the eighth baron (1601–1658). Stafford dedicated his *Guide of Honor* (1634) to him.

# *To one admiring her selfe in a Looking-Glasse*

Faire Lady when you see the Grace
Of Beauty in your Looking-Glasse:
A stately forhead, smooth and high,
And full of Princely Majesty.
A sparkling eye, no gemme so faire,
Whose lustre dimmes the *Cyprian* starre.
A glorious cheeke divinely sweet,
Wherein both Roses kindly meet.
A cherry Lip that would entice
Even Gods to kisse at any price.
You thinke no beauty is so rare
That with your shaddow might compare.
That your reflection is alone,
The thing that men most dote upon.
Madam, alas your Glasse doth lye,
And you are much deceiv'd; for I
A beauty know of richer grace,
(Sweet be not angry) 'tis your face.
Hence then ô learne more milde to bee,
And leave to lay your blame on mee;
If me your reall substance move;
When you so much your Shaddow Love.
Wise nature would not let your eye
Looke on her owne bright majestie;
Which had you once but gaz'd upon,
You could, except your selfe, love none:
What then you cannot love, let me,
That face I can, you cannot see.
  Now you have what to love, you'l say
What then is left for me I pray?

TO ONE ADMIRING HER SELFE.
6 *Cyprian starre:* the planet Venus.
8 *both:* i.e. red and white.

My face sweet hart if it please thee;
That which you can, I cannot see:
So either love shall gaine his due,
Your's sweet in mee, and mine in you.

## *A Maske for Lydia*

Sweet *Lydia* take this maske, and shroud
Thy face within the silken cloud,
And veile those powerfull Skies:
For he whose gazing dares so high Aspire,
Makes burning glasses of his eyes,
And sets his heart on fire.

Vaile, *Lydia* vaile, for unto mee
There is no basiliske but thee.
Thy very lookes doe kill:
Yet in those lookes so fixt is my delight,
Poore soule (alas) I languish still
In absence of thy sight.

Close up those eyes, or we shall finde
Too great a lustre strike us blinde:
Or if a Ray so good
Ought to be seene, let it but then appeare
When Eagles doe produce their brood,
To try their young ones there.

Or if thou would'st have me to know
How great a brightnesse thou canst shew;
When they have lost the Sun;
Then doe thou rise, and give the world this theme,
*Sol* from th' *Hesperides* is run,
And back hath whipt his teame.

A MASKE FOR LYDIA.
8 *basiliske:* a fabulous, reptilian monster, whose breath and look were fatal.
17 *Eagles:* The eagle tested its offspring by having them look at the sun.

Yet through the *Goat* when he shall stray,
Thou through the *Crab* must take thy way;
For should you both shine bright
In the same *Tropick*, we poore moles should get
Not so much comfort by the light,
As torment by the heat.

Where's *Lydia* now? where shall I seeke
Her charming lip, her tempting cheeke
That my affections bow'd?
So dark a sable hath ecclipst my faire,
That I can gaze upon the cloud,
That durst not see the Star.

But yet me thinkes my thoughts begin
To say there lies a white within,
Though black her pride controule:
And what care I how black a face I see,
So there be whitenesse in the soule,
Still such an *Ethiop* be.

## *Upon Love fondly refus'd for Conscience sake*

Nature, Creations law, is judg'd by sense,
Not by the Tyrant conscience.
Then our commission gives us leave to doe
What youth and pleasure prompts us to:
For we must question else heavens great decree,
And taxe it with a Treachery;
If things made sweet to tempt our appetite
Should with a guilt stain the delight.
Higher powers rule us, our selves can nothing doe;
Who made us love made't lawfull too.
It was not love, but love transform'd to vice
Ravish'd by envious Avarice,

UPON LOVE FONDLY REFUS'D.
7 *If:* Whether.

Made women first impropriate; all were free,
  Inclosures mans Inventions be.
I'th' golden age no action could be found
  For trespasse on my neighbours ground:
'Twas just with any Fayre to mixe our blood;
  The best is most diffusive good.
She that confines her beams to one mans sight,
  Is a darke Lanthorne to a glorious Light.
Say, does the Virgin-spring lesse chast appear
  Cause many Thirsts are quenched there?
Or have you not with the same odours met
  When more have smelt your violet?
The Phenix is not angry at her nest,
  Cause her Perfumes make others blest:
Though Incense to th' eternal Gods be meant,
  Yet mortalls Rivall in the sent.
Man is the Lord of creatures, yet we see
  That all his vassals loves are free;
The severe wedlocks fetters doe not bind
  The Pard's inflam'd, and amorous mind;
But that he may be like a Bridegroome led
  Even to the Royall Lyons bed.
The birds may for a yeare their loves confine,
  But make new choyce each *Valentine*.
If our affections then more servile be
  Then are our slaves, where's mans soveraignty?
Why then by pleasing more, should you lesse please,
  And spare the sweets, being more sweet then these?
If the fresh Trunk have sap enough to give
  That each insertive branch may live;
The Gardner grafts not only Apples there,
  But addes the Warden and the Peare;
The Peach, and Apricock together grow,
  The Cherry, and the Damson too.

13 *impropriate:* the private possessions of individual men.
32 *Pard's:* leopard's.
44 *warden:* a kind of baking pear.

Till he hath made by skilfull husbandry
  An intire Orchard of one Tree.
So least our Paradise perfection want,
  We may as well inoculate as plant.
What's Conscience but a Beldams midnight theme?
  Or nodding nurses idle dreame?
So feign'd, as are the Goblins, Elves, and Fairies
  To watch their Orchards, and their Dairies.
For who can tell when first her reigne begun?
  I' th' state of innocence was none:
And since large conscience (as the proverb shewes)
  In the same sense with bad one goes,
The lesse the better then, whence this will fall,
  'Tis to be perfect to have none at all.
Suppose it be a vertue, rich and pure,
  'Tis not for Spring, or Summer sure,
Nor yet for Autumne; Love must have his prime,
  His warmer heats, and harvest time.
Till we have flourish'd, growne, and reap'd our wishes,
  What Conscience dares oppose our kisses?
But when times colder hand leads us neare home,
  Then let that winter-vertue come:
Frost is till then prodigious; we may doe
  What youth and pleasure prompts us to.

50 *inoculate:* engraft.

# WILLIAM HABINGTON
## 1605–1654

## *To Roses in the bosome of* Castara

Yee blushing Virgins happie are
In the chaste Nunn'ry of her brests,
For hee'd prophane so chaste a faire,
Who ere should call them *Cupids* nests.

Transplanted thus how bright yee grow,
How rich a perfume doe yee yeeld?
In some close garden, Cowslips so
Are sweeter then ith' open field.

In those white Cloysters live secure
From the rude blasts of wanton breath,
Each houre more innocent and pure,
Till you shall wither into death.

Then that which living gave you roome,
Your glorious sepulcher shall be.
There wants no marble for a tombe,
Whose brest hath marble beene to me.

## *To* CASTARA

Doe not their prophane Orgies heare,
Who but to wealth no altars reare.
The soule's oft poys'ned through the eare.

*Castara* rather seeke to dwell
Ith' silence of a private cell.
Rich discontent's a glorious hell.

TO CASTARA.
2 *but:* except.

Yet *Hindlip* doth not want extent
Of roome (though not magnificent)
To give free welcome to content.

There shalt thou see the earely Spring,
That wealthy stocke of nature bring,
Of which the Sybils bookes did sing.

From fruitlesse Palmes shall honey flow,
And barren Winter Harvest show,
While Lillies in his bosome grow,

No North-winde shall the corne infest,
But the soft spirit of the East,
Our sent with perfum'd banquets feast.

A Satyre here and there shall trip,
In hope to purchase leave to sip
Sweete Nectar from a Fairies lip.

The Nimphs with quivers shall adorne
Their active sides and rouse the morne
With the shrill musicke of their horne.

Wakened with which, and viewing thee,
Faire *Daphne* her faire selfe shall free,
From the chaste prison of a tree:

And with *Narcissus* (to thy face
Who humbly will ascribe all grace)
Shall once againe pursue the chase.

So they whose wisdome did discusse
Of these as fictions: shall in us
Finde, they were more then fabulous.

7 *Hindlip:* Habington's family estate, three miles from Worcester.

## *To a Wanton*

In vaine faire sorceresse, thy eyes speake charmes,
In vaine thou mak'st loose circles with thy armes.
I'me 'bove thy spels. No magicke him can move,
In whom *Castara* hath inspir'd her love.
As she, keepe thou strict cent'nell o're thy eare,
Lest it the whispers of soft Courtiers heare;
Reade not his raptures, whose invention must
Write journey worke, both for his Patrons lust,
And his owne plush: let no admirer feast
His eye oth' naked banquet of thy brest.
If this faire president, nor yet my want
Of love, to answer thine, make thee recant
Thy sorc'ries; Pity shall to justice turne,
And judge thee, witch, in thy owne flames to burne.

## *A Dialogue betweene* Araphill *and* Castara

ARAPH. Dost not thou *Castara* read
Am'rous volumes in my eyes?
Doth not every motion plead
What I'de shew, and yet disguise?
Sences act each others part.
Eyes, as tongues, reveale the heart.

TO A WANTON.
7 *his raptures:* perhaps an allusion to Carew's poem, "A Rapture."
11 *If . . . president:* If neither this fair precedent (Castara).
14 *flames:* Witches burned enemies in effigy in order to injure them.
A DIALOGUE: *Araphill* is "the lover of the 'chaste altar' (Castara)." This is one of the four dialogue poems in Habington's sequence.

CAST. I saw love as lightning breake
From thy eyes, and was content
Oft to heare thy silence speake.
Silent love is eloquent.
So the sence of learning heares,
The dumbe musicke of the Spheares.

ARAPH. Then there's mercy in your kinde,
Listning to an unfain'd love.
Or strives he to tame the wind,
Who would your compassion move?
No y'are pittious as y're faire.
Heaven relents, o'recome by prayer.

CAST. But loose man too prodigall
Is in the expence of vowes;
And thinks to him kingdomes fall
When the heart of woman bowes:
Frailty to your armes may yeeld;
Who resists you wins the field.

ARAPH. Triumph not to see me bleede,
Let the Bore chas'd from his den,
On the wounds of mankinde feede,
Your soft sexe should pitty men.
Malice well may practise Art,
Love hath a transparent heart.

CAST. Yet is love all one deceit,
A warme frost, a frozen fire.
She with in her selfe is great,
Who is slave to no desire.
Let youth act, and age advise,
And then love may finde his eyes.

ARAPH. *Hymens* torch yeelds a dim light,
When ambition joynes our hands,
A proud day, but mournefull night,
She sustaines, who marries lands.

Wealth slaves man, but for their Ore,
Th'Indians had beene free, though poore.

CAST. And yet wealth the fuell is
Which maintaines the nuptiall fire,
And in honour there's a blisse,
Th'are immortall who aspire.
But truth sayes no joyes are sweete,
But where hearts united meete.

ARAPH. Roses breath not such a sent,
To perfume the neighb'ring groves;
As when you affirme content,
In no spheare of glory moves.
Glory narrow soules combines:
Noble hearts Love onely joynes.

## *Upon* Castara's *absence*

T'is madnesse to give Physicke to the dead;
Then leave me friends: Yet haply you'd here read
A lecture; but I'le not dissected be,
T'instruct your Art by my anatomie.
But still you trust your sense, sweare you discry
No difference in me. All's deceit oth'eye,
Some spirit hath a body fram'd in th'ayre,
Like mine, which he doth to delude you weare:
Else heaven by miracle makes me survive
My selfe, to keepe in me poore Love alive.
But I am dead, yet let none question where
My best part rests, and with a sigh or teare,
Prophane the Pompe, when they my corps interre,
My soule imparadis'd, for 'tis with her.

UPON CASTARA'S ABSENCE.
1 *Physicke:* medicine.
3–4 *I'le . . . anatomie:* Perhaps an echo of Donne's "The Dampe."

## *To* CASTARA,
## *Ventring to walke too farre in the neighbouring wood*

Dare not too farre *Castara,* for the shade
This courteous thicket yeelds, hath man betray'd
A prey to wolves: to the wilde powers oth' wood,
Oft travellers pay tribute with their blood.
If carelesse of thy selfe of me take care,
For like a ship where all the fortunes are
Of an advent'rous merchant; I must be,
If thou should'st perish banquerout in thee.
My feares have mockt me. Tygers when they shall
Behold so bright a face, will humbly fall
In adoration of thee. Fierce they are
To the deform'd, obsequious to the faire.
  Yet venter not; tis nobler farre to sway
  The heart of man, than beasts, who man obey.

## *To the World*
## *The Perfection of Love*

You who are earth, and cannot rise
    Above your sence,
Boasting the envyed wealth which lyes
Bright in your Mistris lips or eyes,
Betray a pittyed eloquence.

TO CASTARA.
  8 *banquerout:* bankrupt.
TO THE WORLD: This poem echoes Donne's "The Extasie" in lines 17–20 and 26–30.

That which doth joyne our soules, so light
　　And quicke doth move.
That like the Eagle in his flight,
It doth transcend all humane sight,
Lost in the element of Love.

You Poets reach not this, who sing
　　The praise of dust
But kneaded, when by theft you bring
The rose and Lilly from the Spring
T'adorne the wrinckled face of lust.

When we speake Love, nor art, nor wit
　　We glosse upon:
Our soules engender, and beget
*Ideas,* which you counterfeit
In your dull propagation.

While Time seven ages shall disperse,
　　Wee'le talke of Love,
And when our tongues hold no commerse
Our thoughts shall mutually converse.
And yet the blood no rebell prove.

And though we be of severall kind
　　Fit for offence:
Yet are we so by Love refin'd,
From impure drosse we are all mind.
Death could not more have conquer'd sence.

How suddenly those flames expire
　　Which scorch our clay?
*Prometheus*-like when we steale fire
From heaven 'tis endlesse and intire
It may know age, but not decay.

## *The Description of* CASTARA

Like the Violet which alone
Prospers in some happy shade:
My *Castara* lives unknowne,
To no looser eye betray'd,
  For shee's to her selfe untrue,
  Who delights ith' publicke view.

Such is her beauty, as no arts
Have enricht with borrowed grace.
Her high birth no pride imparts,
For she blushes in her place.
  Folly boasts a glorious blood,
  She is noblest being good.

Cautious she knew never yet
What a wanton courtship meant:
Not speaks loud to boast her wit,
In her silence eloquent.
  Of her selfe survey she takes,
  But 'tweene men no difference makes.

She obeyes with speedy will
Her grave Parents wise commands.
And so innocent, that ill,
She nor acts, nor understands.
  Womens feete runne still astray,
  If once to ill they know the way.

THE DESCRIPTION OF CASTARA: This is the last poem in the first part of *Castara*. In the second part Araphill celebrates his love for Castara after they are married.

She sailes by that rocke, the Court,
Where oft honour splits her mast:
And retir'dnesse thinks the port,
Where her fame may anchor cast.
  Vertue safely cannot sit,
  Where vice is enthron'd for wit.

She holds that dayes pleasure best,
Where sinne waits not on delight,
Without maske, or ball, or feast,
Sweetly spends a winters night.
  O're that darknesse, whence 'tis thrust,
  Prayer and sleepe oft govern lust.

She her throne makes reason climbe,
While wild passions captive lie.
And each article of time,
Her pure thoughts to heaven flie:
  All her vowes religious be,
  And her love she vowes to me.

## To DEATH, CASTARA *being sicke*

Hence prophane grim man, nor dare
To approach so neere my faire.
Marble vaults, and gloomy caves,
Church-yards, Charnell houses, graves,
Where the living loath to be,
Heaven hath design'd to thee.
  But if needs 'mongst us thou'lt rage,
Let thy fury feed on age.
Wrinckled browes, and withered thighs,
May supply thy sacrifice.
Yet perhaps as thou flew'st by,
A flamed dart shot from her eye,

Sing'd thy wings with wanton fire,
Whence th'art forc't to hover nigh her.
If Love so mistooke his aime,
Gently welcome in the flame:
They who loath'd thee, when they see
Where thou harbor'st will love thee.
Onely I, such is my fate,
Must thee as a rivall hate,
Court her gently, learne to prove
Nimble in the thefts of love.
Gaze on th'errors of her haire:
Touch her lip; but oh beware,
Lest too ravenous of thy blisse,
Thou shouldst murder with a kisse.

## *To a Friend, Inviting him to a meeting upon promise*

May you drinke beare, or that adult'rate wine
Which makes the zeale of Amsterdam divine;
If you make breach of promise. I have now
So rich a Sacke, that even your selfe will bow
T'adore my *Genius*. Of this wine should Prynne
Drinke but a plenteous glasse, he would beginne
A health to *Shakespeares* ghost. But you may bring
Some excuse forth, and answer me the King
To day will give you audience, or that on
Affaires of state, you and some serious Don

TO DEATH.

23 *errors . . . haire:* strands of hair that are awry.

*Title:* This poem, the title of which recalls Jonson's "Inviting a Friend to Supper," is a reply to a poem by Habington's friend, James Shirley, entitled "Two Gentlemen that broke their promise of a meeting, made when they drank Claret."

TO A FRIEND.

2 *Amsterdam divine:* the English pilgrims who had fled to Holland.

5 *Prynne:* William Prynne (1600–1669) notorious Puritan pamphleteer whose *Histriomastix* (1633) was a violent attack on the stage.

10 *Don:* Spanish envoy.

Are to resolve; or else perhaps you'le sin
So farre, as to leave word y'are not within.
The least of these, will make me onely thinke
Him subtle, who can in his closet drinke
Drunke even alone, and thus made wise create
As dangerous plots as the Low Countrey state,
Projecting for such baits, as shall draw ore
To *Holland*, all the Herrings from our shore.
But y'are too full of candor: and I know
Will sooner stones at *Salis'bury* casements throw,
Or buy up for the silenc'd Levits, all
The rich impropriations, then let pall
So pure Canary, and breake such an oath:
Since charity is sinn'd against in both.
Come therefore blest even in the Lollards zeale,
Who canst with conscience safe, 'fore hen and veale
Say grace in Latine; while I faintly sing
A Penitentiall verse in oyle and Ling.
Come then, and bring with you prepar'd for fight,
Unmixt Canary, Heaven send both prove right!
This I am sure: My sacke will disingage
All humane thoughts, inspire so high a rage,
That *Hypocrene* shall henceforth Poets lacke,
Since more Enthusiasmes are in my sacke.
Heightned with which, my raptures shall commend,
How good *Castara* is, how deare my friend.

17 *ore:* over.

20 *Salis'bury:* In 1630 the town recorder of this city had broken windows in a church there. He considered them idolatrous.

21 *Levits:* Puritan ministers silenced by the government and deprived of their parishes.

25 *Lollards:* fifteenth-century English followers of Wyclif. Habington uses the term loosely to mean "Puritans."

28 *Ling:* Lenten fare.

# *To* CASTARA
## *Upon Beautie*

*Castara,* see that dust, the sportive wind
So wantons with. 'Tis happ'ly all you'le finde
Left of some beauty: and how still it flies,
To trouble, as it did in life, our eyes.
O empty boast of flesh? Though our heires gild
The farre fetch Phrigian marble, which shall build
A burthen to our ashes, yet will death
Betray them to the sport of every breath.
Dost thou, poor relique of our frailty, still
Swell up with glory? Or is it thy skill,
To mocke weake man, whom every wind of praise
Into the aire, doth 'bove his center raise.
  If so, mocke on, And tell him that his lust
  To beauty's, madnesse. For it courts but dust.

## *His Muse speakes to him*

Thy vowes are heard, and thy *Castara's* fame
Is writ as faire ith' Register of Fame,
As th'ancient beauties which translated are
By Poets up to heaven; each there a starre.
And though Imperiall *Tiber* boast alone
*Ovids Corinna,* and to *Arn* is knowne
But *Petrarchs Laura;* while our famous Thames
Doth murmur *Sydneyes Stella* to her streames.
Yet hast thou *Severne* left, and she can bring
As many quires of Swans, as they to sing

TO CASTARA. UPON BEAUTIE.
6 *farre fetch:* fetched from farre.

Thy glorious love: Which living shall by thee
The onely Sov'raigne of those waters be.
  Dead in loves firmament, no starre shall shine
  So nobly faire, so purely chaste as thine.

## *Against them who lay unchastity to the sex of Women*

They meet but with unwholesome Springs,
And Summers which infectious are:
They heare but when the Meremaid sings,
And onely see the falling starre:
    Who ever dare,
Affirme no woman chaste and faire.

Goe cure your feavers: and you'le say
The Dog-dayes scorch not all the yeare:
In Copper Mines no longer stay,
But travell to the West, and there
    The right ones see:
And grant all gold's not Alchimie.

What mad man 'cause the glow-wormes flame
Is cold, sweares there's no warmth in fire?
'Cause some make forfeit of their name,
And slave themselves to mans desire;
    Shall the sex free
From guilt, damn'd to the bondage be?

AGAINST THEM WHO LAY UNCHASTITY: This poem is Habington's reply to Donne's "Goe, and catche a falling starre."
10 *the West:* i.e. Worcestershire.

Nor grieve *Castara*, though 'twere fraile,
Thy Vertue then would brighter shine,
When thy example should prevaile,
And every womans faith be thine,
And were there none;
'Tis Majesty to rule alone.

## *To* CASTARA,
## *Upon an embrace*

'Bout th' Husband Oke, the Vine
Thus wreathes to kisse his leavy face:
Their streames thus Rivers joyne,
And lose themselves in the embrace.
But Trees want sence when they infold,
And Waters when they meet, are cold.

Thus Turtles bill, and grone
Their loves into each others eare:
Two flames thus burne in one,
When their curl'd heads to heaven they reare.
But Birds want soule though not desire:
And flames materiall soone expire.

If not prophane; we'll say
When Angels close, their joyes are such.
For we no love obey
That's bastard to a fleshly touch.
Let's close *Castara* then, since thus
We patterne Angels, and they us.

TO CASTARA.
7 *Turtles:* turtledoves.

## *To the Right Honourable the Countesse of* C.

Should the cold *Muscovit,* whose furre and stove
Can scarse prepare him heate enough for love,
But view the wonder of your presence, he
Would scorne his winters sharpest injury:
And trace the naked groves, till he found bayse
To write the beautious triumphs of your prayse.
As a dull Poet even he would say,
Th'unclouded Sun had never showne them day
Till that bright minute; that he now admires
No more why the coy Spring so soone retires
From their unhappy clyme; It doth pursue
The Sun, and he derives his light from you.
Hee'd tell you how the fetter'd Baltick Sea
Is set at freedome, while the yce away
Doth melt at your approach; how by so faire
Harmonious beauty, their rude manners are
Reduc't to order; how to them you bring
The wealthiest mines below, above the Spring.
Thus would his wonder speake. For he would want
Religion to beleeve, there were a Saint
Within, and all he saw was but the shrine.
But I here pay my vowes to the devine
Pure essence there inclos'd, which if it were
Not hid in a faire cloud, but might appeare
In its full lustre, would make Nature live
In a state equall to her primitive.

TO THE RIGHT HONOURABLE: Lucy Hay (1599–1660), the Countess of Carlisle, Castara's cousin. Habington added a number of epistolary poems like this to the second (1635) and third (1640) editions of *Castara.*

5 *bayse:* the laurel. Here the word is equivalent to "poetic inspiration."

But sweetly thats obscur'd. Yet though our eye
Cannot the splendor of your soule descry
In true perfection, by a glimmering light,
Your language yeelds us, we can guesse how bright
The Sunne within you shines, and curse th'unkind
Eclipse, or else our selves for being blinde.
How hastily doth Nature build up man
To leave him so imperfect? For he can
See nought beyond his sence; she doth controule
So farre his sight he nere discern'd a soule.
For had yours beene the object of his eye;
It had turn'd wonder to Idolatry.

## *To* CASTARA

Give me a heart where no impure
  Disorder'd passions rage,
Which jealousie doth not obscure,
Nor vanity t'expence ingage,
Nor wooed to madnesse by queint oathes,
Or the fine Rhetoricke of cloathes,
Which not the softnesse of the age
To vice or folly doth decline;
Give me that heart (*Castara*) for 'tis thine.

Take thou a heart where no new looke
  Provokes new appetite:
With no fresh charme of beauty tooke,
Or wanton stratagem of wit;
Not Idly wandring here and there,
Led by an am'rous eye or eare,
Ayming each beautious marke to hit;
Which vertue doth to one confine:
Take thou that heart, *Castara*, for 'tis mine.

27 *thats obscured:* Although Habington may not have intended to allude to the fact, the Countess of Carlisle was hardly famed for her virtue.

And now my heart is lodg'd with thee,
Observe but how it still
Doth listen how thine doth with me;
And guard it well, for else it will
Runne hither backe: not to be where
I am, but 'cause thy heart is here.
But without discipline, or skill
Our hearts shall freely 'tweene us move;
Should thou or I want hearts, wee'd breath by love.

# *To* CASTARA
## *Of true delight*

Why doth the eare so tempt the voyce,
That cunningly divides the ayre?
Why doth the pallate buy the choyce
Delights oth' sea, to enrich her fare?

As soone as I, my eare obey
The Eccho's lost even with the breath.
And when the sewer takes away
I'm left with no more taste, then death.

Be curious in pursuite of eyes
To procreate new loves with thine;
Satiety makes sence despise
What superstition thought divine.

Quicke fancy how it mockes delight?
As we conceive, things are not such,
The glow-worme is as warme as bright,
Till the deceitfull flame we touch.

TO CASTARA: Allott (*Poems*, p. lviii) describes this as "the only poem in *Castara* which produces a mental echo and seems to possess a secondary layer of meaning."

7 *sewer:* attendant at a meal.

When I have sold my heart to lust
And bought repentance with a kisse
I find the malice of my dust,
That told me hell contain'd a blisse.

The Rose yeelds her sweete blandishment
Lost in the fold of lovers wreathes,
The violet enchants the sent
When earely in the Spring she breaths.

But winter comes and makes each flowre
Shrinke from the pillow where it growes,
Or an intruding cold hath powre
To scorne the perfume of the Rose.

Our sences like false glasses show
Smooth beauty where browes wrinkled are,
And makes the cosen'd fancy glow.
Chaste vertue's onely true and faire.

## *Elegie,* 6

Goe stop the swift-wing'd moments in their flight
To their yet unknowne coast, goe hinder night
From its approach on day, and force day rise
From the faire East of some bright beauties eyes:
Else vaunt not the proud miracle of verse.
It hath no powre. For mine from his blacke herse
Redeemes not *Talbot,* who could as the breath
Of winter, coffin'd lyes; silent as death,

31 *cosen'd:* cheated.

*Title:* One of a group of eight elegies on Talbot which Habington added to the second edition of *Castara.* George Talbot (d. 1634) was the brother of John, the tenth Earl of Shrewsbury.

ELEGIE, 6.
7 *could:* cold.

Stealing on th'Anch'rit, who even wants an eare
To breath into his soft expiring prayer.
For had thy life beene by thy vertues spun
Out to a length, thou hadst out-liv'd the Sunne
And clos'd the worlds great eye: or were not all
Our wonders fiction, from thy funerall
Thou hadst received new life, and liv'd to be
The conqueror o're death, inspir'd by me.
But all we Poets glory in, is vaine
And empty triumph: Art cannot regaine
One poore hour lost, nor reskew a small flye
By a fooles finger destinate to dye.
Live then in thy true life (great soule) for set
At liberty by death thou owest no debt
T'exacting Nature: Live, freed from the sport
Of time and fortune in yand' starry court
A glorious Potentate, while we below
But fashion wayes to mitigate our woe.
We follow campes, and to our hopes propose
Th'insulting victor; not remembring those
Dismembred trunkes who gave him victory
By a loath'd fate: We covetous Merchants be
And to our aymes pretend treasure and sway,
Forgetfull of the treasons of the Sea.
The shootings of a wounded conscience
We patiently sustaine to serve our sence
With a short pleasure; So we empire gaine
And rule the fate of businesse, the sad paine
Of action we contemne, and the affright
Which with pale visions still attends our night.
Our joyes false apparitions, but our feares
Are certaine prophecies. And till our eares
Reach that caelestiall musique, which thine now
So cheerefully receive, we must allow
No comfort to our griefes: from which to be
Exempted, is in death to follow thee.

9 *Anch'rit:* anchorite, hermit.
24 *yand':* yon.

## *Nox nocti indicat Scientiam.* David

When I survay the bright
Coelestiall spheare:
So rich with jewels hung, that night
Doth like an Aethiop bride appeare.

My soule her wings doth spread
And heaven-ward flies,
Th'Almighty's Mysteries to read
In the large volumes of the skies.

For the bright firmament
Shootes forth no flame
So silent, but is eloquent
In speaking the Creators name.

No unregarded star
Contracts its light
Into so small a Charactar,
Remov'd far from our humane sight:

But if we stedfast looke,
We shall discerne
In it as in some holy booke,
How man may heavenly knowledge learne.

It tells the Conqueror,
That farre-strecht powre
Which his proud dangers traffique for,
Is but the triumph of an houre.

NOX NOCTI INDICAT: One of a group of directly religious poems that form the third part of *Castara*. The quotation is from the Psalms, 48:3 in the Vulgate ("Night points out knowledge to the night").

15 *Charactar:* magical sign or emblem.

That from the farthest North;
Some Nation may
Yet undiscovered issue forth,
And ore his new got conquest sway.

Some Nation yet shut in
With hils of ice
May be let out to scourge his sinne
'Till they shall equall him in vice.

And then they likewise shall
Their ruine have,
For as your selves your Empires fall,
And every Kingdome hath a grave.

Thus those Coelestiall fires,
Though seeming mute
The fallacie of our desires
And all the pride of life confute.

For they have watcht since first
The World had birth:
And found sinne in it selfe accurst,
And nothing permanent on earth.

# EDMUND WALLER
1606–1687

# Poems, &c.

Written upon ſeveral

# OCCASIONS,

And to ſeveral

# PERSONS:

BY

EDMOND WALLER, Eſq;

*Licenſed*, May 18. 1686.

*ROGER L'ESTRANGE.*

The Fifth Edition, with ſeveral Additions

*Never before Printed.*

*Non ego mordaci diſtrinxi carmine quenquam,*
*Nulla venenato littera Miſta ioco eſt.*

Printed for *H. Herringman*, and are to be ſold by *J. Knight* and *F. Saunders* at the *Blew Anchor* in the Lower Walk of the *New Exchange*. 1686.

## *Song*

Go lovely Rose,
Tell her that wastes her time and me,
That now she knows,
When I resemble her to thee,
How sweet and fair she seems to be.

Tell her that's young,
And shuns to have her Graces spy'd,
That hadst thou sprung
In Desarts, where no men abide,
Thou must have uncommended dy'd.

Small is the worth
Of Beauty from the light retir'd;
Bid her come forth,
Suffer her self to be desir'd,
And not blush so to be admir'd.

Then die, that she,
The common fate of all things rare,
May read in thee;
How small a part of time they share,
That are so wondrous sweet and fair.

## *The Battel of the* Summer-Islands
## Cant. I.

*What Fruits they have, and how Heaven smiles*
*Upon those late discovered Isles.*

Aid me *Bellona*, while the dreadful Fight
Betwixt a Nation and two Whales I write:
Seas stain'd with goar, I sing, advent'rous toyl,
And how these Monsters did disarm an Isle.
*Bermudas* wall'd with Rocks, who does not know,
That happy Island, where huge Lemons grow,
And Orange trees which Golden Fruit do bear,
Th' Hesperian Garden boasts of none so fair?
Where shining Pearl, Coral, and many a pound,
On the rich Shore, of Amber-greece is found:
The lofty Cedar, which to Heaven aspires,
The Prince of Trees, is fewel for their Fires:
The smoak by which their loaded spits do turn,
For incense might, on Sacred Altars burn:
Their private Roofs on od'rous Timber born,
Such as might Palaces for Kings adorn.
The sweet *Palmettas* a new *Bacchus* yield,
With Leaves as ample as the broadest shield:
Under the shadow of whose friendly Boughs
They sit carowsing, where their Liquor grows.

THE BATTEL: The Bermudas were called the "Summer Islands" after Sir George Somers who was wrecked upon them in 1609 while sailing to Virginia. Waller's poem playfully embroiders upon accounts of the islands which filtered back to England.

1 *Bellona:* the goddess of war.

10 *Amber-greece:* not the yellow fossil resin (amber), but "ambergris," a gray, waxlike substance found floating in tropical seas and as a morbid secretion in the intestines of whales.

15 *born:* borne.

Figs there unplanted through the Fields do grow,
Such as fierce *Cato* did the *Romans* show,
With the rare Fruit inviting them to spoil
*Carthage* the Mistress of so rich a soil.
The Naked Rocks are not unfruitful there,
But at some constant seasons every year,
Their barren tops with luscious Food abound,
And with the eggs of various Fowls are crown'd:
Tobacco is the worst of things, which they
To *English* Land-lords as their Tribute pay:
Such is the Mould, that the Blest Tenant feeds
On precious Fruits, and pays his Rent in Weeds:
With candid Plantines, and the jucy Pine,
On choicest Melons and sweet Grapes they dine;
And with Potatoes fat their wanton Swine.
Nature these Cates with such a lavish hand
Pours out among them, that our courser Land
Tastes of that bounty, and does Cloth return,
Which not for Warmth, but Ornament is worn:
For the kind Spring which but salutes us here,
Inhabits there, and courts them all the year:
Ripe Fruits and blossoms on the same Trees live;
At once they promise, what at once they give:
So sweet the Air, so moderate the Clime;
None sickly lives, or dies before his time.
Heaven sure has kept this spot of earth uncurst,
To shew how all things were Created first.
The tardy Plants in our cold Orchards plac'd,
Reserve their Fruit for the next ages taste:
There a small grain in some few Months will be
A firm, a lofty, and a spacious Tree:
The *Palma Christi*, and the fair *Papah*,
Now but a seed (preventing Natures law)

22 *Cato:* Marcus Porcius Cato (234–149 B.C.), arch-foe of Carthage in the Punic wars.
53 *preventing:* anticipating.

In half the Circle of the hasty year
Project a shade, and lovely fruit do wear:
And as their Trees in our dull Region set
But faintly grow, and no perfection get;
So in this *Northern* Tract our hoarser Throats
Utter unripe and ill-constrained notes:
Where the supporter of the Poets style,
*Phoebus,* on them eternally does smile.
O how I long! my careless Limbs to lay
Under the Plantanes shade, and all the day
With am'rous Airs my fancy entertain,
Invoke the Muses, and improve my vein!
No passion there in my free breast should move,
None but the sweet and best of passions, Love:
There while I sing, if gentle Love be by
That tunes my Lute, and winds the Strings so high,
With the sweet sound of *Sacharissa's* name,
I'll make the listning Savages grow tame.
But while I do these pleasing dreams indite,
I am diverted from the promis'd fight.

## Canto II.

*Of their alarm, and how their Foes*
*Discovered were, this* Canto *shows.*

Though Rocks so high about this Island rise,
That well they may the num'rous Turk despise;
Yet is no humane fate exempt from fear,
Which shakes their hearts, while through the Isle they hear
A lasting noise, as horrid and as loud
As Thunder makes, before it breaks the Cloud.

70 *Sacharissa:* The lady praised in many of Waller's lyrics. He derived her name from *saccharum* (sugar).

Three days they dread this murmur, e're they know
From what blind cause th'unwonted sound may grow:
At length Two Monsters of unequal size,
Hard by the shoar a Fisher-man espies;
Two mighty Whales, which swelling Seas had tost,
And left them prisoners on the rocky Coast;
One as a Mountain vast, and with her came
A Cub not much inferior to his Dame:
Here in a Pool among the Rocks engag'd,
They roar'd like Lions, caught in toyls, and rag'd:
The man knew what they were, who heretofore
Had seen the like lie murdered on the shore,
By the wild fury of some Tempest cast
The fate of ships and shipwrackt men to taste.
As careless Dames whom Wine and Sleep betray
To frantick dreams their Infants overlay:
So there sometimes the raging Ocean fails,
And her own brood exposes; when the Whales
Against sharp Rocks like reeling vessels quasht,
Though huge as Mountains, are in pieces dasht;
Along the shore their dreadful Limbs lie scatter'd,
Like Hills with Earthquakes shaken, torn, & shatter'd.
Hearts sure of Brass they had, who tempted first
Rude Seas that spare not what themselves have nurst.
  The welcome news through all the Nation spread,
  To sudden joy and hope converts their dread.
What lately was their publique terror, they
Behold with glad eyes, as a certain prey;
Dispose already of th'untaken spoil,
And as the purchase of their future toil,
These share the Bones, and they divide the Oyl;
So was the Huntsman by the Bear opprest,
Whose Hide he sold before he caught the Beast.
  They man their Boats, and all their young men arm
With whatsoever may the Monsters harm;

CANTO II.
22 *overlay:* lie upon, and hence smother.

Pikes, Halberts, Spits, and Darts that wound so far,
The Tools of Peace, and Instruments of War:
Now was the time for vig'rous Lads to show
What love or honor could invite them too;
A goodly Theatre where Rocks are round
With reverend age, and lovely Lasses, crown'd:
Such was the Lake which held this dreadful pair
Within the bounds of noble *Warwicks* share:
*Warwicks* bold Earl, than which no title bears
A greater sound among our British Peers;
And worthy he the memory to renew,
The fate and honor to that title due;
Whose brave adventures have transferr'd his name,
And through the new world spread his growing fame.
  But how they fought, & what their valour gain'd,
  Shall in another Canto be contain'd.

## Canto III.

*The bloody fight, successless toyl,*
*And how the Fishes sack'd the Isle.*

The Boat which on the first assault did go
Struck with a harping Iron the younger fo;
Who when he felt his side so rudely goar'd,
Loud as the Sea that nourish't him he roar'd.
As a broad Bream to please some curious tast,
While yet alive in boyling water cast,
Vex't with unwonted heat, bounds, flings about
The scorching brass, and hurls the liquor out:
So with the barbed Javelins stung, he raves,
And scourges with his tayl the suffering waves:

49 *Warwicks:* Robert Rich, Earl of Warwick (1587–1658), who was one of the principal proprietors of the Bermudas.

CANTO III.

5 *Bream:* a fresh water fish.

7 *bounds:* This is the reading of the first (1645) edition; the 1686 text has *boyls.*

Like *Spencer's Talus* with his Iron flayl,
He threatens ruin with his pondrous tayl;
Dissolving at one stroke the battered Boat,
And down the men fall drenched in the Moat:
With every fierce encounter they are forc't
To quit their Boats, and fare like men unhorst.
The bigger Whale like some huge Carrack lay,
Which wanteth Sea room, with her foes to play;
Slowly she swims, and when provok'd she wo'd
Advance her tail, her head salutes the mud;
The shallow water doth her force infringe,
And renders vain her tails impetuous swinge:
The shining steel her tender sides receive,
And there like Bees they all their weapons leave.
This sees the Cub, and does himself oppose
Betwixt his cumbred mother and her foes:
With desperate courage he receives her wounds,
And men and boats his active tayl confounds.
Their forces joyn'd, the Seas with billows fill,
And make a tempest, though the winds be still.
Now would the men with half their hoped prey
Be well content, and wish this Cub away:
Their wish they have; he to direct his dam
Unto the gap through which they thither came,
Before her swims, and quits the hostile Lake,
A pris'ner there, but for his mothers sake.
She by the Rocks compell'd to stay behind,
Is by the vastness of her bulk confin'd.
They shout for joy, and now on her alone
Their fury falls, and all their Darts are thrown.
Their Lances spent; one bolder than the rest
With his broad sword provok'd the sluggish beast:
Her oily side devours both blade and heft,
And there his Steel the bold Bermudian left.

11 *Talus:* Sir Artegal's squire in the fifth book of Spenser's *Faerie Queene.*
17 *Carrack:* galleon.
22 *swinge:* sweep.

Courage the rest from his example take,
And now they change the colour of the Lake:
Blood flows in Rivers from her wounded side,
As if they would prevent the tardy tide,
And raise the flood to that propitious height,
As might convey her from this fatal streight.
She swims in blood, and blood do's spouting throw
To Heaven, that Heaven mens cruelties might know.
Their fixed Javelins in her side she wears,
And on her back a grove of Pikes appears:
You would have thought, had you the monster seen
Thus drest, she had another Island been.
Roaring she tears the air with such a noise,
(As well resembled the conspiring voice
Of routed Armies, when the field is won)
To reach the ears of her escaped son.
He (though a league removed from the fo)
Hastes to her aid; the pious Trojan so
Neglecting for *Creusas* life his own,
Repeats the danger of the burning Town.
The men amazed blush to see the seed
Of monsters, human piety exceed:
Well proves this kindness what the Grecians sung,
That Loves bright mother from the Ocean sprung.
Their courage droops, and hopeless now they wish
For composition with th'unconquer'd fish:
So she their weapons would restore again,
Through Rocks they'd hew her passage to the main.
But how instructed in each others mind,
Or what commerce can men with monsters find?
Not daring to approach their wounded foe,
Whom her couragious son protected so,

62 *Trojan:* Aeneas, who returned to burning Troy to seek his wife Creusa (*Aeneid* II.749 ff.).

64 *Repeats:* Seeks again.

68 *Loves . . . mother:* Venus.

They charge their Muskets, and with hot desire
Of full revenge, renew the fight with fire:
Standing a looff, with lead they bruise the scales,
And tear the flesh of the incensed Whales.
But no success their fierce endeavours found,
Nor this way could they give one fatal wound.
Now to their Fort they are about to send
For the loud Engines which their Isle defend.
But what those pieces fram'd to batter walls
Would have effected on those mighty Whales,
Great *Neptune* will not have us know, who sends
A tyde so high, that it relieves his friends.
And thus they parted with exchange of harms;
Much blood the Monsters lost, and they their Arms.

## *To Phillis*

*Phillis,* why should we delay
Pleasures shorter than the day?
Could we (which we never can)
Stretch our lives beyond their span;
Beauty like a shadow flies,
And our youth before us dies;
Or would youth and beauty stay,
Love hath wings, and will away.
Love hath swifter wings than Time;
Change in love to Heaven does clime.
Gods that never change their state,
Vary oft their love and hate.
  *Phillis,* to this truth we owe,
All the love betwixt us two:
Let not you and I require
What has been our past desire;
On what Shepherds you have smil'd,
Or what Nymphs I have beguil'd;

Leave it to the Planets too,
What we shall hereafter do;
For the joys we now may prove,
Take advice of present love.

## *Song*

Stay *Phoebus*, stay,
The world to which you flie so fast,
Conveying day
From us to them, can pay your hast,
With no such object, nor salute your rise
With no such wonder, as *de Mornay's* eyes.

Well do's this prove,
The error of those antique books
Which made you move,
About the world; her charming looks
Would fix your beams, and make it ever day,
Did not the rowling Earth snatch her away.

## *On a Girdle*

That which her slender waste confin'd,
Shall now my joyful Temples bind;
No Monarch but would give his Crown,
His Arms might do what this has done.

SONG.

6 *de Mornay:* apparently a court beauty of the time.

8 *error:* the old Ptolemaic theory which made the earth the center of the universe.

It was my Heaven's extreamest Sphear,
The Pale which held that lovely Dear;
My Joy, my Grief, my Hope, my Love,
Did all within this Circle move.

A narrow compass, and yet there
Dwelt all that's good, and all that's fair:
Give me but what this Riban bound,
Take all the rest the Sun goes round.

## *At Penshurst*

Had *Sacharissa* liv'd when Mortals made
Choice of their Deities, this Sacred shade
Had held an Altar to her power, that gave
The Peace and Glory which these allays have:
Embroidred so with Flowers where she stood,
That it became a Garden of a Wood:
Her presence has such more than humane Grace,
That it can civilize the rudest place;
And beauty too, and order can impart,
Where Nature ne'r intended it, nor Art.
The Plants acknowledge this, and her admire
No less than those of old, did *Orpheus*'s Lire:
If she sit down, with tops all towards her bow'd,
They round about her into Arbors crowd;
Or if she walk, in even ranks they stand,
Like some well-Marshall'd and obsequious band.
*Amphion* so made stones and timber leap
Into fair Figures from a confus'd heap:

AT PENSHURST: For Penshurst, see Jonson's "To Penshurst."

1 *Sacharissa:* Lady Dorothy Sidney.

17 *Amphion:* King of Thebes and husband of Niobe. The magical power of his music built the walls of Troy.

And in the symmetry of her parts is found
A power, like that of harmony in sound.
  Ye lofty Beeches, tell this matchless Dame,
That if together ye fed all one Flame,
It could not equalize the hundredth part
Of what her Eyes have kindled in my heart.
Go Boy, and carve this passion on the Bark
Of yonder Tree, which stands the sacred mark
Of Noble *Sidneys* birth; when such benign,
Such more than-mortal making stars did shine;
That there they cannot but for ever prove
The monument and pledge of humble Love:
His humble Love, whose hope shall ne'r rise higher
Than for a pardon that he dares admire.

## At Penshurst

While in the Park I sing, the listning Deer
Attend my passion, and forget to fear.
When to the Beeches I report my flame,
They bow their Heads as if they felt the same:
To Gods appealing, when I reach their bowrs
With loud complaints, they answer me in showrs.
To thee a wild and cruel Soul is given,
More deaf than Trees, and prouder than the Heav'n.
Loves Foe profest, why dost thou falsly feign
Thy self a *Sidney?* from which Noble strain
He sprung, that could so far exalt the name
Of Love, and warm our Nation with his Flame,
That all we can of Love or high desire,
Seems but the smoak of am'rous *Sidneys* fire.
Nor call her Mother, who so well do's prove,
One breast may hold both Chastity and Love.

27 *Sidneys birth:* See Jonson's poem, lines 13–16.

Never can she, that so exceeds the Spring
In Joy and Bounty, be suppos'd to bring
One so destructive; to no humane stock
We owe this fierce unkindness, but the Rock,
That cloven Rock produc'd thee, by whose side
Nature to recompence the fatal pride
Of such stern beauty, plac'd those healing springs,
Which not more help, than that destruction brings.
Thy heart no ruder than the rugged stone,
I might like *Orpheus* with my numerous moan
Melt to compassion; now my trait'rous song,
With thee conspires to do the Singer wrong:
While thus I suffer not my self to lose
The memory of what augments my woes:
But with my own breath still foment the Fire,
With flames as high as fancy can aspire.
This last complaint th'indulgent ears did pierce
Of just *Apollo*, President of Verse:
Highly concerned, that the Muse should bring
Damage to one whom he had taught to sing;
Thus he advis'd me, on yon aged Tree
Hang up thy Lute, and hy thee to the Sea,
That there with wonders thy diverted mind
Some truce at least may with this passion find.
Ah cruel Nymph! from whom her humble Swain
Flies for relief unto the raging Main;
And from the Winds and Tempests do's expect
A milder fate, than from her cold neglect:
Yet there he'll pray that the unkind may prove
Blest in her choice; and vows this endless Love
Springs from no hope of what she can confer,
But from those gifts which Heav'n has heap'd on her.

AT PENSHURST.

20 *Rock:* Lady Sidney was born at Sion. The mineral waters of Tunbridge Wells issue from the foot of a hill called Mount Sion.

## *To a very young Lady*

Why came I so untimely forth
Into a world, which wanting thee
Could entertain us with no worth
Or shadow of felicity?
  That time should me so far remove
  From that which I was born to love.

Yet fairest blossom do not slight
That age which you may know so soon;
The Rosy Morn resigns her light,
And milder Glory to the Noon:
  And then what wonders shall you do,
  Whose dawning Beauty warms us so?

Hope waits upon the flowry prime,
And Summer though it be less gay,
Yet is not lookt on as a time
Of declination or decay.
  For with a full hand That does bring
  All that was promis'd by the Spring.

## *To the mutable Fair*

Here *Caelia* for thy sake I part
With all that grew so near my heart;
The passion that I had for thee,
The Faith, the Love, the Constancy,
And that I may successful prove
Transform my self to what you love.
  Fool that I was so much to prize
Those simple virtues you despise,

Fool that with such dull Arrows strove,
Or hop'd to reach a flying Dove;
For you that are in motion still
Decline our force, and mock our skill.
Who like *Don Quixot* do advance
Against a Wind-mill our vain Launce.
  Now will I wander through the Air,
Mount, make a stoop at every fair,
And with a Fancy unconfin'd
(As lawless as the Sea or Wind)
Pursue you wheresoe'r you fly,
And with your various thoughts comply.
  The formal Stars do travel so,
As we their names and courses know,
And he that on their changes looks,
Would think them govern'd by our Books.
But never were the clouds reduc'd
To any Art; the motions us'd
By those free vapors are so light,
So frequent, that the conquer'd sight
Despairs to find the rules that guide
Those gilded shadows as they slide.
And therefore of the spacious Air
*Joves* royal consort had the care:
And by that power did once escape,
Declining bold *Ixions* rape;
She with her own resemblance grac'd
A shining cloud which he embrac'd.
  Such was that Image, so it smil'd
With seeming kindness which beguil'd
Your *Thirsis* lately when he thought
He had his fleeting *Caelia* caught.

TO THE MUTABLE FAIR.

16 *make a stoop:* fall on (like a falcon).

26 The 1686 edition reads "To any Art the motion us'd."

34 *Ixions:* When Ixion fell in love with Hera, Zeus formed a cloud (Nephele) to resemble her.

'Twas shap'd like her, but for the fair
He fill'd his Arms with yielding Air:
A fate for which he grieves the less,
Because the gods had like success.
For in their story one (we see)
Pursues a Nymph, and takes a Tree:
A second with a Lovers haste
Soon overtakes whom he had chac'd;
But she that did a Virgin seem,
Possest appears a wandring stream:
For his supposed love a third
Lays greedy hold upon a bird;
And stands amaz'd to find his dear,
A wild Inhabitant of the air.
To these old tales such Nymphs as you
Give credit, and still make them new,
The Am'rous now like wonders find
In the swift changes of your mind.
But *Caelia* if you apprehend
The Muse of your incensed friend;
Nor would that he record your blame,
And make it live, repeat the same,
Again deceive him, and again,
And then he swears he'll not complain.
For still to be deluded so,
Is all the pleasure Lovers know,
Who, (like good Faulkners) take delight,
Not in the quarrey, but the flight.

# *On St. James's Park, as lately improved by His Majesty*

Of the first Paradice there's nothing found,
Plants set by Heav'n are vanisht, & the ground;
Yet the description lasts; who knows the fate
Of lines that shall this Paradice relate?
  Instead of Rivers rowling by the side
Of Eden's Garden, here flows in the Tyde;
The Sea which always serv'd his Empire, now
Pays Tribute to our Prince's pleasure too:
Of famous Cities we the Founders know;
But Rivers old, as Seas, to which they go,
Are Nature's bounty; 'tis of more Renown
To make a River than to build a Town.
For future shade young Trees upon the banks
Of the new stream appear in even ranks:
The voice of *Orpheus* or *Amphion*'s hand
In better order could not make them stand;
May they increase as fast, and spread their boughs,
As the high Fame of their great Owner grows!
May he live long enough to see them all
Dark shadows cast, and as his Palace tall
Methinks I see the love that shall be made,
The Lovers walking in that amorous shade,
The Gallants dancing by the Rivers side,
They bathe in Summer, and in Winter slide.
Methinks I hear the Musick in the Boats,
And the loud Eccho which returns the Notes,

ON ST. JAMES PARK: Waller's poem was first published in 1661.

6 *here . . . Tyde:* Among the improvements made by Charles II was a stream of water let into the park from the Thames.

Whilst over head a flock of new sprung Fowl
Hangs in the Air, and does the Sun controul:
Darkning the sky they hover o're, and shrowd
The wanton Sailors with a feather'd cloud:
Beneath a shole of silver Fishes glides,
And plays about the gilded Barges sides;
The Ladies angling in the Chrystal Lake,
Feast on the waters with the prey they take;
At once victorious with their Lines and Eyes
They make the Fishes and the Men their prize;
A thousand *Cupids* on the Billows ride,
And Sea-Nymphs enter with the swelling Tide,
From *Thetis* sent as Spies to make report,
And tell the wonders of her Soveraign's Court,
All that can living feed the greedy Eye,
Or dead the Palat, here you may descry,
The choicest things that furnisht *Noah*'s Ark,
Or *Peter*'s sheet, inhabiting this Park:
All with a border of rich Fruit-trees crown'd,
Whose loaded branches hide the lofty mound.
Such various ways the spacious Allies lead,
My doubtful Muse knows not what path to tread:
Yonder the harvest of cold months laid up,
Gives a fresh coolness to the Royal Cup,
There Ice, like Chrystal, firm, and never lost,
Tempers hot *July* with *Decembers* Frost,
Winters dark Prison, whence he cannot flie,
Though the warm Spring his enemy draws nigh:
Strange! that extremes should thus preserve the snow
High on the *Alps*, or in deep Caves below.
  Here a well-polisht Mall gives us the joy
To see our Prince his matchless force imploy;

44 *Peter's sheet:* See Luke 5:4–6; Peter's net was filled with "a great multitude of fishes."

57 *Mall:* The following lines allude to the game of pall-mall, much favored by Charles II. The player tried to drive a boxwood ball through an iron ring which was suspended above a long alley; whoever could do this in the fewest number of strokes won the game.

His manly posture and his graceful meen
Vigor and Youth in all his motion seen,
His shape so lovely, and his limbs so strong,
Confirm our hopes we shall obey him long:
No sooner has he toucht the flying Ball,
But 'tis already more than half the Mall;
And such a fury from his arm has got
As from a smoaking Culverin 'twere shot.
  Nere this my Muse, what most delights her, sees,
A living Gallery of aged Trees;
Bold Sons of earth that thrust their arms so high,
As if once more they would invade the Sky;
In such green Palaces the first Kings reign'd,
Slept in their shades, and Angels entertain'd:
With such old Counsellors they did advise,
And by frequenting sacred Groves grew wise;
Free from th'impediments of light and noise
Man thus retir'd his nobler thoughts imploys:
Here *Charles* contrives the ordering of his States,
Here he resolves his neighb'ring Princes fates:
What Nation shall have Peace, where War be made
Determin'd is in this oraculous shade;
The World from *India* to the frozen *North*,
Concern'd in what this Solitude brings forth.
His Fancy objects from his view receives,
The prospect thought and contemplation gives:
That seat of Empire here salutes his eye,
To which three Kingdoms do themselves apply,
The structure by a Prelate rais'd, *Whitehall*,
Built with the fortune of *Rome*'s Capitol;
Both disproportion'd to the present State
Of their proud Founders, were approv'd by Fate;

59 *meen:* mien, manner.
66 *Culverin:* a large cannon.
87 *a Prelate:* Cardinal Wolsey (1472–1530), Lord Chancellor under Henry VIII.

From hence he does that antique Pile behold,
Where Royal heads receive the sacred gold;
It gives them Crowns, and does their ashes keep;
There made like gods, like mortals there they sleep
Making the circle of their Reign complete,
Those Suns of Empire, where they rise they set:
When others fell, this standing did presage
The Crown should triumph over popular rage,
Hard by that House where all our Ills were shap'd,
Th'auspicious Temple stood, and yet escap'd.
So Snow on *AEtna* does unmelted lie,
Whence rowling flames and scatter'd cinders flie;
The distant Countrey in the ruine shares,
What falls from Heav'n the burning Mountain spares.
Next, that capacious Hall he sees the room,
Where the whole Nation does for Justice come.
Under whose large roof flourishes the Gown,
And Judges grave on high Tribunals frown.
Here like the peoples Pastor he does go,
His flock subjected to his view below;
On which reflecting in his mighty mind,
No private passion does Indulgence find;
The pleasures of his Youth suspended are,
And made a Sacrifice to publick care;
Here free from Court compliances he walks,
And with himself, his best adviser, talks;
How peaceful Olive may his Temples shade,
For mending Laws, and for restoring Trade;
Or how his Brows may be with Laurel charg'd,
For Nations conquer'd, and our Bounds inlarg'd:
Of ancient Prudence here he ruminates,
Of rising Kingdoms, and of falling States;
What ruling Arts gave Great *Augustus* Fame,
And how *Alcides* purchas'd such a name:

91 *antique Pile:* Westminster Abbey.
99 *that House:* Parliament.
105 *Hall:* Westminster Hall.
124 *Alcides:* Hercules.

His eyes upon his native Palace bent
Close by, suggest a greater argument,
His thoughts rise higher when he does reflect
On what the world may from that Star expect
Which at his Birth appear'd to let us see
Day for his sake could with the Night agree;
A Prince on whom such different lights did smile,
Born, the divided world to reconcile:
Whatever Heaven or high extracted blood
Could promise or foretell, he will make good;
Reform these Nations, and improve them more,
Than this fair Park from what it was before.

## *To Mr.* Henry Lawes, *who had then newly set a Song of mine in the Year 1635*

Verse makes *Heroick* Virtue live,
But you can Life to Verses give:
As when in open Air we blow,
The Breath (though strain'd) sounds flat and low;
But if a Trumpet take the blast,
It lifts it high, and makes it last:
So in your Ayrs our Numbers drest
Make a shrill sally from the Brest
Of Nymphs, who singing what we pen'd,
Our passions to themselves commend,
While Love victorious with thy Art
Governs at once their Voice and Heart;
You by the help of Tune and Time,
Can make that Song that was but Rime.
*Noy* pleading, no man doubts the Cause;
Or questions Verses set by *LAWS*.

TO MR. HENRY LAWES: For Henry Lawes, see below, Lovelace, "To Lucasta, Going beyond the Seas," note.

15 *Noy:* William Noye (1577–1634), famous seventeenth-century lawyer, who prosecuted William Prynne in 1634. He had been made Attorney General by Charles I in 1631.

As a Church-window thick with Paint,
Lets in a light but dim and faint;
So others with Division hide
The light of Sence, the Poets pride,
But you alone may truly boast
That not a Syllable is lost;
The Writers and the Setters skill
At once the ravisht Ears do fill.
Let those which only warble long,
And Gargle in their Throats a Song,
Content themselves with *UT, RE, MI,*
Let Words and Sence be set by thee.

## *Of English Verse*

Poets may boast [as safely-Vain]
Their work shall with the world remain:
Both bound together, live, or die,
The Verses and the Prophecy.

But who can hope his Lines should long
Last in a daily-changing Tongue?
While they are new, Envy prevails,
And as that dies, our Language fails.

When Architects have done their part,
The Matter may betray their Art;
Time, if we use ill-chosen Stone,
Soon brings a well-built Palace down.

19 *Division:* a variation on a musical theme. "Other musicians," Waller says, "obscure the sense of a song with their florid embroidery; Lawes enhances and emphasizes it."

27 *UT:* The first note in the hexachords of Guido d'Arezzo (995?–1050?). The modern Do.

Poets that lasting Marble seek,
Must carve in *Latine* or in *Greek;*
We write in Sand, our Language grows,
And like the Tide our work o'reflows.

*Chaucer* his Sense can only boast,
The glory of his Numbers lost,
Years have defac'd his matchless strain;
And yet he did not sing in vain;

The Beauties which adorn'd that Age,
The shining Subjects of his Rage,
Hoping they should Immortal prove,
Rewarded with success his Love.

This was the generous Poet's scope,
And all an *English* Pen can hope
To make the Fair approve his Flame,
That can so far extend their Fame.

Verse thus design'd has no ill Fate,
If it arrive but at the Date
Of fading Beauty, if it prove
But as long-liv'd as present Love.

## *Of the last Verses in the Book*

When we for Age could neither read nor write,
The Subject made us able to indite.
The Soul with Nobler Resolutions deckt,
The Body stooping, does Herself erect:
No Mortal Parts are requisite to raise
Her, that Unbody'd can her Maker praise.

OF ENGLISH VERSE.

17 *Chaucer:* From the sixteenth to the later eighteenth century, Chaucer's lines were believed to be irregular and rough.

22 *Rage:* poetic inspiration.

The Seas are quiet, when the Winds give o're;
So calm are we, when Passions are no more:
For then we know how vain it was to boast
Of fleeting Things, so certain to be lost.
Clouds of Affection from our younger Eyes
Conceal that emptiness, which Age descries.

The Soul's dark Cottage, batter'd and decay'd,
Let's in new Light thrô chinks that time has made
Stronger by weakness, wiser Men become
As they draw near to their Eternal home:
Leaving the Old, both Worlds at once they view,
That stand upon the Threshold of the New.

——*Miratur Limen Olympi.*
Virgil.

13–14 Cf. Pope, *Dunciad*, IV, 125–26: "And you, my Critics! in the chequered shade, / Admire new light through holes yourselves have made."

19 The motto at the end is from Virgil's *Eclogues* v.56: "Candidus insuetum miratur limen Olympi" (In radiant beauty, he [Daphnis] marvels at Heaven's unfamiliar threshold).

# SIR JOHN SUCKLING
## 1609–1642

# *A Sessions of the Poets*

A Session was held the other day.
And *Apollo* himself was at it (they say)
The Laurel that had been so long reserv'd,
Was now to be given to him best deserv'd.
And

Therefore the wits of the Town came thither,
'Twas strange to see how they flocked together,
Each strongly confident of his own way,
Thought to gain the Laurel away that day.

There *Selden*, and he sate hard by the chair;
*Weniman* not far off, which was very fair;
*Sands* with *Townsend*, for they kept no order;
*Digby* and *Shillingsworth* a little further:
And

There was *Lucans* Translator too, and he
That makes God speak so bigge in's Poetry;
*Selwin* and *Walter*, and *Bartlets* both the brothers;
*Jack Vaughan* and *Porter*, and divers others.

A SESSION OF THE POETS.

10 *Selden:* John Selden (1584–1654), famous jurist and antiquarian scholar.

11 *Weniman:* Sir Francis Wenman, a country gentleman and member of Lord Falkland's circle.

12 *Sands with Townsend:* See the biographies of these poets in this volume.

13 *Digby:* Sir Kenelm Digby (1603–1665); *Shillingsworth:* William Chillingsworth (1602–1644), Protestant theologian and another member of Falkland's group.

15 *Lucans Translator:* Thomas May (1595–1650).

16 *That . . . bigge:* Usually identified as Francis Quarles (1592–1644) whose popular book of *Emblems* first appeared in 1635.

17 Selwin, Walter, and the Bartlets have not been identified.

18 *Vaughan:* Perhaps a John Vaughan of the Inner Temple, a friend of Selden; *Porter:* Endymion Porter (1587–1649), a favorite at court and a prominent patron of poets.

The first that broke silence was good old *Ben*,
Prepar'd before with Canary wine,
And he told them plainly he deserv'd the Bayes,
For his were calld Works, where others were but Plaies.
                                        And
Bid them remember how he had purg'd the Stage
Of errors, that had lasted many an Age,
And he hopes they did not think the *silent Woman*,
The *Fox*, and the *Alchymist* out done by no man.

*Apollo* stopt him there, and bade him not go on,
'Twas merit, he said, and not presumption
Must carry't; at which *Ben* turned about,
And in great choler offer'd to go out:
                                        But
Those that were there thought it not fit
To discontent so ancient a wit;
And therefore *Apollo* call'd him back agen,
And made him mine host of his own new Inne.

*Tom Carew* was next, but he had a fault
That would not well stand with a Laureat;
His Muse was hard bound, and th'issue of's brain
Was seldom brought forth but with trouble and pain.
                                        And
All that were present there did agree,
A Laureat Muse should be easie and free,
Yet sure 'twas not that, but 'twas thought that his Grace
Consider'd he was well he had a Cup-bearers place.

22 *Works:* a jesting reference to Jonson's edition (1616) of his poems and plays as "The Works of Ben Jonson."

36 *new Inne:* a punning allusion to the failure of Jonson's play, *The New Inn.*

37 *Carew:* Suckling's close friend. See below, "Upon my Lady Carliles walking."

*Will. Davenant* asham'd of a foolish mischance
That he had got lately travelling in *France,*
Modestly hoped the handsomnesse of's Muse
Might any deformity about him excuse.
And

Surely the Company would have been content,
If they could have found any President;
But in all their Records either in Verse or Prose,
There was not one Laureat without a nose.

To *Will Bartlet* sure all the wits meant well,
But first they would see how his snow would sell:
*Will* smil'd and swore in their judgements they went lesse,
That concluded of merit upon successe.

Suddenly taking his place agen,
He gave way to *Selwin,* who streight stept in;
But alas! he had been so lately a wit,
That *Apollo* hardly knew him yet.

*Toby Mathews* (pox on him) how came he there?
Was whispering nothing in some-bodies ear:
When he had the honour to be nam'd in Court,
But Sir, you may thank my Lady *Carleil* for't:

For had not her care furnisht you out
With something of handsome, without all doubt
You and your sorry Lady Muse had been
In the number of those that were not let in.

46 *Davenant:* Sir William Davenant (1606–1668), poet and dramatist. His nose had been deformed by syphilis.

56 *snow:* a slang term, perhaps suggesting the white pages of Bartlet's unpublished book.

63 *Mathews:* Sir Tobie Matthew (1577–1655), son of the Archbishop of Canterbury. Famous as a courtier and diplomatist, he became a Roman Catholic priest in 1614. He was a close friend of Lucy, Countess of Carlisle (line 66), herself a patron of many poets.

In haste from the Court two or three came in,
And they brought letters (forsooth) from the Queen,
'Twas discreetly done too, for if th' had come
Without them, th' had scarce been let into the room.

*Suckling* next was call'd, but did not appear,
But strait one whisperd *Apollo* i'th'ear,
That of all men living he cared not for't,
He loved not the Muses so well as his sport;

And prized black eyes, or a lucky hit
At bowls, above all the Trophies of wit;
But *Apollo* was angry, and publiquely said
'Twere fit that a fine were set upon's head.

*Wat Montague* now stood forth to his tryal,
And did not so much as suspect a denial;
But witty *Apollo* asked him first of all
If he understood his own Pastoral.

For if he could do it, 't would plainly appear
He understood more than any man there,
And did merit the Bayes above all the rest,
But the Mounsier was modest, and silence confest.

During these troubles in the Court was hid
One that *Apollo* soon mist, little *Cid;*
And having spied him, call'd him out of the throng,
And advis'd him in his ear not to write so strong.

83 *Montague:* Walter Montagu (1603?–1677), author of *The Shepherd's Paradise* (1633). He became a Roman Catholic in 1635 and ended his life as Abbot of St. Martin near Pontoise.

92 *little Cid:* Sidney Godolphin (1610–1643), a minor poet. He was killed at the skirmish of Chagford during the civil wars. His diminutive stature is often referred to.

*Murrey* was summon'd, but 't was urg'd that he
Was Chief already of another Company.

*Hales* set by himself most gravely did smile
To see them about nothing keep such a coil;
*Apollo* had spied him, but knowing his mind
Past by, and call'd *Faulkland* that sate just behind:
But

He was of late so gone with Divinity,
That he had almost forgot his Poetry,
Though to say the truth (and *Apollo* did know it)
He might have been both his Priest and his Poet.

At length who but an Alderman did appear,
At which *Will. Davenant* began to swear;
But wiser *Apollo* bade him draw nigher,
And when he was mounted a little higher

Openly declared that the best signe
Of good store of wit 's to have good store of coyn,
And without a Syllable more or lesse said,
He put the Laurel on the Aldermans head.

At this all the wits were in such a maze
That for a good while they did nothing but gaze
One upon another, not a man in the place
But had discontent writ in great in his face.

95 *Murrey:* Possibly William Murray (1600?–1651), who became first Earl of Dysart in 1643. He had been educated with Charles I.

97 *Hales:* John Hales (1584–1656), a much-loved fellow of Eton, who was a member of the Falkland circle.

98 *keep . . . coil:* make such a fuss.

100 *Faulkland:* Lucius Cary, second Viscount Falkland (1610?–1643). See Jonson's poem to him and Morison.

117 *in great:* in large letters.

Onely the small Poets clear'd up again,
Out of hope as 't was thought of borrowing,
But sure they were out, for he forfeits his Crown
When he lends any Poets about the Town.

## *Song*

Why so pale and wan fond Lover?
prethee why so pale?
Will, when looking wel can't move her
looking ill prevail?
prethee why so pale?

Why so dull and mute young sinner?
prethee why so mute?
Will, when speaking well can't win her,
saying nothing doe't?
prethee why so mute?

Quit, quit for shame, this will not move,
this cannot take her;
If of her self she will not love,
nothing can make her:
the divel take her.

118 *clear'd:* The 1648 edition of *Fragmenta Aurea* reads *cheer'd.*
SONG: Suckling also used this poem in his play *Aglaura.*

# *Sonnet.* I.

*1.*

Do'st see how unregarded now
that piece of beauty passes?
There was a time when I did vow
to that alone;
but mark the fate of faces;
That red and white works now no more on me
Then if it could not charm or I not see.

2.

And yet the face continues good,
and I have still desires,
Am still the self same flesh and blood,
as apt to melt
and suffer from those fires;
Oh! some kind power unriddle where it lies,
Whether my heart be faulty, or her eyes?

3.

She every day her Man does kill,
and I as often die;
Neither her power then, nor my will
can question'd be,
what is the mystery?
Sure Beauties Empires, like to greater States
Have certain periods set, and hidden fates.

# *Sonnet.* II.

*1.*

Of thee (kind boy) I ask no red and white
to make up my delight,
no odd becomming graces,
Black eyes, or little know-not-whats, in faces;
Make me but mad enough, give me good store
Of Love, for her I Court,
I ask no more,
'Tis love in love that makes the sport.

2.

There's no such thing as that we beauty call,
it is meer cousenage all;
for though some long ago
Like't certain colours mingled so and so,
That doth not tie me now from chusing new,
If I a fancy take
To black and blue,
That fancy doth it beauty make.

3.

Tis not the meat, but 'tis the appetite
makes eating a delight,
and if I like one dish
More then another, that a Pheasant is;

SONNET. II.
10 *cousenage:* trickery.

What in our watches, that in us is found,
So to the height and nick
We up be wound,
No matter by what hand or trick.

## *Sonnet.* III.

*1.*

Oh! for some honest Lovers ghost,
Some kind unbodied post
Sent from the shades below.
I strangely long to know
Whether the nobler Chaplets wear,
Those that their mistresse scorn did bear,
Or those that were us'd kindly.

2.

For what-so-e're they tell us here
To make those sufferings dear,
'Twill there I fear be found,
That to the being crown'd,
T'have lov'd alone will not suffice,
Unlesse we also have been wise,
And have our Loves enjoy'd.

22 *nick:* slot or groove. In *Aglaura* (II.i), Suckling writes: "Like the string of a watch wound up too high, and forc'd above the nicke."

SONNET. III.

2 *post:* messenger.

3.

What posture can we think him in,
That here unlov'd agen
Departs, and's thither gone
Where each sits by his own?
Or how can that *Elizium* be
Where I my Mistresse still must see
Circled in others Armes?

4.

For there the Judges all are just,
And *Sophonisba* must
Be his whom she held dear;
Not his who lov'd her here:
The sweet *Philoclea* since she dy'de
Lies by her *Pirocles* his side,
Not by *Amphialus.*

5.

Some Bayes (perchance) or Myrtle bough
For difference crowns the brow
Of those kind souls that were
The noble Martyrs here;
And if that be the onely odds
(As who can tell) ye kinder Gods,
Give me the Woman here.

19 *Elizium:* the Elysian Fields, the abode of the blest.

23 *Sophonisba:* the daughter of Hasdrubal, the Carthaginian general. She committed suicide (204 B.C.) to avoid being taken from her lover and led to Rome as a captive by Scipio Africanus.

26–28 Philoclea, Pyrocles, and Amphialus are all characters in Sir Philip Sidney's *Arcadia.*

## [*There never yet was woman made*]

1.

There never yet was woman made,
 nor shall, but to be curst;
And oh' that I (fond I) should first
 of any Lover
This truth at my own charge to other fools discover.

2.

You that have promis'd to your selves
 propriety in love,
Know womens hearts like straws do move,
 and what we call
Their sympathy, is but love to jett in general.

3.

All mankind are alike to them;
 and though we iron find
That never with a Loadstone joyn'd,
 'tis not the irons fault,
It is because the loadstone yet was never brought.

THERE NEVER YET WAS: This poem is untitled in the 1646 edition.
 10 *but . . . general:* i.e. "merely their desire to strut before everyone."

*4.*

If where a gentle Bee hath fall'n
and laboured to his power,
A new succeeds not to that Flower,
but passes by;
'Tis to be thought, the gallant else-where loads his thigh.

5.

For still the flowers ready stand,
one buzzes round about,
One lights, one tasts, gets in, gets out
all, all waies use them,
Till all their sweets are gone, and all again refuse them.

## *Song*

*1.*

No, no, fair Heretick, it needs must be
But an ill love in me,
And worse for thee;
For were it in my power,
To love thee now this hower
More then I did the last;
I would then so fall
I might not love at all;
Love that can flow, and can admit increase,
Admits as well an ebbe, and may grow lesse.

SONG: This song was also used in Suckling's *Aglaura.*

2.

True Love is still the same; the Torrid Zones,
And those more frigid ones
It must not know:
For love grown cold or hot,
Is lust, or friendship, not
The thing we have.
For that's a flame would dye
Held down, or up too high:
Then think I love more then I can expresse,
And would love more could I but love thee lesse.

## *Upon my Lady* Carliles *walking in* Hampton-Court garden. Dialogue.

*T.C.* *J.S.*

*Thom.*

Didst thou not find the place inspir'd,
And flow'rs as if they had desir'd
No other Sun, start from their beds,
And for a sight steal out their heads?
Heardst thou not musick when she talk't?
And didst not find that as she walkt
She threw rare perfumes all about
Such as bean-blossoms newly out,
Or chafed spices give?——

UPON MY LADY CARLILES: For Lady Lucy Carlisle, see above, "A Sessions of the Poets," line 63. In the "Dialogue" here "T.C." is Thomas Carew the poet and "J.S." John Suckling himself.

*J. S.*

I must confesse those perfumes (*Tom*)
I did not smell; nor found that from
Her passing by, ought sprung up new,
The flow'rs had all their birth from you;
For I pass't o're the self same walk,
And did not find one single stalk
Of any thing that was to bring
This unknown after after spring.

*Thom.*

Dull and insensible, could'st see
A thing so near a Deity
Move up and down, and feel no change?

*J. S.*

None, and so great, were alike strange,
I had my Thoughts, but not your way,
All are not born (Sir) to the Bay;
Alas! *Tom,* I am flesh and blood,
And was consulting how I could
In spite of masks and hoods descry
The parts deni'd unto the eye;
I was undoing all she wore,
And had she walkt but one turn more,
*Eve* in her first state had not been
More naked, or more plainly seen.

*Thom.*

'T was well for thee she left the place,
There is great danger in that face;
But had'st thou view'd her legg and thigh,
And upon that discovery
Search't after parts that are more dear
(As Fancy seldom stops so near)
No time or age had ever seen
So lost a thing as thou hadst been.

## [*Tis now since I sate down before*]

*1.*

Tis now since I sate down before
    That foolish Fort, a heart;
(Time strangely spent) a Year, and more,
    And still I did my part:

*2.*

Made my approaches, from her hand
    Unto her lip did rise,
And did already understand
    The language of her eyes.

TIS NOW SINCE: This poem has occasionally been called "The Siege," though it has no title in the 1646 edition.

3.

Proceeded on with no lesse Art,
My Tongue was Engineer;
I thought to undermine the heart
By whispering in the ear.

4.

When this did nothing, I brought down
Great Canon-oaths, and shot
A thousand thousand to the Town,
And still it yeelded not.

5.

I then resolv'd to starve the place
By cutting off all kisses,
Praysing and gazing on her face,
And all such little blisses.

6.

To draw her out, and from her strength,
I drew all batteries in:
And brought my self to lie at length
As if no siege had been.

7.

When I had done what man could do,
And thought the place mine owne,
The Enemy lay quiet too,
And smil'd at all was done.

8.

I sent to know from whence, and where,
These hopes, and this relief?
A Spie inform'd, Honour was there,
And did command in chief.

9.

March, march (quoth I) the word straight give,
Lets lose no time, but leave her:
That Giant upon ayre will live,
And hold it out for ever.

10.

To such a place our Camp remove
As will no siege abide;
I hate a fool that starves her Love
Onely to feed her pride.

# A Ballade.

## *Upon a Wedding*

I tell thee *Dick* where I have been,
Where I the rarest things have seen;
Oh things without compare!
Such sights again cannot be found
In any place on English ground,
Be it at Wake, or Fair.

At *Charing-Crosse,* hard by the way
Where we (thou know'st) do sell our Hay,
There is a house with stairs;
And there did I see comming down
Such folk as are not in our Town,
Vorty at least, in Pairs.

Amongst the rest, one Pest'lent fine,
(His beard no bigger though then thine)
Walkt on before the rest:
Our Landlord looks like nothing to him:
The King (God bless him) 'twould undo him,
Should he go still so drest.

A BALLADE: Suckling wrote this poem for the marriage of Roger Boyle, Baron Broghill (1621–1679) and Lady Margaret Howard in 1641.

1 *Dick:* usually identified as the poet Richard Lovelace. Both the speaker and "Dick" are portrayed as rustics, overwhelmed by the spectacle of the wedding.

12 *Vorty:* rustic dialect for "forty."

13 *Pest'lent fine:* confoundedly elegant.

18 *still:* always.

At Course-a-Park, without all doubt,
He should have first been taken out
By all the Maids i'th' Town:
Though lusty *Roger* there had been,
Or little *George* upon the Green,
Or *Vincent* of the Crown.

But wot you what? the youth was going
To make an end of all his woing;
The Parson for him staid:
Yet by his leave (for all his haste)
He did not so much wish all past,
(Perchance) as did the maid.

The maid (and thereby hangs a tale)
For such a maid no Whitson-ale
Could ever yet produce:
No Grape that's kindly ripe, could be
So round, so plump, so soft as she,
Nor half so full of Juyce.

Her finger was so small, the Ring
Would not stay on which they did bring,
It was too wide a Peck:
And to say truth (for out it must)
It lookt like the great Collar (just)
About our young Colts neck.

Her feet beneath her Petticoat,
Like little mice stole in and out,
As if they fear'd the light:
But oh! she dances such a way!
No Sun upon an Easter day
Is half so fine a sight.

19 *Course-a-Park:* a country game involving kissing.
34 *kindly:* grown naturally.
39 *a Peck:* by a lot.

He would have kist her once or twice,
But she would not, she was nice,
She would not do't in sight,
And then she lookt as who should say
I will do what I list to day;
And you shall do't at night.

Her Cheeks so rare a white was on,
No Dazy makes comparison,
(Who sees them is undone)
For streaks of red were mingled there,
Such as are on a Katherne Pear,
(The side that's next the Sun.)

Her lips were red, and one was thin,
Compar'd to that was next her chin;
(Some Bee had stung it newly.)
But (*Dick*) her eyes so guard her face;
I durst no more upon them gaze,
Then on the Sun in *July*.

Her mouth so small when she does speak,
Thou'dst swear her teeth her words did break,
That they might passage get,
But she so handled still the matter,
They came as good as ours, or better,
And are not spent a whit.

If wishing should be any sin,
The Parson himself had guilty bin;
(She lookt that day so purely,)
And did the youth so oft the feat
At night, as some did in conceit,
It would have spoil'd him, surely.

50 *nice:* fastidious.
59 *Katherne Pear:* The Catherine pear is a small, early ripening variety.

Just in the nick the Cook knockt thrice,
And all the waiters in a trice
His summons did obey,
Each serving man with dish in hand,
Marcht boldly up, like our Train'd Band,
Presented, and away.

When all the meat was on the Table,
What man of knife, or teeth, was able
To stay to be intreated?
And this the very reason was,
Before the Parson could say Grace,
The Company was seated.

The bus'nesse of the Kitchin's great,
For it is fit that men should eat;
Nor was it there deni'd:
Passion oh me! how I run on!
There's that that would be thought upon,
(I trow) besides the Bride.

Now hatts fly off, and youths carrouse;
Healths first go round, and then the house,
The Brides came thick and thick:
And when 'twas nam'd anothers health,
Perhaps he made it hers by stealth.
(And who could help it? *Dick*)

O'th' sodain up they rise and dance;
Then sit again and sigh, and glance:
Then dance again and kisse:
Thus sev'ral waies the time did passe,
Till ev'ry Woman wisht her place,
And ev'ry Man wisht his.

83 *Train'd Band:* village militia.
87 *stay:* wait.
107 *wisht her place:* wished to be in her [the bride's place]. The 1648 edition reads *Whilst* for *Till* in this line.

By this time all were stoln aside
To counsel and undresse the Bride;
    But that he must not know:
But yet 'twas thought he ghest her mind,
And did not mean to stay behind
    Above an hour or so.

When in he came (*Dick*) there she lay
Like new-faln snow melting away,
    ('Twas time I trow to part)
Kisses were now the onely stay,
Which soon she gave, as who would say,
    *Good Boy!* with all my heart.

But just as heav'ns would have to crosse it,
In came the Bridemaids with the Posset:
    The Bridegroom eat in spight;
For had he left the Women to't
It would have cost two hours to do't,
    Which were too much that night.

At length the candles out and out,
All that they had not done, they do't,
    What that is, who can tell?
But I beleeve it was no more
Then thou and I have done before
    With *Bridget*, and with *Nell*.

122 *Posset:* a drink made of hot milk, sugar, and spices, curdled with ale or wine.

# Sir *J. S.*

*1.*

Out upon it, I have lov'd
  Three whole days together;
And am like to love three more,
  If it prove fair weather.

*2.*

Time shall moult away his wings
  Ere he shall discover
In the whole wide world agen
  Such a constant Lover.

*3.*

But the spite on't is, no praise
  Is due at all to me:
Love with me had made no staies,
  Had it any been but she.

*4.*

Had it any been but she
  And that very Face,
There had been at least ere this
  A dozen dozen in her place.

SIR J.S.: This and the following two poems are from *The Last Remains* (1659). "Love and Debt" is of doubtful authorship, but may be by Suckling.

## *Love and Debt alike troublesom*

This one request I make to him that sits the clouds above
That I were freely out of debt, as I am out of love:
Then for to dance, to drink and sing, I should be very willing
I should not ow one Lass a kiss, nor ne'r a Knave a shilling.
'Tis only being in Love and Debt, that breaks us of our rest;
And he that is quite out of both, of all the world is blest:
He sees the golden age wherein all things were free and common;
He eats, he drinks, he takes his rest, he fears no man nor woman.
Though *Croesus* compassed great wealth, yet he still craved more,
He was as needy a beggar still, as goes from dore to dore.
Though *Ovid* were a merry man, Love ever kept him sad;
He was as far from happiness, as one that is stark mad.
Our Merchant he in goods is rich, and full of gold and treasure;
But when he thinks upon his Debts, that thought destroys his pleasure.
Our Courtier thinks that he's preferr'd, whom every man envies;
When Love so rumbles in his pate, no sleep comes in his eyes.
Our Gallants case is worst of all, he lies so just betwixt them;
For he's in Love, and he's in Debt, and knows not which most vex him.
But he that can eat Beef, and feed on bread which is so brown
May satisfie his appetite, and owe no man a crown:
And he that is content with Lasses clothed in plain woollen,
May cool his heat in every place, he need not to be sullen,
Nor sigh for love of Lady fair; for this each wise man knows
As good stuff under Flanel lies, as under Silken clothes.

## *A Song*

Hast thou seen the Down in the air,
    when wanton blasts have tost it?
Or the Ship on the Sea,
    when ruder winds have crost it?
Hast thou markt the Crocodiles weeping,
    or the Foxes sleeping?
Or hast viewed the Peacock in his pride,
    or the Dove by his Bride,
    when he courts for his leacherie?
Oh so fickle, oh so vain, oh so false, so false is she!

A SONG: This song parodies the third stanza of "Her Triumph" in Jonson's "Celebration of Charis." It occurs in one of Suckling's unfinished plays, *The Sad One.*

# JOHN CLEVELAND
1613–1658

# *Clievelandi Vindiciæ*;

OR,

# CLIEVELAND'S

## Genuine POEMS,

## Orations, Epiſtles, &c.

Purged from the many

## Falſe & Spurious Ones

Which had uſurped his Name, and from innumerable Errours and Corruptions in the True.

---

To which are added many never Printed before.

---

Publiſhed according to the Author's own Copies.

---

*LONDON*,

Printed for *Nath. Brooke*, at the *Angel* in *Corne-Hill* near the *Royal Exchange*, 1677.

## *Fuscara* or the *Bee Errant*

Nature's Confectioner the Bee,
(Whose Suckets are moist Alchimy;
The Still of his refining Mold
Minting the Garden into Gold)
Having rifled all the Fields
Of what Dainties *Flora* yields.
Ambitious now to take Excise
Of a more fragrant Paradise,
At my *Fuscara's* sleeve arriv'd,
Where all delicious Sweets are hiv'd.
The Airy Freebooter distrains
First on the Violet of her Veins,
Whose Tincture could it be more pure,
His ravenous kiss had made it blewer.
Here did he sit, and Essence quaff,
Till her coy Pulse had beat him off;
That Pulse, which he that feels may know
Whether the World's long liv'd, or no.
The next he preys on is her Palm,
That Alm'ner of transpiring Balm;
So soft, 'tis Air but once remov'd,
Tender as 'twere a Jelly glov'd.
Here, while his canting Drone-pipe scan'd
The mystick Figures of her hand,
He tipples Palmestry, and dines
On all her Fortune-telling Lines:

FUSCARA: The Latin name "Fuscara" means "dark" or "swarthy."

2 *Suckets:* sweetmeats, candied fruit.

11 *distrains:* a legal term meaning to force a debtor to pay up by seizing his property.

20 *Alm'ner:* almoner, who bestows alms; *transpiring:* passing through the pores.

23 *Drone-pipe:* his hum, which sounded like a bagpipe.

He bathes in Bliss, and finds no odds
Betwixt this Nectar and the Gods.
He pearches now upon her Wrist
(A proper Hawk for such a Fist)
Making that Flesh his Bill of Fare,
Which hungry Canibals would spare,
Where Lillies in a lovely brown
Inoculate Carnation.
Her Argent Skin with Or so stream'd,
As if the milky-way were cream'd;
From hence he to the Woodbine bends
That quivers at her fingers ends,
That runs division on the Tree,
Like a thick-branching Pedigree;
So 'tis not her the Bee devours,
It is a pretty Maze of Flowers.
It is the Rose that bleeds, when he
Nibbles his nice Phlebotomy.
About her finger he doth cling
Ith' fashion of a Wedding Ring,
And bids his Comrades of the Swarm
Crawl like a Bracelet 'bout her Arm,
Thus when the hovering Publican
Had suck'd the Toll of all her Span,
(Tuning his Draughts with drowsie Hums,
As *Danes* Carouze by Kettle-drums)
It was decreed (that Posie glean'd)
The small Familiar should be wean'd.
At this the *Errant's* Courage quails;
Yet ayded by his native Sails,
The bold *Columbus* still designs
To find her undiscover'd Mines.
To th'*Indies* of her Arm he flies,
Fraught both with East and Western Prize,

33 *brown:* i.e Fuscara herself.
34 *Inoculate:* Become united with.
35 *Or:* gold.
44 *Phlebotomy:* cutting of a vein.
53 *Posie:* verses written inside the bracelet (line 48).

Which when he had in vain essay'd,
(Arm'd like a Dapper Lancepresade
With Spanish Pike) he broach'd a Pore,
And so both made and heal'd the Sore:
For as in Gummy Trees there's found
A Salve to issue at the Wound;
Of this her breach the like was true,
Hence trickled out a Balsom too.
But oh! What Wasp was't that could prove
*Raviliack* to my Queen of Love?
The King of Bees now jealous grown,
Lest her Beams should melt his Throne,
And finding that his Tribute slacks,
His Burgesses and State of Wax
Turn'd to an Hospital; the Combs
Built Rank and File, like Beadsmens Rooms,
And what they bleed but tart and sowre
Match'd with my *Danae's* golden showre,
Live Hony all, the envious Elf
Stung her, cause sweeter than himself.
  Sweetness and She are so alli'd,
  The Bee committed Paricide.

## *The Senses Festival*

I saw a Vision yesternight
Enough to sate a Seeker's sight,
I wish'd my self a shaker there,
And her quick Pants my trembling Sphere.

62 *Lancepresade:* lance-corporal, lowest ranking non-commissioned officer.
70 *Raviliack:* François Ravaillac (1578–1610), a religious fanatic who assassinated King Henry IV of France.
76 *Beadsmens Rooms:* monastic cells.
78 *Danae:* Jove made love to Danae in the form of a golden shower.

THE SENSES FESTIVAL.

3 *shaker:* possibly alluding to the Shakers, a Quaker sect. The Adamites (line 6) were another sect of the period.

It was a She so glittering bright,
You'd think her Soul an Adamite,
A Person of so rare a frame,
Her Body might be lin'd with th' same.
Beautie's chiefest Maid of Honour,
You may break Lent with looking on her.
  Not the fair Abbess of the Skies
  With all her Nunnery of Eyes
  Can shew me such a glorious Prize.

And yet because 'tis more Renown
To make a shadow shine, she's brown,
A Brown for which Heaven would disband
The Galazie, and Stars be tann'd;
Brown by Reflexion, as her Eye
Deals out the Summer's Livery.
Old dormant Windows must confess
Her Beams, their glimmering Spectacles,
Struck with the Splendor of her face,
Do th'office of a Burning glass.
  Now where such radiant Lights have shown,
  No wonder if her Cheeks be grown
  Sun-burnt, with Lustre of her own.

My Sight took pay; but (thank my Charms)
I now impale her in mine Arms
(Love's Compasses, confining you
Good Angels, to a Circle too.)
Is not the Universe strait lac'd,
When I can clasp it in the Waste?
My amorous Fold about thee hurl'd,
With *Drake* I girdle in the World;
I hoop the Firmament, and make
This my Embrace the Zodiack.

11 *fair Abbess:* the moon.

34 *Drake:* Sir Francis Drake's (1545–1596) circumnavigation of the globe, the first by an Englishman, occurred in 1577–1580.

How could thy Center take my Sense,
When Admiration doth commence
At the extreme Circumference?

Now to the melting Kiss that sips
The Jellied Philtre of her Lips;
So Sweet there is no Tongue can prays't,
Till transsubstantiate with a Taste,
Inspir'd like *Mahomet* from above
By th' Billing of my Heavenly Dove.
Love prints his Signets in her Smacks,
Those ruddy drops of squeezing Wax,
Which wheresoever she imparts,
They're Privy-Seals to take up Hearts.
Our mouths encountring at the sport,
My slippery Soul had quitt the Fort,
But that she stopp'd the Sally-port.

Next to these Sweets, her Lips dispense
(As Twin-conserves of Eloquence)
The Sweet Perfume her Breath affords
Incorporating with her Words.
No Rosary this Votress needs,
Her very Syllables are Beads.
No sooner 'twixt those Rubies born,
But Jewels are in Ear-rings worn.
With what delight her Speech doth enter,
It is a Kiss oth' second Venter.
And I dissolve at what I hear,
As if an other *Rosamond* were
Couch'd in the Labyrinth of my ear.

44 *Mahomet:* Mohammed.

57 *Votress:* dedicated nun.

62 *Venter:* a legal term: one of two or more wives who are sources of offspring to the same person. The first kiss is lip to lip, the second lip (words) to the ear.

64 *Rosamond:* Rosamund Clifford (d. 1176?), the mistress of Henry II. See Drayton's "Epistle of Henry to Rosamond."

Yet that's but a preludious Bliss
Two Souls Pickeering in a Kiss.
Embraces do but draw the Line,
'Tis storming that must take her in.
When Bodies joyn, and Vict'ry hovers
'Twixt the equal fluttering Lovers
This is the Game; make stakes, my Dear!
Heark, how the sprightly Chanticlere
(That Baron Tell-clock of the Night)
Sounds Boute-sel to *Cupid's* Knight.
  Then have at all, the Pass is got,
  For coming off, oh name it not!
  Who would not die upon the spot?

## *The Hecatomb to his Mistress*

Be dumb you Beggars of the rhythming Trade,
Geld your loose wits, & let your Muse be spade.
Charge not the Parish with your bastard Phrase
Of Balm, Elixir, both the *India's,*
Of Shrine, Saint, Sacrifice, and such as these,
Expressions common as your Mistresses.
Hence you Phantastick Postillers in Song,
My Text defeats your Art, ties Nature's tongue,
Scorns all her Tinsoyl'd Metaphors of Pelf,
Illustrated by nothing but her self.
As Spiders travel by their bowels spun
Into a Thread, and when the Race is run,

67 *Pickeering:* marauding, with a pun on "ear."

70–71 *When . . . Lovers:* Cf. Donne, "The Extasie," lines 13–14, "As 'twixt two equall Armies, Fate / Suspends uncertaine victorie."

75 *Boute-sel:* "Boot and saddle."

THE HECATOMB.

2 *spade:* spayed.

7 *Postillers:* commentators on Scripture.

9 *Tinsoyl'd:* punningly, for "tinselled."

Wind up their Journey in a living Clew;
So is it with my Poetry and you.
From your own Essence must I first untwine,
Then twist again each Panegyrick Line.
Reach then a Soaring Quill that I may write,
As with a *Jacob's* Staff to take her height.
Suppose an Angel darting through the Air
Should their encounter a religious Prayer
Mounting to Heaven, that Intelligence
Would for a Sunday-Suit thy Breath condense
Into a Body. Let me crack a string,
And venture higher. Were the Note I sing
Above Heaven's *Ela;* should I then decline,
And with a deep-mouth'd *Gammut* sound the Line
From Pole to Pole, I could not reach her worth,
Nor find an Epithet to shadow't forth.
Metals may blazon common Beauties; she
Makes Pearls and Planets humble Heraldry.
As then a purer Substance is defin'd
But by an heap of Negatives combin'd,
Ask what a Spirit is, you'l hear them cry,
It hath no Matter, no Mortality:
So can I not describe how sweet, how fair,
Only I say, she's not as others are:
For what Perfection we to others grant,
It is her sole Perfection to want.
All other Forms seem in respect of thee
The Almanack's mishap'd Anatomy:
Where *Aries* head and face, *Bull* neck and throat,
The *Scorpion* give the Secrets, *Knees* the Goat;

13 *Clew:* ball of thread.
18 *Jacob's Staff:* an instrument for measuring distances and heights.
20 *their:* there.
22 *Sunday-Suit:* best clothes.
25 *Ela:* the highest note in the scale.
26 *Gammut:* the first or lowest note.
42 *Secrets:* private parts.

A Brief of Limbs foul as those beasts, or are
Their name-sake Signs in their strange Character.
As your Philosophers to every Sense
Marry its Object, yet with some dispense,
And grant them a Polygamy with all,
And these their common Sensibles they call:
So is't with her, who stinted unto none,
Unites all Senses in each action.
The same Beam heats and lights, to see her well
Is both to hear and feel, and taste and smell:
For can you want a Palate in your Eyes,
When each of hers contains the beauteous prize,
*Venus's* Apple? Can your Eyes want Nose,
Seeing each Cheek buds forth a fragrant Rose?
Or can your Sight be deaf to such a quick
And well-tun'd Face, such moving Rhetorick?
Doth not each Look a Flash of Lightning feel,
Which spares the Bodie's sheath, yet melts the steel?
Thy Soul must needs confess, or grant thy Sense
Corrupted with the Object's Excellence.
Sweet Magick, which can make five Senses lie
Conjur'd within the Circle of an Eye!
In whom since all the five are intermixt,
Oh now that *Scaliger* would prove his sixt!
Thou Man of mouth that canst not name a she,
Unless all Nature pay a Subsidy,
Whose Language is a Tax, whose Musk-cat Verse
Voids nought but Flowers for thy Muses Herse,
Fitter than *Celia's* Looks, who in a trice
Canst state the long disputed Paradise,

43 *Brief:* list.

52 *feel:* the 1677 edition has *see.*

66 *Scaliger:* Julius Caesar Scaliger (1484–1558), the great Italian physician and scholar. The sixth sense was the *sensus communis,* or common sense.

70–71 The sense is clearer if the comma at the end of line 70 is placed after "Flowers."

72 *Paradise:* The exact location of the Garden of Eden was much debated by seventeenth-century scholars.

And (what Divines hunt with so cold a scent)
Canst in her bosom find it resident;
Now come aloft, come now, and breath a Vein,
And give some vent unto thy daring strain.
Say the Astrologer who spells the Stars,
In that fair Alphabet reads Peace and Wars,
Mistakes his Globe, and in her brighter eye
Interprets Heaven's Physiognomy.
Call her the Metaphysicks of her Sex,
And say she tortures Wits, as Quartans vex
Physicians; call her the squar'd Circle; say
She is the very Rule of *Algebra:*
What e're thou understand'st not say't of her,
For that's the way to write her Character.
Say this and more, and when thou hop'st to raise
Thy phancy so as to inclose her praise,
Alas poor *Gotham*, with thy Cuckoe-hedge!
*Hyperboles* are here but Sacrilege.
Then roll up Muse what thou hast ravel'd out,
Some Comments clear not, but increase the doubt.
She that affords poor Mortals not a glance
Of Knowledge, but is known by Ignorance.
She that commits a Rape on every Sense,
Whose Breath can countermand a Pestilence.
She that can strike the best Invention dead,
Till baffled Poetry hangs down the head.
She, she it is that doth contain all Bliss,
And makes the World but her *Periphrasis*.

82 *Quartans:* severe fevers.
89 *Gotham:* The madmen of Gotham are proverbial.

## *The Antiplatonick*

For shame thou everlasting Wooer,
Still saying Grace, and ne'r fall to her!
Love that's in Contemplation plac'd
Is *Venus* drawn but to the waste.
Unless your Flame confess its Gender,
And your Parley cause Surrender,
Y'are *Salamanders* of a cold desire,
That live untouch'd amidst the hottest fire:

What though she be a Dame of stone,
The Widow of *Pigmalion:*
An hard and unrelenting she,
As the new-crusted *Niobe;*
Or (what doth more of statue carry)
A Nun of the *Platonick* Quarry?
Love melts the rigor which the Rocks have bred,
A Flint will break upon a Feather-bed.

For shame you pretty Female Elves,
Cease thus to candy up your selves;
No more you Sectaries of the Game,
No more of your calcining Flame.
Women commence by *Cupid's* Dart,
As a King hunting Dubs a Hart.

THE ANTIPLATONICK.

10 *Widow:* as if Pygmalion's "fair lady" became a statue again after his death.

19 *Sectaries of:* heretics in.

20 *calcining:* purifying or refining by reducing to ashes. The term is alchemical.

22 *Dubs:* ennobles. The hart becomes noble because the King hunts it; women (line 21) take their degrees ("commence") when dubbed by the King of Love (Cupid).

Love's Votaries enthral each other's Soul,
Till both of them live but upon Parol.

Virtue's no more in Womankind
But the Green sickness of the Mind.
Philosophy (their new Delight)
A kind of Charcoal Appetite.
There is no Sophistry prevails,
Where all-convincing Love assails;
But the disputing Petticoat will warp,
As Skilful Gamesters are to seek at sharp.

The Souldier, that Man of Iron,
Whom Ribs of Horror all environ;
That's strung with Wire instead of Veins,
In whose Embraces you're in Chains;
Let a Magnetick Girl appear,
Straight he turns *Cupid's* Cuiraseer.
Love storms his Lips, and takes the Fortress in,
For all the bristled Turnpike of his Chin.

Since Love's Artillery then checks
The Breast-works of the firmest Sex:
Come let us in affections riot;
Th'are sickly pleasures keep a diet.
Give me a Lover bold and free,
Not Eunuch'd with Formality,
Like an Embassador that beds a Queen
With the nice caution of a Sword between.

24 *Parol:* with a pun on the literal sense ("word").

26 *Green sickness:* chlorosis.

32 *Gamesters:* fencers; *to . . . sharp:* hard to find when real swordplay is involved.

38 *Cuiraseer:* horse soldier with an armored breastplate.

40 *Turnpike:* spiked barrier across a road.

## *Upon* Phillis *walking in a Morning before Sun-rising*

The sluggish Morn as yet undrest,
My *Phillis* brake from out her East,
As if she'd made a match to run
With *Venus,* usher to the Sun.
The Trees, like Yeomen of the Guard
(Serving her more for Pomp than Ward)
Rank'd on each side, with Loyal Duty,
Weav'd Branches to inclose her Beauty.
The Plants, whose Luxury was lopp'd,
Or Age with Crutches underpropp'd,
(Whose wooden Carkases were grown
To be but Coffins of their own)
Revive, and at her general Dole
Each receives his Ancient Soul.
The winged Choristers began
To chirp their *Mattins,* and the Fan
Of whistling Winds like Organs play'd,
Until their Voluntaries made
The wakened Earth in Odors rise
To be her Morning Sacrifice.
The Flowers call'd out of their Beds,
Start and raise up their drowsie Heads;
And he that for their colour seeks
May see it vaulting to her Cheeks:
Where Roses mix; no Civil War
Divides her *York* and *Lancaster.*
The Marygold (whose Courtier's face
Ecchoes the Sun, and doth unlace

UPON PHILLIS WALKING.

18 *Voluntaries:* musical preludes played spontaneously.

25 *Roses:* alluding to the fifteenth-century Wars of the Roses, which pitted the houses of York and Lancaster against each other.

Her at his rise, at his full stop
Packs and shuts up her gawdy Shop)
Mistakes her Cue, and doth display:
Thus *Phillis* antedates the day.
These Miracles had cramp'd the Sun,
Who fearing that his Kingdom's won,
Powders with Light his frizled Locks
To see what Saint his Lustre mocks.
The trembling Leaves through which he play'd,
Dappling the Walk with light and shade,
Like Lattice-windows give the Spye
Room but to peep with half an eye;
Lest her full Orb his sight should dim,
And bid us all good night in him;
Till she should spend a gentle ray
To force us a new fashion'd day.
  But what religious Palsie's this,
Which makes the Bows devest their bliss,
And that they might her footsteps straw,
Drop their Leaves with shivering awe?
*Phillis* perceiv'd, and (lest her stay
Should wed *October* unto *May*,
And as her Beauty caus'd a Spring,
Devotion might an Autumn bring)
Withdrew her Beams, yet made no Night,
But left the Sun her Curate-light.

46 *Bows:* boughs.
47 *straw:* strew.

## *A Fair Nymph scorning a Black Boy courting her*

*Nymph.* Stand off, and let me take the Air,
Why should the smoke pursue the fair?
*Boy.* My Face is smoke, thence may be guest
What Flames within have scorch'd my breast.
*Nymph.* Thy flaming Love I cannot view
For the dark Lanthorn of thy Hue.
*Boy.* And yet this Lanthorn keeps Love's Taper
Surer than your's that's of white Paper.
What ever Midnight can be here,
The Moon-shine of your Face will clear.
*Nymph.* My Moon of an Eclipse is 'fraid;
If thou should'st interpose thy shade.
*Boy.* Yet one thing, Sweet-heart, I will ask,
Take me for a new fashion'd Mask.
*Nymph.* Done: but my Bargain shall be this,
I'le throw my Mask off when I kiss.
*Boy.* Our curl'd Embraces shall delight
To checker Limbs with black and white.
*Nymph.* Thy Ink, my Paper, make me guess
Our Nuptial bed will prove a Press,
And in our Sports, if any came,
They'l read a wanton Epigram.
*Boy.* Why should my Black thy Love impair?
Let the dark Shop commend the Ware;
Or if thy Love from black forbears,
I'l strive to wash it off with Tears.

A FAIR NYMPH.

6 *For:* Because of.

8 *white paper:* The lady perhaps wears a mask of white paper—but her skin is also a mask.

21 *came:* the 1677 edition has *come.*

*Nymph.* Spare fruitless Tears, since thou must needs
Still wear about thy mourning Weeds.
Tears can no more affection win,
Than wash thy *Aethiopian* Skin.

## *A Young Man to an Old Woman courting him*

Peace Beldam *Eve,* surcease thy Suit,
There's no Temptation in such Fruit.
No rotten Medlars, whilst there be
Whole Orchards in Virginity.
Thy Stock is too much out of date
For tender Plants t'inoculate.
A Match with thee the Bridegroom fears
Would be thought Incest in his years,
Which when compar'd to thine become
Odd Money to thy Grandam Sum.
Can Wedlock know so great a Curse,
As putting Husbands out to Nurse?
How Pond and Rivers would mistake,
And cry new Almanacks for our sake?
Time sure hath wheel'd about his Year,
*December* meeting *Janiveer.*
Th'*Egyptian* Serpent figures Time,
And strip'd, returns into his prime.
If my Affection thou wouldst win,
First cast thy Hieroglyphick Skin.
My Modern Lips know not, alack,
The old Religion of thy *Smack.*
I count that Primitive Embrace,
As out of Fashion, as thy Face;

A YOUNG MAN.

3 *Medlars:* small, brown apples, eaten when they have become pulpy.

6 *t'inoculate:* to engraft.

13 *Pond and Rivers:* Edward Pond and Peregrine Rivers, both of whom produced almanacs.

22 *old Religion:* loosely used to indicate Pre-Reformation Catholicism.

And yet so long 'tis since thy fall,
Thy Fornication's Classical.
Our Sports will differ, thou must play
*Lero,* and I *Alphonso* way.
I'm no Translator, have no vein
To turn a Woman young again;
Unless you'l grant the Taylor's due,
To see the Fore-bodies be new.
I love to wear Clothes that are flush,
Not prefacing old Rags with Plush,
Like Aldermen, or Under-shrieves
With Canvas Backs, and Velvet-Sleeves:
And just such Discord there would be
Betwixt thy Skeleton and me.
Go study Salve and Triacle, ply
Your Tenant's Leg, or his sore eye.
Thus Matrons purchase Credit, thank,
Six penny worth of Mountebank;
Or chew thy Cud on some Delight,
That thou didst taste in Eighty eight;
Or be but Bed-rid once, and then
Thoul't dream thy youthful sins agen:
But if thou needs wilt be my Spouse,
First hearken and attend my Vows.
When *AEtna's* fires shall undergo
The Penance of the *Alps* in Snow;
When *Sol* at one blast of his Horn
Post from the Crab to *Capricorn;*
When the Heavens shuffle all in one,
The Torrid with the Frozen Zone;
When all these Contradictions meet,
Then, *Sybil,* thou and I will greet:

28 *Lero . . . Alphonso:* I have not been able to explain Cleveland's allusion.
32 *Fore-bodies:* front parts of dresses.
33 *flush:* like a flush in card games, with corresponding quality throughout.
35 *Under-shrieves:* under-sheriffs.
44 *Eighty eight:* 1588, the Armada year.

For all these Similies do hold
In my young Heat, and thy dull Cold.
Then, if a Fever be so good
A Pimp as to inflame thy Blood,
*Hymen* shall twist thee and thy Page,
The distinct Tropicks of Man's Age.
  Well, Madam Time, be ever bald,
I'l not thy Perriwig be call'd:
I'l never be 'stead of a Lover,
An aged Chronicle's new Cover.

## *Upon an Hermaphrodite*

Sir, or Madam, choose you whether,
Nature twists you both together,
And makes thy Soul two Garbs confess,
Both Petticoat and Breechess dress;
Thus we chastise the God of Wine
With Water that is Feminine,
Until the cooler Nymph abate
His wrath, and so concorporate.
*Adam,* till his Rib was lost,
Had the Sexes thus ingrost.
When Providence our Sire did cleave,
And out of *Adam* carved *Eve,*
Then did Man 'bout Wedlock treat
To make his Body up compleat.
Thus Matrimony speaks but thee
In a Grave Solemnity:

62 *Tropicks:* i.e. the Tropics of Cancer and Capricorn, the former 23°28′ north and the latter the same distance south of the equator. Between them lies the Torrid Zone.

66 *Cover:* with a pun on the verb *cover* (to copulate).

UPON AN HERMAPHRODITE.

1 *whether:* either of the two.

8 *concorporate:* form one body with.

10 *ingrost:* summed up in himself.

For Man and Wife make but one right
Canonical Hermaphrodite.
Ravel thy Body, and I find
In every Limb a double kind.
Who would not think that Head a pair,
That breeds such Faction in the Hair?
One half so churlish in the Touch,
That rather than endure so much,
I would my tender Limbs apparrel
With *Regulus* his nailed Barrel:
But the other half so small,
And so amorous withal,
That *Cupid* thinks each Hair doth grow
A String for his invisible Bow.
When I look Babies in thine Eyes,
Here *Venus,* there *Adonis* lies;
And though thy Beauty be high Noon,
Thy Orb contains both Sun and Moon.
How many melting Kisses skip,
'Twixt thy upper Brush of Hair,
And thy neather Beard's despair?
When thou speak'st (I would not wrong
Thy Sweetness with a double Tongue)
But in every single Sound
A perfect Dialogue is found.

19 *Ravel:* unravel.

26 *Regulus:* Marcus Attilius Regulus (d. 250 B.C.), Roman consul who, after being captured by the Carthaginians, was sent back to Rome to negotiate for peace or the exchange of prisoners. He advised the Senate against either alternative, returned to Carthage, and died in prison there. Legend says that he was tortured, but Cleveland seems to be adapting a story in Aulus Gellius (*Attic Nights* VII.4): "Tuditanus, however, reports that Regulus was for a long time deprived of sleep and so killed, and that when this became known at Rome, Carthaginian captives of the highest rank were handed over by the Senate to his sons, who shut them in a chest studded with spikes; and that they too were tortured to death by lack of sleep."

31 *Babies . . . Eyes:* the small image of oneself reflected in the eyes of the beloved. A common conceit in Renaissance love poetry.

37 *neather:* lower.

Thy Breasts distinguish one another,
This the Sister, that the Brother.
When thou joyn'st Hands my Ear still phancies
The Nuptial Sound, I *John* take *Frances.*
Feel but the difference soft and rough,
This a Gantlet, that a Muff.
Had sly *Ulysses* at the Sack
Of *Troy* brought thee his Pedler's Pack,
And Weapons too to know *Achilles*
From King *Lycomedes' Phillis*
His Plot had fail'd; this Hand would feel
The Needle, that the Warlike Steel.
When Musick doth thy pace advance,
Thy right Leg takes the left to dance:
Nor is't a Galliard danc'd by one,
But a mixt Dance, though alone.
Thus every Heteroclite part
Changes Gender, but thy Heart;
Nay those which Modesty can mean,
But dare not speak, are Epicene.
That Gamester needs must overcome,
That can play both with *Tib* and *Tom.*
  Thus did Nature's Mintage vary,
Coyning thee a *Philip* and *Mary.*

51 *Lycomedes:* King of Scyros with whom Achilles concealed himself in female attire as a maid (Phillis). Lycomedes' daughter Deidamia became the mother of Achilles' son, Pyrrhus.

65 *Philip and Mary:* Philip of Spain and Mary Tudor. The shilling minted in their reign (1554–55) has the two portraits facing each other.

## *The General Eclipse*

Ladies that guild the glittering Noon,
And by Reflection mend his Ray,
Whose Beauty makes the sprightly Sun
To dance, as upon Easter-day;
  What are you now the Queen's away?

Courageous Eagles, who have whet
Your Eyes upon Majestick Light,
And thence deriv'd such Martial heat,
That still your Looks maintain the Fight;
  What are you since the King's Goodnight?

Cavalier-buds, whom Nature teems,
As a Reserve for *England's* Throne,
Spirits whose double edge redeems
The last Age, and adorns your own;
  What are you now the Prince is gone?

As an obstructed Fountain's head
Cuts the Intail off from the Streams,
And Brooks are disinherited;
Honour and Beauty are mere Dreams,
  Since *Charles* and *Mary* lost their Beams.

Criminal Valors! who commit
Your Gallantry, whose *Poean* brings
A Psalm of Mercy after it;

THE GENERAL ECLIPSE: For the stanza form and theme, cf. Wotton's "On his Mistris, the Queen of Bohemia."

5 *Queen:* Henrietta Maria.

22 *Poean:* paean, song of praise. The gallantry of the cavaliers is ironically viewed as if it involved "committing" sin.

In this sad Solstice of the King's,
Your Victory hath mew'd her wings.

See how your Souldier wears his Cage
Of Iron, like the Captive Turk,
And as the Guerdon of his Rage!
See how your glimmering Peers do lurk,
Or at the best work Journey-work!

Thus 'tis a General Eclipse,
And the whole World is al-a-mort;
Only the House of Commons trips
The Stage in a Triumphant sort,
Now e'n *John Lilburn* take 'em for't.

## *On the Memory of Mr.* Edward King *drown'd in the* Irish *Seas*

I like not tears in tune, nor do I prize
His artificial Grief who scans his eyes.
Mine weep down pious Beads; but why should I
Confine them to the Muses Rosary?
I am no Poet here; my Pen's the Spout
Where the Rain-water of mine eyes run out
In pity of that Name, whose Fate we see
Thus copied out in Grief's Hydrography.

25 *mew'd:* shed. The winged Victory is no longer such.

27 *Turk:* perhaps an allusion to Marlowe's *Tamburlaine,* where the captive Bajazet is shut up in a cage.

32 *al-a-mort:* mortally sick.

35 *John Lilburn:* (1614?–1657), a leader of the Leveller party, often imprisoned for attacking Cromwell as too aristocratic.

*Title:* This poem first appeared in the 1638 volume of elegies, *Justa Edouardo King*, compiled by King's friends at Cambridge. Milton's "Lycidas" was the last and longest poem in the volume. King had been drowned on August 10.

ON THE MEMORY.

2 *scans his eyes:* i.e. adjusts his tears artificially to meter.

The Muses are not Mer-mayds, though upon
His Death the Ocean might turn *Helicon.*
The Sea's too rough for Verse; who rhymes upon't
With *Xerxes* strives to fetter th' Hellespont.
My Tears will keep no Channel, know no Laws
To guide their streams, but like the waves, their cause,
Run with disturbance, till they swallow me
As a Description of his Misery.
But can his spatious Virtue find a Grave
Within the Impostum'd bubble of a Wave?
Whose Learning if we sound, we must confess
The Sea but shallow, and him bottomless.
Could not the Winds to countermand thy death
With their whole Card of Lungs redeem thy breath?
Or some new Island in thy rescue peep
To heave thy Resurrection from the Deep;
That so the World might see thy safety wrought
With no less wonder than thy self was thought?
The famous *Stagirite* (who in his life
Had Nature as familiar as his Wife)
Bequeath'd his Widow to survive with thee
Queen Dowager of all Philosophy.
An ominous Legacy, that did portend
Thy Fate, and Predecessor's second end.
Some have affirm'd that what on Earth we find,
The Sea can parallel for shape and kind.
Books, Arts and Tongues were wanting, but in thee
*Neptune* hath got an University.
We'll dive no more for Pearls; the hope to see
Thy sacred Reliques of Mortality
Shall welcome Storms, and make the Seaman prize
His Shipwrack now more than his Merchandize.

10 *Helicon:* As often in Renaissance verse, Mount Helicon is here confused with the fount (of poetic inspiration) that flows from it.

12 *Xerxes:* Xerxes the Great (519?–465 B.C.), whose great expedition, after bridging the Hellespont and overcoming the Greeks at Thermopylae (480), was eventually defeated at Salamis and Plataea.

18 *Impostum'd:* abscessed, festered.

27 *Stagirite:* Aristotle.

He shall embrace the Waves, and to thy Tomb,
As to a Royaler Exchange shall come.
What can we now expect? Water and Fire,
Both Elements our ruin do conspire;
And that dissolves us which doth us compound,
One *Vatican* was burnt, another drown'd.
We of the Gown our Libraries must toss
To understand the greatness of our Loss;
Be Pupils to our Grief, and so much grow
In Learning, as our Sorrows overflow.
When we have fill'd the Rundlets of our Eyes
We'll issue't forth, and vent such Elegies,
As that our Tears shall seem the *Irish* Seas,
We floating Islands, living *Hebrides.*

## *Mark Anthony*

When as the Nightingale chanted her Vespers,
And the wild Forrester couch'd on the ground;
*Venus* invited me in th'Evening Whispers
Unto a fragrant Field with Roses crown'd;
  Where she before had sent
  My Wishes Complement,
  Unto my Heart's content
  Play'd with me on the Green;
    Never *Mark Anthony*
    Dallied more wantonly
    With the fair *Egyptian* Queen.

First on her cherry Cheeks I mine Eyes feasted,
Thence fear of Surfeiting made me retire;

46 *Vatican:* used loosely for "library."
51 *Rundlets:* large casks.
MARK ANTHONY: Manuscript evidence does not ascribe this poem to Cleveland, but to a certain Sampson Briggs. The "Mock-Song" which follows can, however, be attributed to Cleveland with good authority.

Next on her warmer Lips, which when I tasted
My duller Spirits made active as fire;
  Then we began to dart,
  Each at another's Heart,
  Arrows that knew no smart;
  Sweet Lips and Smiles between.
    Never *Mark Anthony*
    Dallied more wantonly
    With the fair *Egyptian* Queen.

Wanting a Glass to plate her Amber Tresses,
Which like a Bracelet rich decked mine Arm,
Gawdier than *Juno* wears, when as she Graces
*Jove* with Embraces more stately, than warm;
  Then did she peep in mine
  Eyes humour Chrystalline
  I in her Eyes was seen,
  As if we one had been.
    Never *Mark Anthony*
    Dallied more wantonly
    With the fair *Egyptian* Queen.

Mystical Grammar of Amorous Glances;
Feeling of Pulses, the Physick of Love,
Rhetorical Courtings and Musical Dances,
Numbring of Kisses Arithmetick prove
  Eyes, like Astronomy,
  Straight-limb'd Geometry
  In her Art's Ingeny,
  Our Wits were sharp and keen.
    Never *Mark Anthony*
    Dallied more wantonly
    With the fair *Egyptian* Queen.

15 *Made: made me* in the 1677 edition.
23 *plate:* plait, braid.
35 *Physick:* (the art of) medicine.
40 *Ingeny:* ingenuity.

## *The Author's Mock-Song to* Mark Anthony

When as the Nightingale sang *Pluto's Mattins,*
And *Cerberus* cri'd three *Amens* at a Howl,
When Night-wandring Witches put on their Pattins,
Midnight as dark as their Faces are Foul:
  Then did the Furies doom
  That the Night-Mare was come;
  Such a mishapen Groom
  Puts down *Su. Pomfret* clean.
    Never did *Incubus*
    Touch such a filthy *Sus,*
    As this foul Gypsie Quean.

First on her Goosberry Cheeks I mine eys Blasted,
Thence fear of vomiting made me retire
Unto her Blewer Lips, which when I Tasted
My Spirits were duller than Dun in the Mire;
  But when her Breath took place,
  Which went an Usher's pace,
  And made way for her Face,
  You may guess what I mean.
    Never did *Incubus*
    Touch such a filthy *Sus,*
    As this foul Gypsie Quean.

THE AUTHOR'S MOCK-SONG.

1 *Nightingale:* Other early editions read *night-raven.*
3 *Pattins:* clogs, wooden shoes.
5 *doom:* judge.
8 *Su. Pomfret:* probably a well-known harlot.
9 *Incubus:* spirit which lies with women.
10 *Sus:* pig.
11 *Quean:* whore.
12 *Blasted:* ruined.
15 *Dun:* proverbial name for a horse.

Like Snakes engendring were platted her Tresses,
Or like to slimy streaks of Ropy Ale;
Uglier than Envy wears, when she confesses
Her Head is periwig'd with Adder's Tail.
But as soon as she spake,
I heard a Harsh Mandrake:
Laugh not at my Mistake,
Her Head is Epicene.
Never did *Incubus*
Touch such a filthy *Sus,*
As this foul Gypsie Quean.

Mystical Magick of Conjuring Wrinckles;
Feeling of Pulses, the Palmstry of Hags,
Scolding out Belches for Rhetorick Twinckles,
With three Teeth in her Head like to three Gags:
Rainbows about her Eyes,
And her Nose weather-wise,
From them the Almanack lies,
Frost, Pond and Rivers clean.
Never did *Incubus*
Touch such a filthy *Sus,*
As this foul Gypsie Quean.

## *Square-Cap*

Come hither *Apollo's* Bouncing Girl,
And in a whole Hippocrene of Sherry
Let's drink a round till our Brains do whirl,
Tuning our Pipes to make our selves merry;

24 *Ropy:* sticky.

28 *Mandrake:* This double-rooted plant, said to resemble the human form and to emit a shriek when pulled from the ground, was often used to promote conception.

41 *Frost . . . Rivers:* names of contemporary almanac compilers.

*Title:* A "square-cap" is an academic cap, a mortar board. One notes that the girl is a "Cambridge-lass."

SQUARE-CAP.

2 *Hippocrene:* a spring on Mount Helicon.

A *Cambridge*-Lass, *Venus*-like, born of the Froth
Of an old half fill'd Jug of Barly-Broth,
She, she is my Mistress, her Suitors are many,
But she'll have a Square-Cap, if e'r she have any.

And first, for the Plush-sake, the *Monmouth*-Cap Comes
Shaking his Head, like an empty Bottle,
With his new-fangled Oath by *Jupiter's* Thumbs,
That to her Health he'll begin a pottle:
He tells her, that after the Death of his Grannam
He shall have God knows what *per Annum*.
But still she replied, Good Sir *La-bee*,
If ever I have a Man Square-Cap for me.

Then *Calot* Leather-Cap strongly pleads
And fain would derive his Pedigree of fashion.
The *Antipodes* were their Shoes on their Heads,
And why may not we in their Imitation:
Oh! how the Foot-ball noddle would please,
If it were but well toss'd on S. *Thomas* his Lees:
But still she replied Good Sir *La-bee*
If ever I have a Man, Square-Cap for me.

Next comes the Puritan in a Wrought-Cap,
With a long-wasted Conscience towards a Sister,

9 *Plush-sake:* for the sake of the plush, perhaps the material from which the Monmouth-Cap (a round cap worn by soldiers) was made.

12 *pottle:* large drinking vessel.

13 *Grannam:* grandmother.

15 *La-bee:* let me be.

17 *Calot:* the coif worn by a sergeant-at-law.

19 *Antipodes . . . Heads:* Cf. the final stanza of Marvell's "Appleton House," "But now the salmon-fishers moist / Their leathern boats begin to hoist; / And, like Antipodes in shoes, / Have shod their heads in their canoes." *were:* wear.

22 *S. Thomas his Lees:* A university decree of 1632 ordered students of Corpus and Pembroke colleges to play football only on "St. Thomas Layes" or meadows, now the site of Downing College.

25 *Wrought-Cap:* homemade cap.

26 *long-wasted:* easy, loose.

And making a Chappel of Ease of her Lap;
First he said Grace, and then he kiss'd her:
Beloved, quoth he, thou art my Text;
Then falls he to use and Application next,
But then she replied your Text Sir I'll be;
For then I'm sure you'l ne'r handle me.

But see where Sattin-Cap scouts about,
And fain would this Wench in his Fellowship marry,
He told her how such a Man was not put out,
Because his Wedding he closely did carry,
He'll purchase Induction by Simony,
And offers her Money her Incumbent to be,
But still she replied, Good Sir *La-bee,*
If ever, I have a Man Square-Cap for me.

The Lawyer's a Sophister by his Round-Cap,
Nor in their Fallacies are they divided,
The one Milks the Pocket, the other the Tap,
And yet this Wench he fain would have Brided:
Come leave these thred-bare Scholars, quoth he,
And give me Livery and Seisin of thee.
But peace *John-a Nokes,* and leave your Oration,
For I never will be your Impropriation:
I pray you therefore, Good Sir *La-bee;*
For if ever I have a Man, Square-Cap for me.

27 *Chappel of Ease:* chapel built for the convenience of parishioners who live far from the parish church.

33 *Sattin-Cap:* the clerical cap.

36 *closely:* secretly. Marriage, if not concealed, would lead to expulsion from the college fellowship.

46 *Livery and Seisin:* for "livery of seisin," a legal phrase meaning the delivery of property into the corporal possession of a person.

47 *John-a Nokes:* colloquial name for a lawyer.

# SIR JOHN DENHAM
## 1615–1669

# Cooper's Hill

Sure there are Poets which did never dream
Upon *Parnassus,* nor did tast the stream
Of *Helicon,* we therefore may suppose
Those made not Poets, but the Poets those.
And as Courts make not Kings, but Kings the Court,
So where the Muses & their train resort,
*Parnassus* stands; if I can be to thee
A Poet, thou *Parnassus* art to me.
Nor wonder, if (advantag'd in my flight,
By taking wing from thy auspicious height)
Through untrac't ways, and aery paths I fly,
More boundless in my Fancy than my eie:
My eye, which swift as thought contracts the space
That lies between, and first salutes the place
Crown'd with that sacred pile, so vast, so high,
That whether 'tis a part of Earth, or sky,
Uncertain seems, and may be thought a proud
Aspiring mountain, or descending cloud,
*Pauls,* the late theme of such a Muse whose flight
Has bravely reach't and soar'd above thy height:
Now shalt thou stand though sword, or time, or fire,
Or zeal more fierce than they, thy fall conspire,
Secure, whilst thee the best of Poets sings,
Preserv'd from ruine by the best of Kings.
Under his proud survey the City lies,
And like a mist beneath a hill doth rise;
Whose state and wealth the business and the crowd,
Seems at this distance but a darker cloud:
And is to him who rightly things esteems,
No other in effect than what it seems:
Where, with like hast, though several ways, they run
Some to undo, and some to be undone;

COOPER'S HILL.

19 *Pauls:* Denham alludes to Waller's poem, "Upon His Majesty's Repairing of Paul's."

While luxury, and wealth, like war and peace,
Are each the others ruine, and increase;
As Rivers lost in Seas some secret vein
Thence reconveighs, there to be lost again.
Oh happiness of sweet retir'd content!
To be at once secure, and innocent.
*Windsor* the next (where *Mars* with *Venus* dwells.
Beauty with strength) above the Valley swells
Into my eye, and doth it self present
With such an easie and unforc't ascent,
That no stupendious precipice denies
Access, no horror turns away our eyes:
But such a Rise, as doth at once invite
A pleasure, and a reverence from the sight.
Thy mighty Masters Embleme, in whose face
Sate meekness, heightned with Majestick Grace
Such seems thy gentle height, made only proud
To be the basis of that pompous load,
Than which, a nobler weight no Mountain bears,
But *Atlas* only that supports the Sphears.
When Natures hand this ground did thus advance,
'Twas guided by a wiser power than Chance;
Mark't out for such a use, as if 'twere meant
T' invite the builder, and his choice prevent.
Nor can we call it choice, when what we chuse,
Folly, or blindness only could refuse.
A Crown of such Majestick towrs doth Grace
The Gods great Mother, when her heavenly race
Do homage to her, yet she cannot boast
Amongst that numerous, and Celestial host,
More *Hero's* than can *Windsor*, nor doth Fames
Immortal book record more noble names.
Not to look back so far, to whom this Isle
Owes the first Glory of so brave a pile,

56 *prevent:* anticipate.

60 *Mother:* Cybele, an Asian goddess whom the Romans referred to as the Great Mother.

Whether to *Caesar*, *Albanact*, or *Brute*,
The Brittish *Arthur*, or the Danish *Knute*,
(Though this of old no less contest did move,
Then when for *Homers* birth seven Cities strove)
(Like him in birth, thou should'st be like in fame,
As thine his fate, if mine had been his Flame)
But whosoere it was, Nature design'd
First a brave place, and then as brave a mind.
Not to recount those several Kings, to whom
It gave a Cradle, or to whom a Tombe,
But thee (great *Edward*) and thy greater son,
(The lillies which his Father wore, he won)
And thy *Bellona*, who the Consort came
Not only to thy Bed, but to thy Fame,
She to thy Triumph led one Captive King,
And brought that son, which did the second bring.
Then didst thou found that Order (whither love
Or victory thy Royal thoughts did move)
Each was a noble cause, and nothing less,
Than the design, has been the great success:
Which forraign Kings, and Emperors esteem
The second honour to their Diadem.
Had thy great Destiny but given thee skill,
To know as well, as power to act her will,

67 *Albanact, or Brute:* Brutus, the legendary grandson of Aeneas, was reputed to have founded London. His son, Albanact, ruled Scotland after his father's death.

68 *Knute:* Canute (994?–1035), King of Denmark, who conquered all England after the death of Edmund and ruled it from 1018 to 1035.

71 *Like . . . birth:* The "birth" of Windsor is as mysterious as Homer's, and just as many controversies have arisen over it.

77 *Edward . . . son:* King Edward III (1312–1377) and his son, Edward the Black Prince (1330–1376), both born at Windsor Castle.

79 *Bellona:* Mars' sister, the goddess of war. Edward III's queen was Phillipa of Hainaut, whom he married in 1328.

81 *one . . . King:* David II of Scotland, captured at Neville's Cross in 1346.

82 *the second:* John II of France, captured by the Black Prince at Poitiers in 1356.

83 *that Order:* the Order of the Garter, founded by Edward in 1349.

That from those Kings, who then thy captives were,
In after-times should spring a Royal pair
Who should possess all that thy mighty power,
Or thy desires more mighty, did devour;
To whom their better Fate reserves what ere
The Victor hopes for, or the Vanquisht fear;
That bloud, which thou and thy great Grandsire shed,
And all that since these sister Nations bled,
Had been unspilt, had happy *Edward* known
That all the bloud he spilt, had been his own.
When he that Patron chose, in whom are joyn'd
Souldier and Martyr, and his arms confin'd
Within the Azure Circle, he did seem
But to foretell, and prophesie of him,
Who to his Realms that Azure round hath joyn'd,
Which Nature for their bound at first design'd.
That bound, which to the Worlds extreamest ends,
Endless it self, its liquid arms extends;
Nor doth he need those Emblemes which we paint,
But is himself the Souldier and the Saint.
Here should my wonder dwell, & here my praise,
But my fixt thoughts my wandring eye betrays,
Viewing a neighbouring hill, whose top of late
A Chappel crown'd, till in the Common Fate,
The adjoyning Abby fell: (may no such storm
Fall on our times, where ruine must reform.)
Tell me (my Muse) what monstrous dire offence,
What crime could any Christian King incense

92 *a Royal pair:* Charles I and Henrietta Maria, though neither was directly descended from David II or John II.

101 *Patron:* St. George.

103 *Azure Circle:* probably the silver star worn by knights of the Garter, but the original insignia of the order did not contain it. In the middle of the insignia is the red cross of St. George surrounded by a blue garter.

104 *him:* Charles I.

113 *hill:* St. Anne's Hill, where Chertsey Abbey (line 115) once stood.

118 *Christian King:* The allusion is to Henry VIII, during whose reign the monasteries were dissolved.

To such a rage? Was't Luxury, or Lust?
Was he so temperate, so chast, so just?
Were these their crimes? They were his own much more:
But wealth is Crime enough to him that's poor,
Who having spent the Treasures of his Crown,
Condemns their Luxury to feed his own.
And yet this Act, to varnish o're the shame
Of sacriledge, must bear devotions name.
No Crime so bold, but would be understood
A real, or at least a seeming good.
Who fears not to do ill, yet fears the Name,
And free from Conscience, is a slave to Fame.
Thus he the Church at once protects, & spoils:
But Princes swords are sharper than their stiles.
And thus to th'ages past he makes amends,
Their Charity destroys, their Faith defends.
Then did Religion in a lazy Cell,
In empty, airy contemplations dwell;
And like the block, unmoved lay: but ours,
As much too active, like the stork devours.
Is there no temperate Region can be known,
Betwixt their Frigid, and our Torrid Zone?
Could we not wake from that Lethargick dream,
But to be restless in a worse extream?
And for that Lethargy was there no cure,
But to be cast into a Calenture?
Can knowledge have no bound, but must advance
So far, to make us wish for ignorance?
And rather in the dark to grope our way,
Than led by a false guide to erre by day?

121 *their:* the monks'.

132 *stiles:* Denham alludes to Henry VII's defense of the church against Luther, *Assertio Septem Sacramentorum* (1521), which earned him the title "Defender of the Faith."

138 *too active:* The reference is to the enthusiastic religion of the English Puritans.

144 *Calenture:* delirious fever.

Who sees these dismal heaps, but would demand
What barbarous Invader sackt the land?
But when he hears, no Goth, no Turk did bring
This desolation, but a Christian King;
When nothing, but the Name of Zeal, appears
'Twixt our best actions and the worst of theirs,
What does he think our Sacriledge would spare,
When such th'effects of our devotions are?
Parting from thence 'twixt anger, shame, & fear,
Those for whats past, & this for whats too near:
My eye descending from the Hill, surveys
Where *Thames* amongst the wanton vallies strays.
*Thames*, the most lov'd of all the Oceans sons,
By his old Sire to his embraces runs,
Hasting to pay his tribute to the Sea,
Like mortal life to meet Eternity.
Though with those streams he no resemblance hold,
Whose foam is Amber, and their Gravel Gold;
His genuine, and less guilty wealth t' explore,
Search not his bottom, but survey his shore;
Ore which he kindly spreads his spacious wing,
And hatches plenty for th'ensuing Spring.
Nor then destroys it with too fond a stay,
Like Mothers which their Infants overlay.
Nor with a sudden and impetuous wave,
Like profuse Kings, resumes the wealth he gave.
No unexpected inundations spoyl
The mowers hopes, nor mock the plowmans toyl:
But God-like his unwearied Bounty flows;
First loves to do, then loves the Good he does.
Nor are his Blessings to his banks confin'd,
But free, and common, as the Sea or Wind;
When he to boast, or to disperse his stores
Full of the tributes of his grateful shores,

158 *Those:* i.e. anger and shame (line 157); *this:* i.e. fear (of seventeenth-century extremism).
160 *wanton:* rich, luxurious.
174 *resumes:* takes back.

Visits the world, and in his flying towers
Brings home to us, and makes both *Indies* ours;
Finds wealth where 'tis, bestows it where it wants
Cities in deserts, woods in Cities plants.
So that to us no thing, no place is strange,
While his fair bosom is the worlds exchange.
O could I flow like thee, and make thy stream
My great example, as it is my theme!
Though deep, yet clear, though gentle, yet not dull,
Strong without rage, without ore-flowing full.
Heaven her *Eridanus* no more shall boast,
Whose Fame in thine, like lesser Currents lost,
Thy Nobler streams shall visit *Jove's* aboads,
To shine amongst the Stars, and bath the Gods.
Here Nature, whether more intent to please
Us or her self, with strange varieties,
(For things of wonder give no less delight
To the wise Maker's, than beholders sight.
Though these delights from several causes move
For so our children, thus our friends we love)
Wisely she knew, the harmony of things,
As well as that of sounds, from discords springs.
Such was the discord, which did first disperse
Form, order, beauty through the Universe;

183 *flying towers:* speedy merchant ships, with high masts.

189–92 *O could . . . full:* These famous lines were often quoted and imitated in the seventeenth and eighteenth centuries. Denham later prefixed six new lines to these four as they stood in the 1668 edition:

Rome only conquerd halfe the world, but trade
One commonwealth of that and her hath made;
And though the sun his beame extends to all
Yet to his neighbour sheds most liberall;
Least God and Nature partiall should appeare
Commerse makes everything grow everywhere.

See James M. Osborn, "New Poems by Sir John Denham," *Times Literary Supplement,* September 1, 1966, p. 788. The verses are quoted here with Mr. Osborn's permission.

194 *Eridanus:* the Greek name for the river Po; *her* refers to Rome and its empire.

While driness moysture, coldness heat resists,
All that we have, and that we are, subsists.
While the steep horrid roughness of the Wood
Strives with the gentle calmness of the flood.
Such huge extreams when Nature doth unite,
Wonder from thence results, from thence delight.
The stream is so transparent, pure, and clear,
That had the self-enamour'd youth gaz'd here,
So fatally deceiv'd he had not been,
While he the bottom, not his face had seen.
But his proud head the aery Mountain hides
Among the Clouds; his shoulders, and his sides
A shady mantle cloaths; his curled brows
Frown on the gentle stream, which calmly flows,
While winds and storms his lofty forehead beat:
The common fate of all that's high or great.
Low at his foot a spacious plain is plac't,
Between the mountain and the stream embrac't:
Which shade and shelter from the Hill derives,
While the kind river wealth and beauty gives;
And in the mixture of all these appears
Variety, which all the rest indears.
This scene had some bold Greek, or British Bard
Beheld of old, what stories had we heard,
Of Fairies, Satyrs, and the Nymphs their Dames,
Their feasts, their revels, & their amorous flames:
'Tis still the same, although their aery shape
All but a quick Poetick sight escape.
There *Faunus* and *Sylvanus* keep their Courts,
And thither all the horned hoast resorts,
To graze the ranker mead, that noble heard
On whose sublime and shady fronts is rear'd
Natures great Master-piece; to shew how soon
Great things are made, but sooner are undone.

209 *horrid:* shaggy.
214 *youth:* Narcissus.

Here have I seen the King, when great affairs
Give leave to slacken, and unbend his cares,
Attended to the Chase by all the flower
Of youth, whose hopes a Nobler prey devour:
Pleasure with Praise, & danger, they would buy,
And wish a foe that would not only fly.
The stagg now conscious of his fatal Growth,
At once indulgent to his fear and sloth,
To some dark covert his retreat had made,
Where no mans eye, nor heavens should invade
His soft repose; when th'unexpected sound
Of dogs, and men, his wakeful ear doth wound.
Rouz'd with the noise, he scarce believes his ear,
Willing to think th'illusions of his fear
Had given this false Alarm, but straight his view
Confirms, that more than all he fears is true.
Betray'd in all his strengths, the wood beset,
All instruments, all Arts of ruine met;
He calls to mind his strength, and then his speed,
His winged heels, and then his armed head;
With these t' avoid, with that his Fate to meet:
But fear prevails, and bids him trust his feet.
So fast he flyes, that his reviewing eye
Has lost the chasers, and his ear the cry;
Exulting, till he finds, their Nobler sense
Their disporportion'd speed does recompense.
Then curses his conspiring feet, whose scent
Betrays that safety which their swiftness lent.
Then tries his friends, among the baser herd,
Where he so lately was obey'd, and fear'd,
His safety seeks: the herd, unkindly wise,
Or chases him from thence, or from him flies.
Like a declining States-man, left forlorn
To his friends pity, and pursuers scorn,
With shame remembers, while himself was one
Of the same herd, himself the same had done.

263 *reviewing:* looking back.

Thence to the coverts, & the conscious Groves,
The scenes of his past triumphs, and his loves;
Sadly surveying where he rang'd alone
Prince of the soyl, and all the herd his own;
And like a bold Knight Errant did proclaim
Combat to all, and bore away the Dame;
And taught the woods to eccho to the stream
His dreadful challenge, and his clashing beam.
Yet faintly now declines the fatal strife;
So much his love was dearer than his life.
Now every leaf, and every moving breath
Presents a foe, and every foe a death.
Wearied, forsaken, and pursu'd, at last
All safety in despair of safety plac'd,
Courage he thence resumes, resolv'd to bear
All their assaults, since 'tis in vain to fear.
And now too late he wishes for the fight
That strength he wasted in Ignoble flight:
But when he sees the eager chase renew'd,
Himself by dogs, the dogs by men pursu'd;
He straight revokes his bold resolve, and more
Repents his courage, than his fear before;
Finds that uncertain waies unsafest are,
And Doubt a greater mischief than Despair.
Then to the stream, when neither friends, nor force,
Nor speed, nor Art avail, he shapes his course;
Thinks not their rage so desperate t'assay
An Element more merciless than they.
But fearless they pursue, nor can the floud
Quench their dire thirst; alas, they thirst for bloud.
So towards a Ship the oarefin'd Gallies ply,
Which wanting Sea to ride, or wind to fly,
Stands but to fall reveng'd on those that dare
Tempt the last fury of extream despair.

277 *conscious:* i.e. sharing in (and sympathizing with) the stag's knowledge.
284 *beam:* the main trunk of the stag's antlers.
307 *oarefin'd:* with oars like fins.

So fares the Stagg among th'enraged Hounds,
Repels their force, and wounds returns for wounds.
And as a Hero, whom his baser foes
In troops surround, now these assails, now those,
Though prodigal of life, disdains to die
By common hands; but if he can descry
Some nobler foes approach, to him he calls,
And begs his Fate, and then contented falls.
So when the King a mortal shaft lets fly
From his unerring hand, then glad to dy,
Proud of the wound, to it resigns his bloud,
And stains the Crystal with a Purple floud.
This a more Innocent, and happy chase,
Than when of old, but in the self-same place,
Fair liberty pursu'd, and meant a Prey
To lawless power, here turn'd, and stood at bay.
When in that remedy all hope was plac't
Which was, or should have been at least, the last.
Here was the Charter seal'd, wherein the Crown
All marks of Arbitrary power lays down:
Tyrant and slave, those names of hate and fear,
The happier stile of King and Subject bear:
Happy, when both to the same Center move,
When Kings give liberty, and Subjects love.
Therefore not long in force this Charter stood;
Wanting that seal, it must be seal'd in bloud.
The Subjects arm'd, the more their Princes gave,
Th'advantage only took the more to crave.
Till Kings by giving, give themselves away,
And even that power, that should deny, betray.
"Who gives constrain'd, but his own fear reviles
"Not thank't, but scorn'd; nor are they gifts, but spoils.
Thus Kings, by grasping more than they could hold,
First made their Subjects by oppression bold:

324 *place:* Runnymede, where the Magna Charta (above, line 329) was signed in 1215.

341–42 Denham's quotation has not been identified.

And popular sway, by forcing Kings to give
More than was fit for Subjects to receive,
Ran to the same extreams; and one excess
Made both, by striving to be greater, less.
When a calm River rais'd with sudden rains,
Or Snows dissolv'd, oreflows th'adjoyning Plains,
The Husbandmen with high-rais'd banks secure
Their greedy hopes, and this he can endure.
But if with Bays and Dams they strive to force
His channel to a new, or narrow course;
No longer then within his banks he dwells,
First to a Torrent, then a Deluge swells:
Stronger, and fiercer by restraint he roars,
And knows no bound, but makes his power his shores.

## On Mr Abraham Cowley
### *His Death and Burial amongst the Ancient Poets*

Old *Chaucer*, like the morning Star,
To us discovers day from far,
His light those Mists and Clouds dissolv'd,
Which our dark Nation long involv'd;
But he descending to the shades,
Darkness again the Age invades.
Next (like *Aurora*) *Spencer* rose,
Whose purple blush the day foreshows;
The other three, with his own fires,
*Phoebus*, the Poets God, inspires;

352 *he:* the river.
ON MR ABRAHAM COWLEY: Cowley died on July 28, 1667. He was buried in Westminster Abbey with great pomp.
4 *involv'd:* enveloped.

By *Shakespear's, Johnson's, Fletcher's* lines;
Our Stages lustre *Rome's* outshines:
These Poets neer our Princes sleep,
And in one Grave their Mansion keep;
They liv'd to see so many days,
Till time had blasted all their Bays:
But cursed be the fatal hour
That pluckt the fairest, sweetest flower
That in the Muses Garden grew,
And amongst wither'd Lawrels threw.
Time, which made them their Fame outlive,
To *Cowly* scarce did ripeness give.
Old Mother Wit, and Nature gave
*Shakespear* and *Fletcher* all they have;
In *Spencer*, and in *Johnson*, Art,
Of slower Nature got the start;
But both in him so equal are,
None knows which bears the happy'st share;
To him no Author was unknown,
Yet what he wrote was all his own;
He melted not the ancient Gold,
Nor with *Ben Johnson* did make bold
To plunder all the *Roman* stores
Of Poets, and of Orators:
*Horace* his wit, and *Virgil's* state,
He did not steal, but emulate,
And when he would like them appear,
Their Garb, but not their Cloaths, did wear:
He not from *Rome* alone, but *Greece*,
Like *Jason* brought the Golden Fleece;
To him that Language (though to none
Of th'others) as his own was known.
On a stiff gale (as *Flaccus* sings)
The *Theban* Swan extends his wings,

14 *in one grave:* Shakespeare, of course, was not buried in the Abbey.
43 *Flaccus:* The allusion is to Horace *Odes* IV.ii.25–27.

When through th'aetherial Clouds he flies,
To the same pitch our Swan doth rise;
Old *Pindar's* flights by him are reacht,
When on that gale his wings are strecht;
His fancy and his judgment such,
Each to the other seem'd too much,
His severe judgment (giving Law)
His modest fancy kept in awe:
As rigid Husbands jealous are,
When they believe their Wives too fair.
His English stream so pure did flow,
As all that saw, and tasted, know.
But for his Latin vein, so clear,
Strong, full, and high it doth appear,
That were immortal *Virgil* here,
Him, for his judge, he would not fear;
Of that great Portraicture, so true
A Copy Pencil never drew.
My Muse her Song had ended here,
But both their Genii strait appear,
Joy and amazement her did strike,
Two Twins she never saw so like.
'Twas taught by wise *Pythagoras*,
One Soul might through more Bodies pass;
Seeing such Transmigration here,
She thought it not a Fable there.
Such a resemblance of all parts,
Life, Death, Age, Fortune, Nature, Arts,
Then lights her Torch at theirs, to tell,
And shew the world this Parallel,
Fixt and contemplative their looks,
Still turning over Natures Books:
Their works chast, moral, and divine,
Where profit and delight combine;
They guilding dirt, in noble verse
Rustick Philosophy rehearse;
When Heroes, Gods, or God-like Kings
They praise, on their exalted wings,

To the Celestial orbs they climb,
And with the Harmonious sphears keep time;
Nor did their actions fall behind
Their words, but with like candour shin'd,
Each drew fair Characters, yet none
Of these they feign'd, excels their own;
Both by two generous Princes lov'd,
Who knew, and judg'd what they approv'd:
Yet having each the same desire,
Both from the busie throng retire,
Their Bodies to their Minds resign'd,
Car'd not to propagate their Kind:
Yet though both fell before their hour,
Time on their off-spring hath no power,
Nor fire, nor fate their Bays shall blast,
Nor Death's dark vail their day o'recast.

89 *two . . . Princes:* Virgil by Augustus, Cowley by Charles II, who lamented the poet's death.

# RICHARD LOVELACE
1618–1657

# Song
## Set by Mr. *Henry Lawes*
## To Lucasta,
## *Going beyond the Seas*

I.

If to be absent were to be
Away from thee;
Or that when I am gone,
You or I were alone;
Then my *Lucasta* might I crave
Pity from blustring winde, or swallowing wave.

II.

But I'le not sigh one blast or gale
To swell my saile,
Or pay a teare to swage
The foaming blew-Gods rage;
For whether he will let me passe
Or no, I'm still as happy as I was.

SONG: Henry Lawes (1596–1662), the composer who wrote the music for Milton's *Comus* (1634). His three books of airs were published in 1653, 1655, and 1658. Efforts to identify Lovelace's "Lucasta" have been fruitless. The name (*lux casta,* chaste light) may owe something to Habington's "Castara."

9 *swage:* assuage.

III.

Though Seas and Land betwixt us both,
Our Faith and Troth,
Like separated soules,
All time and space controules:
Above the highest sphere wee meet
Unseene, unknowne, and greet as Angels greet.

IV.

So then we doe anticipate
Our after-fate,
And are alive i'th' skies,
If thus our lips and eyes
Can speake like spirits unconfin'd
In Heav'n, their earthy bodies left behind.

## Song
## Set by Mr. *John Laniere*
## To Lucasta,
## *Going to the Warres*

I.

Tell me not (Sweet) I am unkinde,
That from the Nunnerie
Of thy chaste breast, and quiet minde,
To Warre and Armes I flie.

SONG: John Laniere (d. 1650), a court musician of the period.

II.

True; a new Mistresse now I chase,
The first Foe in the Field;
And with a stronger Faith imbrace
A Sword, a Horse, a Shield.

III.

Yet this Inconstancy is such,
As you too shall adore;
I could not love thee (Deare) so much,
Lov'd I not Honour more.

## Song
## Set by Mr. *Henry Lawes*
## To Amarantha,
## *That she would dishevell her haire*

I.

*Amarantha* sweet and faire
Ah brade no more that shining haire!
As my curious hand or eye,
Hovering round thee let it flye.

II.

Let it flye as unconfin'd
As it's calme Ravisher, the winde;
Who hath left his darling th'East,
To wanton o're that spicie Neast.

III.

Ev'ry Tresse must be confest
But neatly tangled at the best;
Like a Clue of golden thread,
Most excellently ravelled.

IV.

Doe not then winde up that light
In Ribands, and o're-cloud in Night;
Like the Sun in's early ray,
But shake your head and scatter day.

V.

See 'tis broke! Within this Grove
The Bower, and the walkes of Love,
Weary lye we downe and rest,
And fanne each others panting breast.

VI.

Heere wee'l strippe and coole our fire
In Creame below, in milke-baths higher:
And when all Well's are drawne dry,
I'le drink a teare out of thine eye.

SONG.
11 *Clue:* ball.

VII.

Which our very Joyes shall leave
That sorrowes thus we can deceive;
Or our very sorrowes weepe,
*That joyes so ripe, so little keepe.*

# Ode
## Set by Dr. *John Wilson*
## To Lucasta
## *The Rose*

I.

Sweet serene skye-like Flower,
Haste to adorn her Bower:
From thy long clowdy bed,
Shoot forth thy damaske head.

II.

New-startled blush of *Flora!*
The griefe of pale *Aurora,*
Who will contest no more;
Haste, haste, to strowe her floore.

ODE: John Wilson (1595–1674), a famous lutenist and singer in the court of Charles I.

III.

Vermilion Ball that's given
From lip to lip in Heaven;
Loves Couches cover-led:
Haste, haste, to make her bed.

IV.

Deare Ofspring of pleas'd *Venus,*
And Jollie, plumpe *Silenus;*
Haste, haste, to decke the Haire
Of th'only, sweetly Faire.

V.

See! Rosie is her Bower,
Her floore is all this Flower;
Her Bed a Rosie nest
By a Bed of Roses prest.

VI.

But early as she dresses,
Why fly you her bright Tresses?
Ah! I have found I feare;
Because her Cheekes are neere.

11 *cover-led:* coverlet.

## Gratiana *dauncing and singing*

I.

See! with what constant Motion
Even, and glorious, as the Sunne,
  *Gratiana* steeres that Noble Frame,
Soft as her breast, sweet as her voyce
That gave each winding Law and poyze,
  And swifter then the wings of Fame.

II.

She beat the happy Pavement
By such a Starre made Firmament,
  Which now no more the Roofe envies;
But swells up high with *Atlas* ev'n
Bearing the brighter, nobler Heav'n,
  And in her, all the Dieties.

III.

Each step trod out a Lovers thought
And the Ambitious hopes he brought,
  Chain'd to her brave feet with such arts;
Such sweet command, and gentle awe,
As when she ceas'd, we sighing saw
  The floore lay pav'd with broken hearts.

IV.

So did she move; so did she sing
Like the Harmonious spheres that bring
  Unto their Rounds their musick's ayd;
Which she performed such a way,
As all th' inamour'd world will say
  The *Graces* daunced, and *Apollo* play'd.

## The Scrutinie
## Song
## Set by Mr. *Thomas Charles*

I.

Why should you sweare I am forsworn,
  Since thine I vow'd to be?
Lady it is already Morn,
  And 'twas last night I swore to thee
That fond impossibility.

II.

Have I not lov'd thee much and long,
  A tedious twelve houres space?
I must all other Beauties wrong,
  And rob thee of a new imbrace;
Could I still dote upon thy Face.

III.

Not, but all joy in thy browne haire,
By others may be found;
But I must search the black and faire
Like skilfull Minerallist's that sound
For Treasure in un-plow'd-up ground.

IV.

Then, if when I have lov'd my round,
Thou prov'st the pleasant she;
With spoyles of meaner Beauties crown'd,
I laden will returne to thee,
Ev'n sated with Varietie.

## *The Grasse-hopper*
## To my Noble Friend, Mr. Charles Cotton
## Ode

I.

Oh thou that swing'st upon the waving haire
Of some well-filled Oaten Beard,
Drunke ev'ry night with a Delicious teare
Dropt thee from Heav'n, where now th'art reard.

THE GRASSE-HOPPER: Charles Cotton (1630–1687), a minor poet.

II.

The Joyes of Earth and Ayre are thine intire,
That with thy feet and wings dost hop and flye;
And when thy Poppy workes thou dost retire
To thy Carv'd Acron-bed to lye.

III.

Up with the Day, the Sun thou welcomst then,
Sportst in the guilt-plats of his Beames,
And all these merry dayes mak'st merry men,
Thy selfe, and Melancholy streames.

IV.

But ah the Sickle! Golden Eares are Cropt;
*Ceres* and *Bacchus* bid good night;
Sharpe frosty fingers all your Flowr's have topt,
And what sithes spar'd, Winds shave off quite.

V.

Poore verdant foole! and now green Ice! thy Joys
Large and as lasting, as thy Peirch of Grasse,
Bid us lay in 'gainst Winter, Raine, and poize
Their flouds, with an o'reflowing glasse.

8 *Acron-bed:* acorn bed.
10 *guilt-plats:* golden or gilded rays.
11–12: The grasshopper makes men, himself, and melancholy streams merry.
19 *poize:* counterbalance.

VI.

Thou best of *Men* and *Friends!* we will create
A Genuine Summer in each others breast;
And spite of this cold Time and frosen Fate
Thaw us a warme seate to our rest.

VII.

Our sacred harthes shall burne eternally
As Vestall Flames, the North-wind, he
Shall strike his frost-stretch'd Winges, dissolve and flye
This *AEtna* in Epitome.

VIII.

Dropping *December* shall come weeping in,
Bewayle th'usurping of his Raigne;
But when in show'rs of old Greeke we beginne,
Shall crie, he hath his Crowne againe!

IX.

Night as cleare *Hesper* shall our Tapers whip
From the light Casements where we play,
And the darke Hagge from her black mantle strip,
And sticke there everlasting Day.

27 *strike:* best taken as meaning "spread." Even the North-wind will be driven away by the warmth which the poet and his friend create.
33 *Hesper:* the planet Venus.

X.

Thus richer then untempted Kings are we,
  That asking nothing, nothing need:
Though Lord of all what Seas imbrace; yet he
  That wants himselfe, is poore indeed.

## *LUCASTA Weeping*
## Song
## Set by Mr. *John Laneere*

I.

*Lucasta* wept, and still the bright
  Inamour'd God of Day,
With his soft Handkercher of Light,
  Kist the wet Pearles away.

II.

But when her Teares his heate or'e came,
  In Cloudes he quensht his Beames,
And griev'd, wept out his Eye of Flame,
  So drowned her sad Streames.

III.

At this she smil'd, when straight the Sun
  Cleer'd, with her kinde desires;
And by her eyes Reflection,
  Kindled againe his Fires.

# To Lucasta
## *From Prison*
## An Epode

I.

Long in thy Shackels, liberty,
I ask not from these walls, but thee;
Left for a while anothers Bride
To fancy all the world beside.

II.

Yet e're I doe begin to love,
See! How I all my objects prove;
Then my free Soule to that confine,
'Twere possible I might call mine.

III.

First I would be in love with *Peace*,
And her rich swelling breasts increase;
But how alas! how may that be,
Despising Earth, will she love me?

TO LUCASTA.
2 *thee:* i.e. Lucasta.

IV.

Faine would I be in love with *War*,
  As my deare Just avenging star;
But War is lov'd so ev'ry where,
  Ev'n He disdaines a Lodging here.

V.

Thee and thy wounds I would bemoane
  Faire thorough-shot *Religion;*
But he lives only that kills thee,
  And who so bindes thy hands, is free.

VI.

I would love a *Parliament*
  As a maine Prop from Heav'n sent;
But ah! Who's he that would be wedded
  To th' fairest body that's beheaded?

VII.

Next would I court my *Liberty*,
  And then my Birth-right, *Property;*
But can that be, when it is knowne
  There's nothing you can call your owne?

VIII.

A *Reformation* I would have,
As for our griefes a *Sov'raigne* salve;
That is, a cleansing of each wheele
Of State, that yet some rust doth feele:

IX.

But not a Reformation so,
As to reforme were to ore'throw;
Like Watches by unskilfull men
Disjoynted, and set ill againe.

X.

The *Publick Faith* I would adore,
But she is banke-rupt of her store;
Nor how to trust her can I see,
For she that couzens all, must me.

XI.

Since then none of these can be
Fit objects for my Love and me;
What then remaines, but th'only spring
Of all our loves and joyes? The KING.

37 *Publick Faith:* Money was borrowed by the government "on the public faith," which became the butt of many contemporary jokes.
40 *couzens:* cheats.

XII.

He who being the whole Ball
  Of Day to Earth, lends it to all;
When seeking to ecclipse his right,
  Blinded, we stand in our owne light.

XIII.

And now an universall mist
  Of Error is spread or'e each breast,
With such a fury edg'd, as is
  Not found in th'inwards of th'Abysse.

XIV.

Oh from thy glorious Starry Waine
  Dispense on me one sacred Beame
To light me where I soone may see
  How to serve you, and you trust me.

## To Lucasta
## Ode *Lyrick*

I.

Ah *Lucasta*, why so Bright!
Spread with early streaked light!
If still vailed from our sight,
What is't but eternall night?

II.

Ah *Lucasta,* why so Chaste!
With that vigour, ripenes grac't!
Not to be by Man imbrac't
Makes that Royall coyne imbace't,
And this golden Orchard waste.

III.

Ah *Lucasta,* why so Great!
That thy crammed coffers sweat;
Yet not owner of a seat
May shelter you from Natures heat,
And your earthly joyes compleat.

IV.

Ah *Lucasta,* why so Good!
Blest with an unstained flood
Flowing both through soule and blood;
If it be not understood,
'Tis a Diamond in mud.

V.

*Lucasta!* stay! why dost thou flye?
Thou art not Bright, but to the eye,
Nor Chaste, but in the Mariage-tye,
Nor Great, but in this Treasurie,
Nor Good, but in that sanctitie.

TO LUCASTA.
8 *imbace't:* debased.

VI.

Harder then the Orient stone,
Like an Apparition,
Or as a pale shadow gone
Dumbe and deafe she hence is flowne.

VII.

Then receive this equall dombe,
Virgins strow no teare or bloome,
No one dig the *Parian* wombe;
Raise her marble heart ith' roome,
And tis both her Coarse and Tombe.

## *Against the Love of Great Ones*

Unhappy youth betrayd by Fate
To such a Love hath *Sainted Hate*,
And *damned* those *Caelestiall* bands
Are onely knit with equal hands;
The Love of Great Ones? 'Tis a Love
Gods are incapable to prove;
For where there is a Joy uneven,
There never, never can be Heav'n:
'Tis such a Love as is not sent
To Fiends as yet for punishment;
*Ixion* willingly doth feele
The Gyre of his eternal wheele,

29 *dombe:* doom.
33 *Coarse:* corpse.
AGAINST THE LOVE.
12 *Gyre:* turning. Ixion was tortured in the underworld by being bound on a wheel that turned forever.

Nor would he now exchange his paine
For Cloudes and Goddesses againe.

Wouldst thou with tempests lye? Then bow
To th' rougher furrows of her brow;
Or make a Thunder-bolt thy Choyce?
Then catch at her more fatal Voyce;
Or 'gender with the Lightning? trye
The subtler Flashes of her eye:
Poore *Semele* wel knew the same,
Who both imbrac't her God and Flame;
And not alone in Soule did burne,
But in this Love did Ashes turne.

How il doth Majesty injoy
The Bow and Gaity oth' Boy,
As if the *Purple-roabe* should sit,
And sentence give ith' Chayr of *Wit.*

Say ever-dying wretch to whom
Each answer is a certaine dombe,
What is it that you would possesse,
The *Countes*, or the naked *Besse*?
Would you her *Gowne*, or *Title* do?
Her *Box*, or *Gem*, her *Thing* or *show*?
If you meane *Her*, the very *Her*
Abstracted from her caracter;
Unhappy Boy! you may as soone
With fawning wanton with the Moone,
Or with an amorous Complaint
Get prostitute your very Saint;
Not that we are not mortal, or
Fly *Venus* Altars, or abhor
The selfesame Knack for which you pine;
But we (defend us!) are divine,

21 *Semele:* The mother of Dionysius. Zeus, at Hera's suggestion, visited her in all the splendor of his divinity and she was consumed by lightning.

Female, but Madam borne, and come
From a right-honourable Wombe:
Shal we then mingle with the base,
And bring a silver-tinsell race?
Whilst th'issue Noble wil not passe,
The Gold allayd (almost halfe brasse)
And th' blood in each veine doth appeare,
Part thick *Booreinn*, part *Lady* Cleare:
Like to the sordid Insects sprung
From Father *Sun*, and Mother *Dung;*
Yet lose we not the hold we have,
But faster graspe the trembling slave;
Play at Baloon with's heart, and winde
The strings like scaines, steale into his minde
Ten thousand *Hells*, and *feigned Joyes*
Far worse then they, whilst like whipt Boys,
After this scourge hee's hush with Toys.

This heard Sir, play stil in her eyes,
And be a dying Lives, like Flyes
Caught by their Angle-legs, and whom
The Torch laughs peece-meale to consume.

50 *allayd:* alloyed, and hence debased.
52 *Booreinn:* a peasant woman.
57 *Baloon:* game played with a large, inflated ball.
58 *scaines:* skeins.

# To Althea, *From Prison* Song Set by Dr. *John Wilson*

I.

When Love with unconfined wings
  Hovers within my Gates;
And my divine *Althea* brings
  To whisper at the Grates:
When I lye tangled in her haire,
  And fetterd to her eye;
The *Gods* that wanton in the Aire,
  Know no such Liberty.

II.

When flowing Cups run swiftly round
  With no allaying *Thames*,
Our carelesse heads with Roses bound,
  Our hearts with Loyall Flames;
When thirsty griefe in Wine we steepe,
  When Healths and draughts go free,
Fishes that tipple in the Deepe,
  Know no such Libertie.

III.

When (like committed Linnets) I
  With shriller throat shall sing
The sweetnes, Mercy, Majesty,
  And glories of my KING;
When I shall voyce aloud, how Good
  He is, how Great should be;
Inlarged Winds that curle the Flood,
  Know no such Liberty.

IV.

Stone Walls doe not a Prison make,
  Nor I'ron bars a Cage;
Mindes innocent and quiet take
  That for an Hermitage;
If I have freedome in my Love,
  And in my soule am free;
Angels alone that sore above
  Injoy such Liberty.

## *A Black patch on* Lucasta's *Face*

Dull as I was, to think that a Court Fly,
  Presum'd so neer her Eye;
  When 'twas th'industrious Bee
Mistook her glorious Face for Paradise,
To summe up all his Chymistry of Spice;
  With a brave pride and honour led,
  Neer both her Suns he makes his bed;
And though a Spark struggles to rise as red:

Then AEmulates the gay
Daughter of Day,
Acts the *Romantick Phoenix* fate:
When now with all his Sweets lay'd out in state,
*Lucasta* scatters but one Heat,
And all the Aromatick pills do sweat,
And Gums calcin'd, themselves to powder beat;
Which a fresh gale of Air
Conveys into her Hair;
Then chaft he's set on fire,
And in these holy flames doth glad expire;
And that black marble Tablet there
So neer her either Sphere,
Was plac'd; nor foyl, nor Ornament,
But the sweet little Bees large Monument.

## *Love made in the first Age:* *To* Chloris

1.

In the Nativity of time,
*Chloris!* it was not thought a Crime
In direct *Hebrew* for to woe.
Now wee make Love, as all on fire,
Ring Retrograde our lowd Desire,
And Court in *English* Backward too.

LOVE MADE.

3 *Hebrew:* often thought, in the seventeenth century, to be the original language of mankind. In contrast to the "backward" English (line 6), it is written from right to left.

2.

Thrice happy was that golden Age,
When Complement was constru'd Rage,
  And fine words in the Center hid;
When cursed *No* stain'd no Maids Blisse,
And all discourse was summ'd in *Yes*,
  And Nought forbad, but to forbid.

3.

Love then unstinted, Love did sip,
And Cherries pluck'd fresh from the Lip,
  On Cheeks and Roses free he fed;
Lasses like *Autumne* Plums did drop,
And Lads, indifferently did crop
  A Flower, and a Maiden-head.

4.

Then unconfined each did Tipple
Wine from the Bunch, Milk from the Nipple,
  Paps tractable as Udders were;
Then equally the wholsome Jellies,
Were squeez'd from Olive-Trees, and Bellies,
  Nor Suits of Trespasse did they fear.

5.

A fragrant Bank of Straw-berries,
Diaper'd with Violets Eyes,
  Was Table, Table-cloth, and Fare;

No Pallace to the Clouds did swell,
Each humble Princesse then did dwell
  In the *Piazza* of her Hair.

6.

Both broken Faith, and th' cause of it,
All damning Gold was damn'd to th' Pit;
  Their Troth seal'd with a Clasp and Kisse,
Lasted untill that extreem day,
In which they smil'd their Souls away,
  And in each other breath'd new blisse.

7.

Because no fault, there was no tear;
No grone did grate the granting Ear;
  No false foul breath their Del'cat smell:
No Serpent kiss poyson'd the Tast,
Each touch was naturally Chast,
  And their mere Sense a Miracle.

8.

Naked as their own innocence,
And unimbroyder'd from Offence
  They went, above poor Riches, gay;
On softer than the Cignets Down,
In beds they tumbled of their own;
  For each within the other lay.

9.

Thus did they live: Thus did they love,
Repeating only joyes Above;
And Angels were, but with Cloaths on,
Which they would put off cheerfully,
To bathe them in the *Galaxie*,
Then gird them with the Heavenly Zone.

10.

Now, *CHLORIS!* miserably crave,
The offer'd blisse you would not have;
Which evermore I must deny,
Whilst ravish'd with these Noble Dreams,
And crowned with mine own soft Beams,
Injoying of my self I lye.

# ABRAHAM COWLEY
1618–1667

THE

# WORKS

OF

# Mr Abraham Cowley.

Consisting of

*Those which were formerly Printed:*

AND

*Those which he Design'd for the Press,*

Now Published out of the Authors

*ORIGINAL COPIES.*

LONDON,

Printed by *J. M.* for *Henry Herringman*, at the Sign of the *Blew Anchor* in the Lower Walk of the *New Exchange.* 1668.

# The Motto

## *Tentanda via est, &c.*

What shall I do to be for ever known,
And make the *Age to come* my own?
I shall like *Beasts* or *Common People* dy,
Unless you write my *Elegy;*
Whilst others *Great,* by being *Born* are grown,
Their *Mothers Labour,* not their own.
In this Scale *Gold,* in th'other *Fame* does ly,
The *weight* of *that,* mounts this so *high.*
These men are *Fortunes Jewels,* moulded bright;
Brought forth with their own fire and light.
If I, her *vulgar stone* for either look;
Out of *my self* it must be *strook.*
Yet I must on; what sounds is't strikes mine ear?
Sure I *Fames Trumpet* hear.
It sounds like the *last Trumpet:* for it can
Raise up the *bur'ied Man.*
Unpast *Alpes* stop me, but I'll cut through all,
And march, the *Muses Hannibal.*
Hence all the *flattering vanities* that lay
*Nets* of *Roses* in the way.
Hence the desire of *Honors,* or *Estate;*
And all, that is not above *Fate,*
Hence *Love* himself, that *Tyrant* of my days,
Which intercepts my coming praise.
Come my best *Friends,* my *Books,* and lead me on;
'Tis time that I were gon.

THE MOTTO: The "motto" (*tentanda via est, &c.*) is from Virgil's *Georgics* III.8 f., "I must essay a path whereby I, too, may rise from earth and fly victorious on the lips of men." Cowley's poem stands first in the "Miscellanies" section of the 1668 folio.

18 *Hannibal:* The Carthaginian general (247–183 B.C.), sworn enemy of Rome. His troops crossed the Alps in 218.

Welcome, great *Stagirite,* and teach me now
    All I was born to know.
Thy *Scholars vict'ries* thou dost far out-do;
    *He* conquer'd th' *Earth,* the whole *World you.*
Welcome learn'd *Cicero,* whose blest *Tongue* and *Wit*
    Preserves *Romes greatness yet.*
Thou art the *first* of *Ora'tors;* only he
    Who best can *praise Thee, next* must be.
Welcome the *Mantu'an Swan, Virgil* the *Wise,*
    Whose verse *walks highest,* but not flies.
Who brought green *Poesie* to her perfect Age;
    And made that *Art* which was a *Rage.*
Tell me, ye mighty *Three,* what shall I do
    To be like one of you.
But you have climb'd the *Mountains* top, there sit
    On the calm flour'ishing head of it,
And whilst with wearied steps we upward go,
    See *Us,* and *Clouds* below.

## Ode
### *Of Wit*

1.

Tell me, O tell, what kind of thing is *Wit,*
        Thou who *Master* art of it.
For the *First matter* loves *Variety* less;
Less *Women* love't, either in *Love* or *Dress.*

29 *Thy Scholars:* Alexander the Great (356–323 B.C.), Aristotle's pupil.

35 *Mantu'an Swan:* Virgil (70–19 B.C.) was born near Mantua.

2 *Thou . . . Master:* The poem is not addressed to any individual, but to an ideal poet, a figure whom Cowley aspires to become.

3 *First matter:* a philosophic term designating "that from which all else was created." Wit loves variety more than either the first matter or women (both infinitely various) do.

A thousand different shapes it bears,
*Comely* in thousand shapes appears.
Yonder we saw it plain, and here 'tis now,
Like *Spirits* in a *Place,* we know not *How.*

2.

*London* that vents of *false Ware* so much store,
In no *Ware* deceives us more.
For men led by the *Colour,* and the *Shape,*
Like *Zeuxes Birds* fly to the painted *Grape;*
Some things do through our Judgment pass
As through a *Multiplying Glass.*
And sometimes, if the *Object* be too far,
We take a *Falling Meteor* for a *Star.*

3.

Hence 'tis a *Wit* that greatest *word* of *Fame*
Grows such a common Name.
And *Wits* by our *Creation* they become,
Just so, as *Tit'lar Bishops* made at *Rome.*
'Tis not a *Tale,* 'tis not a *Jest*
Admir'd with *Laughter* at a feast,
Nor florid *Talk* which can that *Title* gain;
The *Proofs* of *Wit* for ever must remain.

4.

'Tis not to force some lifeless *Verses* meet
With their five gowty feet.
All ev'ry where, like *Mans,* must be the *Soul,*
And *Reason* the *Inferior Powers* controul.

ODE OF WIT.

12 *Zeuxes:* Zeuxes, late fifth-century B.C. Greek painter; Parrhasius tells the story of his painting a bunch of grapes so realistically that birds picked at them.

14 *Multiplying:* enlarging, magnifying.

20 *Tit'lar:* bishops with a title, but no see.

Such were the *Numbers* which could call
The *Stones* into the *Theban* wall.
Such *Miracles* are ceast; and now we see
No *Towns* or *Houses* rais'd by *Poetrie.*

5.

Yet 'tis not to adorn, and gild each part;
That shows more *Cost,* then *Art.*
*Jewels* at *Nose* and *Lips* but ill appear;
Rather then *all things Wit,* let *none* be there.
Several *Lights* will not be seen,
If there be nothing else between.
Men doubt, because they stand so thick i' th' skie,
If those be *Stars* which paint the *Galaxie.*

6.

'Tis not when two like words make up one noise;
Jests for *Dutch Men,* and *English Boys,*
In which who finds out *Wit,* the same may see
In *An'grams* and *Acrostiques Poetrie.*
Much less can that have any place
At which a *Virgin* hides her face,
Such *Dross* the *Fire* must purge away; 'tis just
The *Author blush,* there where the *Reader* must.

7.

'Tis not such *Lines* as almost crack the *Stage*
When *Bajazet* begins to rage.

30 *Theban wall:* Amphion, the legendary Greek musician, who is said to have built the walls of Thebes through the power of his lyre.

37 *Several:* separated.

50 *Bajazet:* Turkish sultan (1347–1403). Cowley alludes to Marlowe's *Tamburlaine,* in which Bajazet rants and raves on the stage.

Nor a tall *Meta'phor* in the *Bombast way,*
Nor the dry chips of short lung'd *Seneca.*
    Nor upon all things to obtrude,
    And force some odd *Similitude.*
What is it then, which like the *Power Divine*
We only can by *Negatives* define?

8.

In a true piece of *Wit* all things must be,
    Yet all things there *agree.*
As in the *Ark,* joyn'd without force or strife,
All *Creatures* dwelt; all *Creatures* that had *Life.*
    Or as the *Primitive Forms* of all
    (If we compare great things with small)
Which without *Discord* or *Confusion* lie,
In that strange *Mirror* of the *Deitie.*

9.

But *Love* that moulds *One Man* up out of *Two,*
    Makes me forget and injure you.
I took *you* for *my self* sure when I thought
That you in any thing were to be *Taught.*
    Correct my error with thy Pen;
    And if any ask me then,
What thing right *Wit,* and height of *Genius* is,
I'll onely shew your *Lines,* and say, *'Tis This.*

## *On the Death of Mr.* William Hervey

*Immodicis brevis est aetas,*
*&c rara Senectus.* Mart.

1.

It was a dismal, and a fearful night,
Scarce could the Morn drive on th'unwilling Light,
When *Sleep, Deaths Image,* left my troubled brest,
    By something *liker Death* possest.
My eyes with Tears did uncommanded flow,
    And on my Soul hung the dull weight
    Of some *Intolerable Fate.*
What Bell was that? Ah me! Too much I know.

2.

My sweet *Companion,* and my gentle *Peere,*
Why hast thou left me thus unkindly here,
Thy *end* for ever, and my *Life* to moan;
    O thou hast left me all alone!
Thy *Soul* and *Body* when *Deaths Agonie*
    Besieg'd around thy noble heart,
    Did not with more reluctance part
Then I, my dearest *Friend,* do part from *Thee.*

ON THE DEATH: William Hervey, Cowley's friend at Cambridge, died in Pembroke College on May 16, 1642. For the Latin epigraph, see Martial VI.29.7: "To those of outstanding talents, life is short and old age rarely met with."

3.

My dearest *Friend*, would I had dy'd for thee!
*Life* and this *World* henceforth will tedious bee.
Nor shall I know hereafter what to do
    If once my *Griefs* prove *tedious* too.
Silent and sad I walk about all day,
    As sullen *Ghosts* stalk speechless by
    Where their hid *Treasures* ly;
Alas, my *Treasure's* gone, why do I stay?

4.

He was my *Friend*, the truest *Friend* on earth;
A strong and mighty *Influence* joyn'd our *Birth*.
Nor did we envy the most sounding *Name*
    By *Friendship* giv'n of old to *Fame*.
None but his *Brethren* he, and *Sisters* knew,
    Whom the kind youth preferr'd to Me;
    And ev'n in that we did agree,
For much above my self I lov'd them too.

5.

Say, for you saw us, ye immortal *Lights*,
How oft unweari'd have we spent the Nights?
Till the *Ledaean Stars* so fam'd for *Love*,
    Wondred at us from above.
We spent them not in toys, in lusts, or wine;
    But search of deep *Philosophy*,
    *Wit, Eloquence,* and *Poetry*,
Arts which I lov'd, for they, my *Friend*, were *Thine*.

35 *Ledaean Stars:* Castor and Pollux, the twin sons of Leda.

6.

Ye fields of *Cambridge*, our dear *Cambridge*, say,
Have ye not seen us walking every day?
Was there a *Tree* about which did not know
    The *Love* betwixt us two?
Henceforth, ye gentle *Trees*, for ever fade;
    Or your sad branches thicker joyn,
    And into darksome shades combine,
*Dark* as the *Grave* wherein my *Friend* is laid.

7.

Henceforth no learned *Youths* beneath you sing,
Till all the tuneful *Birds* to'your boughs they bring;
No tuneful *Birds* play with their wonted chear,
    And call the learned *Youths* to hear,
No whistling *Winds* through the glad branches fly,
    But all with sad solemnitie,
    *Mute* and unmoved be,
*Mute* as the *Grave* wherein my *Friend* does ly.

8.

To him my *Muse* made haste with every strain
Whilst it was new, and *warm*, yet from the *Brain*.
He lov'd my worthless *Rhimes*, and like a *Friend*
    Would find out something to *commend*.
Hence now, my *Muse*, thou canst not me delight;
    Be this my latest verse
    With which I now adorn his *Herse*,
And this my *Grief*, without *thy* help shall write.

9.

Had I a wreath of *Bays* about my brow,
I should contemn that flourishing honor now,
Condemn it to the *Fire,* and joy to hear
    It rage and crackle there.
Instead of *Bays,* crown with sad *Cypress* me;
    *Cypress* which *Tombs* does beautifie;
    Not *Phoebus* griev'd so much as I
For him, who first was made that mournful *Tree.*

10.

Large was his *Soul;* as large a *Soul* as ere
Submitted to *inform* a *Body* here.
High as the Place 'twas shortly'in *Heav'n* to have,
    But low, and humble as his *Grave.*
So *high* that all the *Virtues* there did come
    As to their chiefest seat
    Conspicuous, and great;
So *low* that for *Me* too it made a room.

11.

He scorn'd this busie world below, and all
That we, *Mistaken Mortals,* Pleasure call;
Was fill'd with inn'ocent *Gallantry* and *Truth,*
    Triumphant ore the sins of *Youth.*
He like the *Stars,* to which he now is gone,
    That shine with beams like *Flame,*
    Yet burn not with the same,
Had all the *Light* of *Youth,* of the *Fire* none.

72 *him:* the youth Cyparissus, loved by Apollo (Phoebus). He was turned into a cypress tree.

12.

*Knowledge* he only sought, and so soon caught,
As if for him *Knowledge* had rather *sought.*
Nor did more *Learning* ever crowded lie
    In such a short *Mortalitie.*
When ere the skilful *Youth* discourst or writ,
    Still did the *Notions* throng
    About his eloquent Tongue,
Nor could his *Ink* flow faster then his *Wit.*

13.

So strong a *Wit* did *Nature* to him frame,
As all things but his *Judgement* overcame;
His *Judgement* like the heav'nly *Moon* did show,
    Temp'ring that mighty *Sea* below.
Oh had he liv'd in *Learnings World*, what bound
    Would have been able to controul
    His over-powering Soul?
We'have lost in him *Arts* that not yet are *found.*

14.

His *Mirth* was the pure *Spirits* of various Wit,
Yet never did his *God* or *Friends* forget.
And when deep talk and wisdom came in view,
    Retir'd and gave to them their due.
For the rich help of *Books* he always took,
    Though his own searching mind before
    Was so with *Notions* written ore
As if wise *Nature* had made that her *Book.*

15.

So many *Virtues* joyn'd in him, as we
Can scarce pick here and there in *Historie.*
More then old *Writers Practice* ere could reach,
As much as they could ever *teach.*
These did *Religion, Queen* of Virtues sway,
And all their sacred *Motions* steare,
Just like the First and *Highest Sphere*
Which wheels about, and turns all *Heav'n* one way.

16.

With as much Zeal, Devotion, Pietie,
He always *Liv'd,* as other Saints do *Dye.*
Still with his soul severe account he kept,
Weeping all *Debts* out ere he slept.
Then down in peace and innocence he lay,
Like the *Suns* laborious light,
Which still in *Water* sets at Night,
*Unsullied* with his *Journey* of the *Day.*

17.

Wondrous young Man, why wert thou made so good,
To be snatcht hence ere better *understood?*
Snatcht before half of thee enough was seen!
*Thou Ripe,* and yet thy *Life* but *Green!*
Nor could thy Friends take their last sad Farewel,
But Danger and *Infectious Death*
Malitiously seiz'd on that Breath
Where *Life, Spirit, Pleasure* always us'd to dwell.

18.

But happy Thou, ta'ne from this frantick age,
Where *Igno'rance* and *Hypocrisie* does rage!
A fitter *time* for Heav'n no soul ere chose,
The place now onely free from those.
There 'mong the *Blest* thou dost for ever shine,
And wheresoere thou casts thy view
Upon that white and radiant crew,
See'st not a *Soul* cloath'd with more *Light* then *Thine.*

19.

And if the glorious *Saints* cease not to know
Their wretched Friends who *fight* with *Life* below;
Thy Flame to *Me* does still the same abide,
Onely more pure and rarifi'd.
There whilst immortal Hymns thou dost reherse,
Thou dost with holy pity see
Our dull and earthly *Poesie,*
Where *Grief* and *Mis'ery* can be join'd with *Verse.*

## *To Sir* William Davenant
## *Upon his two first Books of* Gondibert, *finished before his voyage to* America

Methinks *Heroick Poesie* till now
Like some fantastick *Fairy Land* did show,
*Gods, Devils, Nymphs, Witches* and *Gyants race,*
And all but *Man* in *Mans chief work* had place.

TO SIR WILLIAM: Sir William Davenant (1606–1668), dramatist and soldier. Cowley was in exile with him at Paris from 1646–1650. His epic poem, *Gondibert,* appeared in 1650; he sailed for Maryland in the same year, but was captured and imprisoned.

Thou like some worthy *Knight* with sacred Arms
Dost drive the *Monsters* thence, and end the *Charms.*
Instead of those dost *Men* and *Manners* plant,
The things which that rich *Soil* did chiefly want.
Yet ev'en thy *Mortals* do their *Gods* excell,
Taught by thy *Muse* to *Fight* and *Love* so well.
By fatal hands whilst *present Empires* fall,
Thine from the Grave *past Monarchies* recall.
So much more thanks from humane kind does merit
The *Poets Fury,* then the *Zelots Spirit.*
And from the *Grave* thou mak'est this *Empire* rise,
Not like some dreadful *Ghost* t'affright our Eyes,
But with more Luster and triumphant state,
Then when it *crown'd* at proud *Verona* sate.
So will our *God rebuild* mans perisht frame,
And raise him up much *Better,* yet the *same.*
So *God-like Poets* do past things reherse,
Not *change,* but *Heighten* Nature by their Verse.
With shame, methinks, great *Italy* must see
Her *Conqu'erors* rais'ed to *Life* again by *Thee.*
Rais'd by such pow'erful Verse, that ancient *Rome*
May blush no less to see her *Wit o'recome.*
Some men their *Fancies* like their *Faith* derive,
And think all Ill but that which *Rome* does give.
The Marks of *Old* and *Catholick* would find,
To the same *Chair* would *Truth* and *Fiction* bind.
Thou in those beaten pathes disdain'st to tred,
And scorn'st to *Live* by robbing of the *Dead.*
Since Time does all things change, thou think'st not fit
This latter *Age* should see *all New but Wit.*
Thy *Fancy* like a *Flame* its way does make,
And leave bright *Tracks* for following Pens to take.

14 *Zelots Spirit:* Probably alluding to the execution of Charles I in 1649.
18 *Verona:* The action of *Gondibert* is set against a background of civil war in medieval Lombardy.

Sure 'twas this noble boldness of the *Muse*
Did thy desire to seek new *Worlds* infuse,
And ne're did Heav'n so much a *Voyage* bless,
If thou canst *Plant* but *there* with like success.

## *Reason*
## *The use of it in* Divine *Matters*

1.

Some *blind* themselves, 'cause possibly they may
  Be led by others a right way;
They build on *Sands*, which if unmov'd they find,
  'Tis but because there was no *Wind*.
Less hard 'tis, not to *Erre our selves*, then know
  If our *Fore-fathers err'd* or no.
When we trust *Men* concerning *God*, we then
  Trust not *God* concerning *Men*.

2.

*Visions* and *Inspirations* some expect
  Their course here to direct,
Like senseless *Chymists* their own wealth destroy,
  *Imaginary Gold* t'enjoy.
So *Stars appear* to drop to us from skie,
  And gild the passage as they fly:
But when they fall, and meet th'opposing ground,
  What but a sordid *Slime* is found?

REASON.
11 *Chymists:* alchemists.

3.

Sometimes their *Fancies* they 'bove *Reason* set,
And *Fast,* that they may *Dream* of meat.
Sometimes *ill Spi'rits* their sickly souls delude,
And *Bastard-Forms* obtrude.
So *Endors* wretched *Sorceress,* although,
She *Saul* through his disguise did know,
Yet when the *Dev'il* comes up *disguis'd,* she cries,
Behold, the *Gods* arise.

4.

In vain, alas, these outward Hopes are try'd;
*Reason* within's our onely *Guide.*
*Reason,* which (God be prais'd!) still *Walks,* for all
It's old Original *Fall.*
And since it self the boundless *Godhead* joyn'd
With a *Reasonable Mind,*
It plainly shows that *Mysteries Divine*
May with our *Reason* joyn.

5.

The *Holy Book,* like the eighth *Sphere,* does shine
With thousand Lights of *Truth Divine.*
So numberless the *Stars,* that to the Eye,
It makes but all one *Galaxie.*
Yet *Reason* must assist too, for in *Seas*
So vast and dangerous as these,
Our course by *Stars above* we cannot know,
Without the *Compass* too *below.*

21 *Endors:* For the Witch of Endor, see I Samuel 28, especially 28:27, "And the woman said unto Saul, I saw gods ascending out of the earth."

33 *eighth sphere:* in the Ptolemaic system, the sphere of the fixed stars.

6.

Though *Reason* cannot through *Faiths Myst'eries* see,
  It sees that *There* and *such* they be;
Leads to *Heav'ens Door,* and there does humbly keep,
  And there through *Chinks* and *Key-holes* peep.
Though it, like *Moses,* by a sad command
  Must not come in to th' *Holy Land,*
Yet thither it infallibly does *Guid,*
  And from afar 'tis all *Descry'd.*

## *On the Death of* Mr. Crashaw

*Poet* and *Saint!* to thee alone are given
The two most sacred *Names* of *Earth* and *Heaven.*
The hard and rarest *Union* which can be
Next that of *Godhead* with *Humanitie.*
Long did the *Muses* banisht *Slaves* abide,
And built vain *Pyramids* to mortal pride;
Like *Moses* Thou (though Spells and Charms withstand)
Hast brought them nobly home back to their *Holy Land.*
  Ah wretched *We, Poets of Earth!* but *Thou*
Were *Living* the same *Poet* which thou'rt *Now.*
Whilst *Angels* sing to thee their ayres divine,
And joy in an applause so great as *thine.*
Equal society with them to hold,
Thou need'st not make *new Songs,* but say the *Old.*
And they (kind Spirits!) shall all rejoyce to see
How little less then *They, Exalted Man* may be.

45 *Moses:* Cf. below, "Ode to the Royal Society," lines 93 ff.
*Title:* Richard Crashaw (1612/13–1649), died at Loreto, Italy (cf. line 40, below).

Still the old *Heathen Gods* in *Numbers* dwell,
The *Heav'enliest* thing on Earth still keeps up *Hell.*
Nor have we yet quite purg'd the *Christian Land;*
Still *Idols* here, like *Calves* at *Bethel* stand.
And though *Pans Death* long since all *Oracles* broke,
Yet still in Rhyme the *Fiend Apollo* spoke:
Nay with the worst of Heathen dotage We
(Vain men!) the *Monster Woman Deifie;*
Find *Stars,* and tye our *Fates* there in a *Face,*
And *Paradise* in them by whom we *lost* it, place.
What different faults corrupt our *Muses* thus?
*Wanton* as *Girles,* as *old Wives, Fabulous!*
  Thy spotless *Muse,* like *Mary,* did contain
The boundless *Godhead;* she did well disdain
That her *eternal Verse* employ'd should be
On a less subject then *Eternitie;*
And for a sacred *Mistress* scorn'd to take,
But her whom *God* himself scorn'd not his *Spouse* to make.
It (in a kind) *her Miracle* did do;
A fruitful *Mother* was, and *Virgin* too.
  How well (blest Swan) did Fate contrive thy death;
And made thee render up thy tuneful breath
In thy great *Mistress* Arms? thou most divine
And richest *Offering* of *Loretto's Shrine!*
Where like some holy *Sacrifice* t'expire,
A *Fever* burns thee, and *Love* lights the *Fire.*
*Angels* (they say) brought the fam'ed *Chappel* there,
And bore the sacred Load in Triumph through the air.
'Tis surer much they brought thee there, and *They,*
And *Thou,* their charge, went *singing* all the way.
  Pardon, my *Mother Church,* if I consent
That *Angels* led him when from thee he went,

ON THE DEATH.

20 *Bethel:* For the Israelites' worship of these golden calves, see I Kings 28:9 and II Kings 10:27–28.

22 *Apollo:* Though no longer active as an oracle, Apollo still speaks as the god of (pagan) poetry.

48 *from . . . went:* Crashaw became a convert to Roman Catholicism about 1645.

For even in *Error* sure no *Danger* is
When joyn'd with so much *Piety* as *His.*
Ah, mighty *God,* with shame I speak't, and grief,
Ah that our greatest *Faults* were in *Belief!*
And our weak *Reason* were ev'en weaker yet,
Rather then thus our *Wills* too strong for it.
His *Faith* perhaps in some nice Tenents might
Be wrong; his *Life,* I'm sure, was *in the right.*
And I my self a *Catholick* will be,
So far at least, great *Saint,* to *Pray* to thee.
  Hail, *Bard Triumphant!* and some care bestow
On *us,* the *Poets Militant* Below!
Oppos'ed by our old En'emy, adverse *Chance,*
Attacqu'ed by *Envy,* and by *Ignorance,*
Enchain'd by *Beauty,* tortur'd by *Desires,*
Expos'd by *Tyrant-Love* to savage *Beasts* and *Fires.*
Thou from low earth in nobler *Flames* didst rise,
And like *Elijah,* mount *Alive* the skies.
*Elisha*-like (but with a wish much less,
More fit thy *Greatness,* and my *Littleness*)
Lo here I beg (I whom thou once didst prove
So humble to *Esteem,* so Good to *Love*)
Not that thy *Spirit* might on me *Doubled* be,
I ask but *Half* thy mighty *Spirit* for Me.
And when my *Muse* soars with so strong a Wing,
'Twill learn of things *Divine,* and first of *Thee* to sing.

55 *nice Tenents:* finer points of dogma.

60 *Poets Militant:* Cowley is adopting the old threefold division of the faithful: the "Church militant" consists of Christians alive on earth, the "Church triumphant" of those in Heaven, and the "Church suffering" of those in Purgatory.

66–67 *Elijah . . . Elisha:* See II Kings 2:11, "And Elijah went up by a whirlwind into heaven." Elisha, Elijah's successor, had asked that "a double portion of thy [Elijah's] spirit be upon me." (II Kings 2:10). Cf. line 71, above.

# *The Duel*

Yes, I will love then, I will love,
I will not now *Loves Rebel* prove,
Though I was once his *Enemy;*
Though ill-advis'd and stubborn I,
Did to the Combate him defy,
An Helmet, Spear, and mighty shield,
Like some new *Ajax* I did wield.
*Love* in one hand his *Bow* did take,
In th'other hand a *Dart* did shake.
But yet in vain the *Dart* did throw,
In vain he often drew the *Bow.*
So well my *Armour* did resist,
So oft by flight the blow I mist.
But when I thought all danger past,
His *Quiver* empty'd quite at last,
Instead of *Arrow,* or of *Dart,*
He shot *Himself* into my Heart.
The *Living* and the *Killing Arrow*
Ran through the skin, the Flesh, the *Blood,*
And broke the Bones, and scorcht the Marrow,
No *Trench* or *Work* of *Life* withstood.
In vain I now the *Walls* maintain,
I set out *Guards* and *Scouts* in vain,
Since th'*En'emy* does within remain.
In vain a *Breastplate* now I wear,
Since in my *Breast* the Foe I bear.
In vain my *Feet* their swiftness try;
For from the *Body* can they fly?

THE DUEL: "The Duel" is one of a series of eleven poems, all of them imitations of Anacreon, which Cowley included in the "Miscellanies" section of the 1668 folio.

## *The Request*

1.

I' have often wisht to love; what shall I do?
Me still the *cruel Boy* does *spare;*
And I a double task must bear,
First to woo *him,* and then a *Mistress* too.
Come at last and strike for shame;
If thou art any thing besides a *name.*
I'le think Thee else no *God* to be;
But *Poets* rather *Gods,* who first *created Thee.*

2.

I ask not one in whom all beauties grow,
Let me but *love,* what e're she be,
She cannot seem *deform'd* to *me;*
And I would have her seem to *others* so.
Desire takes wings and strait does fly,
It stays not *dully* to inquire the *Why.*
That *Happy* thing a *Lover* grown,
I shall not see with *others* Eyes, scarce with *mine own.*

3.

If she be coy and scorn my noble fire,
If her chill heart I cannot move,
Why I'le *enjoy* the very *Love,*
And make a *Mistress* of my own *Desire.*

THE REQUEST: This and the five following poems are from Cowley's collection of love poems, *The Mistress,* first published in 1647.

Flames their most vigorous heat do hold,
And purest light, if compast round with *cold:*
So when sharp *Winter* means most harm,
The springing Plants are by the *Snow* it self kept warm.

4.

But do not touch my heart, and so be gone;
Strike deep thy burning arrows in:
*Lukewarmness* I account a sin,
As great in *Love,* as in *Religion.*
Come arm'd with flames, for I would prove
All the extremities of mighty Love.
Th'excess of heat is but a fable;
We know the *torrid* Zone is now found *habitable.*

5.

Among the Woods and Forrests thou art found,
There *Bores* and *Lyons* thou dost tame;
Is not my heart a nobler game?
Let *Venus, Men;* and *Beasts, Diana* wound.
Thou dost the Birds thy *Subjects* make;
Thy nimble *feathers* do their *wings* o'retake:
Thou all the *Spring* their Songs dost hear,
Make *me Love* too, I'll *sing* to' thee all the *year.*

38 *feathers:* i.e. those on Cupid's wings.

6.

What service can *mute Fishes* do to Thee?
Yet against them thy Dart prevails,
Piercing the armour of their *Scales;*
And still thy *Sea-born Mother* lives i'th' Sea.
Dost thou deny onely to me
The no-great privilege of *Captivitie?*
I *beg* or *challenge* here thy Bow;
Either thy *pity* to me, or else thine *anger* show.

7.

Come; or I'll teach the world to scorn that Bow:
I'll teach them thousand *wholesome arts*
Both to resist and cure thy darts,
More then thy skilful *Ovid* e're did know.
Musick of sighs thou shalt not hear,
Nor drink one wretched *Lovers* tasteful *Tear:*
Nay, unless soon thou woundest me,
My Verses shall not onely *wound,* but *murther* Thee.

44 *Sea-born Mother:* Hesiod describes the birth of Aphrodite (Venus); she sprang from the foam of the sea which formed about the severed member of Uranus after Cronos had mutilated him.

52 *Ovid:* alluding to Ovid's *Art of Love.*

## *Written in Juice of Lemmon*

1.

Whilst what I write I do not see,
I dare thus, even to *you*, write *Poetry.*
Ah foolish Muse, which do'st so high aspire,
And know'st her judgment well
How much it does thy power excel,
Yet dar'st be read by, thy just doom, the *Fire.*

2.

Alas, thou think'st thy self secure,
Because thy form is *Innocent* and *Pure:*
Like *Hypocrites,* which seem unspotted here;
But when they sadly come to dye,
And the last *Fire* their Truth must try,
*Scrauld* o're like thee, and *blotted* they appear.

3.

Go then, but reverently go,
And, since thou needs must *sin, confess* it too:
Confess't, and with humility clothe thy shame,
For thou, who else must burned be
An *Heretick,* if she pardon thee,
May'st like a *Martyr* then *enjoy* the *Flame.*

WRITTEN IN JUICE.
6 *Fire:* Its heat would make the writing in lemon juice visible.

4.

But if her *wisdom* grow severe,
And suffer not her *goodness* to be there;
If her large mercies cruelly it restrain;
Be not discourag'd, but require
A more gentle *Ordeal Fire*,
And bid her by *Loves-Flames* read it again.

5.

Strange power of heat, thou yet dost show
Like winter earth, *naked*, or *cloath'd* with *Snow*,
But, as the quickning *Sun* approaching near,
The *Plants* arise up by degrees,
A sudden paint adorns the trees,
And all kind *Natures Characters* appear.

6.

So, nothing yet in Thee is seen,
But when a *Genial heat* warms thee within,
A new-born *Wood* of various Lines there grows;
Here buds an A, and there a B,
Here sprouts a V, and there a T,
And all the flourishing *Letters* stand in *Rows*.

7.

Still, silly *Paper*, thou wilt think
That all this might as well be writ with *Ink*.
Oh no; there's sense in this, and *Mysterie;*
Thou now maist change thy *Authors* name,
And to her *Hand* lay noble claim;
For as *She Reads*, she *Makes* the words in Thee.

8.

Yet if thine own unworthiness
Will still, that thou art mine, not Hers, confess;
Consume thy self with Fire before her Eyes,
And so her *Grace* or *Pity* move;
The *Gods*, though *Beasts* they do not Love,
Yet like them when they'r burnt in *Sacrifice*.

## *The Change*

1.

*Love* in her Sunny Eyes does basking play;
*Love* walks the pleasant Mazes of her Hair;
*Love* does on both her Lips for ever stray;
And *sows* and *reaps* a thousand *kisses* there.
In all her outward parts *Love's* always seen;
But, oh, He never went within.

2.

Within *Love's* foes, his greatest foes abide,
Malice, Inconstancy, and Pride.
So the Earths face, Trees, Herbs, and Flowers do dress,
With other beauties numberless:
But at the *Center, Darkness* is, and *Hell;*
There wicked *Spirits,* and there the *Damned* dwell.

3.

With me alas, quite contrary it fares;
*Darkness* and *Death* lies in my weeping eyes,
Despair and Paleness in my face appears,
And Grief, and Fear, Love's greatest Enemies;
But, like the *Persian-Tyrant, Love* within
  Keeps his proud *Court,* and ne're is seen.

4.

Oh take *my Heart,* and by that means you'll prove
  Within, too stor'd enough of *Love:*
Give me but Yours, I'll by that change so thrive,
  That *Love* in all my parts shall live.
So powerful is this change, it render can,
My *outside Woman,* and your *inside Man.*

## *Leaving Me, and then loving Many*

So Men, who once have cast the *Truth* away,
Forsook by *God,* do strange wild lusts obey;
So the vain *Gentiles,* when they left t' adore
*One Deity,* could not stop at thousands more.
Their zeal was senseless strait, and boundless grown;
They worshipt many a *Beast,* and many a *Stone.*
Ah fair *Apostate!* couldst thou think to flee
From *Truth* and *Goodness,* yet keep *Unity?*
I reign'd alone; and my blest *Self* could call
The *Universal Monarch* of her *All.*

THE CHANGE.
20 "You too will be stored with enough Love within."
LEAVING ME.
3 *left:* ceased.

Mine, mine her fair *East-Indies* were above,
Where those *Suns* rise that chear the world of Love;
Where beauties shine like Gems of richest price;
Where *Coral* grows, and every *breath* is *spice:*
Mine too her rich *West-Indies* were below,
Where *Mines* of gold and endless treasures grow.
But, as, when the *Pellaean Conquerour* dy'd,
Many small *Princes* did his *Crown* divide,
So, since my *Love* his vanquisht world forsook,
Murther'd by poysons from her falshood took,
An hundred petty *Kings* claim each their part,
And rend that glorious *Empire* of her *Heart.*

## *The Soul*

1.

If mine *Eyes* do e're declare
They have seen a second thing that's *fair;*
Or *Ears,* that they have *Musick* found,
Besides thy *Voice,* in any *Sound;*
If my *Tast* do ever meet,
After thy *Kiss,* with ought that's *sweet;*
If my 'abused *Touch* allow
Ought to be *smooth,* or *soft,* but *You;*
If, what seasonable Springs,
Or the Eastern Summer brings,
Do my *Smell* perswade at all,
Ought *Perfume,* but thy *Breath* to call;
If all my *senses Objects* be
Not *contracted* into *Thee,*

17 *Pellaean Conquerour:* Achilles.

And so through *Thee* more powe'rful pass,
As *Beams* do through a *Burning-Glass;*
If all things that in *Nature* are
Either soft, or sweet, or fair,
Be not in Thee so *'Epitomiz'd,*
That nought *material's* not compriz'd;
May I as worthless seem to *Thee*
As all, but *Thou,* appears to *Me.*

**2.**

If I ever *Anger* know,
Till some *wrong* be done to *You;*
If *Gods* or *Kings* my *Envy* move,
Without their *Crowns crown'd* by thy *Love;*
If ever I an *Hope* admit,
Without thy *Image* stampt on it;
Or any *Fear,* till I begin
To find that *You'r* concern'd therein;
If a *Joy* e're come to me,
That *Tasts* of any thing but *Thee;*
If any *Sorrow* touch my Mind,
Whilst You are *well,* and not *unkind;*
If I a minutes space debate,
Whether I shall curse and hate
The things beneath thy hatred fall,
Though all the *World, My self* and *all;*
And for *Love,* if ever I
Approach to it again so nigh,
As to allow a *Toleration*
To the least *glimmering Inclination;*
If thou alone do'st not controul
All those *Tyrants* of my Soul,

THE SOUL.

16 *Burning-Glass:* magnifying glass.
20 "That no material fails to be comprized, or summed up, in thee."

And to thy Beauties ty'st them so,
That constant they as *Habits* grow;
If any *Passion* of my Heart,
By any *force*, or any *art*,
Be brought to move one step from *Thee*,
Mayst Thou no *Passion* have for *Me*.

3.

If my busie *'Imagination*
Do not *Thee* in all things fashion;
So that all fair *Species* be
*Hieroglyphick* marks of *Thee;*
If when She her sports does keep
(The lower Soul being all asleep)
She play one *Dream* with all her art,
Where Thou hast not the longest part.
If ought get place in my *Remembrance*,
Without some badge of thy resemblance;
So that thy parts become to me
A kind of *Art* of *Memory*.
If my Understanding do
Seek any *Knowledge* but of You,
If she do near thy *Body* prize
Her *Bodies* of *Philosophies*,
If She to the *Will* do show
Ought *desirable* but You,
Or if *That* would not *rebel*,
Should she another doctrine tell;
If my *Will* do not resign
All her *Liberty* to thine;
If she would not follow *Thee*,
Though *Fate* and *Thou* shouldst *disagree;*
And if (for I a curse will give,
Such as shall force thee to believe)
My *Soul* be not entirely Thine;
May thy dear *Body* ne're be Mine.

## *The Dissembler*

1.

*Unhurt, untoucht* did I complain;
And terrifi'd all others with the pain:
But now I feel the *mighty evil;*
Ah, there's no *fooling* with *the Devil!*
So wanton men, whilst others they would fright,
Themselves have met a real *Spright.*

2.

I thought, I'll swear, an handsome ly
Had been no *sin* at all in *Poetry:*
But now I suffer an *Arrest,*
For words were spoke by me in *jest.*
Dull, sottish *God* of *Love,* and can it be
Thou understand'st not *Raillery?*

3.

*Darts,* and *Wounds,* and *Flame,* and *Heat,*
I nam'd but for the *Rhime,* or the *Conceit.*
Nor meant my Verse should raised be,
To this sad fame of *Prophesie;*
*Truth* gives a *dull propriety* to my stile,
And all the *Metaphors* does spoil.

4.

In things, where *Fancy* much does reign,
'Tis dangerous too cunningly to *feign.*
The *Play* at last a *Truth* does grow,
And *Custom* into *Nature* go.
By this curst art of begging I became
*Lame,* with *counterfeiting Lame.*

5.

My Lines of amorous desire
I wrote to kindle and blow others fire:
And 'twas a *barbarous delight*
My *Fancy* promis'd from the sight;
But now, by *Love,* the mighty *Phalaris,* I
My *burning Bull* the first do try.

## *The Extasie*

1.

I leave *Mortality,* and things below;
I have no time in *Complements* to wast,
*Farewel* to'ye all in hast,
For I am *call'd* to go.
A *Whirlwind* bears up my dull Feet,
Th'officious *Clouds* beneath them meet.
And (Lo!) I *mount,* and (Lo!)
How small the biggest Parts of *Earths* proud *Tittle* show!

THE DISSEMBLER.

29 *Phalaris:* The tyrant of Acragas (c. 570–544 B.C.), who put his victims in a hollow brazen bull, where he roasted them alive.

THE EXTASIE: The poem is one of Cowley's imitations of Pindar.

2.

Where shall I find the noble *Brittish* Land?
Lo, I at last a *Northern Spec* espie,
Which in the *Sea* does lie,
And seems a *Grain* o'th' *Sand!*
For this will any *sin,* or *Bleed?*
Of *Civil Wars* is this the *Meed?*
And is it this, alas, which we
(Oh *Irony* of *Words!*) do call *Great Britanie?*

3.

I pass by th'arched *Magazins,* which hold
Th' eternal stores of *Frost,* and *Rain,* and *Snow;*
*Dry,* and *secure* I go,
Nor shake with *Fear,* or *Cold.*
Without *affright* or *wonder*
I meet *Clouds* charg'd with *Thunder,*
And *Lightnings* in my way
Like harmles *Lambent Fiers* about my Temples play.

4.

Now into'a gentle *Sea* of rowling *Flame*
I'm *plung'ed,* and still mount higher there,
As *Flames* mount up through *aire.*
So perfect, yet so tame,
So great, so pure, so bright a fire
Was that unfortunate desire,
My faithful *Breast* did cover,
Then, when I was of late a wretched *Mortal Lover.*

14 *Meed:* reward.
17 *arched Magazins:* vaults of heaven.

5.

Through several *Orbs* which one fair *Planet* bear,
Where I behold distinctly as I pass
The *Hints* of *Galilaeos Glass,*
I touch at last the spangled *Sphaere.*
Here all th'extended *Skie*
Is but one *Galaxie,*
'Tis all so bright and gay,
And the *joynt Eyes* of *Night* make up a perfect *Day.*

6.

Where am I now? *Angels* and *God* is here;
An unexhausted *Ocean* of *delight*
Swallows my *senses* quite,
And drowns all *What,* or *How,* or *Where.*
Not *Paul,* who first did thither pass,
And this great *Worlds Columbus* was,
The *tyrannous pleasure* could express.
Oh, 'tis *too much* for *Man!* but let it ne're be *less.*

7.

The mighty' *Elijah* mounted so on high,
That second Man, who *leapt* the *Ditch* where all
The rest of Mankind *fall,*
And went not *downwards* to the *skie.*

35 *Galilaeos Glass:* Galileo's use of the telescope dates from 1609.

45 *Paul:* Cf. I Corinthians 2:9, "Eye hath not seen, nor ear heard, neither have entered into the heart of man, the things which God hath prepared for them that love him."

49 *Elijah:* Cf. II Kings 1–2.

With much of pomp and show
(As Conquering *Kings* in *Triumph* go)
Did he to *Heav'en* approach,
And wondrous was his *Way*, and wondrous was his *Coach.*

8.

'Twas gawdy all, and rich in every part,
Of *Essences* of *Gems,* and *Spirit* of *Gold*
Was its *substantial mold;*
Drawn forth by *Chymique Angels* art,
Here with *Moon-beams* 'twas *silver'd* bright,
There double-*gilt* with the *Suns* light
And mystique Shapes cut round in it,
*Figures* that did transcend a *Vulgar Angels* wit.

9.

The *Horses* were of temper'd *Lightning* made,
Of all that in *Heav'ens* beauteous *Pastures* feed,
The noblest, sprightfulst breed,
And *flaming Mains* their *Necks* array'd.
They all were shod with *Diamond,*
Not such as *here* are found,
But such *light solid* ones as shine
On the *Transparent Rocks* o'th' *Heaven Chrystalline.*

10.

Thus mounted the great *Prophet* to the skies;
Astonisht Men who oft had seen *Stars fall,*
Or that which so they call,
Wondred from hence to see one *rise.*

64 *Vulgar:* ordinary, common.

The soft *Clouds* melted him a way,
The *Snow* and *Frosts* which in it lay
A while the scared *footsteps* bore,
The *Wheels* and *Horses Hoofs* hizz'd as they past them ore.

11.

He past by th' *Moon* and *Planets*, and did fright
All the *Worlds* there which at this *Meteor* gaz'ed,
And their *Astrologers* amaz'd
With th'unexampled sight.
But where he stopt will ne're be known,
Till *Phoenix Nature* aged grown
To'a better *Being* do aspire,
And mount *herself*, like *Him*, to' *Eternitie* in *Fire*.

## *To the* Royal Society

1.

Philosophy the great and only Heir
Of all that Human Knowledge which has bin
Unforfeited by Mans rebellious Sin,
Though full of years He do appear,
(Philosophy, I say, and call it, He,
For whatso'ere the Painters Fancy be,
It a Male-virtue seemes to me)

86 *Phoenix:* The legendary Egyptian bird which returns to its nest every five hundred years, there to be consumed by fire. Out of the ashes, the new phoenix is born.

TO THE ROYAL SOCIETY: The Royal Society, which had begun to meet as a "philosophical college" in the 1640s, was officially incorporated in 1662. Cowley wrote his ode at the request of friends for inclusion in Thomas Sprat's *History of the Royal Society* (1667).

Has still been kept in Nonage till of late,
Nor manag'd or enjoy'd his vast Estate:
Three or four thousand years one would have thought,
To ripeness and perfection might have brought
  A Science so well bred and nurst,
And of such hopeful parts too at the first.
But, oh, the Guardians and the Tutors then
(Some negligent, and some ambitious men)
  Would ne're consent to set him Free,
Or his own Natural Powers to let him see,
Lest that should put an end to their Autoritie.

2.

That his own business he might quite forget,
They' amus'd him with the sports of wanton Wit,
With the Desserts of Poetry they fed him,
In stead of solid meats t'encrease his force;
In stead of vigorous exercise they led him
Into the pleasant Labyrinths of ever-fresh Discourse:
  In stead of carrying him to see
The Riches which doe hoorded for him lie
  In Natures endless Treasurie,
  They chose his Eye to entertain
  (His curious but not covetous Eye)
With painted Scenes, and Pageants of the Brain.
Some few exalted Spirits this latter Age has shown,
That labour'd to assert the Liberty
(From Guardians, who were now Usurpers grown)
Of this old *Minor* still, Captiv'd Philosophy;
  But 'twas Rebellion call'd to fight
  For such a long-oppressed Right.

19–30 Cowley here contrasts ancient and medieval philosophy (especially the latter) with the new experimental science (natural philosophy) of his own day.

*Bacon* at last, a mighty Man, arose
  Whom a wise King and Nature chose
  Lord Chancellour of both their Lawes,
And boldly undertook the injur'd Pupils cause.

3.

Autority, which did a Body boast,
Though 'twas but Air condens'd, and stalk'd about,
Like some old Giants more Gigantic Ghost,
  To terrifie the Learned Rout
With the plain Magick of true Reasons Light,
  He chac'd out of our sight,
Nor suffer'd Living *Men* to be misled
  By the vain shadows of the Dead:
To Graves, from whence it rose, the conquer'd Phantome fled;
  He broke that Monstrous God which stood
In midst of th' Orchard, and the whole did claim,
  Which with a useless Sith of Wood,
  And something else not worth a name,
  (Both vast for shew, yet neither fit
  Or to Defend, or to Beget;
  Ridiculous and senceless Terrors!) made
Children and superstitious Men afraid.
  The Orchard's open now, and free;
*Bacon* has broke that Scar-crow Deitie;
  Come, enter, all that will,
Behold the rip'ned Fruit, come gather now your Fill.
  Yet still, methinks, we fain would be
  Catching at the Forbidden Tree,
  We would be like the Deitie,

37 *Bacon:* Francis Bacon, Lord Verulam (1561–1626), in Cowley's eyes the first champion of the new science.

52 *Sith:* scythe.

53 *something else:* a phallus. The false god overthrown by Bacon is pictured as an obscene pagan deity.

When Truth and Falshood, Good and Evil, we
Without the Sences aid within our selves would see;
  For 'tis God only who can find
  All Nature in his Mind.

4.

From Words, which are but Pictures of the Thought,
Though we our Thoughts from them perversly drew,
To things, the Minds right Object, he it brought,
Like foolish Birds to painted Grapes we flew;
He sought and gather'd for our use the True;
And when on heaps the chosen Bunches lay,
He prest them wisely the Mechanick way,
Till all their juyce did in one Vessel joyn,
Ferment into a Nourishment Divine,
  The thirsty Souls refreshing Wine.
Who to the life an exact Piece would make,
Must not from others Work a Copy take;
  No, not from *Rubens* or *Vandike;*
Much less content himself to make it like
Th'Idaeas and the Images which lie
In his own Fancy, or his Memory.
  No, he before his sight must place
  The Natural and Living Face;
  The real object must command
Each Judgment of his Eye, and Motion of his Hand.

72 *painted grapes:* See above, "Of Wit," line 12 and note.
75 *the Mechanick way:* by the use of a machine.
81 *Rubens or Vandike:* Peter Paul Rubens (1577–1640) and Sir Anthony Van Dyke (1599–1641), great portrait artists of the seventeenth century.
83 *Idaeas:* mental images.

5.

From these and all long Errors of the way,
In which our wandring Praedecessors went,
And like th'old *Hebrews* many years did stray
  In Desarts but of small extent,
*Bacon,* like *Moses,* led us forth at last,
  The barren Wilderness he past,
  Did on the very Border stand
Of the blest promis'd Land,
And from the Mountains Top of his Exalted Wit,
  Saw it himself, and shew'd us it.
But Life did never to one Man allow
Time to Discover Worlds, and Conquer too;
Nor can so short a Line sufficient be
To fadome the vast depths of Natures Sea:
  The work he did we ought t'admire,
And were unjust if we should more require
From his few years, divided 'twixt th'Excess
Of low Affliction, and high Happiness.
For who on things remote can fix his sight,
That's alwayes in a Triumph, or a Fight?

6.

From you, great Champions, we expect to get
These spacious Countries but discover'd yet;
Countries where yet in stead of Nature, we
Her Images and Idols worship'd see:
These large and wealthy Regions to subdue,
Though Learning has whole Armies at command,
  Quarter'd about in every Land,

110 *but . . . yet:* which have just been discovered.

A better Troop she ne're together drew.
   Methinks, like *Gideon's* little Band,
   God with Design has pickt out you,
To do these noble Wonders by a Few:
When the whole Host he saw, They are (said he)
   Too many to O'rcome for Me;
   And now he chuses out his Men,
   Much in the way that he did then:
   Not those many whom he found
   Idely extended on the ground,
   To drink with their dejected head
The Stream just so as by their Mouths it fled:
   No, but those Few who took the waters up,
And made of their laborious Hands the Cup.

7.

Thus you prepar'd; and in the glorious Fight
   Their wondrous pattern too you take:
Their old and empty Pitchers first they brake,
And with their Hands then lifted up the Light.
   Io! Sound too the Trumpets here!
Already your victorious Lights appear;
New Scenes of Heaven already we espy,
And Crowds of golden Worlds on high;
Which from the spacious Plains of Earth and Sea;
   Could never yet discover'd be

117 *Gideon's:* Cf. Judges 6:27–28, where Gideon with a band of only ten men, casts down the Midianite altar of Baal. So too, in Judges 7, Gideon overcomes a huge enemy host with only three hundred men.

126–29 *To drink . . . the Cup:* Gideon's three hundred were chosen by the Lord because they "lapped, putting their hand to their mouth; but all the rest of the people bowed down upon their knees to drink water" (Judges 7:6).

132–33 *Pitchers . . . Light:* "And the three companies [of one hundred men each] blew the trumpets, and brake the pitchers, and held the lamps in their left hands, and the trumpets in their right hands to blow withal: and they cried, The sword of the LORD, and of Gideon" (Judges 7:20).

134 *Io:* The Roman and Greek shout of triumphant joy.

By Sailers or *Chaldaeans* watchful Eye.
Natures great Workes no distance can obscure,
No smalness her near Objects can secure
  Y' have taught the curious Sight to press
  Into the privatest recess
Of her imperceptible Littleness.
  Y' have learn'd to Read her smallest Hand,
And well begun her deepest Sense to Understand.

8.

Mischief and true Dishonour fall on those
Who would to laughter or to scorn expose
So Virtuous and so Noble a Design,
So Human for its Use, for Knowledge so Divine.
The things which these proud men despise, and call
  Impertinent, and vain, and small,
Those smallest things of Nature let me know,
Rather than all their greatest Actions Doe.
Whoever would Deposed Truth advance
  Into the Throne usurp'd from it,
Must feel at first the Blows of Ignorance,
  And the sharp Points of Envious Wit.
So when by various turns of the Celestial Dance,
  In many thousand years
  A Star, so long unknown, appears,
Though Heaven it self more beauteous by it grow,
It troubles and alarms the World below,
Does to the Wise a Star, to Fools a Meteor show.

140 *Chaldaeans:* famed as astronomers in the ancient East.

9.

With Courage and Success you the bold work begin;
Your Cradle has not Idle bin:
None e're but *Hercules* and you could be
At five years Age worthy a History.
And ne're did Fortune better yet
Th' Historian to the Story fit:
As you from all Old Errors free
And purge the Body of Philosophy;
So from all Modern Folies He
Has vindicated Eloquence and Wit.
His candid Stile like a clean Stream does slide,
And his bright Fancy all the way
Does like the Sun-shine in it play;
It does like *Thames,* the best of Rivers, glide,
Where the God does not rudely overturn,
But gently pour the Crystal Urn,
And with judicious hand does the whole Current Guide.
T' has all the Beauties Nature can impart,
And all the comely Dress without the paint of Art.

168 *Hercules:* alluding to the story of the infant Hercules strangling the serpents in his cradle.
171 *Th' Historian:* Thomas Sprat.

# THOMAS STANLEY
## 1625–1678

## Chang'd, yet Constant

Wrong me no more
In thy complaint,
Blam'd for Inconstancy;
I vow'd t'adore
The fairest Saint,
Nor chang'd whilst thou wert she:
But if another Thee outshine,
Th'Inconstancy is onely Thine.

To be by such
Blind Fools admir'd
Gives thee but small esteem,
By whom as much
Thou'dst be desir'd
Didst thou lesse beautious seem;
Sure why they love they know not well,
Who why they should not cannot tell.

Women are by
Themselves betray'd,
And to their short joyes cruel,
Who foolishly
Themselves perswade
Flames can outlast their fuel;
None (though Platonick their pretence)
With Reason love unlesse by Sence.

And He, by whose
Command to Thee
I did my heart resigne,
Now bids me choose
A Deity
Diviner far then thine;
No power can Love from Beauty sever;
I'me still Loves subject, thine was never.

The fairest She
Whom none surpasse
To love hath onely right,
And such to me
Thy Beauty was
Till one I found more bright;
But 'twere as impious to adore
Thee now, as not t'have done't before.

Nor is it just
By rules of Love
Thou should'st deny to quit
A heart that must
Anothers prove
Ev'n in thy right to it;
Must not thy Subjects Captives be
To her who triumphs over Thee?

Cease then in vain
To blot my name
With forg'd Apostasie,
Thine is that stain
Who dar'st to claim
What others ask of Thee.
Of Lovers they are onely true
Who pay their Hearts where they are due.

## Celia Singing

Roses in breathing forth their scent,
Or Stars their borrowed ornament;
Nymphs in the Watery Sphear that move,
Or Angels in their orbs above;
The winged Chariot of the Light,
Or the slow silent wheels of Night;

The shade, which from the swifter Sun,
Doth in a circular motion run;
Or souls that their eternal Rest do keep,
Make far more noise then *Caelia's* Breath in sleep.

But if the Angel which inspires
This subtile frame with active fires
Should mould this Breath to words, and those
Into a Harmony dispose;
The Musick of this heavenly sphear,
Would steal each soul out at the Ear,
And into Plants and Stones infuse
A life that Cherubins would choose;
And with new Powers invert the Laws of Fate,
Kill those that live, and dead things animate.

## The Repulse

Not that by this disdain
I am releas'd,
And freed from thy tyrannick chain,
Do I my self think blest;

Nor that thy Flame shall burn
No more; for know
That I shall into ashes turn,
Before this fire doth so.

Nor yet that unconfin'd
I now may rove,
And with new beauties please my mind;
But that thou ne'r didst love:

For since thou hast no part
    Felt of this flame,
I onely from thy tyrant heart
    Repuls'd, not banish'd am.

To lose what once was mine
    Would grieve me more
Then those inconstant sweets of thine
    Had pleas'd my soul before.

Now I have lost the blisse
    I ne'r possest;
And spight of fate am blest in this,
    That I was never blest.

## The Divorce

Dear, back my wounded heart restore,
    And turn away thy powerful eyes;
Flatter my willing soul no more,
    Love must not hope what Fate denies.

Take, take away thy smiles and kisses,
    Thy Love wounds deeper then Disdain,
For he that sees the Heaven he misses,
    Sustains two Hels, of losse and pain.

Shouldst thou some others suit prefer,
    I might return thy scorn to thee,
And learn Apostasie of her
    Who taught me first Idolatry.

THE REPULSE.
21 *have:* All the early editions read *have not.*

Or in thy unrelenting breast
  Should I disdain or coynesse move,
He by thy hate might be releas't,
  Who now is prisoner to thy love.

Since then unkind Fate will divorce
  Those whom Affection long united,
Be thou as cruel as this force,
  And I in death shall be delighted.

Thus whilst so many suppliants woo
  And beg they may thy pitty prove,
I onely for thy scorn do sue,
  'Tis charity here not to love.

## The Bracelet

Rebellious fools that scorn to bow
  Beneath Loves easie sway,
Whose stubborn wils no laws allow,
  Disdaining to obay,
Mark but this wreath of hair and you shall see
None that might wear such fetters would be free.

I once could boast a soul like you
  As unconfin'd as aire;
But mine, which force could not subdue,
  Was caught within this snare;
And (by my self betray'd) I for this gold,
A heart that many storms withstood, have sold.

THE BRACELET: Stanley's poem should be compared with Donne's "The Funerall."

11 *this gold:* i.e. the golden hair of which the bracelet is made.

No longer now wise Art enquire
(With this vain search delighted)
How souls that humane breasts inspire
Are to their frames united;
Material chains such spirits well may bind,
When this soft brayd can tie both Arm and Mind.

Now (Beauties) I defie your charm,
Rul'd by more powerful Art,
This mystick wreath which crowns my Arm,
Defends my vanquisht Heart;
And I, subdu'd by one more fair, shall be
Secur'd from Conquest by Captivity.

## The Exequies

Draw neer
You Lovers that complain
Of Fortune or Disdain,
And to my Ashes lend a tear;
Melt the hard marble with your grones,
And soften the relentlesse Stones,
Whose cold imbraces the sad Subject hide
Of all Loves cruelties, and Beauties Pride.

No Verse
No Epicedium bring,
Nor peaceful Requiem sing,
To charm the terrours of my Herse;
No prophane Numbers must flow neer
The sacred silence that dwells here;
Vast Griefs are dumb, softly, oh softly mourn
Lest you disturb the Peace attends my Urn.

THE EXEQUIES: *Exequies:* funeral rites.
10 *Epicedium:* funeral ode.

Yet strew
Upon my dismall Grave,
Such offerings as you have,
Forsaken Cypresse and sad Ewe;
For kinder Flowers can take no Birth
Or growth from such unhappy Earth.
Weep only o're my Dust, and say, Here lies
To Love and Fate an equal Sacrifice.

## Song

I prethee let my heart alone
Since now tis rais'd above thee
Not all the Beauty thou dost own
Again can make me love thee:

He that was shipwrack'd once before
By such a Syrens call,
And yet neglects to shun that shore,
Deserves his second fall.

Each flatt'ring kiss, each tempting smile
Thou dost in vain bestow,
Some other Lovers might beguile
Who not thy falsehood know.

But I am proof against all art,
No vowes shall e're perswade me
Twice to present a wounded Heart
To her that hath betray'd me.

Could I again be brought to love
Thy form though more divine,
I might thy scorn as justly move,
As now thou sufferest mine.

20 *Ewe:* yew.

## The Relapse

Oh turn away those cruel Eyes,
  The stars of my undoing.
Or death in such a bright disguise,
  May tempt a second wooing.

Punish their blindly impious Pride,
  Who dare contemn thy glory;
It was my fall that deifi'd
  Thy name, and seal'd thy Story.

Yet no new sufferings can prepare
  A higher praise to crown thee;
Though my first death proclaim thee fair,
  My second will unthrone thee.

Lovers will doubt thou canst entice
  No other for thy fuel,
And if thou burn one Victime twice,
  Both think thee poor and cruel.

## Expectation

Chide, chide no more away
The fleeting daughters of the day,
Nor with impatient thoughts out-run
  The lasie Sun,
Or think the houres do move too slow;
  Delay is kind,
And we too soon shall find
That which we seek, yet fear to know.

The mystick dark decrees
Unfold not of the Destinies,
Nor boldly seek to antedate
The laws of Fate,
Thy anxious search awhile forbeare,
Suppresse thy haste,
And know that Time at last
Will crowne thy hope, or fix thy fear.

# JOHN DRYDEN
1631–1700

# Religio Laici

Dim, as the borrow'd beams of Moon and Stars
To *lonely, weary, wandring* Travellers
Is *Reason* to the *Soul:* And as on high
Those rowling Fires *discover* but the Sky
Not light us *here;* So *Reason's* glimmering Ray
Was lent, not to *assure* our *doubtfull* way,
But *guide* us upward to a *better Day.*
And as those nightly Tapers disappear
When Day's bright Lord ascends our Hemisphere;
So pale grows *Reason* at *Religions* sight;
So *dyes,* and so *dissolves* in *Supernatural Light.*
Some few, whose Lamp shone brighter, have been led
From Cause to Cause to *Natures* secret head;
And found that *one first principle* must be:
But *what,* or *who,* that UNIVERSAL HE;
Whether some *Soul* incompassing this Ball,
*Unmade, unmov'd;* yet *making, moving All;*
Or various *Atom's* interfering Dance
Leapt into *Form,* (the Noble work of *Chance;*)
Or this great *All* was from *Eternity;*
Not ev'n the *Stagirite* himself could see;
And *Epicurus Guess'd* as well as He:
As *blindly grop'd* they for a *future State,*
As *rashly Judg'd* of *Providence* and *Fate:*
But least of all could their Endeavours find
What most concern'd the good of Humane kind:

RELIGIO LAICI: In the subtitle to his poem, Dryden translated "Religio Laici" as "A Laymans Faith" and appended the motto "Ornari res ipsa negat; contenta doceri," which is taken from Manilius' *Astronomicon* 3.39: "The thing itself refuses to be decked out ornately; it is happy merely to be taught." Dryden's long prose preface, in which he discusses Anglicanism as a middle way between Deism and Roman Catholicism, is not printed here.

18 *interfering:* colliding.

21 *Stagirite:* Aristotle.

For *Happiness* was never to be found;
But vanish'd from 'em, like Enchanted ground.
One thought *Content* the Good to be enjoy'd:
This, every little *Accident* destroy'd:
The *wiser Madmen* did for *Vertue* toyl:
A Thorny, or at best a barren Soil:
In *Pleasure* some their glutton Souls would steep;
But found their Line too short, the Well too deep;
And leaky Vessels which no *Bliss* cou'd keep.
Thus, *anxious Thoughts* in *endless Circles* roul,
Without a *Centre* where to fix the *Soul:*
In this wilde Maze their vain Endeavours end:
How can the *less* the *Greater* comprehend?
Or *finite Reason* reach *Infinity?*
For what cou'd *Fathom* GOD were *more* than *He.*
The *Deist* thinks he stands on firmer ground,
Cries, *eureka:* the mighty Secret's found:
*God* is that *Spring* of *Good; Supreme,* and *Best,*
*We,* made to *serve,* and in that Service *blest;*
If so, some *Rules* of Worship must be given,
Distributed alike to all by Heaven:
Else *God* were *partial,* and to *some* deny'd
The Means His Justice shou'd for *all* provide.
This *general Worship* is to *PRAISE,* and *PRAY:*
One part to *borrow* Blessings, one to *pay:*
And when frail Nature slides into *Offence,*
The *Sacrifice* for *Crimes* is *Penitence.*
Yet, since th'Effects of Providence, we find
Are variously dispensed to Humane kind;
That *Vice Triumphs* and *Vertue suffers* here,
(A Brand that Sovereign justice cannot bear;)
Our Reason prompts us to a *future* State,
The *last Appeal* from *Fortune,* and from *Fate:*
Where God's all-righteous ways will be declar'd;
The *Bad* meet *Punishment,* the *Good, Reward.*
Thus Man by his own strength to Heaven wou'd soar:
And wou'd not be Obliged to God for more.

Vain, wretched Creature, how art thou misled
To think thy Wit these God-like notions bred!
These Truths are not the product of thy Mind,
But dropt from Heaven, and of a Nobler kind.
*Reveal'd Religion* first inform'd thy sight,
And *Reason* saw not till *Faith* sprung the Light.
Hence all thy *Natural Worship* takes the *Source:*
'Tis *Revelation* what thou thinkst *Discourse.*
Else how com'st *Thou* to see these truths so clear,
Which so obscure to *Heathens* did appear?
Not *Plato* these, nor *Aristotle* found.
Nor he whose wisedom *Oracles* renown'd.
Hast thou a Wit so deep, or so sublime,
Or canst thou lower dive, or higher climb?
Canst *Thou,* by *Reason,* more of *God-head* know
Than *Plutarch, Seneca,* or *Cicero?*
Those Gyant Wits, in happyer Ages born,
(When *Arms,* and *Arts* did *Greece* and *Rome* adorn,)
Knew no such *Systeme:* no such Piles cou'd raise
Of *Natural Worship,* built on *Pray'r* and *Praise,*
*To One sole GOD:*
Nor did Remorse, to Expiate Sin, prescribe:
But slew their fellow Creatures for a Bribe:
The guiltless *Victim* groan'd for their Offence;
And *Cruelty,* and *Blood,* was *Penitence.*
If *Sheep* and *Oxen* cou'd Attone for Men
Ah! at how cheap a rate the *Rich* might Sin!
And great Oppressours might Heavens Wrath beguile
By offering his own Creatures for a Spoil!
   Dar'st thou, poor Worm, offend *Infinity?*
And must the Terms of Peace be given by *Thee?*
Then *Thou* art *Justice* in the *last Appeal;*
*Thy easie God* instructs Thee to *rebell:*
And, like a King remote, and weak, must take
What Satisfaction *Thou* art pleased to make.

75 *he:* probably Socrates, whom the Delphic oracle proclaimed to be the wisest man in Greece.

But if there be a *Pow'r* too *Just,* and *strong*
To wink at *Crimes* and bear unpunish'd *Wrong;*
Look humbly upward, see his Will disclose:
The *Forfeit* first, and then the *Fine* impose:
A *Mulct thy* poverty cou'd never pay
Had not *Eternal Wisedom* found the way:
And with Coelestial Wealth supply'd thy Store:
*His Justice* makes the *Fine, his Mercy* quits the *Score.*
See God descending in thy Humane Frame;
Th'*offended,* suff'ring in th'*Offenders* name:
All thy Misdeeds to him imputed see,
And all his Righteousness devolv'd on thee.
For granting we have Sin'd, and that th'offence
Of *Man,* is made against *Omnipotence,*
Some Price, that bears *proportion,* must be paid;
And *Infinite* with *Infinite* be weigh'd.
See then the *Deist lost: Remorse* for *Vice,*
*Not* paid, or *paid, inadequate* in price:
What farther means can *Reason* now direct,
Or what Relief from *humane Wit* expect?
*That* shews us *sick;* and sadly are we sure
*Still* to be *Sick,* till *Heav'n* reveal the *Cure:*
If then *Heaven's Will* must needs be understood,
(Which must, if we want *Cure,* and *Heaven,* be *Good*)
Let all Records of *Will reveal'd* be shown;
With *Scripture,* all in equal ballance thrown,
And *our one Sacred Book* will be *That one.*
*Proof* needs not here; for whether we compare
That Impious, Idle, Superstitious Ware
Of *Rites, Lustrations, Offerings,* (which before,
In various Ages, various Countries bore)
With *Christian Faith* and *Vertues,* we shall find
None answ'ring the great ends of humane kind
But *This one Rule of Life;* That shews us best
How *God* may be *appeas'd,* and *Mortals blest.*

103 *Mulct:* a fine imposed (usually unfairly) for an offense.
128 *Lustrations:* expiatory sacrifices.

Whether from length of *Time* its worth we draw,
The *World* is scarce more *Ancient* than the *Law:*
Heav'ns early Care prescrib'd for every Age;
First, in the *Soul,* and after, in the *Page.*
Or, whether more abstractedly we look,
Or on the *Writers,* or the *written Book,*
Whence, but from *Heav'n,* cou'd men unskill'd in Arts,
In several Ages born, in several parts,
Weave such *agreeing Truths?* or *how,* or *why*
Shou'd *all* conspire to cheat us with a *Lye?*
*Unask'd* their *Pains, ungratefull* their *Advice,*
*Starving* their *Gain,* and *Martyrdom* their *Price.*
 If on the Book it self we cast our view,
Concurrent Heathens prove the Story *True:*
The *Doctrine, Miracles;* which must convince,
For *Heav'n in Them* appeals to *humane Sense:*
And though they *prove* not, they *Confirm* the Cause,
When what is *Taught* agrees with *Natures Laws.*
 Then for the *Style; Majestick* and *Divine,*
It speaks no less than God in every Line:
*Commanding words;* whose *Force* is still the same
As the first *Fiat* that produc'd our Frame.
All Faiths *beside,* or did by *Arms* ascend;
Or *Sense* indulg'd has made *Mankind* their *Friend:*
This *onely* Doctrine does our *Lusts* oppose:
Unfed by Natures Soil, in which it grows;
Cross to our *Interests,* curbing Sense, and Sin;
Oppress'd without, and undermin'd within,
It thrives through pain; its own Tormentours tires;
And with a stubborn patience still aspires.
To what can *Reason* such Effects assign,
Transcending *Nature,* but to *Laws Divine?*
Which in that Sacred Volume are contain'd;
Sufficient, clear, and for that use ordained.

139 *Book:* i.e. the Bible.
155 *Fiat:* "Let there be made," God's words in the first chapter of Genesis.
160 *Cross:* antipathetic.

But stay: the *Deist* here will urge anew,
No *Supernatural Worship* can be *True:*
Because a *general Law* is that alone
Which must to *all* and every *where* be known:
A Style so large as not *this* Book can claim,
Nor ought that bears *reveal'd* Religions *Name.*
'Tis said the sound of a *Messiah's Birth*
Is gone through all the habitable Earth:
But still that Text must be confin'd alone
To what was *Then* inhabited, and known:
And what Provision cou'd from *thence* accrue
To *Indian* Souls, and Worlds discover'd *New?*
In other parts it helps, that Ages past,
The Scriptures there were *known,* and were *imbrac'd,*
Till Sin spread once again the Shades of Night:
What's that to these who never *saw* the Light?
Of all Objections this indeed is chief
To startle Reason, stagger frail Belief:
We grant, 'tis true, that Heav'n from humane Sense
Has hid the secret paths of *Providence:*
But *boundless Wisedom, boundless Mercy,* may
Find ev'n for those *be-wildred* Souls, a *way:*
If from his *Nature Foes* may Pity claim,
Much more may *Strangers* who ne'er heard his *Name.*
And though *no Name* be for *Salvation* known,
But that of His *Eternal Sons* alone;
Who knows how far transcending Goodness can
Extend the *Merits* of *that Son* to *Man?*
Who knows what *Reasons* may his *Mercy* lead;
Or *Ignorance invincible* may plead?
Not onely *Charity* bids hope the *best,*
But *more* the great Apostle has exprest:
*That, if the* Gentiles, (whom no Law inspir'd,)
*By Nature did what* was by *Law requir'd;*

173 *ought:* aught.
199 *great Apostle:* St. Paul. Cf. Romans 2:14–15.

*They, who the written Rule had never known,*
*Were to themselves both Rule and Law alone:*
*To Natures plain indictment they shall plead;*
*And, by their Conscience, be condemn'd or freed.*
Most Righteous Doom! because a *Rule reveal'd*
Is *none* to *Those,* from whom it was *conceal'd.*
Then those who follow'd *Reasons* Dictates right;
Liv'd up, and lifted high their *Natural Light;*
With *Socrates* may see their Maker's Face,
While Thousand *Rubrick-Martyrs* want a place.
  Nor does it baulk my *Charity,* to find
Th'*Egyptian* Bishop of another mind:
For, though his *Creed Eternal Truth* contains,
'Tis hard for *Man* to doom to *endless pains*
All who believ'd not all, his Zeal requir'd;
Unless he first cou'd prove he was inspir'd.
Then let us either think he meant to say
*This Faith,* where *publish'd,* was the onely way;
Or else conclude that, *Arius* to confute,
The good old Man, too eager in dispute,
Flew high; and, as his *Christian* Fury rose,
Damn'd all for *Hereticks* who durst *oppose.*
  Thus far my Charity this path has try'd;
(A much unskilfull, but well meaning guide:)
Yet what they are, ev'n these crude thoughts were bred
By reading that, which better thou hast read,
Thy Matchless Author's work: which thou, my Friend,
By well translating better dost commend:

211 *Rubrick-Martyrs:* "official" martyrs, mentioned in the liturgical rubrics.

213 *Egyptian Bishop:* St. Athanasius (293?–373), Patriarch of Alexandria from 328 to 373, and lifelong opponent of the Arian heresy (line 220), which held that God is unknowable and that Christ is not fully divine. The "Athanasian Creed" (line 214) was not composed by Athanasius, but originated in the fifth or sixth century.

228 *Matchless Author:* Richard Simon's *Critical History of the Old Testament* (1678), which was translated by Dryden's friend, Henry Dickinson, in 1682. Simon's work, which effected a revolution in biblical studies, was attacked by both Catholics and Protestants.

Those youthfull hours which, of thy Equals most
In *Toys* have *squander'd,* or in Vice have *lost,*
Those hours hast thou to Nobler use employ'd;
And the severe Delights of Truth enjoy'd.
Witness this weighty Book, in which appears
The crabbed Toil of many thoughtfull years,
Spent by thy Authour in the Sifting Care
Of *Rabbins'* old Sophisticated Ware
From Gold Divine, which he who well can sort
May afterwards make *Algebra* a Sport.
A Treasure which, if *Country-Curates* buy,
They *Junius,* and *Tremellius* may defy:
Save pains in various readings, and Translations;
And without *Hebrew* make most learn'd quotations.
A Work so full with various Learning fraught,
So nicely pondred, yet so strongly wrought,
As Natures height and Arts last hand requir'd:
As much as Man cou'd compass, uninspir'd.
Where we may see what *Errours* have been made
Both in the *Copiers* and *Translaters Trade:*
How *Jewish, Popish,* Interests have prevail'd,
And where *Infallibility* has *fail'd.*
  For some, who have his secret meaning ghes'd,
Have found our Author not too *much* a *Priest:*
For *Fashion-sake* he seems to have recourse
To *Pope,* and *Councils,* and *Traditions* force:
But he that *old* Traditions cou'd subdue,
Cou'd not but find the weakness of the *New:*
If *Scripture,* though deriv'd from *heav'nly birth,*
Has been but carelesly preserved on *Earth;*
If *God's own People,* who of *God* before
Knew what we know, and had been promis'd more,
In fuller Terms, of Heaven's assisting Care,
And who did neither *Time,* nor *Study* spare

241 *Junius . . . Tremellius:* Franciscus Junius (1545–1602) and Emmanuel Tremellius (d. 1580). Their translation of the Bible into Latin was widely circulated.

To keep this Book *untainted, unperplext;*
Let in gross *Errours* to corrupt the *Text:*
Omitted *paragraphs,* embroyl'd the *Sense;*
With vain *Traditions* stopt the gaping Fence,
Which every common hand pull'd up with ease:
What Safety from such *brushwood-helps* as these?
If *written words* from time are not secur'd,
How can we think have *oral Sounds* endur'd?
Which *thus* transmitted, if *one* Mouth has fail'd,
*Immortal Lyes* on *Ages* are intail'd:
And that some such have been, is prov'd too plain;
If we consider *Interest, Church,* and *Gain.*
  Oh but, says one, *Tradition* set aside,
Where can we hope for an *unerring Guid?*
For since th'*original* Scripture has been lost,
*All* Copies *disagreeing, maim'd* the *most,*
Or *Christian Faith* can have no *certain* ground,
Or *Truth* in *Church Tradition* must be found.
  Such an *Omniscient* Church we wish indeed;
'Twere worth *Both Testaments,* and cast in the *Creed:*
But if *this Mother* be a *Guid* so sure,
As can all *doubts resolve,* all *truth secure,*
Then her *Infallibility,* as well
Where Copies are *corrupt,* or *lame,* can tell;
Restore *lost Canon* with as little pains,
As *truly explicate* what still *remains:*
Which yet no *Council* dare *pretend* to doe;
Unless like *Esdras,* they could *write* it new:
Strange Confidence, still to *interpret* true,
Yet not be sure that all they have explain'd,
Is in the blest *Original* contain'd.

266 *embroyl'd:* confused.

269 *brush-wood-helps:* mere twigs or branches (the "vain Traditions" of line 267) in contrast to the stout fence posts of the original, uncorrupted texts.

291 *Esdras:* Ezra, the Hebrew scribe and priest of the fifth century B.C. The Book of Ezra, which is at least partially attributed to him, gives a continuous account of postexilic Jewish history. See II Esdras 14.

More Safe, and much more modest 'tis, to say
*God wou'd not leave Mankind without a way:*
And that the *Scriptures,* though not *every where*
Free from Corruption, or intire, or clear,
Are uncorrupt, sufficient, clear, intire,
In *all* things which our needfull *Faith* require.
If *others* in the *same Glass better* see
'Tis for *Themselves* they look, but not for *me:*
For *MY* Salvation must its Doom receive
Not from what *OTHERS,* but what *I* believe.
  Must *all Tradition* then be set aside?
This to affirm were Ignorance, or Pride.
Are there not many points, some needfull sure
To saving Faith, that Scripture leaves obscure?
Which every Sect will wrest a several way
(For what *one* Sect interprets, *all* Sects *may:*)
We hold, and say we prove from Scripture plain,
That *Christ* is *GOD;* the bold *Socinian*
From the *same* Scripture urges he's but *MAN.*
Now what Appeal can end th'important Suit;
*Both* parts *talk* loudly, but the *Rule* is *mute?*
  Shall I speak plain, and in a Nation free
Assume an honest *Layman's Liberty?*
I think (according to my little Skill,
To my own Mother-Church submitting still:)
That many have been sav'd, and many may,
Who never heard this Question brought in play.
Th'*unletter'd* Christian, who believes in *gross,*
Plods on to *Heaven;* and ne'er is at a loss:
For the *Streight-gate* would be made *streighter* yet,
Were *none* admitted there but men of *Wit.*

301 *others . . . see:* Cf. I Corinthians 13:12, "For now we see through a glass, darkly, but then face to face."

312 *Socinian:* a follower of Lelio Sozzini (1525–1562) and his nephew Fausto (1539–1604), who developed the anti-Trinitarian theology of Socianism.

324 *Streight-gate:* Cf. Matthew 7:14, "Because strait is the gate, and narrow is the way, which leadeth unto life, and few there be that find it."

The few, by Nature form'd, with Learning fraught,
Born to instruct, as others to be taught,
Must Study well the Sacred Page; and see
Which Doctrine, this, or that, does best agree
With the whole *Tenour* of the Work Divine:
And plainlyest points to Heaven's reveal'd Design:
*Which* Exposition flows from *genuine Sense;*
And which is *forc'd* by *Wit* and *Eloquence.*
Not that Traditions parts are useless here:
When general, old, disinteress'd and clear:
That Ancient Fathers thus expound the Page,
Gives *Truth* the reverend Majesty of *Age,*
*Confirms* its force, by biding every *Test;*
For best *Authority's* next *Rules* are best.
And still the nearer to the Spring we go
More limpid, more unsoyl'd the Waters flow.
Thus, *first Traditions* were a proof alone;
Cou'd we be *certain* such they *were,* so *known:*
But since some Flaws in long descent may be,
They make not *Truth* but *Probability.*
Even *Arius* and *Pelagius* durst provoke
To what the *Centuries preceding* spoke.
Such difference is there in an oft-told Tale:
But Truth by its own Sinews will prevail.
*Tradition written* therefore more commends
*Authority,* than what from *Voice* descends:
And this, as perfect as its kind can be,
Rouls down to us the Sacred History:
Which, from the *Universal Church receiv'd,*
Is *try'd,* and *after,* for its *self* believ'd.
 The partial *Papists* wou'd infer from hence,
*Their* Church, in last resort, shou'd Judge the *Sense.*

339 This line has been variously interpreted; it may mean: "it is best, after the rules are observed, to rely on the best authorities."

346 *Pelagius:* The British monk (360–420?), who opposed St. Augustine's doctrine of predestination and asserted the total freedom of the will to do good or evil. For Arius, see above, line 213 and note. *provoke:* appeal.

But first they wou'd assume, with wondrous Art,
*Themselves* to be the *whole,* who are but *part*
Of that vast Frame, the Church; yet grant they were
The handers down, can they from thence infer
A right t' interpret? or wou'd they alone
Who brought the Present, claim it for their own?
The *Book's* a *Common Largess* to *Mankind;*
Not more for *them,* than *every* Man design'd:
The *welcome News* is in the *Letter* found;
The *Carrier's* not Commission'd to *expound.*
It *speaks* it *Self,* and what it does contain,
In all things *needfull* to be *known, is plain.*
In times o'ergrown with Rust and Ignorance,
A gainfull Trade their Clergy did advance:
When want of Learning kept the *Laymen* low,
And none but *Priests* were *Authoriz'd* to *know:*
When what small Knowledge was, in them did dwell;
And he a *God* who cou'd but *Reade* or *Spell;*
Then *Mother Church* did mightily prevail:
She parcel'd out the Bible by *retail:*
But still *expounded* what She *sold* or *gave;*
To keep it in *her Power* to *Damn* and *Save:*
*Scripture* was *scarce,* and as the Market went,
Poor *Laymen* took *Salvation* on *Content;*
As needy men take Money, good or bad:
*God's* Word they had not, but the *Priests* they had.
Yet, whate'er *false Conveyances* they made,
The *Lawyer* still was *certain* to be paid.
In those dark times they learn'd their knack so well,
That by long use they grew *Infallible:*
At last, a knowing Age began t' enquire
If *they* the *Book,* or *That* did *them* inspire:
And, making narrower search they found, thô late,
That what they thought the *Priest's,* was *Their Estate:*
Taught by the *Will produc'd,* (the written Word)
How long they had been *cheated* on *Record.*

384 *Conveyances:* dispositions of property.

Then, every man who saw the Title fair,
Claim'd a Child's part, and put in for a Share:
Consulted Soberly his private good;
And sav'd himself as cheap as e'er he cou'd.
'Tis true, my Friend, (and far be Flattery hence)
This good had full as bad a Consequence:
The Book thus put in every vulgar hand,
Which each presum'd he best cou'd understand,
The *Common Rule* was made the *common Prey;*
And at the mercy of the *Rabble* lay.
The tender Page with horney Fists was gaul'd;
And he was gifted most that loudest baul'd:
The *Spirit* gave the *Doctoral Degree:*
And every member of a *Company*
Was of *his Trade* and of the *Bible free.*
Plain *Truths* enough for needfull *use* they found;
But men wou'd still be itching to *expound:*
Each was ambitious of th'obscurest place,
No measure ta'n from *Knowledge,* all from GRACE.
*Study* and *Pains* were now no more their Care;
*Texts* were explain'd by *Fasting,* and by *Prayer:*
This was the Fruit the *private Spirit* brought;
Occasion'd by *great Zeal,* and *little Thought.*
While Crouds unlearn'd, with rude Devotion warm,
About the Sacred Viands buz and swarm,
The *Fly-blown Text* creates a *crawling Brood;*
And turns to *Maggots* what was meant for *Food.*
*A Thousand daily Sects rise up, and dye;*
*A Thousand more the perish'd Race supply.*
So all we make of Heavens discover'd Will
Is, not to have it, or to use it ill.
The Danger's much the same; on several Shelves
If *others* wreck *us,* or *we* wreck our *selves.*
What then remains, but, waving each Extreme,
The Tides of Ignorance, and Pride to stem?

427 *waving:* waiving.

Neither so rich a Treasure to forgo;
Nor proudly seek beyond our pow'r to know:
Faith is not built on disquisitions vain;
The things we *must* believe, are *few*, and *plain:*
But since men *will* believe more than they *need;*
And every man will make *himself* a Creed:
In doubtfull questions 'tis the safest way
To learn what unsuspected Ancients say:
For 'tis not likely *we* shou'd higher Soar
In search of Heav'n, than *all the Church before:*
Nor can we be deceiv'd, unless we see
The *Scripture,* and the *Fathers disagree.*
If after all, they stand suspected still,
(For no man's Faith depends upon his Will;)
'Tis some Relief, that points not clearly known,
Without much hazard may be let alone:
And, after hearing what our Church can say,
If still our Reason runs another way,
That private Reason 'tis more Just to curb,
Than by Disputes the publick Peace disturb.
For points obscure are of small use to learn:
But *Common quiet* is *Mankind's concern.*
  Thus have I made my own Opinions clear:
Yet neither Praise expect, not Censure fear:
And this unpolish'd, rugged Verse, I chose;
As fittest for Discourse, and nearest prose:
For while from *Sacred Truth* I do not swerve,
*Tom Sternhold's* or *Tom Shadwell's Rhimes* will serve.

FINIS.

456 *Sternhold's:* Thomas Sternhold (d. 1549), one of the versifiers of the Psalms in the Anglican Prayer Book. *Shadwell's:* Thomas Shadwell (1642?–1692), dramatist and poet, the butt of Dryden's satire in *Mac Flecknoe* (1682).

# COMMENTARY

The following general works on seventeenth-century poetry can be profitably consulted:


D. C. Allen, *Image and Meaning: Metaphoric Traditions in Renaissance Poetry,* Johns Hopkins Press, 1960.

A. Alvarez, *The School of Donne,* New York, Pantheon, 1962.

Douglas Bush, *English Literature in the Earlier Seventeenth Century, 1600–1660,* 2nd ed. rev., Oxford University Press, 1962.

T. S. Eliot, *Selected Essays, 1917–1932,* New York, Harcourt, 1932.

R. Ellrodt, *Les Poètes Métaphysiques Anglais,* 3 vols., Paris, 1960.

H. J. C. Grierson, ed., *Metaphysical Lyrics and Poems of the Seventeenth Century, Donne to Butler,* Oxford University Press, 1921.

Samuel Johnson, *Lives of the Poets,* London, 1779–81.

W. R. Keast, ed., *Seventeenth Century English Poetry: Modern Essays in Criticism,* Oxford University Press, 1962.

F. R. Leavis, *Revaluation: Tradition & Development in English Poetry,* London, Chatto, 1936.

R. L. Sharp, *From Donne to Dryden: The Revolt against Metaphysical Poetry,* University of North Carolina Press, 1940.

Rosemond Tuve, *Elizabethan and Metaphysical Imagery: Renaissance Poetic and Twentieth-Century Critics,* University of Chicago Press, 1947.

Ruth Wallerstein, *Studies in Seventeenth Century Poetic,* University of Wisconsin Press, 1950.

G. Williamson, *The Donne Tradition: A Study in English Poetry from Donne to the death of Cowley,* Harvard University Press, 1930.


## MICHAEL DRAYTON

LIFE Born in Warwickshire in 1563, and thus a year older than Shakespeare, Drayton was not to die until 1631, the year of Donne's death. He was brought up as a page in the household of Sir Henry Goodere, and remained devoted to the family throughout his life. For the most part, Drayton was fortunate enough to find a number of generous, upper-class patrons and, except for a brief period (1597–1602) when he was forced to write as a dramatic hack, his life moved tranquilly between London and country estates. Drayton tried almost every current poetic genre at one time or other in his career and, always the professional poet, often drastically revised his early efforts in later editions. His long topographical poem, *Poly-Olbion*, appeared in 1612, with a second part in 1622.

EDITION J. W. Hebel, Kathleen Tillotson, and B. H. Newdigate, *Works*, 5 vols., Shakespeare Head Press, 1931–41. A convenient and scholarly selection, with a good critical introduction, is that of John Buxton, *The Poems*, 2 vols., Harvard University Press, 1953.

TEXT *The Epistle of Rosamond* is taken from the edition of 1619, the *Epistle to Reynolds* from that of 1627, and the selections from *The Muse's Elizium* from the edition of 1630.

STUDIES B. H. Newdigate, *Michael Drayton and His Circle*, Oxford, Blackwell, 1941.

## HENRY WOTTON

LIFE Wotton was born in 1568 at Boughton Hall in Kent. He was educated at Winchester and at New College and Queen's College, Oxford (B.A. 1588). It was at Oxford that his lifelong friendship with Donne began. Between 1588 and 1595, Wotton toured on the Continent. He served the Earl of Essex until 1599, when he left England for Venice as Essex fell from favor. Under James I, Wotton was well received at court. In 1604 he accepted appointment as ambassador to Venice, where he served for almost twenty years. It was at the beginning of his formal diplomatic career that Wotton uttered the maxim for which he is most famous: "An ambassador is an honest man, sent to lie abroad for the good of his country." In 1624 he became Provost of Eton, holding that position until his death in early December, 1639.

EDITION There is no modern edition of Wotton's verse, which first appeared in the *Reliquae Wottonianae*, 1651. The texts given here are taken from the first edition.

STUDIES The standard study is L. P. Smith's *Life and Letters of Sir Henry Wotton*, 2 vols., Oxford University Press, 1907. Izaak Walton's *Life of Wotton* was first printed as a preface to the *Reliquae* of 1651.

## BEN JONSON

LIFE Born in London in 1572 or 73, Jonson attended Westminster School, where he studied under the antiquarian William Camden. He left school about 1588, working as a bricklayer's apprentice, and serving as a soldier in the Low Countries. By 1597 he had entered the London dramatic circle, first as an actor, but soon as a playwright. *Every Man in his Humour* and *The Case Is Altered* were both acted in 1598. In the same year Jonson was imprisoned for killing an actor in a duel; while in jail, he became a convert to Roman Catholicism, a faith he held to for twelve years. Between 1598 and 1616 most of Jonson's best plays appeared. But by 1606 he had also begun writing masques for the court, often working with the designer, Inigo Jones, with whom he was to feud violently. Jonson's later years were marred by a series of misfortunes: a fire which destroyed his books (1623), poverty, and ill-health. Yet these years also marked the founding of the various "clubs," where the Sons of Ben met at the Mermaid and other taverns in London. Most of these self-styled disciples contributed to the volume (*Jonsonus Virbius*) of thirty-three elegies which was published in 1638, the year after his death.

EDITION C. H. Herford, Percy and Evelyn Simpson, *Works*, 11 vols., Oxford University Press, 1925–52.

TEXT The texts presented here follow those established by William B. Hunter, Jr. in *The Complete Poetry of Ben Jonson*, New York, Anchor Books, 1963. *The Epigrammes* and *The Forrest* first appeared in the *Works* of 1616, which also contained a number of the dramatic lyrics. *Under-wood* was published posthumously in the *Works* of 1640–41. The texts of *Pans Anniversarie* and *Pleasure Reconciled to Vertue* are taken from the 1640 folio edition of Jonson's *Works*.

STUDIES The first volume of Herford and Simpson's edition contains a full scholarly biography.

Marchette G. Chute, *Ben Jonson of Westminster*, New York, Dutton, 1953.

G. B. Johnston, *Ben Jonson: Poet*, Columbia University Press, 1945.

Hugh Maclean, "Ben Jonson's Poems: Notes on the Ordered Society," in *Essays in English Literature from the Renaissance to the Victorian Age Presented to A. S. P. Woodhouse*, eds. M. MacLure and F. W. Watt, University of Toronto Press, 1964.

Wesley Trimpi, *Ben Jonson's Poems: A Study of the Plain Style,* Stanford University Press, 1962.

R. S. Walker, "Ben Jonson's Lyric Poetry," *Criterion,* XII (1933–34).

Geoffrey Walton, *Metaphysical to Augustan: Studies in Tone and Sensibility in the Seventeenth Century,* London, Bowes, 1955.

For Jonson's masques, see the recent studies by John C. Meagher (*Method and Meaning in Jonson's Masques,* Notre Dame University Press, 1966) and Stephen Orgel (*The Jonsonian Masque,* Harvard University Press, 1965).

## GEORGE SANDYS

LIFE Sandys, the youngest son of Edwin Sandys, Archbishop of York, was born at Bishopthorpe, Yorkshire, on March 2, 1578. He matriculated at St. Mary Hall, Oxford, in 1589, but does not seem to have taken a degree. In 1610 he set out on an extensive tour, which took him to France, Venice, Turkey, Egypt, Palestine, and Rome. In 1615 Sandys published an account of his travels. He became interested, with his brother Edwin, in colonial enterprise; in 1621 he was appointed treasurer of the Virginia Company and resided in the colony for a number of years. His translation of the *Metamorphoses* was begun before he sailed and an edition of the first five books, now lost, may have been printed in 1621. The complete version first appeared in 1626, and the elaborate folio edition, with notes and allegorical commentary, was published in 1632. Sandys became a gentleman of the privy chamber early in the reign of Charles I and soon joined the circle of Lucius Cary, Lord Falkland. His later years were spent on poetical paraphrases of the Bible. The *Paraphrase upon the Psalmes* appeared in 1636, with King, Godolphin, Carew, Waller, and others writing commendatory verses to the second edition of 1638. Sandys died, unmarried, at Boxley Abbey, Kent, in 1644.

EDITION AND TEXT There is no reliable modern edition of Sandys. The selection given here is taken from the 1632 edition of his *Ovid's Metamorphoses.*

STUDIES The best analysis of Sandys' versification is that of Ruth Wallerstein in "The Development of the Rhetoric and Metre of the Heroic Couplet," *Publications of the Modern Language Association,* L (1935), 166–209. His diction is discussed by G. Tillotson, *On the Poetry of Pope,* Oxford University Press, 1938. There is a biography by R. B.

Davis, *George Sandys, Poet-Adventurer: A Study in Anglo-American Culture in the Seventeenth Century,* Columbia University Press, 1955.

## RICHARD CORBETT

LIFE Corbett, perhaps the most poetically frivolous of the Sons of Ben, was born at Ewell, Surrey, in 1582. Educated at Westminster School, he went up to Oxford in 1598, there to remain, for the most part at Christ Church, for the next thirty years. Corbett rose fairly rapidly in the University hierarchy and achieved early fame as both a wit and a preacher. In 1619, when Jonson received his honorary degree, he stayed with Corbett at Christ Church. Corbett became Dean of his college in 1620 and proved himself an adept seeker for patronage. He married Anne Hutten about 1623; she died in 1628. In the latter year, mainly through the efforts of the Duke of Buckingham, Corbett was appointed Bishop of Oxford. He was translated to Norwich in 1632, where he died in 1635.

EDITION J. A. W. Bennett and H. R. Trevor-Roper, *The Poems,* Oxford University Press, 1955.

TEXT The selections given here are based on the two early editions of Corbett's poems, *Certain Elegant Poems* (1647) and *Poëtica Stromata* (1648).

## HERBERT OF CHERBURY

LIFE Herbert's early life (until 1621) is enthusiastically recorded by himself in his *Autobiography* (see the edition by Sidney Lee, London, 1885 and 1906). Born at Eyton on Severn in 1583, Edward was the eldest brother of George Herbert, ten years his junior. He studied at Oxford for a time after his father's death in 1596, but was resident in London by 1600. Knighted by King James, he set out on a continental tour, with Aurelian Townshend as his companion, in 1608. For the next decade he pursued a courtly and military career, both at home and abroad. In 1619 he became ambassador to France, serving there until 1624. Created Lord Herbert in 1629, he dropped from public life shortly after. Historical and philosophical studies occupied most of his remaining years. His important Latin treatise *De Veritate* had been printed in Paris in 1623, and in 1645 he issued *Religio Laici* and *De*

*Causis Errorum.* His *History of Henry VIII* was first published in 1649, a year after his death.

EDITION G. C. Moore Smith, *Poems English and Latin,* Oxford University Press, 1923.

TEXT The present selections are based on the first edition of 1665, *Occasional Verses.*

## AURELIAN TOWNSHEND

LIFE Townshend was born not later than 1583. He was in Sir Robert Cecil's service from 1600 to 1603, traveling in France and Italy. In 1608, Townshend was again on the Continent, this time as a companion of Edward Herbert, afterwards Lord Herbert of Cherbury. By 1622 he had married and was living in London. His two masques, *Albion's Triumph* and *Tempe Restored* (to the latter Townshend contributed only the songs) were produced and printed in 1632. Townshend's later years seem to have been spent in poverty and he has often been remembered as described in 1642: "a poor and pocky poet, who would be glad to sell a hundred verses now at sixpence apiece, fifty shillings an hundred verses." His death probably occurred about 1651.

EDITION E. K. Chambers, *Aurelian Townshend's Poems and Masks,* Oxford University Press, 1912. For new texts of poems by Townshend, see G. C. Moore Smith, "Aurelian Townshend," *Modern Language Review,* XII (1917), 421–27.

TEXT Townshend's poems were not published in a collected edition during his lifetime. The selections given here follow Chambers, who based his on printed songbooks and a few contemporary manuscripts.

## ROBERT HERRICK

LIFE Herrick was born at London in 1591, the seventh child of Nicholas Herrick, a goldsmith. His father died a year later and nothing is known of the poet until 1607 when he was apprenticed to his uncle, Sir William Herrick. But in 1613 Herrick entered St. John's, Cambridge, taking his B.A. in 1617 and M.A. in 1620. He was ordained priest in 1623, but apparently received no benefice until he was appointed to Dean Prior, Devonshire, in 1629. It was probably during the 1620s that Herrick became intimate with Jonson and the other Sons of Ben in London. He remained at his vicarage until 1647, when he was expelled for his support of the king. The *Hesperides* and *Noble Numbers* appeared together in 1648. Herrick was probably supported by relatives until 1660, when he returned to his vicarage. He died in 1674 and was buried at Dean Prior.

EDITION L. C. Martin, *Poems*, Oxford University Press, 1956.

TEXT The poems are presented here as edited by J. Max Patrick in *The Complete Poetry of Robert Herrick*, New York, Anchor Books, 1963.

STUDIES Floris Delattre, *Robert Herrick*, Paris, 1912. Sydney Musgrove, *The Universe of Robert Herrick*, Auckland, 1950.

## HENRY KING

LIFE King was born in 1592 at Worminghall, Buckinghamshire. His father, John, a royal chaplain and a close friend of John Donne, became Bishop of London in 1611. Educated, like Jonson, at Westminster School, King proceeded to Christ Church, Oxford, in 1608, receiving his B.A. in 1611, M.A., in 1614, and later his B.D. and D.D. in 1625. He married Anne Berkeley in 1616; it is her death (January 5, 1624) that is commemorated in King's greatest poem, "The Exequy." King, who had been appointed in 1616 to a prebendary at St. Paul's, was a close friend of Donne and served as executor of the latter's will. He became an esteemed preacher in the 1630s and was elected Bishop of Chichester in 1641. Deprived in 1643, he lived in retirement until restored to his see in 1660. He died in 1669.

EDITION Margaret Crum, *The Poems*, Oxford University Press, 1965, the first edition to adopt the text and arrangement of the manuscripts.

TEXT The selections given here are based on the 1657 edition of *Poems, Elegies, Paradoxes, and Sonnets*. As Miss Crum notes, the text of this edition agrees very closely with the manuscripts.

STUDIES L. Mason, "Life and Works of Henry King," in *Transactions of the Connecticut Academy of Arts and Sciences*, XVIII (1913).

John Sparrow, introduction to his edition of the *Poems*, Nonesuch Press, 1925.

Rosemond Tuve, *Elizabethan and Metaphysical Imagery*, University of Chicago Press, 1947.

## THOMAS CAREW

LIFE Carew was born in late 1594 or early 1595, probably at West Wickham, Kent. He matriculated at Merton College, Oxford, in 1608, taking his B.A. in January 1611. Carew evidently intended to enter the legal (his father's) profession and he was admitted to the Middle Temple in 1612. But by 1613 he was on the Continent, serving as a secretary to Sir Dudley Carleton, the English ambassador to Venice. He returned to England late in 1615, and then went to the Netherlands with Carleton in the following year. While there, Carew fell into disgrace with his patron, who sent him back to England (August 1616). After his father's death in 1618, Carew continued his career as a courtier. He traveled to France with Herbert of Cherbury in 1619 and may have remained there until 1624. In 1630, he was made a gentleman of the privy chamber to Charles I. His masque, *Coelum Britannicum,* was performed at court in February 1634. Carew's life at court seems to have been quite free and easy. He was friendly with the "tribe of Ben" and a close associate of Suckling. He died in March 1640.

EDITION Rhodes Dunlap, *The Poems, with his masque Coelum Britannicum,* Oxford University Press, 1949.

TEXT Except for the elegy on Donne, which is taken from the 1633 edition of Donne's *Poems,* the texts of the poems given here are based on the 1640 edition of Carew's *Poems.*

STUDIES R. A. Blanshard, "Thomas Carew and the Cavalier Poets," *Transactions of the Wisconsin Academy of Sciences, Arts and Letters,* XLIII (1954), 97 ff. and "Carew and Jonson," *Studies in Philology,* LII (1955), 195 ff.

E. I. Selig, *The Flourishing Wreath,* Yale University Press, 1958.

C. J. Sembower, "A Note on the Verse Structure of Carew," *Studies in Language and Literature in Celebration of the Seventieth Birthday of James Morgan Hart,* New York, Holt, 1910, 456 ff.

## THOMAS RANDOLPH

LIFE Randolph was born at Newnham, Northamptonshire, in 1605. He is said to have begun writing verse at the age of nine. Educated at Westminster School and Trinity College, Cambridge, he received his

B.A. in 1628 (M.A. 1631). Randolph was celebrated as a wit at the university, a good fellow and merry companion. By 1630 he belonged officially to the "tribe of Ben" and in that year his two Cambridge plays, *Aristippus* and *The Pedler* were published. In 1632, his *Jealous Lovers* was presented before the king at the University. Randolph had settled in London by late 1632 and he lived there, working as a dramatist, until his death in March 1635. *Amyntas,* his best play, was acted in 1633.

EDITION J. J. Parry, *The Poems and Amyntas,* Yale University Press, 1917.

TEXT *Poems, With the Muses Looking-glasse and Amyntas,* Oxford, 1638.

## WILLIAM HABINGTON

LIFE Habington was born, of a recusant family, on November 4, 1605, the eve of the Gunpowder Plot. His father, Thomas, was implicated in the attempt, and was the only one of the ringleaders who was reprieved. Habington was educated at St. Omer and at Paris and, by 1629, was living in London. In early 1634, he married Lucy Herbert, the "Castara" of his poems. In 1640, Habington's play, *The Queene of Arragon,* was produced at court, and in the following year his two historical works, *The Historie of Edward the Fourth* and *Observations Upon Historie* were published. At the opening of the civil war, Habington retired to his estate at Hindlip, Worcestershire. He died there in 1654.

EDITION K. Allott, *The Poems,* Liverpool University Press, 1948.

TEXT *Castara* appeared in three editions (1634, 1635, 1640), each with new material, during Habington's lifetime. The texts given here are based on the edition of 1640.

## EDMUND WALLER

LIFE Waller was born at Coleshill, Buckinghamshire, on March 3, 1606. He was educated at Eton and Cambridge, but did not take a degree. In 1622 he was admitted to Lincoln's Inn and his career in Parliament began about this time. In 1631 he married the wealthy heiress, Anne Banks (d. 1634). Between 1636 and 1639 Waller addressed a number of his poems to Lady Dorothy Sidney (Sacharissa). During the revolution, Waller stuck to a position of constitutional royalism. His plot to seize London for the king was discovered in 1643, but he escaped with banishment and a heavy fine. Before leaving England for Paris in late 1644, he married his second wife, Mary Bracey. Waller was pardoned in 1651, returning to London in that year. At the Restoration, he was again elected to Parliament and held his seat until his death on October 21, 1687.

EDITION The most recent edition of Waller's poems is that by G. Thorn Drury, 2 vols., London, 1893.

TEXT The selections given here are taken from the 1686 edition, the fifth and last printed in Waller's lifetime.

STUDIES Alexander W. Allison, *Toward an Augustan Poetic: Edmund Waller's "Reform" of English Poetry,* University of Kentucky Press, 1962.

Warren L. Chernaik, "Waller's 'Panegyric to My Lord Protector' and the Poetry of Praise," *Studies in English Literature,* IV (1964), 109–24.

## JOHN SUCKLING

LIFE Suckling was the son of Sir John Suckling, who became secretary of state in 1622. He was educated at Trinity College, Cambridge and inherited his father's extensive estates in 1627. After traveling in France and Italy, he returned to England and was knighted in 1630. Suckling served under Gustavus Adolphus in 1631–32 and thereafter threw himself into the life of Charles's court. He produced his play, *Aglaura,* at great expense in 1637. In 1641, he set on foot "the first army plot," but managed to escape to Paris, where he died in 1642.

EDITION There is no reliable modern edition of Suckling's poems, but they are being edited by Thomas Clayton for the Oxford University Press.

TEXT Suckling's poems were published in *Fragmenta Aurea* (1646 and 1648) and in *The Last Remains* (1659). The texts here follow the 1646 edition, except for the last three poems, which are taken from the *Remains.*

STUDIES L. A. Beaurline, "The Canon of Sir John Suckling's Poems," *Studies in Philology,* LVIII (1960), 492–518, and "New Poems by Sir John Suckling," *Studies in Philology,* LIX (1962), 651–57.

Herbert Berry, *Sir John Suckling's Poems and Letters from Manuscript,*

University of Western Ontario Studies in Humanities, vol. 1, London, Ontario, 1960.

F. O. Henderson, "Traditions of *Précieux* and Libertin in Suckling's Poetry," *English Literary History*, IV (1937).

## JOHN CLEVELAND

LIFE Cleveland (or Cleiveland) was born at Loughborough, Leicestershire, in 1613. He entered Cambridge in 1627 (B.A. 1631, M.A. 1635). In 1634 he became a fellow of St. John's and a Reader in Rhetoric. When Cromwell was a candidate for Parliament from Cambridge in 1641, Cleveland opposed him in a long speech. In 1645, he was ejected from the University and his loss was mourned by his pupils. He joined the Royalist army and became judge-advocate at Newark until its surrender in 1646. Cleveland lived with friends for some years, but was arrested and imprisoned for three months in 1655. He died in April, 1658.

EDITION Brian Morris and Eleanor Withington, *The Poems*, Oxford University Press, 1967.

TEXT The poems given here are based on the 1677 edition, *Clievelandi Vindiciae*. Miss Withington has demonstrated that this is easily the most authoritative of the early editions. See her article in *Bulletin of the New York Public Library*, LXVII (1963), 307–27 and 377–94.

## JOHN DENHAM

LIFE Denham was born in Dublin in 1615, the son of a Baron of the Exchequer. He attended Trinity College, Oxford, from 1631 to 1634, and then proceeded to Lincoln's Inn. Denham showed an early aptitude for gambling and several anecdotes about his exploits are preserved. At his father's death in 1639, he inherited a sizable estate. Not an extreme Royalist, Denham nevertheless sided with the Stuarts throughout the war. His tragedy, *The Sophy*, appeared in 1642, and in that year the first and shorter version of *Cooper's Hill* was published. After the Restoration, Denham became Surveyor of the king's works. In 1666, a year after his second marriage, Denham went temporarily mad, remaining at least eccentric until his death in 1669. His second wife's affair with the Duke of York culminated in her death, apparently from poison, in 1667.

EDITION T. H. Banks, *The Poetical Works,* Yale University Press, 1928.

TEXT *Cooper's Hill* first appeared in its full form in 1655. The text followed here is that of *Poems and Translations,* 1668, the last edition appearing in Denham's lifetime.

## RICHARD LOVELACE

LIFE Lovelace was born in 1618, probably in Holland. He was educated at the Charterhouse School, where he was Crashaw's contemporary, and at Worcester College, Oxford, where he was given an honorary M.A. by Charles I in 1636. Lovelace soon became a favorite at the court, beginning his military career during the Scottish expeditions of 1639 and 1640. He had probably met Suckling in 1636 or 1637. In 1642, Lovelace's pronounced Royalist sympathies brought him out of retirement in Kent to deliver the Kentish Petition at Blackheath. He was arrested and imprisoned for two months. When released on bail, he went abroad, spending much of 1643–46 in Holland and France. In June, 1648, Lovelace was again in prison, not to be released until April of the next year. Very little is known about the last years of his life, but the seventeenth-century stories of his dire poverty have been discredited by modern scholarship. His death occurred in late 1656 or early 1657.

EDITION C. H. Wilkinson, *The Poems,* 2 vols., Oxford University Press, 1925; revised in one volume, 1953 (Oxford).

TEXT *Lucasta,* 1649, and *Lucasta, Posthume Poems,* 1659.

## ABRAHAM COWLEY

LIFE Cowley was born in London in 1618 and was educated at Westminster School and Trinity College, Cambridge (B.A. 1639, M.A. 1642). But already, in 1633, Cowley had published *Poetical Blossoms,* a precocious volume of poems which was reprinted, with additions, in 1636 and 1637. While at the University, Cowley wrote several plays and worked on his epic, the *Davideis.* In 1643–44 he was ejected from his fellowship at Cambridge and moved to Oxford. The exiled court employed him on several missions and he himself lived in exile from 1646 to 1656. A collection of love poems, *The Mistress,* was published in 1647. Cowley was arrested in 1656 and remained under bail until the Restoration. A collected edition of his poetry appeared in 1656.

Cowley was active in the formation of the Royal Society and was one of its first members. He lived in retirement from 1665, when he received a grant of land from the crown, until his death on July 28, 1667.

EDITION A. R. Waller, *English Works,* 2 vols., Cambridge English Classics, Cambridge University Press, 1905–6.

TEXT The text of the poems given here is that of the 1668 folio edition, posthumously produced by Cowley's close friend, Thomas Sprat.

STUDIES Samuel Johnson's famous essay (*Lives of the Poets,* 1779) should be consulted for both Cowley and Cleveland. There is a good biography by A. H. Nethercot, *Abraham Cowley: The Muse's Hannibal,* Oxford University Press, 1931, and a full study by R. B. Hinman, *Abraham Cowley's World of Order,* Harvard University Press, 1960. For Cowley's "Pindaric" odes, see Harvey D. Goldstein, "Anglorum Pindarus: Model and Milieu," *Comparative Literature,* XVII (1965), 299–310.

## THOMAS STANLEY

LIFE Stanley was born at Cumberlow, Essex, in 1625. He entered Cambridge in 1639 and was incorporated at Oxford the following year. At the outbreak of the war he left England, traveling in France for some years. By 1646 he was back in London, meeting there regularly with a group of friends that included Shirley, Sherburne, and perhaps Lovelace. A collection of his poems was published privately in 1647 and a much enlarged and revised edition appeared in 1651. Thereafter Stanley devoted himself to translation and classical scholarship. In 1661 he became, with Dryden and others, a charter member of the Royal Society. He died in 1678.

EDITION G. M. Crump, *The Poems and Translations,* Oxford University Press, 1962.

TEXT The text of "Expectation" is that of the 1647 *Poems and Translations.* The other selections are based on the text of the 1651 *Poems.*

## JOHN DRYDEN

LIFE Dryden was born in 1631 and educated at Westminster School and Trinity College, Cambridge (B.A. 1654). His first poem, an elegy on the death of Lord Hastings, appeared in 1649. From 1663 until 1679 (and again in the 1690s) he produced a number of heroic plays and comedies. When published, many of these were prefaced with some of his finest prose essays. In the early 1680s he turned to heroic satire with *Absalom and Achitophel* (1681), *The Medal* (1682), and *Mac Flecknoe* (1682). *The Hind and the Panther,* a defense of his conversion to Roman Catholicism, appeared in 1687. Dryden was poet laureate and royal historiographer from 1670 to 1689. In the last decade of his life he produced his translations of Persius, Juvenal, Virgil, and Chaucer. *Fables, Ancient and Modern,* a noble finish to a great career, was published in 1700, the year of his death.

EDITIONS James Kinsley, *The Poems,* 4 vols., Oxford University Press, 1958. Many other editions. For Dryden's prose, see W. P. Ker, *The Essays,* 2 vols., Oxford University Press, 1900.

TEXT The text of *Religio Laici* is taken from the first edition of 1682.

STUDIES Louis I. Bredvold, *The Intellectual Milieu of John Dryden: Studies in Some Aspects of Seventeenth-Century Thought,* University of Michigan Press, 1934.

Elias Chiasson, "Dryden's Apparent Skepticism in *Religio Laici,*" *Harvard Theological Review,* LIV (1961), 207–21.

Thomas H. Fujimaira, "Dryden's *Religio Laici,*" *Publications of the Modern Language Association,* LXXVI (1961), 205–17.

Victor M. Hamm, "Dryden's *Religio Laici* and Roman Catholic Apologetics." *Publications of the Modern Language Association,* LXXX (1965), 190–98.

Arthur W. Hoffman, *John Dryden's Imagery,* University of Florida Press, 1962.

Martin Price, *To the Palace of Wisdom,* New York, Doubleday, 1964, Anchor Books, 1965.

# INDEX

*Authors' names are printed in small capitals, titles of poems in italics, and first lines of poems in Roman.*